Law and War

Law and War

Magistrates in the Great War

Jonathan Swan

Pen & Sword
MILITARY

First published in Great Britain in 2017 by
Pen & Sword Military
an imprint of
Pen & Sword Books Ltd
47 Church Street
Barnsley
South Yorkshire
S70 2AS

ISBN 978 1 47385 337 9

A CIP catalogue record for this book is available from the British Library

Typeset in Ehrhardt by
Mac Style Ltd, Bridlington, East Yorkshire
Printed and bound in Malta by Gutenberg Press

Pen & Sword Books Ltd incorporates the imprints of Pen & Sword
Archaeology, Atlas, Aviation, Battleground, Discovery, Family History,
History, Maritime, Military, Naval, Politics, Railways, Select, Transport,
True Crime, Fiction, Frontline Books, Leo Cooper, Praetorian Press,
Seaforth Publishing and Wharncliffe.

For a complete list of Pen & Sword titles please contact
PEN & SWORD BOOKS LIMITED
47 Church Street, Barnsley, South Yorkshire, S70 2AS, England
E-mail: enquiries@pen-and-sword.co.uk
Website: www.pen-and-sword.co.uk

Contents

To my wife, Rebecca, the fount of law and justice in the Swan household.

List of Plates

Preface
by His Honour Richard Seymour QC

In the summer of 1914 the British Government, legislators and the naval and military authorities realized that, for the first time in the history of the nation, it was going to be necessary for a high degree of legal regulation of activities in the United Kingdom to equip the country better to fight a war and to respond to the novel challenge of an enemy likely to be able to affect life in this country without necessarily invading. England had not been invaded successfully since 1066. There had been no serious threat of invasion for over a hundred years. No one, it seems, had given serious thought previously to what legal powers might be needed, and by whom, in the event that there was a threat of invasion or a need to compel citizens to collaborate in order effectively for the nation to be able to fight a war in Europe, still less throughout the world. Certainly there was no existing Parliamentary legislation in force which dealt with these matters, and no such legislation had ever been passed before. There were no precedents.

The first important legal question, as the likelihood of war increased in the summer of 1914, was not so much what laws to make, as how to make them. In other words, what powers of what body were to be used to make the new laws. There were, in principle, two possible sources of law-making power, the royal prerogative and Parliament. Another important question was whether either of these possible sources of law-making power permitted the delegation of law-making powers to someone else, and, if so, to whom and on what terms. Certainly, as things turned out, it was necessary for large numbers of regulations and orders dealing in detail with a vast range of matters to be produced, and often amended, speedily, and it was beyond the capacity of a legislative body to consider such a range of considerations and so much material as swiftly as was required. Unless much could be delegated, the making of the relevant laws could not be achieved. A further important issue was the mechanism by which whatever laws were made were to be enforced. That question involved considering what powers might be possessed by what authority to create new forms of court or tribunal.

Although very important in the period before Parliament established its present predominance as the source of new laws, and still important in some areas, the concept of the royal prerogative is difficult. Essentially it is the residue of the royal powers of the Norman kings, that is to say, what is left in the hands of the Crown (in modern times the Government, rather than the monarch personally), after centuries of Parliamentary development during which Parliament has progressively arrogated to itself power to intervene in ever-widening areas of national life. In 1914 it was unclear what limits, if any, there had been to the royal powers of the Norman kings, and the precise scope of what was left to the Crown was even less clear, save in well-established areas, such as foreign policy. As Parliament developed, it was accepted that Parliament could legislate, and thereby make law. However, although Parliament could change the English common law – and limit the royal prerogative – in any respects it chose, to the extent that Parliament did not choose to exercise that power, the English common law, including the royal prerogative, continued to be the law of the land. That remains the position today.

After the English Civil War the wars in which the country became involved were abroad. The decision to go to war, or not, was taken by the Government of the day in the exercise of the royal prerogative. Although there were occasionally invasion scares, no one gave much attention to what should be the legal consequences of an invasion. No one seems to have given any attention at all to the consequences in England of going to war abroad, because, apart from by suffering increases in taxation, the population in England was unlikely to be much affected.

There is probably a right, as an aspect of the royal prerogative, for the Government to take steps in an emergency to protect the country and its citizens. In 1914 the extent of that right – that is to say, what exactly the Government had power to do – was, and remains, obscure. However, as Jonathan Swan explains in this book, the first thoughts of the Government at the start of the First World War were to seek to use royal prerogative powers. In the end the Parliamentary legislative route was adopted as the way of making laws, delegating powers to make laws and providing for enforcement by delegated authorities. However, Parliament's first attempts resulted in conferring wide-ranging powers upon the naval and military authorities, leaving it up to those authorities to decide which powers to exercise and how to enforce them – in effect a form of martial law.

In this book Jonathan Swan considers, thoroughly and with some very interesting insights, what did happen and what consequences were produced. Readers will form their own conclusions in the light of the comprehensive material assembled in the book. If they were to decide that, faced with an unprecedented situation, Parliament initially reacted hysterically and proceeded on an ill-considered, and somewhat irrational course, they may not be alone.

Introduction

Police Courts 1917

At the present day the police court is a court of justice, a place where the prosecutor and the defendant are heard, the facts weighed, the law applied, and judgment given. This is an important business, but it grows into one of enormous consequence when it is realised that here the claims of society to exemplary punishment, to the reformation of the criminal, are weighed against the temptations, the need of mercy, the right to personal liberty, and the whole complex of internal and external circumstance which has made the accused what he is. Often the scales have to be applied in an attempt to measure the imponderables, the claim of the State to service and obedience, against the right of the individual to lead his own life, to develop his own soul as his conscience directs.

Parliament makes the law. The Courts of summary jurisdiction do most of the enforcing of it. The war has cast a myriad new duties on the justice. He must go into complicated questions of nationality. He fixes the legal liability to military service. He decides whether any condition has been imposed upon the purchase of a specified article of food, whether the bread has been baked less or more than twelve hours, and whether a light inside a house is improperly visible outside.

We have difficult times now before us, and all that makes for confidence in the administration of justice must be jealously fostered. It must be remembered that for every criminal case before a higher court there are a hundred before justices, that apart from crime properly so-called numbers of people come into collision with constituted authority and get 'summoned'.

Bearing all these things in mind it is obvious that Courts of summary jurisdiction must, if they are to continue to do good work, retain the confidence of the public. Doing justice is one of the finest things that man has it in him to do; a pretence of justice is a vile sham; but humankind being what it is, the appearance is nearly as important as the reality.[1]

These words appeared in the *Justice of the Peace* in the penultimate year of the First World War but resonate clearly and immediately with the modern magistrate. This weekly journal, still published today as *Criminal Law & Justice Weekly*, was written for magistrates and other court users and informed its readers about current practice in the courts of summary jurisdiction. It introduced and explained new laws and regulations, highlighted interesting cases, answered questions about points of law and, although essentially conservative, drew attention to some of the inconsistencies of wartime legislation. The statute books contained the law as defined by Parliament, and the newspapers reported the stories of the people in the dock, but the *Justice of the Peace* illustrated the concerns of 'the great unpaid' – the lay magistrates who had to interpret and apply the law in those difficult times.

Although the office of justice of the peace can be traced back to 1361 in the reign of King Edward III, the magistrates' court as we understand it today developed from the reforms to the system of summary justice which began in the middle of the nineteenth century. Increasing powers had been given to magistrates to hear and determine simple cases and soon the local police court or petty sessions became the forum in which many people saw and experienced the law in action. And not just for criminal matters, but for many forms of legal redress: quarrelsome disputes between neighbours, landlords and tenants, masters and servants, husbands and wives, but in many cases they simply provided straightforward – and free – legal advice. The magistracy itself had been reformed and working-class men were found on the bench in increasing numbers, although women were not appointed until 1919.

But war brought a new dimension to the work of the courts. In August and September 1914 the Parliamentary legislators worked at a frantic pace to bring in statute law to deal with a nation at war and for the first time in a century facing a genuine prospect of invasion. Unlike Continental systems of *l'état de siege* or *Notrecht* which were systems of emergency law which had actually been tested in times of war, we had the Riot Act, 1714, designed to deal with isolated cases of civil disorder; indeed, legal thinking was based around 'the enemy within', going back to the Stuart rebellions and the English Civil War, citizens rebelling against the state. Even our imperial experience was limited – as lands were brought into the British Empire we imposed English legal systems, magistrates and judges. Foreign wars, such as the Crimean (1853–6), were offensive campaigns in enemy territory. The Boer War (1899–1902) was fought in a grey area of British colonies in South Africa but, again, with the enemy within – 'disloyal subjects'. The reaction from Parliament to the new European war was the Defence of the Realm Act, 1914, but was this an abrogation of civil liberty and the imposition of martial law, as has been claimed?

This book examines the impact of wartime legislation on the people of this country: not from the law reports, judges and learned counsel, or the accounts of the major trials in the higher courts, but from the stories of ordinary people: housewives, shopkeepers, soldiers and children, very few of whom were representatives of the 'criminal classes'. The early period was marked by a flurry of new legislation which often illustrated a lack of knowledge of existing law, and many of the orders and regulations were clumsily implemented at a local or regional level which rarely matched existing police and judicial boundaries, and led to substantial difficulties in operation and to inconsistencies in sentencing. As will be seen, responsibility for these regulations rested variously with the 'competent naval or military authority', the War Office, the Home Secretary, the Central Control Board, the military tribunals, the munitions tribunals, or the Food Controller, and underneath all of this sat the magistrates, trying to make sense of it all and to do justice to those before them.

This book is arranged thematically and to an extent chronologically. Chapter 1 provides an introduction to the criminal legal system of 1914, with its police courts, petty sessions, quarter sessions and assizes, as well as the wide range of work undertaken by the magistrates' courts. The selection and appointment of magistrates had been challenged and reformed by the Liberal government and, despite the absence of women the bench was becoming more representative of society.

Chapter 2 looks at the sentencing options available for magistrates. Justice was fast and punishment was very straightforward, with the same formula we use today: fine or imprisonment. The latter was much more widely used, particularly for fine defaulters. Probation was very much an innovation (1907) and magistrates were still learning how to use it effectively. The power to imprison youngsters had been removed in the Children Act, 1908, but juvenile offenders could be birched or sent to reformatory or industrial schools for several years.

Chapter 3 follows the transition to war, with the implementation of existing legislation for the mobilization, transport and billeting of the reserves and Territorial forces, to the rapid development and implementation of new emergency laws, often badly drafted and poorly understood.

Chapter 4 examines three legal systems: that of martial law, military law, and civil (criminal) law. Although we are primarily interested in the magistrates' courts, early Defence of the Realm Act cases were tried by courts-martial and the distinction between military and civil procedure needs to be established.

Chapter 5 explores the origins and impact of the Defence of the Realm Act (DoRA) and its amendments and its myriad subsidiary regulations. Initially an emergency response to the fears of invasion, the early regulations were replaced with a much wider set that gave almost unrestrained powers to the naval and military authorities and government departments and kept the courts busy for the rest of the war.

Chapter 6 is concerned with the Aliens (Restriction) Act, 1914 and the treatment of the tens of thousands of Germans, Austrians and Turks ordinarily resident in this country. Cautiously tolerated for the first few months of the war, and controlled through rigorous registration, the sinking of the *Lusitania* by a German submarine in early 1915 and subsequent public disorder brought about an urgent need to intern enemy aliens. The legal basis for this was the common law principle that they were His Majesty's enemies – effectively prisoners of war – and this made them the responsibility of the War Office rather than the Home Office.

Chapter 7 begins with a recognition that alcohol use and abuse was several orders of magnitude greater than anything seen today: public houses were open from early in the morning until late at night (in London they were only closed between 12.30 am and 5 am), and men – and women – routinely drank at breakfast and lunchtimes, and at times in between, even when at work. The impact on industry was enormous. Magistrates found their existing licensing powers insufficient and the Defence of the Realm Act regulations had limited geographical application, so the Intoxicating Liquor (Temporary Restrictions) Act, 1914 was enacted, some of the effects of which were not amended until 2003. Sensitive to the fears of prohibition and the influence of the abstinence campaigners, the government used the theme of 'efficiency' to justify and promote a new attitude to alcohol consumption, and a new and separate Defence of the Realm (Liquor Control) Act, 1915 created the Central Control Board to oversee and coordinate the patchwork of orders in place around the country. They also worked with the powerful and influential brewing industry to both reduce production and alcohol content.

Chapter 8 looks at the one regulation that had more impact on the community than any other, and brought thousands of people into court. The first lighting controls (the term 'blackout' was not used in the First World War) were introduced almost casually, as the feasibility of attack from the air was unknown, but the first Zeppelin raids of 1915 removed any doubts about the threat. Uniquely, the DoRA lighting regulation was the only one under the direct control of the Home Secretary himself, who eventually imposed a system of control orders for the whole country.

Chapter 9 considers the transition of a civilian community into a 'military and industrial machine'. In 1914 both the regular and the Territorial forces were much more in the public eye and the magistrates' courts routinely dealt with deserters and absentees. With the rush of recruits in response to Kitchener's appeal, justices worked in shifts to assist with the process of attestation. In an attempt to resolve the conflicting demands for 'men and munitions' the National Registration Act, 1915 required everyone in the country to register their age and occupation but many, correctly, saw this as a prelude to compulsory military service. With the failure of the voluntary Group (or Derby) Scheme to secure enough recruits, the Military Service Act, 1916 placed every man of military age (18–41) in the Army Reserve, and those not in military service were expected to undertake 'work of a national importance', in munitions or industry. By the end of the war every adult in the country had been registered and categorized, ready for military or national service at the government's call.

Chapter 10 looks at the changing social conditions brought about by the war and in particular the effects on women and families. Youth crime increased rapidly, variously attributed to the absence of fathers and male teachers on military service, mothers absent on munitions work, and the subversive influence of the cinema. Other opportunities for criminal behaviour arose through abuse of the generous scheme of military separation and family allowances, and women, earning their own money for the first time, turning to drink. Given the limited sentencing options at the time, magistrates increasingly turned to the use of the relatively new option of probation.

Chapter 11 looks at the nonsensical food regulations implemented in astonishing numbers in the last year of the war. Learning none of the lessons from the DoRA, lighting, licensing or registration experiences, a barrage of confusing and badly-drafted orders was fired off from the office of the Food Controller, at times on a daily basis. The orders were promulgated in the limited-circulation *London Gazette* and policed by local authority inspectors, and producers, shopkeepers, consumers and magistrates struggled to keep up with seasonal and regional regulations with the inevitable result that many found themselves in court.

Chapter 12 takes a broad view of crime and punishment during the war. The regular police were rapidly depleted at the outset as many officers were reservists and were called up, and others were young and fit and keen to serve. Their place was taken by an army of special constables who, with warrant card, armlet and truncheon, took on the responsibility for registering aliens, enforcing the lighting and licensing controls, patrolling the streets and a host of other duties. The Criminal Justice Act, 1914 brought about changes to sentencing options and the courts at all levels saw their criminal workload decrease, and some of the prisons were closed. And then there were the magistrates themselves: many did join the forces and several lost their lives. Others fell foul of the regulations and found themselves appearing before their colleagues. For some magisterial duties were not enough, and they joined the special constabulary or the Volunteers. And most served quietly and conscientiously for the duration.

Chapter 13 reflects on the impact of the wartime legislation and considers its legacy, in terms of the Second World War and today. The delegation of powers under the Defence of the Realm Act and the lack of parliamentary oversight was regarded as unconstitutional, and the relationship of the military to the civil authorities and the courts has been subject to close scrutiny over the years, and is clearly defined in modern legislation.

The sourcebooks and journals for understanding the criminal justice system at the start of the First World War are Atkinson's *Magistrates' Practice*, 10th edition, 1913; Wigram's *Justice's Note-book*, 9th edition, 1910; Alexander's *The Administration of Criminal Justice*, 1915; 'Middlesex Magistrate', *The Justice of the Peace and his Functions; on and off the Bench*, J. M. Dent & Sons, 1911; and, a name familiar to the modern magistrate, Stone's *Justices' Manual*, 46th edition, 1914. Published legislation is found in the *Public General Statutes* and, with commentary, in Chitty's *Annual Statutes* (which also includes DoRA and other regulations). Discussion about magisterial practice, legal commentary, and legislative updates are to be found in the *Justice of the Peace* (first published in 1837 and now titled *Criminal Law & Justice Weekly*). The mighty *Defence of the Realm Manual, revised to 31 August 1918*, by Charles Cook/BiblioLife, contains both the Defence of the Realm Acts and amendments, and the full set of regulations. The *Food Control Manual*, 1918 is a separate publication. The principles and practice of military law can be found in the *Manual of Military Law*, War Office, 1907, which contains the Army Act, 1881 and the Rules of Procedure; and the *King's Regulations and Orders for the Army*, HMSO 1912. *Hansard* is the official report of proceedings in the House of Commons and House of Lords, and provides an insight into the thinking of the politicians in framing wartime legislation. The *London Gazette* published all the Acts and regulations and was the official source of information used by the authorities. Court registers are held by many local records offices but prove to be frustratingly lacking in detail, merely listing names, offences, and sentences. The real character of the magistrates' court and the people using it comes from the local newspapers, which often carry verbatim accounts of the proceedings. The excellent online British Newspaper Archive[2] provides a wealth of such information. I am immensely grateful to the Deputy Justices Clerk, East Group London, who has so kindly given me access to the legal libraries at Stratford and Thames Magistrates' Courts. I am very grateful to His Honour Richard Seymour QC for his continued interest and support for this book, and I am indebted to my editor, Stephen Chumbley, for his hard work on the manuscript and proofs. Extensive endnotes are provided with each chapter with references to the source material, but where legislation is quoted it is derived directly from the relevant Act.

At the time of the First World War, our country was called the United Kingdom of Great Britain and Ireland. The legal system in Scotland was and is different to that in

England and Wales, and Ireland had considerable legal problems of its own (including the imposition of martial law in 1916 following the Easter Rising). Given that this book is about summary jurisdiction and the magistrates' courts, I have reluctantly decided to concentrate on the system as practised in England and Wales, with the inclusion of Scottish cases and examples where they fit into general practice.

Many of the sentences imposed were financial penalties and used the pre-decimal coinage system of pounds, shillings and pence (Lsd). There were twelve pennies in a shilling, and twenty shillings in a pound, with a shilling being equivalent to 5p in modern money. Slightly confusingly, fines of £1 or £2 are often recorded as 20s and 40s. For larger amounts the guinea was used, which was a unit of twenty-one shillings. There were a number of low-denomination coins – the farthing was one quarter of a penny, next was the half penny or 'ha'penny', followed by the 'thrupenny bit', the sixpence or 'tanner', the one-shilling 'bob', the two-shilling florin (usually described as 'two bob'), the half crown, worth two and six, and the pocket-bursting crown (5s). The 10s half sovereign and £1 sovereign coins were replaced at the outbreak of war by the new 10s and £1 notes.

Costs of one pound ten shillings and sixpence would be written £1 10s 6d; but it isn't particularly helpful to restate this in modern terms as £1.52½. 1914 values can be converted to today's prices using tools such as the Bank of England inflation calculator.[3] This suggests that £1 in 1914 is worth about £104 today, but there was significant inflation during the war so that the 1918 pound is worth about £51. I have avoided the tedium of converting every amount into modern currency: a simple rule of thumb is to add two zeroes to any 1914 price in pounds, and to add two zeroes and then halve any 1918 value. In 1914 a labourer earned around 20s a week, a skilled tradesman 40s, so the impact of a 10s fine can be appreciated. Notwithstanding inflation, wages more than doubled during the war, and 'war bonuses' (temporary pay rises for the duration of the war only) substantially increased take-home pay, with munitions work being especially lucrative.

Rates of Wages of Typical Classes of Labour, July 1914 (*Hansard*, 13 July 1923)

INDUSTRY	Per week
Building (40 large towns)	
Bricklayers	40s
Painters	36s
Labourers	26s
Engineering (16 of the principal districts)	
Fitters and turners	38s
Labourers	22s
Shipbuilding (9 of the principal districts)	
Shipwrights	41s
Ship joiners	40s
Labourers	22s

INDUSTRY	Per week
Railway service	
Engine drivers	45s to 50s
Ticket collectors	23s to 27s
Goods porters	19s to 23s
Road transport	
Tram drivers (50 of the principal districts)	30s
One-horse carters (12 large towns)	25s
Printing (27 large towns)	
Hand compositors and machine minders	35s
Bookbinders and machine rulers	33s
Agriculture (England and Wales)	
Ordinary labourers	14s to 22s
Dock labour (10 of the principal ports)	Per day
Ordinary cargo workers	4s 6d to 6s 8d
Shipping (foreign-going vessels)	Per month
Able seamen	£5 to £5 10s
Firemen	£5 10s to £6

Other imperial measurements are shown as described at the time: acres, hundredweights (cwt), pounds weight (lbs), feet, yards and miles. Another archaism is the use of the male pronoun to describe both sexes, for which I apologize in advance as it occurs so frequently in the narrative, along with 'chairman', rather than 'chair'.

By 1918 there were some four million men serving in the British Army, with another 450,000 in the Royal Navy. Across most of the country the army was the most visible service, and so most of the references to His Majesty's Forces in this book are in fact to soldiers, rather than sailors.

My interest in this subject arose from the research I carried out for my previous book, Chelmsford in the Great War',[4] as I saw the way in which all aspects of life on the home front were permeated by increasingly intrusive rules, restrictions and regulations, and seemingly petty infractions of which ended up in the magistrates' court. I wrote an article for The Magistrate, the Journal of the Magistrates' Association, and gave a presentation on the subject, and this inspired me to research the subject further. I have now served as a justice of the peace in east London (Stratford and Thames) for nearly two decades and chair both the adult and youth benches. In this time I have witnessed many changes to the law and its practice – the Human Rights Act of 1998 and implementation in 2000; new forms of community penalties such as anti-social behaviour orders; the recognition of domestic violence as a distinct area of judicial practice; changes to sentencing powers to deal with the prevalence of knife crime; and even technological changes, as we have now (May 2016) been issued with bench iPads. But through all this the 'job' has remained the same: to deliver justice to our community, to listen to the voice of the inarticulate, to sift through conflicting accounts of the same event and determine the truth, and, where necessary, to punish but hopefully rehabilitate. Reading through countless case studies and reports for my research for this book I have been struck by the number of occasions that the common sense and humanity of the justices has been displayed and I would hope that Mr Leycester and Mr Booth, the magistrates for Thames Court during the First World War, would recognize these same qualities on our bench today.

Chapter 1

Summary Justice 1914

Petty Sessions Reports
Tamworth County
Tuesday 28 July 1914
Staffordshire

Before Lieutenant Colonel E.S.P. Wolferstan (chairman), Mr T. Levett-Prinsep, and Mr T.F. Cheatle

On the Scenic Whirlwind
George H. Houghton, an attendant at the Fair ground at Tamworth, was charged with stealing two shillings and fourpence, the moneys of Alexander Sutherland, engineer's apprentice, 27 Marmion Street, Tamworth, on July 27. Prosecutor stated that at 10 p.m. he was in the Fair ground, Lady Meadow, and went on what was known as 'the Scenic Whirlwind.' Accused was engaged on the machine, taking money. Prosecutor tendered him a half-crown piece to pay one penny each for himself and a young lady, and he expected 2s. 4d. change. Accused asked him if he had less change, and he replied 'No.' Accused then went to another part of the machine, and did not come back with the change. Later prosecutor went to him and asked him for it, and accused denied that he had taken half-a-crown from him and said that he was not on that portion of the machine at the time. Prosecutor had no doubt about the accused being the man. On the application of Inspector Hall, accused was remanded until next Tuesday.[1]

This news report is just one of the matters reported from Tamworth Petty Sessions court on Tuesday, 28 July 1914. There were several cases of drunkenness, a man was accused of beating his wife, two men were charged with stealing mushrooms, and there was an application for an occasional licence to sell intoxicants at Drayton Manor for the Fazeley Cricket Club sports day. It was typical of the routine work undertaken by magistrates across England and Wales at that time, and indeed is still representative of the bread-and-butter work of the modern magistrates' court. But although the offences may still be the same, the processes and procedures of the magistrates' courts – the courts of summary jurisdiction – require further exploration.

Houghton's case is a good example. This prosecution was brought by the laying of an information by Alexander Sutherland, 17, motivated, no doubt, by the wish to stand up for his own honour before his sweetheart. Once Houghton had been remanded into custody, he next appeared before Lieutenant Colonel Wolferstan and Mr F. Moseley at the Tamworth County Police Court on Tuesday 4 August. Sutherland's evidence was read out again, and he added that the accused told him he could wait all night and still not get his money back.

The young lady, Lucy Vickers, gave evidence corroborating the half crown and the failure to give any change. Sutherland had then gone to PC Hulme and complained. The police officer interviewed Houghton who told him he had only been given one half crown that session, from a man 'wearing a billy-cock hat'.[2] He was then taken to the police station by which time Houghton was realizing the trouble that was brewing for him, and he offered to pay the half crown back because he did not want to go to gaol again. He then made a statement admitting that he had taken the money.

The magistrates listened as Houghton told them that he was trying to lead a straight life and it was not his fault he had made a slip. However, despite the comprehensive presentation of the evidence this was not the trial. Colonel Wolferstan and his colleagues decided to send him to the Staffordshire Quarter Sessions or Assizes, whichever came first, for sentencing, and remanded him in custody. And so, on Tuesday, 20 October 1914, Houghton was brought into the third court at the Shirehall in Stafford, Mr Henry S. Staveley Hill JP MP presiding.[3] The facts were presented and the prisoner was found guilty, and sentenced to three months' imprisonment as prisoner number 5198 in Stafford Gaol.

In 1913 there were 731,648 prosecutions in the courts of summary justice, resulting in 569,947 convictions. 75,291 were discharged, and the remaining 85,810 were dealt with by means of recognizances or probation orders.[4] Only 127 cases were appealed to the quarter sessions, and only 54 were successful.

There were 216 boroughs and 95 counties and liberties across the country, with 1,053 courts of summary jurisdiction and in 1912 there were 23,039 lay justices of the peace in England and Wales. The typical bench was becoming more diverse. The property qualification had been removed from municipal appointments in the local authority reforms of 1882, and following successful experiments in the Duchy of Lancaster working-class magistrates ('artisans') were beginning to make their presence known on municipal benches around the country.[5] The new Liberal government of 1906 abolished the remaining property qualification for county magistrates with the Justice of the Peace Act, 1906, and challenged the existing Conservative Unionist domination of the magistracy by appointing considerable numbers of their own members. In the previous five years of Tory government there had been 6,032 new magistrates appointed; in the first year alone of the Liberal administration there were no fewer than 3,218. The Liberals were supported by the then Labour Representation Committee (which with twenty-nine seats became the Labour Party after the 1906 election) who were rewarded by the appointment of a number of Labour magistrates, including Mr Albert Bellamy, an engine driver on the London & North Western Railway in Stockport.[6] Such men were often politically active, as union leaders or councillors, and in response to the large number of Liberal appointments the Lord Chancellor warned, 'It is one thing to correct monopolies and open the Bench to the honourable ambition of men of all parties. It is quite a different thing to treat the position of justice as merely of mainly a reward for political service.'[7]

The perception of political bias and the 'considerable and widespread want of confidence in the justices of the peace as present selected' resulted in the 1910 Royal Commission on the Selection of Justices of the Peace. It was predicated on three assumptions, firstly, that in a large proportion of cases, particularly in the counties, they were drawn from the propertied classes; secondly, that benches of justices were becoming mere juries, with the clerk informing them of the law and of the evidence – this was especially pronounced with the *ex officio* mayoral appointments, who lacked experience; and thirdly, the distorting effect of reasonably blatant political appointments.[8] The Commission interviewed many senior legal and political figures, and reached a number of conclusions, which included:

- Anyone recommending persons for appointment as Justices should decline to recognize political or religious options as any ground of disqualification or qualification.
- Persons appointed to the office should be men of moral and good personal character, general ability, business habits, independent judgement, and common sense.
- It is in the public interest that persons of every social grade should be appointed Justices of the Peace, and that working men with a first-hand knowledge of the conditions of life among their own class should be appointed to county as well as the borough benches.[9]

They also presented a vision of the courts of summary jurisdiction:

> [The court] should be a place where all kinds of people, good and bad, high and low, can be sure of meeting with courtesy and sympathy, with impartial consideration and well-weighed judgement, and appeal to, and faith in, their better nature. The court should be a place with a bracing and elevating tone and atmosphere, not depressing or humiliating. People should come there for moral assistance, or for a helping hand, rather than for revenge or punishment. In a word a court should be a centre for regenerative influences. And the justices who preside over it should befit agents of such influence.

One of the most important results of the Commission's work was the formation of Advisory Committees in the course of 1911. They were to assist the Lords Lieutenant in identifying and recommending individuals for nomination to the Lord Chancellor. The members were supposedly more representative and with local knowledge of their communities, but the Warwickshire Advisory Committee seems to have been made up of the usual 'great and good' and probably as remote from the people as it was possible to be. Under the chairmanship of the Lord Lieutenant, the Marquis of Hertford, the committee comprised:

> Lord Algernon Percy, Deputy Lieutenant and justice of the peace since 1892.
> Sir Michael Lakin, Bart. Alderman on the county council, and JP since 1880.
> Mr J. Stratford Dugdale, KC, Recorder of Birmingham and JP since 1878.

Mr Stanes Brocket Henry Chamberlayne, JP since 1881.
Rev. William MacGregor, member of the county council and JP since 1893.
Mr Thomas Hunter, member of the county council, active in Liberal politics and
JP since 1901.[10]

County magistrates were appointed by the Lord Chancellor on the recommendation
of the Lord Lieutenant of the county (who probably knew the candidate socially), and
in boroughs names were proposed by the town council, trades unions, or the local
MP. With the abolition of property qualifications the magistracy was opened up to
a much broader cross section of society, but there were some restrictions: holders of
liquor licences were disqualified, as were pawnbrokers (who received and disposed of
distrained goods on behalf of the bailiffs), and there was a semi-formal ban on newspaper
proprietors. Clergymen were discouraged – as Lord Campbell suggested to the Royal
Commission, it would be supposed that the gentleman would be 'too much occupied by
his spiritual functions to be able to devote sufficient time to the duties of the bench'.[11]
The commissioners also discovered that there was a widespread and not inaccurate view
that most of the magistrates did very little work, and some were only after 'the honour
of the magic letters after their name'.

Under the Qualification of Women (County and Borough Councils) Act, 1907 women
were not permitted to become magistrates, even if they held office as mayor of the local
council. Dr Elizabeth Garrett Anderson was elected mayor of Aldeburgh in 1908 and
1909, and Mrs H. Partington was the mayor of Glossop in 1916, succeeding her late
husband who had himself been mayor for three years in succession.[12] Dukinfield Town
Council elected Mrs Kenyon as mayor in 1917; none of these ladies were permitted to
accept the *ex officio* seat on the bench.

In August 1914 fourteen new magistrates were appointed to the Commission of the
Peace for West Hartlepool and were representative of many similar appointments at the
time:

Mr Walter Andrew, paper merchant (Liberal).
Mr E. Birks, head of the firm of Birks Bros., grocers (Conservative).
Mr William Brankstone, blacksmith (Liberal-Labour).
Mr C.H. Ford, shipowner and broker (Liberal).
Mr J.T. Furness, eldest son of the late Alderman T. Furness and a nephew of the
late Lord Furness (Liberal).
Mr Maurice S. Gibb, manager of the Central Marine Engine Works (Conservative).
Mr A.B. Horsley, of the firm of Geo. Horsley and Co., shipowners and timber
merchants (Liberal).
Mr R. Reid, shipyard plater (Conservative-Labour).
Mr I.J. Robinson, auctioneer (Liberal).
Dr E. Swanwick, medical practitioner (Liberal).
Mr J.S. Stainsby, newspaper compositor (Liberal-Labour).
Mr H. Weatherall, clerk, a prominent temperance and social worker (Liberal).
Captain Willis, shipowner, chairman of the Pilotage Board (Conservative).

Mr Somerville-Woodiwis, dentist, a prominent member of the local Roman Catholic community (Independent).[13]

On appointment the new magistrate usually had to pay a fee, which for county magistrates was £2 and magistrates appointed *ex officio* 5s, although the exact amounts varied across the country. Training did not exist, which Wigram (a JP himself) pointed out in the preface to his *Justice's Note-book*, 'His appointment upon the Commission implies no knowledge of the Statutes at large … his sole credentials are the instincts and education of an English gentleman'.[14] The 1906 Act required that the man should possess 'education and intelligence', which Lord Lansdowne recognized did not include a 'knowledge of dead languages' but simply the ability to differentiate between 'mere assertion and matters of proved fact'.[15] The new magistrate made an oath of allegiance and the judicial oath before the Mayor, or at quarter sessions:

I, A. B., swear by Almighty God that I will be faithful and bear true allegiance to His Majesty King George the Fifth, his heirs and successors according to law.

I, A. B., swear by Almighty God that I will well and truly serve our Sovereign Lord, King George the Fifth, in the office of Justice of the Peace, and I will do right to all manner of people after the laws and usages of this realm without fear or favour, affection or ill-will.

The administrative unit for the magistracy was the commission of the peace for the county or borough, but in practice these were subdivided into petty sessional divisions (following the Courts Act 2003 these were replaced with Local Justice Areas from 2005) and the magistrate performed his duties at this level. As Atkinson put it, 'as a matter of custom, courtesy and convenience, and in some cases express enactment, its members do not concern themselves with any affairs … as having arisen within another division'.[16] At the time there was, if not a hierarchy, certainly a distinction between county and borough magistrates. County justices could sit at borough courts ('concurrent jurisdiction') but not vice versa, and they also sat at quarter sessions, which in the boroughs were run by the legally-qualified Recorder. A sitting of the justices at a police court or any other place appointed, was deemed a 'petty sessions of the peace' in a petty sessional division. County justices could also appoint places as occasional court houses (excluding licensed premises), including police stations, but any such place had to be an 'open court', with public access, and had to comprise at least two justices (Summary Jurisdiction Act, 1879). The justices of the petty sessional division appointed or elected a chair, which in the boroughs was the Mayor. For the purposes of each sitting the magistrates would elect a chair for each bench for the day, usually the senior magistrate unless a stipendiary was present. Archaically the work of the magistrates was done at quarter sessions; petty sessions, licensing and other duties were described as 'out of sessions'.

The London metropolitan or police magistrates were a special class of magistrate under the Metropolitan Police Courts Act, 1839. Legally trained and qualified, with at least seven years' standing as a barrister, they were appointed by the King on the nomination of the Home Secretary and were given the power, when sitting alone, 'to do any act, and exercise any jurisdiction, which can be done or exercised by two or more ordinary justices'. Under the Municipal Corporations Act, 1882 a local authority could apply to the Home Secretary to appoint stipendiary magistrates. The relationship between lay justices and their paid colleagues had some tensions. There were twenty-seven London police magistrates, sitting at fourteen police courts, and nineteen stipendiaries in the rest of England and Wales. Some believed that they were drawn 'exclusively from a class that has never known want', and were 'remote from the life of the poor', which seems an odd criticism given that the county magistrates in particular were almost exclusively men of wealth and standing and, despite the reforms of the Liberal government, staunchly Conservative. Indeed it was argued that the lay magistrates were either businessmen with other interests and in an undue hurry to work their way through the court lists, or gentlemen of leisure, quite content to draw out the proceedings.[17]

Although recommended practice for lay justices was to sit as a bench of two as a minimum (and in practice there could often be as many as five or six), they had more extensive powers when sitting alone than today. Under the Indictable Offences Act, 1848 a single lay magistrate could receive a charge and issue a summons or warrant and, if the accused was present, conduct the initial hearing to assess the strength of the evidence for a subsequent trial, or discharge him. The single magistrate could also remand a prisoner into custody or set bail.

There were two aspects to the duties of the lay magistrate: *judicial*, in matters relating to the determination of criminal complaint and offence; and *administrative* (or 'ministerial'), which were civil functions. The ministerial acts were non-discretionary, so, for example, a justice was not allowed to refuse an application for a warrant (assuming it had been filled in correctly and paid for). Other acts included the signing of a summons, the hearing of a statutory declaration, receiving and hearing an information or complaint, allow the poor rates, and attesting recruits. None of these involve a 'decision', judicial or otherwise.

Although many ministerial duties had been handed over to the borough and county councils there was a regular annual calendar of business for the courts of summary jurisdiction. This included the scheduling of the quarter sessions, as well as the licensing, watch and lunacy committees, returns to the Home Secretary on fines, fees and other sums received. Much of the non-judicial, administrative work of the courts was dealt with in 'special sessions'. Most were fixed in the justices' annual calendar, but additional sessions could be held for special reasons. These sessions covered:

1. Granting of licences for alehouses, beerhouses, wine and refreshment houses, and licences for billiard tables; held in the first fourteen days of February each year, the precise date must be fixed at a petty sessions held at least twenty-one days before.
2. Transferring such licences, not less than four nor more than eight special sessions must be fixed, to be held on dates appointed at the annual licensing meeting.
3. Appointing parochial constables, between 24 March and 9 April. In boroughs the justices could appoint special constables during October.

4. Reviewing and allowing the lists of jurors, within the last seven days of September. Notice of the sessions must be given before 20 August.
5. Hearing appeals against parochial rates; special sessions to be held at least four times a year. Twenty eight days' public notice to be given, by fixing a notice on church doors.
6. Appointing justices to act as 'judicial authorities' under the Lunacy Act, 1890, in October. Special sessions must also be held for appointing visitors and for licensing private asylums.
7. Appointing overseers of the poor, annually on 25 March or within fourteen days thereafter.

The justices' prison visiting committee was appointed each year in the first week after 28 December and its members were given free access to the local prison and to the prisoners, and they had a limited rôle in the exercise of prison discipline.

The magistrates' or police court, or court of petty sessions, was a court of summary jurisdiction and dealt with the vast majority of prosecutions in the first instance. The magistrates conducted the preliminary examination of prisoners charged with indictable offences to be referred to the quarter sessions or assizes. In general terms, they dealt with non-indictable offences. Much of the procedure was first set down in the Summary Jurisdiction Act, 1848 (also known as the Jervis Act), which defined the rôle of lay justices in criminal and civil matters. The Summary Jurisdiction Act, 1879 required that offences triable by a court of summary jurisdiction must be 'heard, tried, determined and adjudged' by a bench consisting of two or more justices.[18]

The common law descriptions of offences as either felonies or misdemeanours were becoming slightly archaic by 1914, with the use instead of indictable and summary offences. Felonies were originally crimes which were punishable by forfeiture of land or goods, but in general usage were those which carried the death penalty and, in later days, transportation and latterly penal servitude. Examples include murder, manslaughter, rape, arson, treason, burglary, and kidnapping, and these offences were sent directly from the magistrates' courts to the assizes. It was a common law duty for any person witnessing a felony or attempted felony to arrest the offender. Misdemeanours, according to Wigram, include 'every possible act of misbehaviour cognisable by courts which does not amount to a felony',[19] and, in general usage, were indictable offences which were not felonies. Summary offences were therefore neither felonies nor misdemeanours. This terminology was abolished under the Criminal Law Act, 1967, when the term 'arrestable offence' was introduced.

Proceedings began with the process of laying or preferring a complaint or an information before the justices. A *complaint* would relate to the payment of money or the performance of an act (or not), in the sense of a civil matter which might result in an order but not a conviction. Examples would include the recovery of maintenance for a bastard child or deserted wife, or of ejectment (eviction) of tenants from a property for non-payment of rent. An *information* was the preliminary step in criminal proceedings, and could be brought by the police, by an individual (the 'party aggrieved'), or by an agency or authority, such as the Poor Law Guardians at the workhouse. The information did not need to be in writing but in practice this was strongly recommended if the alleged offence was punishable by imprisonment or fine, and if the magistrates were to issue a warrant the information was to be given on oath. There was no public duty to prosecute, in the sense of the modern Crown Prosecution Service, and victims of assault or theft were required to initiate any prosecution themselves. A police officer had the duty of keeping the peace: if he saw two men fighting it was his duty to break them up, but he was not required to prosecute.[20]

The magistrates could decide if a summons or warrant was necessary; the former was given or served to the defendant in person and notified them of the complaint and gave a date and time to appear at the court. An individual laying a complaint or an information could pay 2s for a summons which would be recovered as the costs imposed on a successful prosecution (unless the defendant was imprisoned). A warrant was likely to be granted if the magistrate believed that the defendant was likely to abscond on being served, or had no fixed abode, and it was given to the police, providing authority to arrest and detain the defendant and to bring them to court as soon as possible after the warrant was executed. If the individual named in the warrant resided in, or was likely to have removed to, an area outside the magistrate's jurisdiction, the document had to be given to a local magistrate who would endorse and sign on the back of the paper, a process known as 'backing'. This was not required if in 'fresh pursuit', where the person named in the warrant was actually being followed at the time. The content of the information had to include one offence only, and the name of the alleged offender. The exact details of the offence were not, at this stage, material. Witnesses could also be summoned, or brought in under warrant, but warrants could not be issued for complaints, which were summons only.

Police officers, and indeed members of the public, were empowered to arrest anyone 'found offending'; in addition to felonies in progress or believed to be likely, the Town Police Clauses Act, 1847 provided a whole series of minor offences for which the miscreant was liable to have their collar felt, including having an unmuzzled ferocious dog, driving cattle 'furiously', leaving a shop awning less than eight feet off the ground, or placing any line, cord or pole across any street, or hanging or placing any clothes thereon. Those arrested would be taken to the police station and detained until the next magistrates' court, or no more than forty hours. This Act, although largely repealed, is still in force today and used for activities such as street processions.

A police officer could make an arrest with or without a warrant, and 'charged' the person by stating the offence of which he was accused, or by reading the information on the warrant. He was also required to provide the caution that 'You need not say anything in answer to the charge, but whatever you may say will be taken down in writing and may be used against you at your trial'. The arrested person was then taken to the police station and detained until he could be taken to before the magistrates. Alternatively the defendant could be given bail, which involved the giving of recognizances by the offender and, if necessary, by one or more individuals providing sureties. The recognizance (pronounced 'reconnaissance') was the obligation to attend court at a certain date and time. The surety was an amount offered by the defendant or others, to be paid to the court if the recognizance was breached. If others were standing as sureties they had to attend the police station or court to make the appropriate declaration, and the police and magistrates had to be satisfied in all cases that they had the means to pay the amount specified. Failure to attend as required led to the recognizance being 'estreated' ('extracted') and the sureties became His Majesty's absolute debtors, and fully liable for the sums promised.

The police brought the majority of prosecutions to court, to the extent, as seen, that the term 'police court' became synonymous with 'magistrates' court', and by law the London stipendiaries were known as police magistrates. Many of those involved in the legal system were unhappy with this apparent relationship, and the implied collusion between the police and the bench.[21] The competence of the police as prosecutors was also challenged, and in one pronouncement the High Court considered it 'very bad practice to allow a policeman to act as an advocate before any tribunal, so that he would have to bring forward only such evidence as he might think fit, and keep back any that he might consider likely to tell in the favour of any person placed upon his trial'.[22] In 1908 the Lord Chief Justice was baffled as to how a police officer 'can stand indifferent and at the same time have … to support the charges brought by his fellows', and worse, how could he be expected to give impartial evidence when 'his superior officer is conducting the case against the prisoner'.[23] The *Justice of the Peace* reminded magistrates that it was their duty to ensure impartiality and to thoroughly challenge any perceived bias in the police management of a prosecution.[24]

The defendant, appearing at court by way of summons, or produced from the cells by warrant, appeared before the magistrates' court (the usual routine was charges in the morning, summonses in the afternoon[25]). A bench consisting of two justices or more was able to impose fines of up to £100 or six months' imprisonment, but if the offence as charged carried a penalty of more than three months the defendant was entitled to a trial by jury and it was the duty of the court to notify him of this right (as we shall see this has implications for offences under the Defence of the Realm Act). If this right was asserted then the procedure was that for indictable offences (below). Some indictable matters could be dealt with at the magistrates' court or the higher court and the defendant had to elect the venue; alternatively, if the matter appeared serious or more complex the bench could decline jurisdiction and transfer the case to the assizes for trial by judge and jury.

Offences could be classified by the venue in which the trial was to take place:

1. Those triable at Quarter Sessions and Assizes, by ordinary procedure:
   a. Indictable, e.g. murder.
   b. Non-indictable, where accused has elected to be tried by jury, on being charged at Petty Sessions with an offence punishable by more than three months' imprisonment.
2. Those triable by justices at Petty Sessions in the exercise of their summary jurisdiction:
   c. Non-indictable offences.
   d. Indictable offences which may be dealt with summarily:
      i.   Offences committed by children.
      ii. Offences committed by young persons.

iii. Certain offences committed by adults, where the value of the property in question is less than 40s and the accused consents.
iv. When the accused pleads guilty.

In this context the Petty Sessions are the formally scheduled court sittings; indictable offences were not dealt with by lay magistrates at the police courts. If the matter was a summary-only offence the clerk then stated the details contained in the information and asked there was any cause why he should not be convicted. If the charge was admitted the magistrates were able to sentence immediately. If the defendant denied the charge and the prosecution was ready the matter could go to an immediate, simplified form of trial. The prosecutor was required to state the case and bring any and all prosecution witnesses as required. The defendant, almost invariably unrepresented, had the right to cross-examine and was often assisted by the court clerk. After the prosecution case closed, the defendant was allowed to give his own evidence, and bring forward witnesses of fact (who were there at the time of the offence), and of character. The prosecution was not permitted to respond unless points of law had been raised, although they could call further witnesses against the defence witnesses. The magistrates then decided to convict or acquit.

This approach seems refreshingly swift and efficient compared to the working of the modern magistrates' court, which, despite many well-intentioned reforms and initiatives, seem to have a culture of adjournment and delay. Although clearly there were cases where the prosecution was not ready to proceed on the day of the first hearing, in most cases they went ahead on the day, and as part of the normal court list. Adjournments, when granted, were very short – typically a week (magistrates were limited to a maximum remand in custody of eight days).

The list of offences recorded at Southend Petty Sessions in October 1914 gives a sense of the wide range of offences before the magistrates:[26]

Driving motor dangerously	Attempted suicide	Dangerous dog
Drunk (and disorderly)	Shop breaking	Permitting drunkenness
Malicious damage	Burglary	Desertion
Assault	Obstruction	Separation
No light on motor	Cattle straying	Ejectment
Cruelty to horse	Travelling without fare	Bastardy
Indecent language	Threats	Neglecting family
Larceny (unspecified)	Illegal pawning	Refusing to quit
Noisy hawking	Drunk in charge of a child	School attendance order
Carriage unattended	No light on cart	Alien failing to register
Embezzlement	False pretences	Absentee without leave
Keeping brothel	Riding on footpath	Army deserter
Prostitute behaving indecently	Allowing chimney to be on fire	Extinguishing light in public
Soliciting prostitution	Exposing person	Receiving army overcoat

The offender charged with an indictable offence appeared before the bench (which could be a single lay justice) on summons or from custody. However the bench was constituted it did not, in law, form a court of petty sessions and the hearing was administrative rather than judicial. In the absence of the modern Crown Prosecution Service (established in 1986 following the Prosecution of Offences Act, 1985) and in recognition of the injustice of the police conducting both the investigation and prosecution of an offence, the magistrates conducted a preliminary examination of the evidence to establish if there was 'a strong or probable presumption' of the defendant's guilt. The accused had no formal right to a defence lawyer at this stage, but, assuming he could afford one, this would not be refused. The hearing opened with the prosecutor stating the facts of the case and the witnesses for the prosecution were called, sworn and examined (and cross-examined) in what was in effect a dress rehearsal of the trial. This live evidence was taken down in writing by the clerk, read back to the witnesses and signed by them. At the end of the presentation of evidence, the clerk or magistrate read back the depositions to the defendant, who was then asked:

The charge against you is [...]. Having heard the evidence, do you wish to say anything in answer to the charge? You are not obliged to say anything unless you desire to do so; but whatever you say will be taken down in writing, and may be given in evidence against you at your trial. And you are also clearly to understand that you have nothing to hope from any promise of favour, and nothing to fear from any threat which may have been held out to you to induce you to make any admission or confession of your guilt; but that whatever you shall now say may be given in evidence against you upon your trial notwithstanding such promise or threat.

Note that this is not actually an invitation to enter a plea, as would be expected today. A standard response was 'I have nothing to say', and this was often recorded, somewhat archaically, in the Latin '*ponit se*' which meant 'I put myself [upon the country or the law]', indicating that he would let his peers in the jury decide the matter.

He would also be asked, at this stage, if he had witnesses of his own to call, and, if present, they too would be called, sworn and examined; otherwise he made his own deposition on oath. The magistrate or magistrates then considered the strength of the case and, if of the opinion that a jury would be unlikely to convict, they could discharge the matter. However, this being an administrative bench, rather than judicial, the prosecution were entitled to bring the case again if they obtained further evidence. If the justices decided that there was a case to answer the matter would be referred to the next quarter sessions or assizes, depending on which was sooner. The defendant could be remanded in custody or given bail. All of the witnesses, including the prosecutor, were then bound over to give evidence at the trial. A 'bill' was prepared and the names of the witnesses endorsed on the back.

The decision to send a case to quarter sessions or to the assizes usually depended on the seriousness of the offence. Judges were, for some reason, unhappy about dealing with what they perceived as trivial matters or, more correctly, 'less important cases', and preferred such matters to go before the quarter sessions. The dates of both were published well in advance, so defendants rarely had to wait more than two or three months. The next hurdle to face was the Grand Jury at quarter sessions.

The original courts of quarter and general sessions had a rôle that went far beyond the judicial processes of trials and appeals. They were the administrative bodies for the counties and exercised powers over the setting of rates, building and repair of roads, bridges and sewers, water supply, lunatic asylums, local prisons, reformatories and industrial schools, as well as several aspects of public health and housing (the full title of the *Justice of the Peace* journal was *Justice of the Peace and Local Government Review*, reflecting this historical origin). Most of these functions were lost when the Municipal Corporations Act, 1882 and Local Government Act, 1888 created the borough and county councils. Magistrates retained some jurisdiction, and although they no longer set the rates they were required to approve them (one of the administrative duties they were not allowed to refuse). The councils' Standing Joint Committees and Watch Committees comprised justices and councillors and were responsible for the police force. Magistrates also formed committees for prison visiting, lunatic asylums and licensing (the latter continued until 2003), and the close relationship between the court and the local authorities was marked by the *ex officio* appointment of the chairman of the county council (1888) and chairman of the district council (1894) to the bench for his year of office and the year after (except for women).[27]

The jurisdiction of the quarter sessions covered all indictable offences with the exception of:

1. Felonies which on a first conviction are punishable by death or penal servitude for life; these matters were dealt with at the assizes. Burglary was originally in this category but was brought into quarter sessions in 1896 for cases which were not grave or difficult.
2. Crimes likely to involve difficult questions of law, such as forgery, bigamy, perjury and libel, and financial offences involving banks, agents and trustees.

County quarter sessions were chaired by a senior magistrate, usually with legal qualifications as a solicitor, and at least one other justice sat with him; in reality the bench was made up of as many magistrates as could attend – sometimes eight or more. Borough quarter sessions were run by the Recorder, a judicial officer with legal qualifications, usually a barrister (King's Counsel) and appointed by the Crown. The administration of the court was in the hands of the Clerk of the Peace. The assizes were presided over by a judge of the High Court.

The ancient institution of the Grand Jury was an assembly of between twelve and twenty-four 'good and loyal' men drawn from the electors' lists of the sessional area by the sheriff, although the Grand Jury at the assizes was usually drawn from the magistrates of the county. At the borough quarter sessions there was no property qualification, but the grand juror at county sessions had to have an income of £10 year. These men (no women) were often 'from the highest positions in the county, freeholders and persons of consequence ranking after the peers'.[28] They were summoned by a precept from the sheriff, and their duties were to 'inquire into, present, do and execute all those things which on the part of our Sovereign Lord the King shall be commended to them'. The Grand Jury at the East Riding Quarter Sessions, Beverley, in April 1914 comprised:

Mr P Kettlewell, merchant, of Howden (foreman).
Mr Geoffrey Henry Brown, merchant, Sutton.
Mr Walter Bell, merchant, Brantlingham.
Mr A.E. Devin, chartered accountant, Hornsea.
Mr Ambrose Good, merchant, Cottingham.
Mr A.B. Hebblethwaite, land agent, Hornsea.
Mr C.A. Montifield, surveyor, Elloughton.
Mr A. Moscrop, farmer, Thorganby Hall.
Mr J.W. Nettleton, farmer, Cottam.
Mr C. Nesfield, famer, Kirbygrindalythe.
Mr R.A. Plimpton, farmer, Walkington.
Mr F.S. Staveley, farmer, Tibthorpe.
Mr D.F. Stubbings, farmer, Boynton.
Mr R. Wilson, gentleman, Norton.
Mr Steward, farmer, Holme-on-Spalding-Moor.
Mr R. Limon, draper, Bridlington.

On assembling at the court house, the grand jurors were sworn:

You, as foreman of this grand inquest for our Sovereign Lord the King for the body of this county of Essex, shall diligently inquire and true presentment make of all such manners and things as shall be given you in charge, or shall otherwise come to your knowledge, touching this present service. The King's counsel, your fellows', and your own, you shall observe and keep secret; you shall present on one through envy, hatred, or malice; neither shall you have anyone unpresented through fear, favour, or affection, gain reward, or the hope thereof but you shall present all things truly and indifferently as they shall come to your knowledge, according to the best of your skill and understanding.

The chairman (in the counties) or the Recorder (in the boroughs) read a Charge, which was usually some lofty statement about crime or the state of the world as they saw it. Mr G.A. Rimington JP, chairman of the Cumberland Quarter Sessions held in Carlisle in April 1914, expressed his fears of civil war.[29] Mr J.S. Dugdale KC, presiding at the Warwick Midsummer Quarter Sessions, 'had not the slightest hesitation in saying that it would be the duty of the Grand Jury to find a true bill in every case'.[30] Mr Samuel Roberts, JP MP, reported to the West Riding Quarter Sessions in January 1914 that he had the honour of sitting on the Royal Commission tasked with reviewing the Grand Jury system, and the duplication of procedure where the Grand Jury reviewed the evidence that the magistrates at petty sessions had already examined.

The men of the Grand Jury, having been sworn in, then retired in strict seclusion to a private room either in the court house or nearby, and examined the bills sent up from the magistrates' courts. In each case they examined the prosecution evidence and witnesses but nothing from the defence case or the accused, with the objective to find that there was a prima facie case against the defendant. If they decided that there was no grounds for prosecution, they wrote 'no true bill' across the face of the bill. If they found that there was a case, they endorsed the back of the bill with 'true bill' and returned it to presiding judge or magistrate in open court. At this point the bill became a formal indictment, and in routine practice, once the Grand Jury had returned all the true bills, the defendants were summoned and entered their pleas; those that pleaded guilty were dealt with by way of a short statement of the facts, representations from defence counsel, if any, and from the defendant, and sentence was passed.

Not guilty pleas required the empanelling of yet another body of men, the twelve 'good men and true' of the Petty Jury, who then heard the trial, at which the prosecution evidence was turned over yet again. This jury, formed of the less exalted names on the electoral register, also needed the property qualification (in the counties, £10 freehold or £20 leasehold per year). The effectiveness and value of the jury system had been investigated in 1913[31] and the report of the committee had confirmed that 'as regards the trial of all criminal cases a jury is still acknowledged everywhere to be for many reasons the tribunal most suitable for determining any question of a prisoner's guilt or innocence'.

At magistrates' courts it was not uncommon for a prosecution to be initiated by an individual, rather than the police, on application for a summons. It was once possible to bring a bill of indictment directly to the Grand Jury without any previous enquiry into the truth of the accusation by the magistrates in the lower court, but the Vexatious Indictments Act, 1859 limited the number of offences permitted to be brought this way, unless the accused was already in custody or the prosecutor had been bailed to attend.[32]

At county quarter sessions the trials were conducted before benches of magistrates. There were no magistrates present at borough quarter sessions or assizes, unless as members of the grand or petty juries.

There were six Circuits for the Assizes: Northern, Western, South-Eastern, Oxford, Midland, and North and South Wales and Chester, with two judges on each circuit. In 1914 Mr Justice Bray, on the South-Eastern Circuit, appeared at Huntingdon on 12 January, Cambridge on the 15th, on the 20th at Ipswich, on the 27th at Norwich and on 3 February at Chelmsford. These were grand affairs – the arrival of the judge was an occasion for civic pageantry, which led to much criticism. Mr Justice Darling, in his contribution to the Royal Commission on the Law's Delays in 1913, described the judge's retinue as consisting of a marshal, clerk, butler, cook, and valet; and the Sheriff had to provide the accommodation and domestic staff, as well as the judge's state coach, 'the ringing of church bells on his lordship's arrival, and the fanfares of trumpeters'.[33] Mr Justice Channell was met at the Midland Station in Nottingham by the High Sheriff, Under-Sheriff and acting Under-Sheriff, and was attended by a mounted escort as he was driven to the judge's lodgings.[34]

Police court, petty sessions, quarter sessions, or assizes: assuming conviction the offender needed to be sentenced.

Summary Offences

Adulteration (of food, drugs, etc)
Assaults: –
  aggravated
  on constable
  common, etc
Betting and gaming
Brothel keeping
Cruelty to animals
Cruelty to children
Diseases of Animals Acts, offences against
Dog, offences in relation to
Education Act, offences against
Explosives, offences in relation to
Fishery laws, offences against
Game laws, offences against: –
  night poaching
  day poaching
  unlawful possession of game, etc
  illegal buying and selling of game
  other offences
Highway Acts, offences against: –
  offence by owners and drivers of carts
  obstructions and nuisances
  heavy locomotives
  motor cars
  bicycles
Housing of the Working Class Acts, offences against
Indecent advertisements
Indecent exposure
Intoxicating liquor laws, offences against: –
  drunkenness, simple
  drunkenness, with aggravation
  unlicensed sale of drink
  habitual drunkards obtaining drink
  offences by licensed persons: –
    (1) permitting drunkenness
    (2) selling drink to children
    (3) selling drink to habitual drunkards
    (4) offences against Closing Regulations
    (5) other offences by licensed persons
  other offences
Labour laws, offences against: –
  intimidation
  breach of contracts
  offfences under Special Trades Acts
  offences under Truck Acts
  Mines Acts
  Factory Acts
  Shops Acts
  Employment of Children Acts
  other Acts for Protection of Labour

Malicious damage: –
    to animals
    to fences, etc
    to trees, shrubs, etc
    to fruit, etc
    other offences
Merchant Shipping Acts, offences against
Military and Naval law, offences against: –
    Army
    Navy
    Territorial Force
Parks, commons, and open spaces, offences in relation to
Pawnbrokers Acts, offences against: –
    offences by pawnbrokers
    unlawful pledging
    other offences
Police Regulations, offences against: –
    Metropolitan Police Acts
    Town Police Acts and other Police Acts
    Borough byelaws
    County byelaws
    Local Acts and byelaws
Poor Law, offences against: –
    neglecting to maintain family, etc
    misbehaviour by paupers
    stealing or destroying workhouses clothes
    other offences
Prevention of Crimes Acts: –
    offences by licence holders
    offences by supervisors
    special offences by twice-convicted persons
Prostitution
Railways, offences in relation to
Revenue laws, offences against
Sanitary law, offences against: –
    Public Health Acts and other General Acts
    Infectious Diseases Act
    Public Health (London) Act, 1891
    Local Acts and Byelaws
Stage Carriage and Cab Regulations, offences against
Stealing: –
    animals
    fences, etc
    trees, shrubs, etc
    fruit, plants, etc
    receiving stolen animals, trees, fruit, etc
Streets and Buildings, offences in relation to
Sunday trading, etc
Tramways Act, offences against
Unlawful possession
Vaccination Acts, offences against

Vagrancy Acts, offences against: –
  begging
  sleeping out
  gaming, etc
  found in inclosed premises, possessing picklocks, etc
  frequenting
  living on prostitute's earnings
  other offences
Weights and Measures Act, offences against
Wild Birds Protection Acts, offences against
Other offences

Indictable Offences Triable at the Court of Summary Jurisdiction

Simple larceny and offences punished as simple larceny
Larceny from the person
Larceny by a servant
Embezzlement
Obtaining by false pretences
Receiving stolen goods
Endangering railway passengers
Destroying railways
Setting fire to commons, etc.
Offences under the Post Office laws
Indecent assault upon a male person under 16
Indecent assault upon a female person under 16
Libel
Habitual drunkenness
Offences in connection with bankruptcy
Other indictable offences committed by children or young persons

Magistrates Sitting Alone: Maximum Fine of 20s or 14 Days

Gaming Act	unauthorized lottery
Poor Law	pauper in workhouse refusing to work; misbehaviour
Vagrancy	neglect to maintain family, desertion of wife and children, etc.
Game	trespass in daytime, refusing name and address
Railway Regulations	wilful trespass on railway, etc.
Improperly conveying animals	
Larceny	first offences only
Malicious damage	first offences only
Drunkenness on highway	
Town & Police Clauses	suffering dog to be at large, street offences, etc.
Sunday Observance	Sunday trading
Profane Oaths	cursing and swearing
Bread	selling otherwise by weight
Prisons	introducing prohibited articles into convict prisons

Indictable Offences

Class I: Offences against the Person	Class II: Offences against Property with Violence	Class III: Offences against Property without Violence	Class IV: Malicious Injuries to Property	Class V: Forgery and Currency Offences	Class VI: Other Offences
Murder	Sacrilege		Arson		Offences against the State and Public Order
Attempt to Murder	Burglary		Setting Fire to Crops, &c		High Treason
Threats or Conspiracy to Murder	Housebreaking		Killing and Maiming Cattle		Treason Felony
Manslaughter	Shopbreaking		Malicious Use, &c, of Explosives		Riot
Felonious Wounding	Attempts to break into Houses, Shops, &c		Destroying Ships		Unlawful Assembly
Endangering Railway Passengers	Entering with intent to commit Felony		Destroying Railways		Other Offences
Endangering Life at Sea	Possession of Housebreaking Tools, &c		Destroying Trees and Shrubs		Offences against Public Justice
Malicious Wounding (Misdemeanours)	Robbery		Other Malicious Injuries		Extortion by Officers, &c
Assault	Extortion by Threats to Accuse				Bribery, &c
Intimidation and Molestation	Extortion by other Threats				Perjury
Cruelty to Children				Forgery and Uttering (Felony)	Escape and Rescue
Abandoning Children under Two Years				Forgery (Misdemeanour)	Other Offences
Child Stealing		Larceny of Horses and Cattle		Coining	Offences against Religion
Procuring Abortion		Larceny from the Person		Uttering Counterfeit Coin	Blasphemy, &c

Concealment of Birth	Larceny in House	Offences against Law of Nations
Unnatural Offences	Larceny by a Servant	Piracy
Attempts to Commit Unnatural Offences	Embezzlement	Slave Trade
Indecency with Males	Larceny of Post Letters	Libel
Rape	Other Aggravated Larcenies	Poaching
Indecent Assaults on Females	Simple Larceny and Minor Larcenies	Indecent Exposure
Defilement of Girls under 13	Obtaining by False Pretences	Keeping Disorderly Houses
Defilement of Girls under 16	Fraud by Agents, &c	Other Nuisances
Incest	Falsifying Accounts	Habitual Drunkenness
Procuration	Other Frauds	Suicide (Attempting to Commit)
Abduction	Receiving Stolen Goods	Other Misdemeanours
Bigamy	Offences in Bankruptcy	

Justices' Annual Calendar

January	Annual Licensing Meeting: licensing magistrates.
	Clubs: secretaries to submit annual return to clerk to the justices.
	Compensation (licensing): return to Secretary of State.
	Coroner of Borough: annual return of inquests.
	County Quarter Sessions: in first whole week after 28 December.
	Crown Fines: quarterly return to Home Office.
	Magistrates: statement of qualification and deaths.
	Parochial Assessments Appeals.
	Police Returns: annual return of number of offences reported to police and proceedings.
	Probation of Offenders Act: appointment of probation officers.
February	Annual Licensing Meeting.
	Compensation (licensing): financial statement to Secretary of State.
	Parish Constables: precept to overseers to prepare list of qualified persons.
	Prisons: visiting committee meeting.
	Probation officers: annual report.
March	Overseers: appointment of overseers.
	Parish Constables: as February.
April	County Quarter Sessions: in first whole week after 31 March.
	Crown Fines: as January.
	Parochial Assessments Appeals: as January.
	Referred Licences and Reports: licensing.
May	Licensing: preliminary meeting.
July	Licences Refused, Lapsed and Granted: returns to Secretary of State.
	County Quarter Sessions: to be held in first whole week after 14 July.
	Crown Fines: as January.
	Parochial Assessments Appeals: as January.
August	Jury lists: notices to churchwardens and overseers.
September	Jurors: production of jury lists.
October	Borough Special Constables: appoint so many special constables as thought fit.
	County Quarter Sessions: to be held in first whole week after 11 October.
	Lunacy: annual appointment of justices in relation to orders for reception of lunatics.
	Parochial Assessments Appeals: as January.
December	County Quarter Sessions: to be held in first whole week after 28 December.
	Prisons: appointment of justices' visiting committee.

Chapter 2

Fourteen Days, with Hard Labour

Sixty-four-year-old David Tatchell was no stranger to Winchester Police Court. His list of convictions, according to Head Constable Sim, was 'beyond count'. PC Eames had seen him coming out of a house in Edgar Road on Sunday, 16 August 1914 and asked him what he had been doing, to which he replied 'The same old thing', which the officer confirmed was begging for food. Tatchell told the magistrates that he had been released from fourteen days in prison on the previous Thursday, and had gone drinking with friends. At the Hampshire Quarter Sessions in July he had been charged with being an incorrigible rogue, but it was found that he had never been convicted as a rogue and vagabond, so had been discharged. He had, however, been convicted as an idle and disorderly person. Sim asked that the bench sentence him as a rogue and vagabond, to which the bench agreed, passing the maximum sentence of three months' hard labour.[1]

The Vagrancy Act, 1824 was passed 'to make further provision for the suppression of vagrancy'. It described a wonderful hierarchy of degeneracy: persons who were unable to maintain themselves and wilfully refused or neglected work, every 'petty Chapman or Pedlar' wandering abroad and trading without a licence, every Common Prostitute wandering in the public streets and highways and behaving in a riotous or indecent manner, and every beggar, could be brought before a magistrate and sentenced with up to one month's hard labour as an Idle and Disorderly Person. Repeat offenders, or fortune tellers, or anyone found wandering without any visible means of subsistence, or indecently exposing his person, might be convicted as a Rogue and Vagabond, with up to three months' imprisonment with hard labour. Repeat offenders, or those having violently resisted arrest as a rogue and vagabond, might graduate to the rank of Incorrigible Rogue, and would be detained in custody until the next quarter sessions could pass this sentence, including imprisonment of up to twelve months, with hard labour.

Most offenders were not vagrants but there was a public perception of the 'criminal classes', although social attitudes to the sociology of crime were gradually changing. The magistrates had a limited range of sentencing options, but were able to dispose of matters in a very flexible way, including the imposition of costs only. A form of conditional discharge existed, in which a recognizance was imposed for the defendant to pay a certain amount or return 'for judgement if called upon to do so', within a set amount of time. A similar disposal was the bind over, in which the offender undertook to be of good behaviour and to keep the peace for a certain time. Probation, introduced in the Probation Act, 1907 (below) could be imposed as an alternative to conviction, or as a post-conviction sentence. Sentencing powers for magistrates at quarter sessions were more extensive than at petty sessions, and included penal servitude (other than for life), imprisonment up to two years with hard labour, fines or, less commonly, whipping.

The Southend Court Register for October 1914 records the following sentences and disposals:

Committed for trial at next assizes.
Committed for 14 days with hard labour.
Committed for 3 months in the second division.
Fined 10s with 2s costs; allowed until Saturday.
Sent to Chelmsford Industrial School until 16 years of age.
Sent to Redhill Reformatory until 19 years of age.
Remanded for lunch in custody (Vagrancy).
Remanded to the workhouse for 14 days.
Costs only; allowed 7 days to pay.
Bound over under supervision for 3 months, condition to go into home selected
    by probation officer.
Bound over on own recognizance for 6 months, to come back for judgement if
    called upon.
Bound over for 12 months.
Dismissed on payment of costs.
To receive 3 strokes of the birch.
Remanded in custody to await military escort.
Ordered back to naval barracks.
Discharged.
Bound over for 12 months to keep the peace especially towards [neighbour].
Separation order 10s per week and costs.
Bastardy order 5s per week until child aged 14.
Order to be sent to Mental Deficiency School.
Ordered to be sent to Training Ship *Cornwall* until 19 years of age.[2]

Fines were very common, but there was very limited flexibility in making payments, and there was a set formula of payment defaults prescribed by the Summary Jurisdiction Act, 1879:

For any sum	Imprisonment not to exceed
Not exceeding 10s	Seven days
Exceeding 10s but not exceeding 20s	Fourteen days
Exceeding 20s but not exceeding £5	One month
Exceeding £5 but not exceeding £20	Two months
Exceeding £20	Three months

A fine of 20s, for example, was to be paid before the court rose that day. The defendant was kept either in the court waiting room or in the cells, and if payment was not forthcoming he would be collected along with the convicted prisoners and taken to the local gaol for the term specified. Someone receiving a fine would hope that there were friends at the back of court who could either pay on their behalf, or get a message out to family or friends – quite often a youngster would be despatched to 'uncle' at the pawnbroker's shop with mother's wedding ring or the family clock.[3] Part payment was accepted, to reduce the term of imprisonment, and this could either be done at the courthouse or at the prison (except on Sundays). As Mr McKenna, the Home Secretary, reported to the House of Commons in April 1914, some 80,000 people a year were sent to prison for the non-payment of fines. Although magistrates had a limited power to allow time to pay, this was rarely exercised, and through his new Criminal Justice Administration Bill McKenna proposed to make deferred payments more routine, and the time given was to be not less than seven days. A further innovation was that under section 5(1) the court was to take into account the means of the offender when imposing a fine.

Non-payment of fines triggered a distress warrant from the court, which allowed the constable to seize and sell the defendant's goods (distraint), to the value specified. He was not permitted to take 'wearing apparel and bedding' of the defendant or his family, nor the tools or implements of his trade. If there were no, or insufficient, goods, the magistrates could commit the person to prison for all or part of the period in proportion to the scale above. It was not uncommon for the defendant, on being given the fine and/or imprisonment sentence, to tell the bench of his situation and to request the imprisonment option immediately. Such imprisonment was to be without hard labour.

Imprisonment was a much more common sentence than now, and often for very short periods. The modern sentencer perhaps considers a term of imprisonment as a means not merely of punishment, but of rehabilitation and the opportunity to engage with drugs or mental health services, or education, or social services, and certainly it is considered a final option, to be imposed only if all community-based options have been exhausted or are inappropriate. The *Magistrates' Court Sentencing Guidelines* (2016)[4] and the *Adult Court Bench Book* (2013)[5] offer step-by-step guidance in determining the offence category and working out the sentencing starting point and range, given the details of the offence, and taking into account the recommendations of the pre-sentence report prepared by the probation service. It is not usual for a defendant to be given an immediate custodial sentence, and current thinking is that imprisonment in some ways is a failure of the system. Many magistrates find it slightly upsetting. The justices of 1914 had no such qualms and saw the prison as a punishment only.

For adults there were two classes of prison – the six convict prisons, for those serving sentences of penal servitude (minimum of three years) at Dartmoor, Portland, Parkhurst, Camp Hill (Isle of Wight), Aylesbury (women only) and Maidstone (convict and local); and the fifty-six local prisons, holding those sentenced to imprisonment for up to two years and those awaiting trial, and those awaiting execution.

Local Prisons

Bedford	Carlisle	Hereford	Liverpool	Portsmouth	Wakefield
Birmingham	Carnarvon	Holloway	Manchester	Preston	Wandsworth
Bodmin	Carmarthen	Hull	Newcastle	Reading	Warwick
Borstal	Chelmsford	Ipswich	Northallerton	Ruthie	Winchester
Brecon	Derby	Knutsford	Northampton	St Albans	Worcester
Bristol	Devizes	Lancaster	Norwich	Shepton Mallet	Wormwood Scrubs
Brixham	Dorchester	Leeds	Nottingham	Shrewsbury	
Cambridge	Durham	Leicester	Oxford	Stafford	
Canterbury	Exeter	Lewes	Pentonville	Swansea	
Cardiff	Gloucester	Lincoln	Plymouth	Usk	

There were criminal lunatic asylums at Broadmoor and Rampton, Borstal Institutions at Borstal, Canterbury, Feltham and Aylesbury (girls only). The two State Inebriate Reformatories were at Warwick and Aylesbury. For young offenders there were the new 'places of detention' provided by local authorities, and there were also 37 reformatories and 136 industrial schools. Under section 13 of the Criminal Justice Act, 1914, a new custodial option was available, that of 'police custody' in a police station for up to five days.

Magistrates at quarter sessions were able to sentence prisoners to penal servitude. This punishment replaced 'transportation beyond the seas' in 1853. These prisoners, correctly known as 'convicts', wore the linen uniform marked with the broad arrow, and served a minimum sentence of three years, although good conduct could earn early release on a 'ticket of leave'. On such release the man was required to regularly report to his local police station and any failure to do so, or conviction for any other indictable offence, resulted in recall to prison to serve the rest of the term. However, and perhaps surprisingly, convicts saw themselves as better off than ordinary prisoners and, indeed, convict prisons were run completely separately. Not least of the differences were that the prison officers were on better pay and conditions, which created a much better environment inside the establishment. Convicts were required to work, and the great breakwaters of Portland Harbour are lasting evidence of their labours – the chairman of the Prison Commission claimed that the value of such work was nearly equal to the maintenance cost of these prisons.[6] Under the Prevention of Crime Act, 1908, there was a new class of imprisonment known as 'preventive detention', which applied to convicts who, in the opinion of the court, had such criminal habits and lifestyle that 'it is expedient for the protection of the public that the offender should be kept in detention for a lengthened period of years'. This sentence, of between five and ten years, was passed at the same time as one of penal servitude and came into force at the time that the prisoner would ordinarily be released on licence. These men were held at Camp Hill on the Isle of Wight.

For summary offences the maximum term of imprisonment was specified in the statute itself, up to a maximum of two years, and could be with or without hard labour. A further distinction, under the Prison Act, 1898 and Criminal Justice Administration Act, 1914,[8] was that prisoners could be placed into one of three divisions. The first division was for offenders such as vaccination objectors and suffragettes, and they were allowed to wear their own clothes and were not required to have their heads shaved. They were also allowed greater visiting rights, more letters, and, if circumstances permitted, they could pay for their own food. Prisoners in the second division were typically those not of the 'criminal classes', and almost invariably first offenders, but the magistrates had to specify, on conviction, that the prisoner was in this class, although those who had been imprisoned in default of recognizances or sureties were automatically put in the second division ('surety prisoners').

Second division prisoners also had rights to wear different clothes, and were kept apart from other prisoners. In the absence of any instructions to the contrary from the sentencing bench, the default was the third and largest division, although in April 1915 under the new Criminal Justice Administration Act the prison authorities were given powers to transfer prisoners from the third to the second division, but only if they were of sufficient moral character so as not to be an adverse influence on the other prisoners.

Whatever the length of the sentence, the 'hard labour' component was restricted to the first twenty-eight days. This time was served in solitary confinement and in silence. If male, between 16 and 60, and medically fit, the prisoner slept – or attempted to sleep – for the first fourteen days without a mattress. During this time the work consisted of picking oakum, which was the untwisting of lengths of old rope, to separate out the fibres; and a certain weight of oakum had to be produced each day, usually between 3 and 4lbs. Other tasks followed, such as making coal sacks, chopping wood or breaking stones. Unproductive labour, such as turning the crank (which was connected to a paddle in a barrel of sand) was, at last, being abolished, although the treadmill, such as at Lewes prison, was still in use for pumping water, sawing wood or operating millstones for grinding flour.[7] In 1908 the Mayor of Maidenhead and his colleague Alderman Truscott sentenced nearly a dozen tramps to hard labour for refusing to work the crank known as the 'Maidenhead Kill Devil'. They determined to find out for themselves why the men objected to this work, so, on a self-imposed diet of eight ounces of bread and a glass of water, they attended the workhouse and operated the crank for the prescribed minute and a half, making five clean cuts through a length of wood held by an inmate in the wood sawing shed. Although several turns of the crank caused them both to pant, they agreed that the work 'certainly wasn't too hard for the class of persons for whom it was intended'.[8]

At the end of the twenty-eight days the prisoner joined the rest of the prison community in 'industrial' labour, such as making hammocks, post bags, nose bags, and ship's fenders. He could also be employed in various domestic duties in the prison, or if he had a trade he might be allowed to carry out piece work.

Defendants in prison awaiting trial were given a separate status under the Prison Rules, 1899 – they were to be kept apart from convicted prisoners and could enjoy certain privileges, such as separate exercise, the retention of books and papers, and communication with legal representatives and friends. With the permission of the Visiting Committee they could pay for a 'sufficient supply of wholesome food', a furnished cell, and even for someone to do their prison chores.

The Children Act, 1908 brought an end to the imprisonment of children under the age of fourteen years for any offence, and a 'young person' (between fourteen and sixteen) was not to be imprisoned unless the court certified that he was of such unruly character, or so depraved, that he could not be held in a 'place of detention'. Provided by the police authorities, these were usually remand homes, reformatories or special facilities attached to local prisons, and periods of detention were limited to a month. The Prevention of Crimes Act, 1908 introduced the Borstal Institutions, for young males between the ages of 16 and 21, convicted of an indictable offence for which he is liable to penal servitude, and that 'by reason of his criminal habits or tendencies, or his association with persons of bad character, it is expedient that he should be subject to detention ... as appears most conducive to his reformation and the repression of crime'. Sentences were to be between one and three years. In the first instance these sentences could only be imposed by the quarter sessions, but magistrates' courts could exercise this option when dealing with boys who had been convicted of offences against the discipline of the reformatory schools. The magistrates could also send youths up to the quarter sessions for sentencing to Borstal, if they were repeat offenders. However, the Prison Commissioners had to assess the suitability of any youth case for treatment in a Borstal.

In 1913 815 persons were sentenced to penal servitude, and 139,060 to imprisonment, of whom 75,152 were imprisoned in default of fines: 90,188 were sentenced to hard labour, 31 were placed in the first division and 1,609 in the second. The daily average of persons held in local prisons was 12,651, 2,552 in the convict prisons, and 870 in Borstals. Less than 1 per cent were serving a term of greater than one year, and around 60 per cent were imprisoned for fourteen days or less.[9]

In their annual report for 1914 the magistrates of the Visiting Committee for Chelmsford Prison recorded that they had made fifty-two visits during the year. There had been one execution, two inmates had been removed to Colchester Asylum, and twenty-five prisoners had been disciplined with the No. 1 Dietary punishment (bread and gruel) for periods in excess of twenty-four hours. One prisoner had assaulted a warden and had received eighteen strokes of the birch. The report was dated 11 January 1915 and they were already able to comment on the 'remarkable diminution in the number of persons admitted to this prison' since the outbreak of the war. In September they had 144 prisoners, and by 21 December there were only 93.[10]

A typical magistrates' court prosecution, whether brought by the police or an individual, could be taken through to conviction and sentence with no legally-qualified representatives on either side. Matters before the quarter sessions and assizes would be prosecuted by a qualified solicitor or barrister appointed by the court, but there was no provision for any defence representation. The Poor Prisoners Defence Act, 1903, provided legal aid for prisoners but only on the basis of the nature of the defence set up by the poor prisoner 'as disclosed in the evidence given or statement made by him'; as previously noted, with the assessment of the strength of the prosecution evidence by both the magistrates and by the grand jury taking place before any trial, the grant of legal aid would require an interesting or complex defence argument. Mr A.J. Ashton, the Recorder at the Manchester Quarter Sessions, described one such case, Frank Carter, charged with stealing three parcels at Victoria Station:

> A prisoner came here and his defence was practically that he was wrong in his head at the time of the alleged offence. It was not the sort of defence which he himself could have developed with the greatest success. The magistrates did not allow the prisoner legal aid, and though I was very doubtful about it I decided to allow counsel to defend the prisoner. The result was that the prisoner's counsel, Mr Lisbona, was able to develop the defence to satisfy the jury that the prisoner was not right in his head. It is an excellent illustration of the value of the Act, and I wish to draw public attention to it.[11]

It had long been felt that the fine and/or imprisonment of offenders was not always the best way of dealing with offenders, particularly at the lower end of the scale and for those who might be diverted from the criminal justice system, especially youths. The Summary Jurisdiction Act, 1879 had introduced the concept of probation for summary offences, and the Probation of First Offenders Act, 1887 was aimed at those finding themselves in court for the first time, and only applied to certain offences. The new and reforming Liberal government of 1906 looked at the problem again, and the result was the Probation of Offenders Act, 1907, a natural and welcome development in the sentencing options available for the magistrates. The Act provided that:

(1) Where any person is charged before a court of summary jurisdiction, with an offence punishable by such a court, and the court thinks that the charge is proved, but is of the opinion that, having regard to the character, antecedents, age, health, or mental condition of the person charged, or to the trivial nature of the offence, or to the extenuating circumstances under which the offence was committed, it is inexpedient to inflict any punishment or any other than nominal punishment, or that it is expedient to release the offender on probation, the court may, without proceeding to conviction, make an order, either

   (i) dismissing the information or charge; or
   (ii) discharging the offender conditionally on his entering into a recognizance (bond) with or without sureties, to be of good behaviour and to appear for conviction and sentence when called on at any time during such period, not exceeding three years, as may be specified in the order.

In relation to modern practice it is notable that the probation order was an alternative to conviction, rather than a sentence; and that the recognizance element would now be described as a conditional discharge. Various conditions could be attached to the order, preventing the offender from association with thieves or other undesirables, or from frequenting particular locations. Abstention from liquor could be required, if alcohol was a factor in the offence. A rather more ambiguous condition was that the probationer should follow an honest and industrious life. The management and supervision of the probation order required a new class of court officer. A model was already in place, known as the police court missionary.

The relationship between liquor and crime was well known, and in 1876 the Church of England Temperance Society began to employ men, and a few women, as police court missionaries.[12] They were to engage with prisoners and defendants before and after their court appearances, to offer support and ideally to secure a promise to take the pledge of abstinence. It didn't take long for magistrates to appreciate the assistance they could provide, in particular to the way in which they could exercise greater familiarity with the poorer and less educated members of the community. Robert Holmes was a police court missionary in Sheffield and wrote an account of his experiences with young offenders in the 1915 classic *My Police Court Friends with the Colours*.

With the introduction of the Probation Act, 1907 the Home Office wanted to know how best to deliver the new services, and if the police court missionaries were to provide the model for the social workers and probation officers to be appointed by the courts. The Metropolitan Police executive branch commissioned the *Police Court Missionaries: review on value of their work*[13] in 1907 and received a decidedly mixed opinion. Superintendent Wells, Westminster Division, believed that they were 'in many instances invaluable' with young persons on being bound over and discharged on condition they go into a home; and were able to provide clothing for a large number of poor children. He offered a case study. On 17 October 1907 May Hayward, aged 25 and of 25 Great Peter Street, was arrested for disorderly conduct and obscene language at Ashley Gardens. She appeared the same day at Westminster police court and managed to speak to Mr Barnett, the police court missionary. She told him she was from South Wales and married to a decorator. She had met George Rees and he enticed her away from her husband to London, and that he had subsequently been living on her earnings as a prostitute. Barnett spoke privately to the magistrate, Mr H. Curtis Bennett, who directed that an information be laid. Hayward paid for a warrant which was then issued and executed. Reece was arrested and remanded until 19 October, when he was sentenced to three months' hard labour as a vagrant and six months' for assaulting her. Barnett received a telegram from her husband saying that he would receive her back with pleasure, so Hayward was discharged and Barnett arranged to send her back home to Swansea.[14]

The Vine Street report was equally favourable. Their police court missionary was in touch with various philanthropic institutions, rescue homes, Homes for Working Lads, and voluntary homes for habitual drunkards. He was even able to assist poor persons requiring surgical appliances but unable to afford them, by referring them to the Surgical Aids Society. The Marylebone Division thought that the missionaries were useful for making enquiries that did not come within the scope of police duties (such as means, employment and references), and they were very useful for follow up work where the police would be resented; in summary a 'handy man about the Court'.

Bow Street was more critical. The missionary took his temperance work seriously and undertook to get the drunkards to sign the pledge, but 'very little good comes of this', however, the 'magistrates I believe hold a high opinion' of him. The missionary in the Finsbury Division covered both Clerkenwell and Old Street police courts but made little impression on Superintendent Hammond, who felt unable to offer any good results traceable to his influences. His colleague, Superintendent Laughlin, held a similarly ambivalent view of Mr Fitzsimmons at the Thames police court. The missionary at West Ham police court was paid for from the Poor Box and at Stratford Petty Sessional Court there were a male and a female missionary funded by the Diocese of St Albans.

There was a general sense that, in simple terms, the police court missionaries were not doing any harm, but most of the senior police officers felt that their rôle was of 'a social character' and that they exerted a certain moral influence. Mr Harwood and Mrs Curtis, who worked at the Tower Bridge police court, were particularly praised for their efforts with young people, wives and families, and in bringing about reconciliations in matrimonial cases. The superintendent of Greenwich Division summarized the potential value of the missionary and the probation officer: 'there can be no doubt that such agencies have become indispensable to the police courts, but as in every other sphere, so much often also depends on the "personal equation". Well-selected men and women can do immense good, but there is the liability to trespass and become meddlesome instead of useful agents.' Mr Hall, of the South Western Police Court (Southwark division) was the exemplar of the police court missionary. He was appointed and paid by the Southwark Diocesan branch of the Church of England Temperance Society and worked under the supervision of the local vicar. He regularly attended the sittings of the court, and administered moral and spiritual advice. He was held in high esteem by the police magistrate, the Hon. John de Grey, who publicly claimed that he 'could not speak too highly of the valuable assistance rendered to the court by that gentleman'.

The police court missionaries, and the new probation officers appointed from 1908, had the following duties:

1. To visit or receive reports from the person under supervision, at such reasonable intervals as may be specified in the probation order, or subject thereto, as the probation officer may think fit;
2. To see that he observes the conditions of his recognizance;
3. To report to the court as to his behaviour;
4. To advise, assist and befriend him, and, when necessary, endeavour to find him suitable employment.

Even in its first few years of operation, the Probation of Offenders Act attracted as much criticism as it did praise. In October 1912 the Home Secretary recognized the underlying principle that 'though an offence against the law has clearly been committed, it is not necessary nor even desirable, that punishment should be imposed on the offender', but in the same circular he warned that juvenile offenders of a 'persistently criminal disposition' were not suitable for repeated probation orders, and to use them would be 'an abuse of the Act'. Cecil Leeson of the Howard League for Penal Reform considered that while the principle of probation was laudable, its administration left much to be desired, which he attributed to its rapid growth. He identified four main factors: unsuitable probation officers, unsuitable cases, probationary periods which were too short for suitable intervention, and the inadequacy of organization and control.[15]

The Children Act, 1908 had reformed the way in which young people were dealt with in the criminal justice system. There was to be a clear separation between adults and youths at all stages, so that youths arrested and denied bail were to be held in 'places of detention', such as a remand home. Although it had been proposed that there should be new and dedicated youth court buildings, in reality the courts operated a separate youth list before or after the adult list. The public were excluded from these hearings, and the names of young offenders were not permitted to be reported. As might be expected, magistrates did not receive any training for managing the juvenile court, and this shortly became one of the arguments in favour of women magistrates. Under the Act the court had several disposals available for the young offender:

1. Dismiss the charge;
2. Discharge on his entering into a recognizance;
3. Discharge and place him under the supervision of a probation officer;
4. Commit him to the care of a relative or other fit person;
5. Send him to an industrial school;
6. Send him to a reformatory school;
7. Order him to be whipped;
8. Order him to pay a fine, damages, or costs;
9. Order his parents or guardian to pay a fine, damages, or costs;
10. Order his parent or guardian to give security for his good behaviour;
11. Commit him to custody in a place of detention provided under this Act;
12. Sentence to imprisonment if he is of an unruly or depraved character;
13. Deal with him by any other manner in which he may legally be dealt with.

Whipping, which was up to six strokes of a birch rod by a police sergeant, was very popular with the public, although its actual efficacy may be doubted. Probation and detention were often seen as weak punishments, particularly when imposed repeatedly on the same juvenile offender to little apparent effect. Offenders between 12 and 16 years of age could be sent to reformatory school in lieu of imprisonment, and for extended periods not less than three or more than five years, it being not uncommon to send the youth away 'until the age of nineteen'. Industrial schools were similar but a juvenile could be sent there for one of several reasons, if the child was:

1. Begging or receiving alms.
2. Found wandering and not having any home or settled place of abode.
3. Found destitute, not being an orphan, with his parent or parents undergoing penal servitude or imprisonment.
4. Under the care of a parent or guardian who by reason of criminal or drunken habits was unfit to have the care of the child.
5. In the company of any reputed thief, or common prostitute.
6. Lodging or residing in a house used by a prostitute for the purposes of prostitution.

There was also an astonishing provision in the Act, where a parent or guardian of a child might claim to the magistrates that he was unable to control his child and that he wished the child to be sent to an industrial school. If they believed this proved, the court could order the boy or girl to be sent to a certified industrial school. The parent in this case was often required to make a contribution to the maintenance costs of the child while at the school. The industrial school, by definition, was to provide the young person with training in some form of mechanical, crafts or agricultural skills and attendance could be by residence or by attendance. One form of industrial school was the training ship, to prepare a boy for life at sea. Unlike the reformatory schools, juveniles could only be sent there until the age of 16.

There were few appeals from decisions of the magistrates' courts, primarily because under the Summary Jurisdiction Act, 1879 it was only possible to appeal a sentence of imprisonment without the option of a fine, provided the defendant pleaded had not guilty (only in 1914 did the Criminal Justice Administration Act grant the right of appeal for any conviction). Although often cited as evidence of the fairness and equity of the process of summary jurisdiction, it must be acknowledged that, at £5, the cost of taking an appeal to the quarter sessions was largely prohibitive. There were mechanisms for the higher courts to challenge the magistrates, and their use seems to have been more common than today. *Mandamus* was used when the justices had failed to carry out the duties of their office – for example, refusing to issue a summons without reason, or refusing to continue proceedings considered futile. Now known as a 'mandatory order', the higher court ordered the magistrates to perform the action. *Certiorari* ('quashing order') allowed the higher court to overturn a sentence or verdict, and also to stop or transfer proceedings for which the magistrates had no jurisdiction. In both cases the review was based on the magistrates' decision-making process, not the decision itself, and so the justices were not required to defend their actions in person, as the clerk's minutes provided sufficient record. Another common form of challenge was the statement of case (now, for some reason, 'case stated') in which the prosecutor could require the magistrates to prepare a written statement of their reasoning for a decision, for higher review. This was often used if there were novel or unusual legal features, particularly if the (untrained) lay magistrates been required to interpret and apply the law to specific circumstances. This happened reasonably frequently during the early days of the emergency legislation and throughout the war as increasing numbers of DoRA-related regulations were introduced. These cases were referred to the King's Bench Division of the High Court, which was the usual venue for full judicial review and legal rulings.

Whatever personal and professional characteristics the lay magistrates possessed, few could claim any legal training. The clerk to the justices had an essential rôle in advising them about the law, but he had many other duties: to take minutes of all the proceedings, to receive and transmit all fines, costs and fees, and generally manage the staff, police, solicitors, ushers, missionaries and probation officers and others attending the court house. This was a substantial position, and not only must the man possess 'education, intelligence and discretion', but also be a solicitor or barrister of not less than fourteen years' standing. As of the Justices' Clerks Act, 1877, the clerk was paid a salary.

The Stratford magistrates wanted to appoint a new justices' clerk in October 1918 and drew up the following description of his duties:

1. [The Clerk] shall make the business of the bench his sole duty and shall personally conduct the business of the court, and shall only be absent by leave of the chairman or of the senior justice present on a previous day.
2. He shall keep all books and papers concerning the business of the bench at the Court House, Stratford.
3. He shall be responsible, under the direction of the chairman, for the annual auditing and printing of 'Arrangements for Business'. The cost of such printing is to be borne by the Mess Fund.
4. He shall pay daily all monies received on account of court business to a bank account entirely separate from any other account, and render an account and pay of the balance to the County Accountant monthly. He shall effect a Guarantee Bond with an Approved Society for the sum of £400, or such other sum as the justices may from time to time require.
5. While holding this appointment he shall not accept any other public appointment without the consent of the justices specially summoned.
6. He shall not act for any person, firm or company connected with the licensing trade, neither shall he prepare any notice in connexion with licensing business coming before the bench.
7. He shall appoint one Assistant Clerk at a salary of not less than £300 per annum. He shall submit the name of the person to be so appointed to the chairman for approval by the bench. He shall provide a clerk for the third court on Saturdays if and when such a court is restarted.
8. He shall defray all expenses for the purchasing and payment of all stamps, stationary books etc. computed to cost £150 per annum.
9. The appointment shall be terminable on three months' notice given at any time.[16]

The clerk had a major responsibility in maintaining the court register, which was, for the historian, a frustratingly brief document. They were in a format determined by the Summary Jurisdiction Rules of 1886 and 1915, and merely recorded the name of the complainant or prosecutor, the name and age of the defendant, the type of offence, and the sentence (if convicted). The magistrates were required to sign each minute. One of the most important aspects of the register was that it was used to provide evidence of previous convictions at the same court; there was no central register of offenders.

The clerk also had the duty of administering the various oaths required for the many applications, warrants, and statutory declarations. The giving of evidence on oath has been a fundamental tenet of the judicial process for centuries, but the method and wording have changed over the years. The 'clerk in spectacles' in Dicken's *Pickwick Papers* had a standard formula: 'Take the book in your right hand this is your name and handwriting you swear that the contents of this your affidavit are true so help you God a shilling you must get change I haven't got it.'[17] The Oaths Act, 1888 introduced the affirmation for those with no religious belief or holding that taking an oath was against their belief, but the standard practice was that the oath was read to the witness while he held a copy of the New Testament (or Old Testament if Jewish); he did not repeat the words, but kissed the book at the end of the declaration. The Oaths Act, 1909 required the witness to either say or repeat the oath in the first person, and dispensed with the kiss ('an exhibition altogether vague and inappropriate').[18] Putting the words of the oath into the mouths of the semi-literate produced some odd results, as noted by the *Justice of the Peace*: apparently it was quite common to swear to tell the 'holy' truth rather than the whole truth, along with 'all the mighty gods' rather than 'almighty God', and one witness was heard to declare that he would tell 'anything but the truth'.[19] A rather dramatic form of declaration was known as the Scottish Oath: holding the holy book and with the other hand uplifted, the witness declared 'I swear by Almighty God, as I shall answer to God at the Great Day of Judgement, that I will speak the truth, the whole truth, and nothing but the truth.' The English version was the more sedate wording we use today: 'I swear by Almighty God that the evidence I shall give shall be the truth, the whole truth, and nothing but the truth', and the affirmation begins 'I do solemnly, sincerely and truly declare and affirm … '.[20] A complainant would use the following in laying the information before the justices: 'I, A. B., swear by Almighty God that the contents of this information, signed by me, are true and correct to the best of my knowledge and belief.'

Considerable amounts of cash flowed through the courts and the clerk was the accounting officer. A table of fees was 'fixed in some conspicuous part of the court' and everything had to be paid for. A man taking out a prosecution against his neighbour had to pay 1s to lay the complaint and 1s for a summons, a stamp for this amount being attached to the court record. On a successful conviction he would hope that the defendant would be ordered to pay these costs, but if he was unable to do so and the bailiffs found that he had no goods or property to recover, the debt was a civil matter, to be taken, if the complainant could afford it, to the county court. The magistrates had no powers to recover costs. They could, on conviction, remit costs against the defendant on grounds of poverty, but usually only in matters prosecuted by the police or other authorities. Fines and fees paid went to the county or borough rates. The clerk managed the court staff including the police officers who were detached for court duties. According to Gamon they included the gaoler-sergeant and assistant gaolers and three or four warrant officers.[21]

The clerk was responsible for the poor box charitable fund maintained by most courts, which could be used to provide immediate assistance to those before the courts. It was not to be used to pay for fines or costs, but bus or train fares, or subsistence contributions on application to the justices. Often filled from the magistrates' own pockets,[22] it was occasionally topped up by wealthier defendants. Mr W. Kilbourne Kay, himself a Worcester magistrate, appeared before his colleagues on a charge of keeping two dogs without a licence. They fined him 20s but he announced he would leave two guineas in the poor box.[23] Walter Bowley, an Ilkeston collier, was awarded 5s from the Sheffield poor box for rescuing a girl, Louisa Wheatley, from the canal (the poor girl was charged with attempted suicide but let off with a caution after promising not to do it again).[24] Arthur Williams put his six-year-old son out in New Street, Birmingham, to beg for money and within an hour the boy had been given three shillings and thirteen pennies, as well as a new jersey and a pair of boots. The magistrates fined him 40s and ordered the boy's takings to be put in the poor box.[25] The poor box lasted a long time – the Stratford Magistrates' Court Poor Box Trust Fund, as with so many others, was finally wound up in 2012 as probation and other services provided the support needed.

The magistrates, and in particular the London stipendiaries, had a social dimension to their work that is not seen today. This can be seen in the accounts of the London police courts left by some of the London police magistrates, such as Cancellor[26] and Waddy,[27] which show the courts dealing with far more than criminal matters and acting as informal arbiter and adviser at the borderline of legal services. The Toynbee Trust commissioned an Oxford academic, Hugh Gamon, to examine the rôle of the police courts in the context of the broader community (published in 1907 as *The London Police Court, today and tomorrow*[28]). He spent twelve months living in the East End of London and visited police courts, prisons, remand homes and Salvation Army hostels and saw the courts working in a way which would be unrecognizable to the modern magistrate. He described the police court as 'a meeting ground for a great diversity of moral standards and social grades', and the magistrate is 'the surgeon at law, diagnosing the complaints and pricking the blisters and ulcers of society'. The court users were 'a motley assortment of applicants, prosecutors, witnesses, complainants, defendants, friends and loafers, bullies and their backers, sufferers with their sympathisers; husbands and wives'. The court sat at 10 am and at 2 pm. Those on bail had to be there and ready to be called on. The first business of the day was the hearing of applications, with the public excluded as the applicants requested their various summons for assault, petty theft and other minor matters. This was, in large part, ministerial work, and one London magistrate, Mr Haden Corser, was known to come down from the bench to sit in a cane chair near the witness box, the better to talk to the humble folk seeking his advice. Gamon tells of the many applicants who simply had no idea of the law nor of the redress they were seeking, and that the London magistrates became the 'Poor Man's Lawyer' giving 'legal and moral advice gratis, as far as time permits', but he was aware that this was not widely practised in the provinces.

Sir James Vaughan, the Chief Magistrate of the London Metropolitan District, described the relationship of the police courts to the working classes:

> To our courts the poor resort with confidence; they come and lay before us their own various troubles and difficulties, and cases of oppression they have met with, and they ask our advice. The confidence thus engendered amongst the people of a district is such that very many wrongs are redressed without issuing any summons at all, simply the magistrate's sending a message by a constable to the party being complained about.[29]

With the outbreak of the war, this public confidence in the courts was to be put to the test. Laws and regulations concerning situations and matters which had never been imagined were about to introduced; sometimes at a bewildering rate, sometimes badly worded, almost all far-reaching and intrusive, in reaction to a form of warfare which had never before been experienced. The net of the law was to be cast wide, and rich and poor, soldier and civilian, were all likely to find themselves before the magistrates.

Chapter 3

Transition to War

The transition to war was marked in the magistrates' courts by an increase in offences of drunkenness. Monday, 3 August was a Bank Holiday, and in view of the emergency in Europe Tuesday and Wednesday were also declared holidays, although officially this only applied to banks.[1] The Middlesbrough bench sat on Wednesday, 4 August and had to deal with fifty-five prisoners, facing sixty-three charges. The chairman remarked that 'no doubt the country was under considerable excitement at the present time', and the fines imposed were smaller than they would normally have been.[2] Birmingham had a lighter list but had fifteen cases of drunkenness.[3] Britain declared war on Germany at 11 pm that night. The following day at Bow Street police court Cissie Frost was charged with obstruction. She had rung the bell at No. 10 Downing Street and had demanded to see the Prime Minister and had refused the duty police officer's request to move away, saying 'I am a suffragette and have a message for Mr Asquith'. She explained to the magistrate that women demanded the franchise now that husbands and sons were being killed. She was fined 20s.[4]

Although Parliamentary legislators were kept busy in the first few months of the war, there was much relevant law already in place. The mass movement of troops by rail had been long anticipated, and legislation had been enacted as far back as 1842 with the Railway Regulation Act requiring railway companies to convey military forces at 'such prices or upon such conditions as may from time to time be contracted', and required the production of the 'route'. The Act was amended in 1844 to specify the fare for a soldier was to be 1d per mile, and an officer (in first class, of course) at 2d per mile. The Cheap Trains Act, 1883 was to 'amend and consolidate the law relating to the conveyance of the Queen's forces by railway'. On 2 August 1914 the War Office announced an Order in Council declaring that the Government would take over control of the railways under the section 16 of the Regulation of the Forces Act, 1871. An executive committee composed of the general managers of the several railway companies was formed, and because of extensive pre-war planning on their part, the transition was almost seamless, with minimal impact on civilian rail traffic in the first weeks of the war. According the Act, the powers of the Secretary of State were to remain in force for one week only, but renewed from week to week if, in the opinion of the minister, the state of emergency was continuing.[5] The newspapers carried a warning:

> We are officially advised that in order to give due effect to the instructions received from the War Office and Admiralty for the movement of troops, etc., it may be necessary to discontinue at short notice a portion of the advertised service or to close certain of the lines against ordinary traffic. Under these circumstances, no responsibility can be taken for any delay or loss that may arise.

For many people their first real wartime experience was the arrival of the Territorials in their towns in vast numbers and all requiring accommodation. The 'competent naval and military authorities' and the police may not have rehearsed an operation of this scale but they had all the legal powers they needed to requisition property and to billet troops on civilians.

The English common law has long held the principle that 'an Englishman's home is his castle' and unlike European systems the privacy of the home was held inviolable. King Charles I used the threat of billeting troops as a means of extracting revenues from recalcitrant towns and guilds long before the English Civil War, and in 1628 an appeal was submitted in the House of Commons requesting that 'every freeman hath, and of a right ought to have, a full and absolute property in his estate, and that therefore the billeting and placing of soldiers in the houses of any such freeman against his will is directly contrary to the said laws'. This and other grievances against the Crown led to the Petition of Right, 1628, which forced the King to recognize the unlawfulness of billeting, martial law and imprisonment without trial. Section 4 of the Petition read:

> VI. And whereas of late great companies of soldiers and mariners have been dispersed into divers counties of the realm, and the inhabitants against their will have been compelled to receive them into their houses, and there to suffer them to sojourn against the laws and customs of this realm, and to the great grievance and vexation of the people.

In 1679 Charles II gave assent to the Disbanding Act (also known as the Billeting Act) which provided that:

> **XXXII: No Officer, &c. to quarter soldiers on any Subject without his Consent, and Subject may refuse to quarter soldiers**
>
> And whereas by the Laws and Customs of this Realme the Inhabitants thereof cannot be compelled against their wills to receive Souldiers into their Houses and to sojourne them there Bee it declared and enacted by the Authoritie aforesaid That noe Officer Military of Civil nor any other person whatever shall from henceforth presume to place quarter or billet any Souldier or Souldiers upon any Subject or Inhabitant of this Realme of any degree quality of profession whatever without his consent And that it shall and may be lawfull for every such Subject and Inhabitant to refuse to sojourne or quarter any Souldier or Souldiers notwithstanding any Command Order or Billeting whatever.

As will be seen in the next chapter, military law evolved into the Mutiny Act and eventually to the Army Act, 1881. The latter legislation was kept in force by the Army (Annual) Act each year, and under its provisions the billeting of soldiers upon civilians was illegal. Somewhat confusingly the first section of Part III of the Army Act, 1881 appeared to suggest the contrary:

102. During the continuance in force of this Act, so much of any law as prohibits, restricts or regulates the quartering or billeting of officers and soldiers on any inhabitant of this realm without his consent is hereby suspended, so far as such quartering or billeting is authorized by this Act.

This apparent contradiction is resolved under section 104(2)(a) 'Provided that an officer or soldier shall not be billeted … in any private house'.

The preamble to the Army (Annual) Act each year stated that 'Whereas the raising or keeping of a standing army within the United Kingdom of Great Britain and Ireland in time of peace, unless it be with the consent of Parliament, is against law', the purpose of the Act being to grant such consent. The peacetime forces were quartered in barracks and camps around the country, such as at the great garrison towns of Aldershot, Colchester and Catterick, and the military establishments such as the Royal Military College, Sandhurst and the Royal Artillery Barracks at Woolwich. Such soldiers, and their Territorial Force comrades, were regularly required to travel to Salisbury Plain and other areas for military exercises, and the powers to obtain accommodation was a well-rehearsed activity covered by section 103(1) in Part III of the Army Act, 1881. Although in the first years of the twentieth century the army routinely used the railways, all army units had an official complement or 'scale' of horses and carts of various descriptions and the Territorials in particular routinely participated in route marches to a nearby location for a weekend under canvas (few units yet had motor vehicles). The military authorities were required to produce a 'route' which was originally an order of the Crown directing a senior officer to move troops, and which required the civil authorities to assist in providing quarters. There were four forms of 'route' (general, district, regimental and deserter) which were printed off as blanks with a lithograph of the Secretary of State's signature. The details of troop movements and especially the numbers of officers, men and horses, were stated on the form which was then signed by an officer of the appropriate rank. The 'route' was presented to police officers and, if necessary, to local magistrates, who would then locate accommodation at inns, hostels, livery stables and retail wine shops, collectively known as 'victualling houses', within a mile or less of the intended line of march. These establishments were then issued with a billet, or note, recording the number men and horses who could stay (the term 'billet' subsequently came to mean the accommodation itself). Although the landlord had no say in the matter, he was entitled to compensation at rates set out in the annual Army Act and was paid at the end of every four days. The original billeting system was meant to be a temporary state of affairs for troops on the move and in the legislation and the *Manual of Military Law* there is nothing to suggest that stays of more than four days were anticipated; there is no mention, for example, about changing bedding.

Under the provisions of the Act, the police were required to maintain a list of victualling houses and make it available for public inspection. It also set out the matter of grievances and complaints, which had to be made to the local justice of the peace. This system worked, and was regularly used in the years before the war, before military motor transport became common.

The annual Army Act was usually passed without comment in Parliament but in 1909 the Secretary of State for War, Richard Haldane, added several new clauses which caused some debate.[6] In addition to creating the Army Council as the executive authority for the Army, he added measures for the impressment of motor vehicles and, significantly, the billeting of troops on civilians. This would only be in cases of emergency when directions had been giving for calling up, or embodying, the Territorial Force. In addition to the powers of the properly authorized general officer or field officer to issue a route demanding accommodation in victualling houses, it was extended to include 'occupiers of all public buildings, *dwelling houses*, warehouses, barns and stables' [author's emphasis]. This permitted the requisition of schools, halls and similar buildings. The *Sheffield Independent* explained:

> Should the need arise constables will arrive at a house and inform the occupant authoritatively that the accommodation afforded by the inns and hotels of the town have been exhausted, and that a number of soldiers must be lodged in it. He is asked how many rooms he can place at the disposal of the military authorities. These are allotted to soldiers who take up their quarters immediately, and a paper is affixed to the door stating that number. Food must be provided to the soldier-lodgers, and the householder must provide it.[7]

One of the criticisms was that in the event of genuine emergency it was highly likely that both prices would rise and that foodstuffs would be in short supply, and the scheme of compensation failed to anticipate this.

With the outbreak of war the burden of locating civilian accommodation under these recent powers was borne by the police. They managed the task with tact and diplomacy; under the Act it was not permitted to order billets in excess of the number required, so the starting point was to find out how many soldiers required accommodation and to approach the larger houses first. As these were filled enquiries could be made in the neighbourhood to find out which households were willing to take soldiers in. They had no detailed registers comparable to those of victualling houses, so the police officer simply interviewed the householder and marked the number of billets available in chalk on the wall of the house. Their work was not helped by many Territorials arriving at their concentration points in a haphazard manner: rather than platoons or companies of officers and men, many turned up in small groups, and some were rather the worse for wear. Technically it was an offence to refuse to provide a billet but the majority seemed to have welcomed the opportunity to help the war effort in this way, and cases of refusal came in future years, and was usually coloured by a bad experience with unclean or unruly soldiers.

There were some problems with billeting arrangements. On 14 August William Young, landlord of the Woolpack Inn on Mildmay Road, was charged at Chelmsford Petty Sessions with refusing accommodation for soldiers under section 110(1) of the Army Act, 1881. Inspector Barrow provided evidence that on Saturday 8 August he had issued a billeting notice for four men of 1 East Anglian Field Ambulance to go to the Woolpack. Later that evening he visited the public house and found that Mrs Young was refusing to accommodate them, claiming she had no room. The policeman sent the soldiers to the Army & Navy Inn on Baddow Road. He stated that since 1906 he had sent forty men and forty horses to be billeted at the Woolpack Inn, and only four men and four horses had ever been taken in. The inspector described the situation that afternoon, when he had received telegrams instructing him to find billets for 270 men. The unfortunate Mr Young didn't find out about the soldiers until after his wife had made the refusal, and found himself charged with the offence. The bench found him guilty, but gave him the minimum fine of £2, with 4s costs, the chairman stating 'we hope licensed victuallers will understand that they must take in these men or find suitable accommodation. It is most necessary that everybody should show loyalty at the present time, and we hope that this case will act as a warning.' Barney Hoggard, of the Queen's Head, Anchor Street, was also in the same court that day, facing the same charge, having refused to take in two Royal Army Medical Corps men, but he then arranged for them to stay elsewhere. The wording of the section 110 offence was 'refusing and neglecting'; the magistrates felt that he had indeed refused to take in the men, but had not neglected them, and so he was acquitted on the technicality.

On 18 January 1915, Rev. Jeremiah Brown, 2, Oliver Villa, Albany Road, of the Gospel Mission Hall, Old Windsor appeared before the Berkshire county magistrates at Windsor Town Hall, charged with refusing to billet two men of 6 East Surrey Regiment. Colour Sergeant Knight had sent the men to his house and they had been sent away. There were 120 men billeted in the same road, with up to five men per house. Brown had previously billeted two men between 24 November and 24 December but had got rid of them for some reason. Brown claimed there was one bedroom for him and his wife, another which was occupied by his daughter, and this room led to the third which was only large enough for a single bed 'which could only be occupied by a lady'. When the constable made the application for rooms his wife was ill with bronchitis and influenza. The lack of proper sanitary arrangements made it impossible for him to accommodate the men even if he had room. The magistrates dismissed the charge.[8]

One incentive for householders to take on soldiers was financial. Army Order 289 of 1914, published on 4 August 1914, set out the rates to be paid for billeting:

1. Pursuant to section 108A(3) of the Army Act, the prices to be paid to an occupier other than the keeper of a victualling house for billets requisitioned in accordance with the provisions of section 108A have been fixed at the rates shown in the subjoined schedule:

Accommodation to be provided		Price to be paid to an occupier other than the keeper of a victualling house
Lodging and attendance for soldiers where meals are furnished		9d night
Breakfast as specified in Part I of the Second Schedule to the Army Act		7½d each
Dinner as so specified	1s	7½d each
Supper as so specified		4½d each

Accommodation to be provided		Price to be paid to an occupier other than the keeper of a victualling house
Where no meals furnished, lodging and attendance, and candles, vinegar, salt, and the use of fire, and the necessary utensils for dressing and eating his meat		9d day
Stable room and ten pounds of oats, twelve pounds of hay, and eight pounds of straw for each horse	2s	7½d per day
Stable room without forage		9d per day
Lodging and attendance for officer Note: an officer must pay for his own food.	3s	0 per night

The following special rates have been fixed for troops accommodated in buildings (other than dwelling houses) where bed and attendance are not provided, and for horses where proper stabling is not provided:

For each officer or soldier		3d night
For each horse		3d night

A revised form (A.B. 123M) for payment of billets is now being issued to all units in lieu of A.B.123.

The rates for victualling houses were lower; these were published in Schedule 1 of the Army (Annual) Act.

Accommodation to be provided		Price to be paid to the keeper of a victualling house
Lodging and attendance for soldiers where meals are furnished		6d night
Breakfast as specified in Part I of the Second Schedule to the Army Act		5d each
Dinner as so specified	1s	1d each
Supper as so specified		3d each
Where no meals furnished, lodging and attendance, and candles, vinegar, salt, and the use of fire, and the necessary utensils for dressing and eating his meat		6d day
Stable room and ten pounds of oats, twelve pounds of hay, and eight pounds of straw for each horse	1s	9d per day
Stable room without forage		6d per day
Lodging and attendance for officer Note: an officer must pay for his own food.	2s	0 per night

Where men were to be supplied with a hot meal, it was to consist of 1¼lb of meat, weighed before cooking, 1lb of bread, 1lb of potatoes or other vegetables, two pints of small beer, vinegar, salt and pepper. The money, and the generous ration, would have been a welcome addition to most households at the time. Mrs Emily Appleby had a number of soldiers billeted in her house on Oak Road, in Luton, and in December 1914 was paid the grand sum of £5 in billeting money. Accompanied by her friend Mrs Mary Kingham she went for a drink at the George. After tea in Dumfries Street they had another drink at the Regent Arms and then went to the corner of Wellington Street to catch a tram home. Mrs Kingham paid the penny for her friend's fare. But when Appleby got home she discovered that £5, in £1 notes, had disappeared from her bag. In a sorry tale that was played out before the Luton magistrates Kingham admitted taking the purse from her bag on the tram, 'on the impulse of the moment'. She offered to pay the money back, and the bench adjourned the matter for a week, to allow the money to be paid.[9]

On 26 September 1914, two young women, the wives of soldiers, appeared in front of Mr Cancellor at Marylebone Police Court. They complained that their landlord had threatened to eject (evict) them as they were unable to pay the rent as they had not yet received their allowances from the War Office (Chapter 10). The magistrate told them to lock their doors securely and sent a court officer to the landlord to warn him not to take any further action.[10] Cancellor had already expressed strong opinions about the rapacious nature of property owners in the current crisis: 'I am afraid that many of you landlords get into a fright about your miserable rent, and the moment you think there is a possibility of your losing it you start to clear out the unfortunate women whose husbands have gone out to fight for their country.'[11] Of course landlords were perfectly – and legally – entitled to their rent, and under the Small Tenements Recovery Act, 1838 were able to eject tenants who had fallen into arrears. The process involved serving a notice to quit, which included a requirement to attend court if any objection was to be lodged, and the magistrates would grant a warrant for ejectment to be executed after twenty-two days.[12] Following a meeting of the Privy Council on Sunday, 2 August, the King had issued a proclamation for the postponement of payments which was designed to stabilize the money markets, which were already in turmoil following weeks of turbulence in stock exchanges around the world. This was the basis for the Postponement of Payments Act, 1914, 'an Act to authorize His Majesty … to suspend temporarily the payment of Bills of Exchange and payments in pursuance of other obligations'. Known generally as the Moratorium, it was rushed through parliament and secured Royal assent by 7.15 pm on Monday, 3 August.[13] It was given a six-month period of operation, and in essence allowed payments on financial instruments to be deferred by thirty days or until 4 September (interest would still be incurred). Although clearly aimed at business it also provided relief to mortgage payers, and to insurance contributions. Taxes and rates were not exempt, however, neither were amounts under £5, which of course included rent.[14] This put magistrates in a difficult position, as they had a duty to enforce payments but, as Cancellor demonstrated, were naturally sympathetic to cases of hardship, especially if rent had been paid promptly and fully in the past. The *Justice of the Peace* advised judicial discretion: if the tenant appeared to be in a temporary difficulty caused by the current crisis, they ought to adjourn the case, or even refuse the ejectment warrant out of hand.[15]

The situation was greatly improved by the Courts (Emergency Powers) Act, passed on 31 August, which restricted the exercise of the powers of creditors under certain conditions. Section 1 (2) gave the court the absolute discretion to stay or defer any notice of ejectment 'upon it being shown that the debtor is unable immediately to make payment by reason of circumstances directly or indirectly attributable to the war';[16] and section 1 (4) specifically applied to all proceedings under the Small Tenements Act. Magistrates were gently reminded that the new legislation did not apply to the payment of fines, recognizances, costs, affiliation orders or maintenance contributions.

On 12 August the *Dundee Courier* reported on a 'wonderful week's work' by both houses of Parliament. They listed:

Postponement of Payments Act.
Currency and Bank Notes Act – the issue of the first £1 notes.
Prize Courts Act.
Aliens (Restriction) Act.
Patents, Designs and Trademarks.
Electoral Disabilities Removal.
Police Reservists.
Metropolitan Police.
Education (Provision of Meals).
Injuries in War.
Army Act.
Unreasonable Withholding of Food Supplies Act.
Defence of the Realm Act.
Housing Bill – to provide work by expenditure of £4m on housing.[17]

Items in bold are dealt with in subsequent chapters. A full list of the Emergency Legislation appears at the end of this chapter.

Most of these acts were passed in a single day, and it is not surprising that many had to return to Parliament for amendment or correction. Given the crisis facing the country, rather incredibly both houses adjourned for the summer recess after business on 10 August and did not resume until 25 August. Parliamentary lawyers were busy during this time, and very shortly Mr McKenna, the Home Secretary, was able to introduce the **Special Constables Act**, and a Bill to 'enable orders to be made in connection with the present war for the restriction of the sale and consumption of intoxicating liquors' which would shortly become the **Intoxicating Liquor (Temporary Restrictions) Act**.[18]

Hansard is a publication which forms the official report of debates in Parliament and it provides a fascinating record of the speed with which this enormous amount of legislation passed through the two chambers. In simple terms, British law is normally introduced by a 'white paper', which is a policy document, usually from the party in government, setting out the purposes of a proposed law or change of law, and often including the law in draft (it may be preceded by a 'green paper' which a more consultative document). It is then presented as a Bill and goes through a first reading which is usually a formality. The second reading is the opportunity for members to consider the draft and is conducted as a parliamentary debate, with the minister responsible for introducing the Bill explaining the key features, followed by a response from the opposition. This may take a considerable time and involve much negotiation. The committee stage follows, where each line, clause and amendment is further debated (the 'committee' is the Public Bill Committee of between sixteen and fifty members, but in August 1914 frequently comprised all the members present in the chamber – 'the House resolves itself into committee'). This committee may request reports and evidence from officials and from counsel and other experts. The report of the committee is presented to the House for further and final debate. If the Bill was introduced and passed the third reading in the House of Commons it then goes to the House of Lords and the process is repeated (and vice versa if the Bill is initiated in the Upper Chamber). The Bill may be sent back to the other house for amendment, but once both houses are satisfied the Bill returns to the first house for any amendments, before finally obtaining Royal Assent.[19]

This book is concerned with the way in which this legislation affected peoples' lives during the war. The Act itself is described as primary legislation, in which Parliament positively enacts provisions it wishes to implement, and the Act may delegate powers to a government department or agency. The detailed implementation is achieved through secondary legislation, using instruments such as statutory rules, regulations and orders. At the time of the Great War these were governed using the language of the Rules Publication Act, 1893 and the terminology, then and now, can be slightly confusing. A regulation is usually the secondary legislation which sets out the details by which the aims of the primary legislation are to be achieved, and by which department, authority or agency (and often prescribing the penalties for offences against the regulation). Slightly confusingly, the Secretary of State or other person with delegated power may make and implement decisions by making an Order, which is also secondary legislation. A critical element of the Rules Publication Act, and of legislative procedure generally, was that draft rules (regulations or orders) were to be laid before Parliament for inspection for forty days, and that members of Parliament and other public bodies were entitled to examine and comment on them. As we shall see, parliamentary scrutiny of secondary legislation, especially in relation to the Orders in Council, was in almost complete abeyance for the duration of the war.

The Postponement of Payments Bill passed through all three stages on 3 August. The Aliens (Restriction) Bill went through on 5 August. The innocuous Defence of the Realm Act was dealt with in minutes on 8 August. When the House resumed two weeks later, no fewer than four of these rushed measures were brought back for amendment: the Chancellor of the Exchequer, Lloyd George, had to apologize for the quality of the new £1 and 10s notes which were 'prepared in haste and which may be easily forged', and so the Currency and Banknotes Act was amended to give the Treasury the power to recall the 'old' notes. The Defence of the Realm (No. 2) Act needed to extend the powers of the military authorities to all areas in which trade was being carried on (it actually covered areas used for training or concentration of forces, and introduced wide-ranging powers for the acquisition and use of land). Mr Runciman, President of the Board of Trade, had to introduce a new Bill to supplement the Unreasonable Withholding of Food Supplies Act, which had failed to provide any authority for the Government to actually ascertain the amount of stocks being withheld. He also had to apologize for the poor drafting of the Patents, Designs and Trademarks (Temporary Rules) Act he had introduced a fortnight previously, and submit an amended Act.[20] It should also be noted that in addition to the emergency legislation Parliament was also dealing with its existing programme of legislation, so that ministers and members were debating Bills such as the River Navigation Improvement (Ireland), Town Charities (Extension) and Places of Worship Enfranchisement. A long-planned and, for the magistracy, important piece of legislation was the Criminal Justice Administration Act, which was passed on 10 August 1914 but was not fully implemented until the following year. The reaction to this raft of legislation was muted. The editor of the *Shoreditch Observer*, noting the lack of comment from MPs, asserted that 'if the position were not so serious the attitude of Parliament would be laughable, because its members have abandoned even the negative function of criticism'.[21]

The transition to war was marked by considerable legal innovation, but much of it was poorly drafted and, in many cases, there was a failure to recognize the extent of available legislation which was already on the statute book and much of which helped the nation make a smooth transition to war. The reservists were brought back into the regular army, the territorials were embodied and mobilized to their concentration points around the country, the railways were effectively nationalized to ensure efficient transport of men and munitions. The justices and the courts were able to deal with absentees and deserters, and to attest the volunteers who were coming forward in their thousands. But would the legal system be able cope with an enemy invader, and warfare on British soil?

Emergency Legislation Passed Between 1 August and 30 September 1914[22]

Aug 1	Notice under Wireless Telegraphy (Foreign Ships) Regulations that an Emergency has arisen.
	Admiralty Regulations for the Prohibition of the Use of Wireless Telegraphy by Merchant Vessels.
Aug 2	Proclamation Postponing Payment of certain Bills of Exchange.
	Order of Secretary of State under Aerial Navigation Acts, 1911 and 1913.
Aug 3	Proclamation Calling out Men of the Royal Naval Reserve and Royal Fleet Reserve, and Officers and Men of Royal Naval Volunteer Reserve.
	Proclamation Extending Services of Time-expired Men in the Royal Navy.
	Proclamation authorizing Admiralty to requisition any British Ship or British Vessel within British Isles or Waters adjacent thereto.
	Proclamation prohibiting Exportation of certain Warlike Stores.
	Proclamation appointing August 4, 5 and 6, Bank Holidays.

	Proclamation of Lord Lieutenant appointing August 4, 5 and 6, Bank Holidays.
	Order in Council calling Officers of the Reserved and Retired Lists into Active Service and Suspending Compulsory Retirement from the Active List.
Aug 4	Notification of a State of War with Germany.
	Proclamation Calling out Army Reserve and Embodying Territorial Force.
	Proclamation continuing Soldiers in Army Service.
	Proclamation regarding the Defence of the Realm.
	Proclamation specifying Articles to be treated as Contraband.
	Order in Council as to Government control of the Railroads of Great Britain.
	Order in Council as to the Detention of German Ships.
	Order in Council for Calling out Militia Reserve of Jersey.
	Proclamation giving Notice of Order in Council Calling out Militia Reserve in Jersey.
	Order of His Majesty authorizing General or Field Officers to issue Billeting Requisitions.
	Order of His Majesty authorizing General or Field Officers to issue Requisitions of Emergency.
	Order of the Lord Lieutenant authorizing general or Field Officers in Ireland to issue Billeting Requisitions.
	Order of the Lord Lieutenant authorizing general or Field Officers in Ireland to issue Requisitions of Emergency.
	Warrant of the Secretary of State empowering the President of the Board of Trade to take possession of all Railroads in Great Britain.
	Army Order 289 of 1914 promulgating Special Rates to be paid for Billeting in cases of Emergency.
Aug 5	Postponement of Payments Act, 1914.
	Aliens Restriction Act, 1914.
	Prize Courts (Procedure) Act, 1914.
	Proclamation as to Trading with the Enemy.
	Proclamation prohibiting British Vessels from carrying Contraband from one Foreign Port to another.
	Proclamation prohibiting Exportation of certain Warlike Stores, Provisions and Victuals.
	Proclamation prohibiting Exportation of Warlike Stores to certain Countries.
	Proclamation as to Financial Assistance to the Enemy.
	Order in Council authorizing the Admiralty to require the Constitution of a Prize Court (Germany).

	Order in Council prescribing the Rules and Tables of Fees to be observed and taken in Prize Proceedings.
	Order in Council as to Royal Indian Marine Vessels 'Hardinge' and 'Dufferin'.
	Aliens Restriction Order.
	Estimate of additional Number of Men required for Army Service.
Aug 6	Currency and Bank Notes Act, 1914.
	Proclamation (First General) under Postponement of Payments Act, 1914.
	Order of Board of Agriculture and Fisheries Suspending Operation of certain Orders.
Aug 7	Electoral Disabilities (Naval and Military Service) Removal Act, 1914.
	Army (Supply of Food, Forage and Stores) Act, 1914.
	Patents, Designs and Trade Marks (Temporary Rules) Act, 1914.
	Notice declaring that Articles III to VIII of the Order in Council of August 4, relating to German Ships in British Ports at the outbreak of hostilities, will not come into operation.
	Notice of proposal to submit the 'Provisional Prize Court Rules, 1914' for making as 'Statutory Rules'.
Aug 8	Defence of the Realm Act, 1914.
Aug 10	Injuries in War (Compensation) Act, 1914.
	Police Reservists (Allowances) Act, 1914.
	Unreasonable Withholding of Food Supplies Act, 1914.
	Housing (No. 2) Act, 1914.
	Special Constables (Scotland) Act, 1914.
	Proclamation prohibiting the Exportation of certain Warlike Stores, Provisions and Victuals.
	Aliens Restriction (No. 2) Order, 1914.
	Order in Council approving scheme under the Injuries in War (Compensation) Act, 1914.
	Order authorizing General or Field Officers to issue Requisitions of Emergency.
Aug 11	Order of the Lord Lieutenant authorizing General or Field Officers in Ireland to issue Requisitions of Emergency.
	Notification as to the Constitution of the Admiralty Transport Arbitration Board.
Aug 12	Notification of a State of War with Austria-Hungary.
	Proclamation extending to Austria-Hungary the scope of certain Proclamations and an Order in Council connected with the War.
	Proclamation (Second General) under Postponement of Payments Act, 1914.

	Order in Council as to Royal Indian Marine Vessels 'Northbrook' and 'Minto'
	Defence of the Realm Regulations, 1914.
	Aliens Restriction (No. 3) Order, 1914.
	Letter from the Chancellor of the Exchequer to the Bank of England as to Assistance in regard to Bills of Exchange.
Aug 13	Royal Warrant under Sign Manual revoking Exequaturs of German or Austro-Hungarian subjects exercising Consular functions for any third Power.
Aug 14	Letter from War Office to Treasury as to Expenditure under Vote of Credit.
Aug 15	Notice declaring that Articles III to VIII of the Order in Council of August 4, as extended by the Proclamation of August 12 to Austro-Hungarian ships in British ports at the outbreak of hostilities, will come into operation.
Aug 20	Proclamation modifying Proclamations relating to Exportation of certain Warlike Stores, Provisions and Victuals.
	Order in Council adopting during the present hostilities the provision of the 'Declaration of London' with Modifications.
	Aliens Restriction (No. 4) Order, 1914.
	Order in Council as to Royal Indian Marine Vessel 'Dalhousie'.
	Order in Council authorizing Admiralty to require the Constitution of a Prize Court (Austria-Hungary).
	Treasury Minute as to the Vote of Credit.
Aug 21	Patents, Designs and Trade Marks (Temporary) Rules, 1914.
	Notice as to Procedure under Rules 2, 3 or Patents, Designs and Trade Marks (Temporary) Rules, 1914.
	Trade Marks (Temporary) Rules, 1914.
Aug 22	Official Announcement in explanation of Trading with the Enemy Proclamation of 5 August.
Aug 27	Arrangements made in accordance with the Currency and Bank Notes Act, 1914, for placing currency notes at the disposal of the banks.
	Letter from the Treasury to the Bank of England as to Assistance in regard to Bills of Exchange.
	Letter from Bank of England in reply to foregoing.
Aug 28	War Loan Act, 1914.
	Special Constables Act, 1914.
	Isle of Man (War Legislation) Act, 1914.
	Defence of the Realm (No. 2) Act, 1914.
	Customs (Exportation Prohibition) Act, 1914.

	Articles of Commerce (Returns, &c) Act, 1914.
	Elementary School Teachers (War Service Superannuation) Act, 1914.
	Police (Scotland) (Limit of Age) Act, 1914.
	Naval Billeting, &c Act, 1914.
	Housing (No.2) (Amendment) Act, 1914.
	Currency and Banknotes (Amendment) Act, 1914.
	Patents, Designs and Trade Marks Temporary Rules (Amendment) Act, 1914.
	Order in Council providing for cancellation of so much of Proclamation of 1900 as relates to Distribution of Net Proceeds of Naval Prizes.
	Order in Council withdrawing certain prohibitions on Exportation of Provisions and Victual to Dominions, &c, 1914.
Aug 31	Slaughter of Animals Act, 1914.
	Death Duties (Killed in War) Act, 1914.
	Intoxicating Liquor (Temporary Restrictions) Act, 1914.
	Courts (Emergency Powers) Act, 1914.
	Notification as to the constitution of the Admiralty Transport Arbitration Board.
Sep 1	Proclamation under Postponement of Payments Act, 1914.
	Defence of the Realm (No. 2) Regulations, 1914.
	Order of Council withdrawing prohibition on Exportation of Jams, Marmalades and Condensed Milk.
Sep 2	Order of Secretary of State as to Carrier and Homing Pigeons.
Sep 3	Proclamation (Third General) under Postponement of Payments Act, 1914.
	Order in Council extending Postponement of Payments Act, 1914 to Isle of Man.
	Order prescribing Limit of Age of Person transferred or appointed to any Police Force in Scotland during continuance of War.
Sep 5	Designs (Temporary) Rules, 1914.
	Statement appearing in the Press as to Assistance in regard to Bills of Exchange.
Sep 7	Patents and Designs (Temporary) Rules, 1914.
	Notice as to Procedure under Rule 1 of the Patents, &c, the Trade Marks, and the Designs (Temporary) Rules.
Sep 8	Order in Council amending Proclamations prohibiting the Exportation of various Articles.
	Courts (Emergency Powers) Rules, 1914, made by Lord Chancellor.
Sep 9	Trading with the Enemy Proclamation (No. 2).

	Aliens Restriction (Consolidation) Order, 1914.
	Special Constables Order, 1914.
	Order in Council extending the Defence of the Realm Acts, 1914 and the Regulations thereunder to the Isle of Man.
	Estimate of Additional Number of Men required for Army Service.
Sep 10	Order of Secretary of State as to Homing and Carrier Pigeons.
	County Court Rule as to the Postponement of Payments Act.
Sep 11	Order in Council prohibiting Exportation of Sugar, &c.
	Directions of Lord Chancellor under Courts (Emergency Powers) Act, 1914.
	Provisional Regulations of the Insurance Commissioners as to men belonging to the Naval Reserves, the Army Reserve, and the Territorial Force.
	Provisional Regulations of the Welsh Insurance Commissioners as to men belonging to the Naval Reserves, the Army Reserve, and the Territorial Force.
Sep 12	Regulations of the Scottish Insurance Commissioners as to men belonging to the Naval Reserves, the Army Reserve, and the Territorial Force.
Sep 15	Treasury Order as to County Court Fees under Courts (Emergency Powers) Rules.
	Army Order XXI as to Special Rates to be paid for Billeting in the cases of Emergency.
Sep 16	Provisional Regulations of the Irish Insurance Commissioners as to men belonging to the Naval Reserves, the Army Reserve, and the Territorial Force.
Sep 17	Proclamation authorizing the Board of Trade to take Possession of Articles of Commerce unreasonably withheld from the Market.
	Courts (Emergency Powers) Order.
	Special Constables (Scotland) Order.
	Order in Council prescribing the Rules and Tables of Fees to be observed and taken in Prize Proceedings.
	Order in Council amending the Defence of the Realm Regulations, 1914.
	Further Directions of the Lord Chancellor to County Courts under the Courts (Emergency Powers) Act.
	Courts (Emergency Powers) Rules, 1914, made by the Lord Chancellor of Ireland.
Sep 18	Prize Courts (Egypt, Zanzibar and Cyprus) Act, 1914.
	Police Constables (Naval and Military Service) Act, 1914.
	National Insurance (Navy and Army) Act, 1914.
	Bills of Exchange Act, 1914.
	Army Pensions Act, 1914.
	Irish Police Constables (Naval and Military Service) Act, 1914.

	Rates (Proceedings for Recovery) Act, 1914.
	Trading with the Enemy Act, 1914.
	Suspensory Act, 1914.
	Navy (Pledging of Certificates) Act, 1914.
	Additional Rule made by Lord Chancellor under Courts (Emergency Powers) Act.
Sep 21	Proclamation specifying Additional Articles to be treated as Contraband of War.
	Order of Secretary of State as to Carrier and Homing Pigeons.
Sep 22	Licence granted by Secretary of State under Trading with the Enemy Proclamation (No. 2).
	Memorandum as to Separation Allowances to Wives and Children of Seamen, Marines, and Naval Reservists.
Sep 23	Licence granted by Board of Trade under Trading with the Enemy Proclamation (No. 2) in connection with patents, designs and trade marks.
Sep 25	Order in Council amending Proclamations and Order in Council prohibiting the Exportation of various Articles.
	Licence granted by Board of Trade under Trading with the Enemy Proclamation (No. 2) respecting payment of freights and other charges in respect of enemy ships.
Sep 27	Board of Trade Announcement as to British Cargoes in Enemy Ships in Neutral Ports.
Sep 28	Act of Sederunt under the Courts (Emergency Powers) Act.
Sep 30	Proclamation (Final) under Postponement of Payments Act.
	Proclamation extending the Prohibitions of the Trading with the Enemy Proclamation (No. 2).
	Order in Council extending Aliens Restriction Act, 1914 to the Isle of Man.
	Aliens Restriction (Isle of Man) Order, 1914.
	Order in Council conferring jurisdiction in matters of Prize on certain British Courts in Egypt, Zanzibar and Cyprus, and authorizing the Admiralty to require the Constitution of Prize Courts.
	Order in Council (Provisional) amending the Rules to be observed in Prize Proceedings.
	National Health Insurance (Officers, Warrant Officers and Soldiers) (Provisional) Regulations, 1914.
Not dated	Modifications effected in the Army Act as applied to Naval Billeting by the Naval Billeting &c Act, 1914.
	Modifications effected in the Army Act as applied to Naval Requisitions of Emergency by the Naval Billeting Act, 1914.
	Increased Rates of Separation Allowances for Wives and Children of Soldiers.

Chapter 4

Civil, Military and Martial Law

One of the most striking geological features of the Jurassic Coast of Dorset is the Isle of Portland, a limestone peninsula stretching some four miles into the English Channel. The eastern side provides a shelter for shipping and the strategic importance of this harbour has been recognized for centuries, and it was home to a large naval base until recent times. It is connected to the mainland by a road along the great Chesil Beach, with the risk of being cut off during winter storms. With a combined civilian and naval population on the island the demand for water has always exceeded the local supply and to overcome this problem Victorian engineers sank boreholes in the chalky downland at the tiny village of Upwey, north of Weymouth, and pumped water to the island through a ten-mile pipeline. At the outbreak of the Great War, the pumping station and its reservoir, along with thousands of similar installations around the country, were designated as 'vulnerable points' and required military protection.

The 3rd Battalion of the Dorsetshire Regiment, formerly the Dorset Militia, was assigned to guard the Portland water supply. A small tented camp was originally set up in fields off Friar Waddon Road, at the top of the chalk scarp above Upwey village, an exposed and somewhat remote location. With the realization that the war might last beyond Christmas, plans were made to erect wooden huts to house a detachment of seventy officers and men. The camp was intended to be reasonably self-contained, with separate mess tents and huts for the officers and NCOs, and a canteen and a pair of forty-bed huts for the men. With deteriorating weather conditions in late November the officers decided to move the men into the huts even though they were unfinished. On the night of Sunday, 29 November 1914, torrential rain lashed the camp and those men not on guard duty spent the evening making 'hilarious use'[1] of the canteen. By about 9.30 pm things were getting out of hand. A fight broke out between one of the NCOs, Sergeant Probert, and a couple of soldiers. Probert retired to his tent, which was then surrounded by an angry mob who pounded the canvas with implements and tools, beating him unconscious inside. Private Wallace Williams, an excitable man of questionable intelligence, ran into a hut crying out that there was a mutiny. He grabbed his rifle and fixed his bayonet and dashed out again. Another man, Alfred Wilson, a corporal despite being only 18 years of age, also seized a rifle and, in an incredible escalation of the situation, opened fire, shooting wildly into the roof and out of the windows. Several other men collected their rifles. In the ensuing mayhem three officers and the company sergeant major attempted to control the situation but had to withdraw, and they ordered the more sober men into trenches for their own safety. An outlying patrol in the nearby village of Broadwey was recalled, and reinforcements from the main camp at Wyke Regis were urgently summoned by telephone. Wilson continued firing indiscriminately out of the hut window while Williams rushed around outside in a frenzy. And at some point, perhaps predictably, Williams was shot in the chest, and he died almost immediately. Another man, Private Lane, was seriously injured.

By the time the commanding officer, Colonel Castleman-Smith, and the reinforcements arrived at about 10 pm the camp had quietened down. Four men, including Wilson, were arrested and taken into military custody at the Red Barracks in Weymouth. The officers discovered that about 100 rounds of ammunition had been fired during the incident. Bullet holes were found in the hut ceilings, doors, and door frames. A local doctor was summoned to examine Williams' body, which was conveyed to Weymouth mortuary. The town coroner, Mr Gustavus Phelps Symes, solicitor and notary public, was duly notified, and he convened an inquest to determine the cause of death.

The hearing took place in the Guildhall in Weymouth on Thursday, 3 December 1914. A jury was sworn in, and they were shown the body, as well as plans of the camp and of the locations of the bullet holes, spent cartridge cases and ammunition clips. Symes gave the jury a very clear warning that they had 'nothing to do with military law or discipline' and that notwithstanding the present state of war, 'any crime committed in this country must be dealt with by civil authorities'. After giving a brief account of the events in the Upwey camp on that evening, the coroner spelled out the law as it applied to the act of homicide: it could only be excused as an unavoidable accident; or that it was in self-defence; or in lawful obedience to the orders of a civil or military authority. If the man acted in malice towards the other, the finding would be murder. In the absence of malice it would be manslaughter.

Corporal Wilson and the three other soldiers were present in court, under military escort. Although Symes warned him of the seriousness of the situation and of his willingness to adjourn the matter until he had obtained legal representation, Wilson refused any assistance. Evidence was then presented by a number of witnesses who described the fighting and the shooting. At the end of the first part of the hearing Symes reached the conclusion that Wilson had been the only man firing a rifle, and he adjourned the court. Williams was given a full military funeral and was buried at Melcombe Regis cemetery on Saturday 5 December 1914.[2]

The inquest resumed the following Thursday, 10 December. After further evidence about the incident and about the dead man, Wilson volunteered to give evidence. After being cautioned and sworn, the coroner questioned him:

Coroner: I wish you to realize the seriousness of the matter. If you were the only one who fired out of the window it must have been you who struck and killed Williams.
Wilson: It must have been, I suppose.
Coroner: You had no ill-feeling towards Williams had you?
Wilson: No sir, in fact I liked the man.
Coroner: So you really do think it must have been you who struck and killed Williams?

Wilson did not answer the question and appeared emotional. The examination continued:

Coroner: Come, bear up. I quite believe what you have said. You have given your evidence in a very straightforward manner. You were so excited you did not know what you were doing.

Wilson: I fired, but I did not know what I was firing at.[3]

After hearing evidence from more of Wilson's comrades, Symes summed up the case for the benefit of the jury by noting that Wilson 'had used a dangerous weapon in such a way as had resulted in the death of a man'; and he could not see what other course was open to the jury other than to return a verdict of manslaughter. After a short retirement, the jury agreed, although they asked that as they found some of the evidence conflicting, and that Wilson had not intended to kill, and that the circumstances were 'extremely exciting', they wished to strongly recommend him to mercy. Wilson was committed to the next assizes on bail of his own recognizance of £10. As he was in the charge of the military authorities he would be remanded into military custody until the Public Prosecutor had considered the case.

Symes was confident that this was a straightforward manslaughter case in which Wilson's admission and the comments of the coroner's jury might convince a trial judge to reach a sentence of a few years' imprisonment. He did not foresee what happened next.

The Winter Assizes were held at the Shirehall in Dorchester on Tuesday, 12 January 1915, before Mr Justice Scrutton. Wilson was brought up from the cells on the coroner's warrant for the manslaughter of Wallace Williams. Mr Elliott, the Crown prosecutor, then announced that there was to be no prosecution, and on behalf of the Director of Public Prosecutions no evidence was to be offered. On 29 December, while in military custody, Wilson and two others had been tried by court-martial for the offence of mutiny under section 7 of the Army Act, 1881. Wilson had been sentenced to six months' hard labour, and Privates Amey and Cattell to three months each (two other men, Privates Parson and Anscombe, had been acquitted). The Crown had taken the view that the same facts had been used to prove the mutiny offence as would be used to prove the manslaughter charge. Having heard from the military prosecutor at the court-martial, Captain Bullock, the learned judge assented: 'although the two charges against the prisoner were different, they were the outcome of the same set of facts, and … he did not think a man should be punished twice for one offence'.[4] Following his direction, the jury found Wilson not guilty and he was dismissed.

Symes was outraged and wrote a furious letter to the *Justice of the Peace*: 'I should think that this is a unique case in our criminal history and that no man has ever before been committed for manslaughter, and escaped being tried altogether on that charge, or that a crime involving manslaughter had not been enquired into by civil magistrates.'[5]

The Wilson case attracted no attention. For a nation at war overwhelmed with emergency legislation it seemed of little matter if an offence was dealt with by a military or a civilian court. With a significant proportion of the male population now under military law, and the Defence of the Realm Act and its subordinate regulations putting the whole country under a form of martial law, the nuances – and the implications – were given little thought.

The *Manual of Military Law*[6] defines military law as 'the law which governs the soldier in peace and in war, at home and abroad'. Section 190, subsection 31 of the Army Act, 1881 defines 'civil court' as 'a court of ordinary criminal jurisdiction, and includes a court of summary jurisdiction'. For our purposes the expressions 'civil law' and 'civil courts' include both systems of criminal and civil law proper.

Historically, armies were raised by the sovereign at times of local or national emergency. In the absence of any concerted invasion since William the Conqueror there was little need for a standing army in this country, although the Crown maintained naval and military forces as a royal prerogative. Such troops were governed by Articles of War which related only to the conduct of the soldiers for the duration of their military service, but with internal armed conflict during the Tudor period the application of military law to civilian communities caused considerable social and political unrest. By the time of the Civil War the right of the monarch to raise and maintain an army without the sanction of the Parliament was overturned. This principle was subsequently enshrined in the Bill of Rights (1689).

It has always been recognized that a soldier, subject to military discipline, has a particular relationship to his superior officers that requires levels of submission and obedience far higher than would be expected of a civilian, and the penalties for breaches of military discipline need to be swift and severe. Mutiny, the refusal of a soldier to obey orders, is clearly and specifically a military offence; nor can a civilian desert. The Glorious Revolution of 1688 saw William III replace King James II. In March the following year the new king ordered 800 Scottish soldiers to embark for Holland from Ipswich, but they refused and declared their loyalty for James and set off to Scotland. James himself had introduced articles which provided for the punishment of offences by courts-martial (excluding the death penalty) but the legal position of the Scottish deserters was unclear. In response to this challenge the first Mutiny Act was passed through all its stages in one day and received Royal Assent on 3 April 1689. This made mutiny, desertion and sedition crimes triable by courts-martial and punishable by death. The Act had an important preamble:

> Whereas the raising or keeping of a standing army within the United Kingdom of Great Britain and Ireland in time of peace, unless it be with the consent of Parliament, is against law.

This law expired after twelve months and so each year, for the next 190 years, the Act was brought back to Parliament to be passed again (although it did lapse between 1698 and 1702 as the nation was at peace). The Mutiny Act covered all British military forces at home in peace and in war; but overseas forces 'in the dominions of the Crown' were also under the Articles of War. The legal position of British forces on foreign or enemy territory was resolved following the Peninsular War in 1813, when the Act and the Articles were extended to cover all troops wherever they were serving. The two aspects of military law were combined into the Army Discipline and Regulation Act, 1879, which itself was repealed and replaced by the Army Act, 1881.

The Army Act began with the same preamble as the Mutiny Act and in itself had no powers – the authority of the Act was re-established each year with the Army (Annual) Act, which was also the instrument by which changes to the Army Act could be made. The Act covers all aspects of military law, crimes and punishment:

Army Act, 1881
Part I: Discipline, Arrest and Trial, Execution of Sentence
Part II: Enlistment
Part III: Billeting and Impressment of Carriages
Part IV: General Provisions
Part V: Application of Military Law, Saving Provisions, and Definitions
Part VI: Commencement and Application of Act, and Repeal

The first forty sections of the Army Act described the offences which were recognized under military law. They were grouped under specific headings, as offences in respect to:

Part I
Military service (sections 4 to 6)
Mutiny and insubordination (ss 7–11)
Desertion, fraudulent enlistment, and absence without leave (ss 12–15)
Disgraceful conduct (ss 16–18)
Drunkenness (s 19)
Persons in custody (ss 20–22)
Property (ss 23–24)
False documents and statements (ss 25–27)
Courts-martial (ss 28–29)
Billeting (s 30)
Impressment of carriages (s 31)
Enlistment (ss 32–34)
Miscellaneous military offences (ss 35–40)
Offences punishable by ordinary law (s 41)

The *Manual of Military Law* was a substantial reference book for officers and military lawyers and, in addition to the text of the Army Act, included the *Rules of Procedure* and many other laws and regulations which applied to the army, including the Geneva Convention and the Riot Act. As a handbook it provided substantial detail on legal procedure, including the various courts-martial. It was supplemented by the *King's Regulations and Orders for the Army*, 1912 (generally known as 'King's Regs') which described the day-to-day operation of the army, including such topics as rank and precedence, dress, clothing and equipment, office work, and military training. Army Orders, since 1907 issued by the Army Council, provided routine administrative instructions. Military clerks and orderly room sergeants developed great expertise in matching breaches of regulations to the relevant sections of the Army Act for disciplinary purposes. And there was always section 40 which related to 'any act, conduct, disorder, or neglect, to the prejudice of good order and military discipline'.

Throughout the evolution of military law it had always been accepted that civil law remained superior. Chapter XII of the *Manual of Military Law* was entitled 'The Relation of Officers and Soldiers to Civil Life' and section 41 of the Army Act, 1881 was 'Offences punishable by ordinary law of England'. It was explicitly acknowledged that a soldier remains a citizen, and if he committed an offence against ordinary criminal law he would be tried and punished as a civilian.

Returning to the Wilson case, the question of how he managed to avoid being charged with manslaughter depends on the relationship of the two legal systems, not necessarily on the distinction between manslaughter and mutiny. Military law was held by legal scholars as an 'indulgence', according to Sir Matthew Hale, and he quoted Sir William Blackstone's *Commentaries on the Laws of England*, 1765.[7] Blackstone went on to suggest that there was a clear use for a military law in times of war, but 'the necessity of order and discipline in an army is the only thing which can give it countenance; and therefore it ought not to be permitted in time of peace, when the King's courts are open for all persons to receive justice according to the laws of the land'. The inference was that soldiers governed themselves using a shadow legal system, including prosecutors and courts, of their own, whereas the real province of the lawyer and the judiciary was the civil court. Wilson's escape from civil prosecution depended on the Director of Public Prosecutions holding that a military court was at least equal to a civilian criminal court, and that the military conviction was equivalent to a civilian conviction. These are bold assertions: section 41 clearly stated that,

> Subject to such regulations for the purpose of preventing interference with the jurisdiction of the civil courts as are in this Act after mentioned, every person who, whilst he is subject to military law, shall commit any of the offences in this section mentioned, shall be deemed guilty of an offence against military law, and, if charged under this section with any such offence (in this Act referred to as a civil offence), shall be liable to be tried by court-martial, and on conviction to be punished as follows; that is to say, …

> (3) If he is convicted of manslaughter or treason-felony, be liable to suffer penal servitude, or such less punishment as in this Act mentioned.

Section (5)(a) also specified that the offence of manslaughter, if committed in the United Kingdom, was not to be tried by court-martial unless on active service or in a place more than 100 miles from a competent civil court. The civilian punishment for manslaughter was penal servitude for life, or for not less than three years.

Wilson was court-martialled, but not for manslaughter. Along with his four comrades he was charged with the section 7 (1) offence of mutiny, in that they 'caused or conspired with any other persons to cause any mutiny or sedition in any forces belonging to His

Majesty's regular, reserve, or auxiliary forces'. On conviction by court-martial the soldier was 'liable to suffer death, or such less punishment as is in this Act mentioned'. The sections of the Army Act are in order of seriousness and the first six relate to offences on active service in the field. Mutiny, then, is the most serious military offence that can be committed in the United Kingdom. As the *Manual of Military Law* states, 'mutiny' is an act of collective insubordination, involving two or more persons, and it goes on to suggest that the charge, being so grave, must be very carefully framed and with very clear evidence to show that there was 'a combined design on their part to resist authority'. In considering the events of the night of 29 November 1914, the officers in the court-martial would have heard evidence of the complete breakdown of military discipline and of the armed resistance of the men. Against this backdrop, the death of Williams was just one incident amongst many of what might arguably be described as a military riot. In this context it is clear that the military authorities were correct to charge – and convict – Wilson of the military offence.

Mutiny is not, of course, a civilian offence, so the question turns on the equivalence of the military tribunal and the civilian courts. Section 162 of the Army Act provided that:

> If a person sentenced by court-martial in pursuance of this Act to punishment for an offence is afterwards tried by a civil court for the same offence that court shall, in awarding punishment, have regard to the military punishment he may already have undergone.

This is an unusual formulation: it was perfectly possible for a military tribunal to take account of a the conviction and sentence passed upon a soldier, but as the Army Act by definition did not apply to civilians, it appears that the civil courts were somehow bound by the Army Act.

According to *Stone's Justices' Manual* a defence is available 'where any man is put in peril more than once for the same act', using the common law principle *autrefois convict* ('double jeopardy'). Section 162 seems to imply that a soldier could be tried and convicted twice, but the second, civil, court need only take account of any military punishment, rather than suggesting that a civil prosecution and trial need not take place following a military conviction. It does, however, suggest that a military conviction and sentence carries the same weight as that of the civil court. Wilson had been convicted, at general court-martial, of the grave offence of mutiny, which carried the death penalty. The manslaughter of Williams formed part of the evidence of mutiny, and therefore the civilian charge was a lesser offence. Even if tried and convicted at the Dorchester Assizes the maximum penalty would have been penal servitude for life, and there had already been representations for leniency from the inquest jury. Ultimately there had been a political or administrative decision by the Director of Public Prosecutions not to proceed with the case. When the prosecution withdrew their evidence, Mr Justice Scrutton had no option but to direct the jury to acquit. The test of the relationship of the two legal systems was expeditiously and frustratingly avoided.

The principle established here is that in both times of peace and of war, there were two parallel legal systems of equal validity. The forty sections of the Army Act covered distinctly military offences, relating specifically to military personnel, property and procedure. Section 41 recognized that soldiers committing civil offences must be dealt with by the civil courts. Civilians, however, were not subject to military law and could neither commit military offences nor be tried at a military tribunal.

The court which heard Wilson's case was a general court-martial. This was the highest level of military tribunal, above the district court-martial and the regimental court-martial. These courts dealt with offences which were too serious to be dealt with summarily, which in military terms means trial and sentencing by the offender's commanding officer. Paragraph 1 of Chapter V of the *Manual of Military Law* explicitly stated that 'none of these tribunals had power to try any person unless he is subject to military law as provided by the Army Act'; and all members of the tribunal were themselves required to be under military law. These courts were called into being as required and most courts-martial comprised ordinary officers whose only qualification was rank and a certain level of time served. The officers did not have to belong to the same regiment or corps – indeed for general and district court-martials it was recommended that they were from different regiments – and could try a man from any from their own or different a unit. The distinctive feature of these courts was speed: once a man was remanded for trial his commanding officer had to take steps for the assembly of a tribunal of the appropriate level within thirty-six hours. He could convene a regimental court-martial under his own powers, otherwise he had to apply to the higher authority without delay. This application would contain a summary of the (prosecution) evidence. The senior officer receiving the application reviewed the charge and the evidence and had the power to dismiss the matter, refer back to a lower tribunal, or to authorize and convene a court-martial. Cases were not to be tried unless there was a reasonable prospect of conviction. At this stage the accused was to be informed of the charges and the procedure to be followed, and of the names of the members of the court. He was entitled to object, with reasonable cause, to any member, including the president. He was also entitled to prepare a defence case, with his own witnesses, and could engage a legal adviser or friend to help him with this. Despite the requirement that the court had to be composed of persons subject to military law, the accused was permitted a civilian solicitor or barrister, and they had the rights to address the court and to examine witnesses.

Although there were qualified lawyers in the army they were not necessarily available for duties at courts-martial. The rôle of 'judge-advocate' was performed by a 'fit person' who 'should be free from all suspicion or bias or prejudice; and should possess some acquaintance with military law and the rules of evidence', but despite his title he was explicitly not an advocate to the judge. The convening officer was required to appoint a judge-advocate for all general courts-martial, but it was optional for district courts-martial. This officer acted as the representative of the Judge Advocate-General (in the Adjutant-General's Branch). His rôle was to provide advice for both the prosecution and the accused on points of law, and to inform the court of any irregularity or informality in the proceedings, the constitution of the court, or the charge. A key rôle was that he was required to sum up the evidence and provide advice to the court before it withdrew to consider its verdict, and it was considered poor practice to ignore the advice of the judge-advocate on any legal point. It was permitted for the general officer commander-in-chief, with the approval of the Army Council, to appoint legal counsel to appear on behalf of the prosecutor, particularly for complex cases.

Recognizing that the members of the tribunal were army officers and not legal experts, the *Manual of Military Law*, *Rules of Procedure* and the *King's Regulations* provide extensive descriptions of court procedure, with such details as the hours of the hearing (between 10 am and 4 pm, or 11 am and 5 pm, and never more than eight hours in one day), and the problem of who sits where. The court-martial was an open court and a short-hand writer took a verbatim account of the proceedings, although the deliberations of the members took place in private.

The general court-martial (GCM), as the highest military court, had the power to award the punishments of death or penal servitude. It was convened by a senior officer whose position carried with it the authority to do so, and in home service this was usually the general officer commander-in-chief of the district. In the United Kingdom the tribunal had to consist of not less than nine officers, each of whom had held a commission for not less than three whole years, and they had to hold the rank of captain or above. The president of the tribunal was appointed by name by the convening officer and had to hold the rank of field officer (lieutenant colonel or above). If any of these requirements were not met, the proceedings would be invalid. GCMs were used for a number of high-profile espionage cases involving civilians (see table) and a number of those convicted were executed.

The district court-martial (DCM) had the power to award punishments of up to two years' imprisonment. It could be convened by the general officer commander-in-chief or by a senior officer to whom he had delegated such powers. A minimum of three officers was required, each of whom must have held a commission for not less than two whole years. Up until March 1915 civilians were routinely tried by DCM; it was rarely used thereafter.

The regimental court-martial (RCM) was to try minor offences the punishment for which was outside the powers of the commanding officer acting summarily, when he could award punishments of up to fourteen days' detention or fines not exceeding ten shillings. By the time of the First World War most simple offences were dealt with by the commanding officer in the orderly room, and more serious matters, and those involving non-commissioned officers and officers, were sent to DCMs. On active service overseas there was also the field general court-martial (FGCM) which was subject to slightly different rules and had sentencing options including field punishment No. 1, in which the defaulter was tied to a cartwheel or a post for a number of hours each day. This court was not used at home, although in the period of martial law imposed in Ireland after the Easter Uprising in 1916, there were 161 field general courts-martial for 'war treason', resulting in 151 convictions and 15 death sentences. They were all civilians.

The sentencing powers of the courts-martial was determined by the level of the tribunal and by the punishments available under the Army Act. Unlike civilian sentencing options, the principle of military punishment was the maintenance of discipline, and so a soldier might receive a particularly severe punishment if his offence was seen as prevalent. Convictions and sentences were required to be confirmed by a superior authority: the general officer commanding-in-chief for a DCM, or the King (or officer with authority from the King) for GCM. Both the finding and the sentence could be sent back for review. The confirming authority also had the power to mitigate, remit, commute or suspend the punishment, but once the punishment had been confirmed only the King or the Commander-in-Chief had the power to overturn the sentence. The confirming officer was responsible for seeing that the punishment was carried into effect, including death sentences.

A soldier sentenced to penal servitude was invariably dismissed from the Army, often 'with ignominy', and he served his sentence in a civilian convict prison. Sentences of imprisonment were to be served in military prisons (such as Colchester and the original 'Glass House' at Aldershot North Camp), or if the soldier was to be discharged, in a civilian local prison. Detention, as a punishment, was usually short term and served either in a military detention barracks or the local barrack detention room.

The military courts-martial ran in parallel with the civilian courts, with several levels of tribunal to deal with the specific issues of military offences. The procedures were fair and robust and with a reasonable degree of judicial impartiality, predicated on the maintenance of military discipline. The distinct jurisdictions of the military and civilian courts was recognized under section 41 of the Army Act, 1881; soldiers on home service committing civilian offences were dealt with by the civil courts. And as stated in the *Manual of Military Law*, the Army Act only applied to persons subject to military law. But what would happen in time of war?

One result of a history free from foreign invasion is that the civil law failed to anticipate the legal effects of a country at war. The existing legislation recognized civil disorder, as a localized and temporary event, which could be managed using the powers of the magistrates to summon the militia. Local authorities – and indeed individuals – had common law powers and duties to prevent riotous assembly and threats to the King's Peace. This included the right to take up arms and to use violence. The sheriff, mayor and magistrates had authority to call out the militia and to appoint special constables. The Riot Act of 1714 brought civil disorder into the statute book and its main objective was the dispersal of the riot. If the disturbance involved a crowd of twelve or more, the magistrate had to proclaim the following:

> Our Sovereign Lord the King chargeth and commandeth all persons, being assembled, immediately to disperse themselves, and peaceably depart to their habitations, or to their lawful business, upon the pains contained in the Act made in the first year of King George for preventing tumults and riotous assemblies.
> God Save the King

At the end of the hour the militia, or local military forces, could and were sent to clear the mob from the streets, and section 3 of the Act indemnified them from any death or injuries caused. Any individuals apprehended were tried in the civil courts, and usually for specific offences such as assault, affray or criminal damage. These powers were sufficient to deal with the Gordon Riots of 1780, the Peterloo Massacre of 1819, and many popular uprisings, protests and strikes up to the period of the First World War. Even with the Jacobite Rising of 1745 and the march of the Scottish forces as far south as Derby it was not felt necessary to impose any new law to deal with this 'invasion' or to view this as anything other than a temporary or local rebellion. The test applied by the legal authorities was that the courts were able to function normally; in the absence of widespread or long term disorder, from whatever cause, there was no requirement for special legislation.

The concept of martial law was not well explored, legally or practically. Blackstone and Hale, above, did not distinguish a difference between 'martial' and 'military' law, and the 'indulgence' was that for both of them, and many other legal thinkers, it was absurd to consider how military law might be applied to a civilian population. Dicey, in his influential *Law of the Constitution*[8] proposed that 'martial law … is unknown in England', and he defined martial law as 'the suspension of ordinary law and the temporary government of the country or parts of it, by military tribunals'. Even with the growth of Empire the problem of 'martial law' was not fully considered. If the army was on offensive operations in foreign or enemy territory, it was governed by the Mutiny Act and the Articles of War. If on peaceable duties in Crown colonies, civil law, modelled of course on English legal institutions, prevailed. With the exportation of Anglo-Saxon common law principles, the governors of overseas territories had a common law duty to preserve the peace, supported by the local Riot Act, and often by a Royal warrant or article of appointment granting them general powers of control in an emergency. There were several cases when such powers were exercised: Canada (1838), Barbados (1816), and Jamaica (1865) which resulted in judicial review in the British High Courts. In all such instances, however, the threat was from the 'enemy within', in the form of rebellion of His Majesty's subjects, rather than from a hostile enemy from without. The notable feature of colonial legal system was the general lack of an efficient and disciplined police force, and such as did exist were likely to be easily overwhelmed by the mob. The imposition of martial law provided the governor with the necessary force to control the civil disorder and restore peace. Whether at home or overseas Riot Act offences were dealt with by the civil courts. Any invocation of the Act was invariably followed by a Parliamentary Act of Indemnity.

In Europe matters were very different. From early times countries such as France, Belgium and the states comprising the German Empire had seen the effects of enemy forces marching across their lands. The French developed a system of law known as *l'état de siege*, or 'State of Siege' (conceptually it translates more accurately as 'State of Emergency'), which was a third way, between civil and military law. Historically derived from the need for effective government of fortified towns isolated from the central authorities, it provided a constitutional framework for the transfer of policing powers from the civil to the military authority and the establishment of military courts. First formulated after the French Revolution, by 1878 it had reached a robust level of development. It was able to be implemented at district or regional level in the French prefectures in response to imminent danger from armed insurrection or war, and required, at national level, cabinet agreement and presidential signature. Importantly, it was limited to a maximum of twelve days and required full parliamentary approval for any extension. The principle was that the military governor assumed control of all civil powers but delegated various duties and responsibilities to the civil authority – usually the mayor – for the management of the civilian population during the emergency. Importantly the decisions of the military and civil authorities were subject to judicial review. Military officers were appointed to the courts to sit alongside the magistrates, and the courts functioned as usual, although a number of specific military/emergency offences were triable: espionage, trading with the enemy, looting and others. Note that these were not a new form of court, but the usual court with additional responsibilities. In Germany there was a corresponding form of law known as *Notrecht* ('emergency law'), which was enshrined in the German Constitution, with Article 68 giving power to the German Emperor to declare a state of war (emergency) in German federal territory. Both *l'état de siege* and *Notrecht* could be used for civil rebellion or military invasion, or for a general state of war.

A very simplistic distinction between the Anglo-Saxon common law and the Continental Roman law systems is that common law tends to rely heavily on precedent: if something apparently new happens, the lawyers consult the law books to see if anything similar has happened in the past to develop new law on the basis of previous experience. Roman law tends to be anticipatory: the jurist tends to take existing law and test it, often with complex hypothetical scenarios, to see if it is consistent (think straight bananas and the European Union). Until the mid-nineteenth century there had been no common law examination of martial law in wartime, but the American Civil War (1861–5) produced several cases which forced the courts to consider how military and civil authorities administer justice when enemy forces are in the country. These cases, and others we will see later, usually began with a writ of *habeas corpus*, a fundamental common law right for the individual held in custody to challenge the courts to show cause for his detention.

President Lincoln used section 9 of Article 1 of the United States Constitution to declare martial law, which sanctioned arbitrary arrest and trial by military commission, and suspending the writ of *habeas corpus* as 'in cases of Rebellion or Invasion the public Safety may require it'. Lincoln's interpretation of position was that civil courts were established to try individuals and small groups 'on charges of crimes well-drafted in law', and not to deal with 'large groups of dissenters, whose actions, damaging to the war effort, did not constitute a defined crime'.

Clement Vallandigham was a Democrat senator for the state of Ohio. He was strongly opposed to the Civil War and was a member of the Copperheads peace movement. On 13 April 1863 the Union general Ambrose Burnside issued General Order Number 38 in the Department of the Ohio, which declared that those declaring sympathies for the enemy would no longer be tolerated and would be arrested and tried as spies or traitors. Vallandigham made speeches against the war and President Lincoln, and on 5 May he was arrested, tried by court-martial the following day, and convicted of 'uttering disloyal statements' and attempting to hinder the prosecution of the war. He was sentenced to two years' confinement in a military prison (he was subsequently banished to Canada). At a subsequent appeal a federal circuit judge upheld his arrest and military trial as a 'valid exercise of the President's war powers'. On his return Vallandigham took the matter to the Supreme Court. The question was to determine if the military proceedings were constitutional, and to issue a writ of *habeas corpus* to the military commission. The court considered the US constitution as it applied to the court system, and noted that there were clear precedents to issue writs of *certiorari* (quashing orders) to lower courts, there was no mention in the constitution of its powers over military courts, and on 15 February the Supreme Court declared that they were 'not authorized to call up proceedings of a military commission'.[9]

This established that decisions of military courts could not be subject to civil judicial review. Lambden Milligan established another precedent. He had been arrested, with others, in Indianapolis on 21 October 1864, for conspiracy against the US (Union) government, offering aid and comfort to Confederates, inciting insurrection, disloyal practices and violations of the rules of war. Milligan and two others were found guilty and were sentenced to be hanged. On 10 May 1865, Milligan's legal counsel issued a writ of *habeas corpus* to the Circuit Court of the United States for the District of Indiana. Two judges reviewed his petition and found themselves unable to agree if the US constitution prohibited civilians from being tried by a military commission. To resolve the dilemma they themselves passed the matter up to the Supreme Court. On 3 April 1866 the Supreme Court found that the military commission did not have the jurisdiction to try or sentence Milligan, and as a civilian not in military service and as a resident of a state in which civilian courts were still functioning, he had a right, when charged with a crime, to be tried and punished according to the law. Mr Justice Davis then made a significant pronouncement that 'martial law can never exist when the courts are open', following a principle stated by the jurist Lord Coke in the seventeenth century: 'peace is when the courts of justice are open'.[10] Martial law should be confined to areas of 'military operations, where war really exists'. They further clarified three classes of military jurisdiction under the US constitution:

1. That to be exercised in both peace and war;
2. That to be exercised in times of foreign war without the boundaries of the United States, or in time of rebellion within the limits of the states or districts occupied by rebels treated as belligerents;
3. That to be exercised in time of invasion or insurrection within the limits of the United States or during rebellion within the limits of the states maintaining adhesion to the National Government, when the public danger requires its exercise.

The first is military law, the second is military government, superseding local law and exercised by the military commander under the direction of the President or sanction of Congress. The third is martial law proper, called into action by Congress or the President, when ordinary law is no longer able to secure public safety.[11]

The subtle constitutional distinction between the two cases is that Vallandigham showed that the Supreme Court could not, of itself, review the decisions of the military commission, but Milligan demonstrated that the Supreme Court could be invited to consider the decisions of military commissions.

The British government had to wait until the Boer War of 1899–1902 to confront the issues of martial law. Both the British and the Dutch had established claims on the lands of southern Africa during the nineteenth century. The Cape Colony was acquired in 1814 and Natal in 1843. The Dutch set up the Boer South African Republic (or Transvaal) in 1852 and Orange Free State in 1854. With the discovery of diamonds in Kimberley in 1866, a rapid influx of non-Boers into Boer territories led to conflict, with the British seeking to acquire or incorporate the two Boer lands. The Boers had no formal or regular army and were essentially a militia or commando force, and declaring war on 11 October 1899 they attacked Kraaipan the next day and quickly penetrated into British territory.

The following was published in December 1899 as a *Memorandum of Rules for the Administration of Martial Law*,[12] advising the civil and military authorities of their powers should martial law be imposed, but this was not, in itself, a declaration of martial law.

Army Order on martial law 7 December 1899
1. Objects
2. Officers with powers
3. Non-interference with civil rights of peaceful colonists
4. Principal offences:
    a. Treasonable or seditious acts and words, or acts and words tending to excite disaffection, disloyalty, or distrust of Government
    b. Enlisting or engaging in the military forces of the enemy
    c. Aiding or abetting the enemy
    d. Carrying on trade with or supplying goods to the enemy. Destroying railways, bridges or telegraphs, and acts endangering the safety of Her Majesty's forces; also the contravention of rules and regulations made by the military authorities under the Proclamation
    e. Being suspected of any of the above offences
5. Procedure
6. Place and time of offences
7. Arrest, trial and sentence
8. Carrying out sentence
9. Armed rebels are to be treated as enemies, and, if taken prisoner, must be tried by military courts

Full declarations of martial law, based on these regulations, followed in Cape Colony, Natal and the Orange River Colony on 31 May 1900, and the Transvaal, following its capture, on 1 September 1900.

Interestingly, the Boers also imposed martial law in their territories. A poster was found with the proclamation of E.R. Grobler, Head Commandant of the Southern Army Division of the Orange Free State Burgher Forces, declaring that martial law of the Free State, as embodied in Law No. 10 of 1899, was in force. 'No one who did not take up an inimical attitude towards the Government of the Orange Free State or South African Republic, or their officers, officials, laws or orders would experience any harm.

Those who refused to subject themselves were thereby granted permission to leave the territory over which martial law had been declared within seven days.'[13]

Martial law, in the third, full, American sense was imposed in the besieged town of Kimberley on 20 December 1899, which provided regulations about the supply of tea, coffee, and other food stuffs issued, and issuing permits for weekly supplies in limited quantities per head. Prices were regulated by Colonel Kekwich and his staff.[14]

The Under-Secretary of State for War, George Wyndham, had offered a definition of martial law as he saw it in the context of the recently-occupied Orange Free State:

> It is the best substitute that can be contrived by those commanding an army of occupation for the civil law has been dislocated and impaired by the very fact that warlike operations are being prosecuted, and it is in that spirit that martial law is administered.[15]

He went on to reassure the House that detailed instructions had been issued for the guidance of officers who administered martial law, and to follow the rules of evidence as used in the civil courts. The sentences of the South African courts-martial had to be confirmed by the Judge Advocate-General as laid out in section 54 of the Army Act, 1881. Subsequently the Secretary of State for the Colonies, Joseph Chamberlain, confirmed that 'the military tribunals were not taking cognisance of offences against the criminal law', and that these were being dealt with by the civil courts.[16]

In January 1900 Lord Kitchener proposed that the object of martial law was 'to enable persons resisting the authority of the government, or aiding and abetting the enemy, to be arrested summarily and punished promptly'; and that when practical, it should 'only supplement, but where the civil government is paralysed, it must necessarily replace, the ordinary civil procedure'.[17] In this he was probably mindful of the US Supreme Court principle that martial law could not exist when the civil courts were open. By the following year he was clearer about the jurisdiction of military tribunals. In April 1901 Kitchener proposed to the Governor of Cape Colony that all overt acts of rebellion should be dealt with by the military courts. The governor and attorney-general were not fully convinced of his arguments, and pointed out the difficulty in preserving the calm, judicial atmosphere of the civil court in the environment of a military tribunal. They conceded that those courts which were open could not adequately deal with the cases of treason and rebellion and were prepared to agree that graver of cases be dealt with by military court. The only persons to be tried by courts-martial should be those charged with:

actively bearing arms with the enemy;
treacherously doing some overt act which endangered the safety of troops;
wrecking or firing on trains;
wanton personal outrages on His Majesty's subjects;
other acts of similar nature or gravity.

On 22 April 1901 Major General Wynne, the commander of Cape Colony district, issued martial law regulation No. 14:

Notice is hereby given that all subjects of his Majesty and all persons residing in the Cape Colony who shall in districts thereof in which martial law prevails:

1. Be actively in arms against his Majesty, or
2. Directly incite others to take up arms against his Majesty, or
3. Actively aid or assist the enemy, or
4. Commit any overt act by which the safety of his Majesty's forces or subjects are endangered,

Shall immediately on arrest be tried by a military court convened by the authority of the General Commanding-in-Chief his Majesty's Forces in South Africa, and shall on conviction be liable to the severest penalties. These penalties include death, penal servitude, imprisonment, and fine. Any person reasonably suspected of such offence is liable to be arrested without warrant, or sent out of the district, to be hereafter dealt with by a military Court.

David François Marais was a British subject residing in the town of Paarl in the Cape Colony. He was a notary public of the Supreme Court, an enrolled agent of the Court of the Resident Magistrate and a licensed auctioneer. He was also sympathetic to the Boer cause. On 15 August 1901 he was arrested in his office by the chief constable, acting on instructions from the military authorities. There was no warrant. He was taken to the town gaol and locked up for the night. On the night of the 19th Lieutenant McCausland collected him and, with a mounted military escort, took him to Lady Grey Bridge Station and then travelled on by train to Beaufort West, 300 miles away. On 21 August Marais wrote to Captain A.G. Boyle, the area military commandant, pointing out that he had now been detained for seven days without any charge against him. Boyle dismissed his letter. Marais was able to instruct lawyers in Cape Town and on 2 September they submitted a petition to the Supreme Court on the basis that his arrest and imprisonment had been effected by military force without warrant or cause assigned, and were consequently illegal, and they requested his release. On 6 September the petition was heard by Justices Buchanan and Jones, who also received an affidavit from Major General Wynne stating that there was a *prima facie* case against Marais and military reasons, which he was not prepared to disclose, for why he should remain in custody. He would be charged as soon as possible, and either discharged or sentenced by the military court. The judges issued a writ of *habeas corpus* to the gaoler at Beaufort West, ordering him to return the authority on which he detained the prisoner on 12 September. The response was that Marais had been arrested and imprisoned by virtue of a warrant that 'authority is hereby given to arrest and lodge in gaol the following persons: D.F. Marais. Signed J.R. Smiley, Staff Officer for Commandant, Paarl, 15.8.1901'. Another affidavit was produced confirming that a sergeant and four privates had brought the petitioner to gaol, with a warrant that the charge was 'contravening martial law regulation, par. 14. sec. 11, of 1.5.1901'. The regulation was not provided in evidence, but it was confirmed as the notice above.

Mr Justice Buchanan, at the Supreme Court, refused the petition, holding that martial law had been proclaimed in both the districts of Paarl and Beaufort West, and that the court could not go behind the necessity for the proclamation of martial law nor the actions of the military authorities. The matter was referred back to London and the Privy Council. On 5 November, 1901 Richard Haldane (later as, Lord Haldane, Lord Chancellor 1912–15), argued in support of the petitioner, and rehearsed the Milligan argument that the civil courts were still open in Paarl and Beaufort West and so Marais should be tried before civil magistrates. He also contended that if the civil courts were sitting then there could be no state of war in the district, and that martial law was used by the Army on behalf of the Crown to use so much force as was necessary to preserve peace and order in a district. He further differentiated military law as that which related to soldiers but not to civilians.[18]

On 18 December 1901, the Privy Council announced that they refused leave for the appeal. They considered the ground that 'whereas some of the courts were open it was impossible to apply the ordinary rule that where actual war is raging the civil courts have no jurisdiction to deal with military action, but where acts of war are in question the military tribunals alone are competent'. They held that 'war in this case was actually raging', and the fact that some courts had been functioning was not sufficient to believe that war was not raging. They maintained that no doubt had ever existed that where war actually prevails the ordinary courts had no jurisdiction over the action of the military authorities'.[19] The decision, as recorded in the *Times Law Report*, was:

> Martial law had been proclaimed in the Cape Colony over the districts in which the petitioner was arrested by the military authorities, and to which he was removed, and actual war was raging. Held, that the civil courts have no jurisdiction over the acts of the military authorities, even though for some purposes the civil courts were permitted to remain open.

Sir Frederick Pollock was one of several leading jurists who felt that further clarification was required. Notwithstanding the declaration of martial law itself, could there be a state of war if, as Haldane was claiming, there was no state of war in the districts involved? Pollock's response was to propose that the nature of warfare itself had changed. He used the scenario of an enemy force landing at York to ask what the Lord Mayor of Bristol should do? The right action would be to prevent suspected persons from landing in the port, and to take control of the railways to prevent undesirable persons travelling north, and to censor telegrams and letters. The mere appearance of peace – and in this example clearly the Bristol courts could continue their ordinary work – did not then mean that there was no state of war. Pollock also carefully stated the nature and objects of 'military law', and concluded that:

> So-called 'martial law', as distinct from military law, is an unlucky name for the justification by the common law of acts done by necessity for the defence of the Commonwealth when there is war within the realm.[20]

Sir William Harcourt KC MP, speaking just after the Marais decision, described martial law as 'an illegal exercise of force necessary upon an emergency to preserve the peace', and as a law only justifiable by emergency – riot, rebellion, or invasion – when there was no other law. He reminded the House of Commons that in the rebellions of 1715 and 1745 the 'traitors' were tried by the law courts, as were those taken during the Monmouth Rebellion of 1685. He made the important distinction that martial law cannot be said to 'supersede the ordinary tribunals inasmuch as it only exists by reason of these tribunals having been already practically superseded'. Martial law, if it were to be imposed in this country, would have to be authorized by an Act of Parliament.[21] When was there a state of war? According to Coke:

> So when by invasion, insurrection or rebellion, or such like, the peaceable course
> of justice is disturbed and stopped up so as the courts of justice be as it were shut
> up, *et silent leges inter arma*, then it is said to be a time of war.

By the end of the Boer War in 1902 there had been 49 death sentences carried out under martial law, with 393 sentences of penal servitude (including commuted death sentences), and a further 1,150 minor cases.[22]

In a strange little exchange in the House of Commons in June 1913, Colonel Josiah Wedgewood, MP, asked the then Secretary of State for War, Colonel John Seely, if 'any arrangements were under consideration by the Home Office or War Office with reference to the possibility or necessity of declaring martial law in the case of mobilisation'. Colonel Seely replied that no such arrangements had been made.[23] And on 1 August 1914 the *Manchester Evening News* featured a column of 'War Terms', in which they explained to their readers that martial law:

> … is the suspension of ordinary law and its replacement by military authority,
> the military commander may take action against any person who offends without
> trying them before the ordinary courts. Thus a proclamation of martial law
> abolishes trial by jury.[24]

Civil law, military law, and 'martial law'. Martial law might work in the colonies, but would it – could it – ever be imposed here?

Chapter 5

Dear Old DoRA

Defence of the Realm
Proclamation, dated August 4, 1914, regarding the Defence of the Realm
1914. No. 1249
BY THE KING
A Proclamation regarding the Defence of the Realm
George R.I.
Whereas by the law of Our Realm it is Our undoubted prerogative and the duty of all Our loyal subjects acting in Our behalf in times of imminent national danger to take all such measures as may be necessary for securing the public safety and the defence of Our Realm:

And whereas the present state of public affairs in Europe is such as to constitute an imminent national danger:

Now, therefore, We strictly command and enjoin Our subjects to obey and conform to all instructions and regulations which may be issued by Us or Our Admiralty or Army Council, or any officer or Our Navy or Army, or any other person acting in Our behalf for securing the objects aforesaid, and not to hinder or obstruct, but to afford all assistance in their power to, any person acting in accordance with any such instructions or regulations or otherwise in the execution of any measures duly taken for securing those objects.

Given at Our Court at Buckingham Palace, this Fourth day of August, in the year of our Lord one thousand nine hundred and fourteen, and in the Fifth year of Our Reign.

God save the King.

Dicey, in his influential *Law of the Constitution*,[1] states that 'Royal proclamations have in no sense the force of law: they serve to call the attention of the public to the law; they cannot of themselves impose on any man any legal obligation or authority not imposed by common law or Act of Parliament'. It was and is a common procedure: there is a proclamation dated 13 May 2016, for 'determining the specifications and designs for a new twenty-five pound gold coin and a two-pound gold coin'.[2]

The significant phrase in the King's proclamation of 4 August is that the country was in 'imminent national danger', and it is this that should be borne in mind when examining the first Defence of the Realm Acts and the regulations which followed. There appears to have been a very genuine fear of invasion, and a sudden recognition that there was nothing in the statute books to provide any guidance for the formulation of new legislation capable of managing the realities of an enemy invader fighting on British soil.

The proclamation itself defers to the control of the naval and military authorities, and for the civilian population to offer all assistance. On Friday, 7 August 1914 the Home Secretary, Mr Reginald McKenna, spoke briefly in the House of Commons about a new Bill. This is the extract from *Hansard*:

The SECRETARY of STATE for the HOME DEPARTMENT (Mr McKenna) I beg to move, 'That leave be given to introduce a Bill to make Regulations during the present war for the Defence of the Realm'. I ask leave to introduce another emergency Bill, the object of which, while it is important, is extremely simple.

We ask for the following powers. Clause 1 provides that: 'His Majesty in Council has power during the continuance of the present War to issue Regulations as to the powers and duties of the Admiralty and Army Council, and of the members of His Majesty's Forces, and other persons acting in His behalf, for securing the public safety and the defence of the Realm; and may be such Regulations authorize the trial by courts-martial and punishment of persons contravening any of the provisions of such Regulations designed:

(a) to prevent persons from communicating with the enemy or obtaining information for that purpose or any purpose, calculated to jeopardise the success of the operations of any of His Majesty's Forces or to assist the enemy; or

(b) to secure the safety of any means of communication, or of railways, docks or harbours;

in like manner as if such persons were subject to military law and had on active service committed an offence under section five of the Army Act'.

Punishment under section 5 of the Army Act would not include the death sentence. Therefore there would always be an opportunity of considering any action taken by the court-martial. The House will readily understand that it is extremely desirable in cases of tapping wires or attempts to blow up bridges that there should be an immediate Court to consider the offence of the offenders. I ask leave to introduce this Bill.

Dr CHAPPLE: Will this Bill be retrospective from the commencement of the war?

Mr McKENNA: No, Sir, it will date from the passing of the Act, and the Regulations will last during the continuance of the war.

Dr CHAPPLE: Will it apply to any offence which has already been committed?

Mr McKENNA: No, it will only apply to offences committed after the passing of the Act.
Question put, and agreed to.

Bill ordered to be brought in by Mr McKenna and the Attorney-General. Presented accordingly, read for the first time, and ordered to be printed.

Bill read a second time.

Mr McKENNA: I beg to move, 'That this House will immediately resolve itself in the Committee on the Bill'.

Question put, and agreed to.

Bill accordingly considered in Committee; reported without Amendment, read the third time, and passed.[3]

Neither Dr Chapple nor any other member of the House queried the phrase 'in like manner as if such persons were subject to military law and had on active service committed an offence under section five of the Army Act'. This simple sentence is probably one of the most implausible in British legislative history. As described in the previous chapter, the distinct jurisdictions of civil and military law were well established in the corpus of constitutional law and through the comments of Coke, Pollock, Dicey, Harcourt and others. With the introduction of the Defence of the Realm Act there were now two classes of offences on the statute books: those which should dealt with by military tribunal, and those which were sent to the normal courts. Did the government take into account the Boer War experience? There was no suggestion of martial law and, as repeatedly emphasized, the civil courts were open. On the face of it this Act seemed more to follow Kitchener's 1901 suggestion, that treason (and rebellion) should be the province of the military courts, as the actions described were beyond criminal: they were simply treasonable.

Section 5 of the Army Act should be considered in full:

Every person subject to military law who on active service commits any of the following offences; that is to say,

1. Without orders from his superior officer leaves the ranks, in order to secure prisoners or horses, or on pretence of taking wounded men to the rear; or
2. Without orders from his superior officer wilfully destroys or damages any property; or
3. Is taken prisoner, by want of due precaution, or through disobedience of orders, or wilful neglect of duty, or having been taken prisoner fails to rejoin His Majesty's service when able to rejoin the same; or
4. Without due authority either holds correspondence with, or gives intelligence to, or sends a flag of truce to the enemy; or
5. By word of mouth or in writing, or by signals, or otherwise, spreads reports calculated to create unnecessary alarm or despondency; or
6. In action, or previously to going into action, uses words calculated to create alarm or despondency,

Shall, on conviction by court-martial be liable to suffer penal servitude, or such less punishment as is in this Act mentioned.

According to *Stone's Justices' Manual*, 'it is a maxim of criminal law that criminal responsibility shall not attach to a man unless it can be shown that the act with which he is charged was done with criminal intent', the principle of *mens rea*. The Army Act defines 'active service' in section 189:

> In this Act, if not inconsistent with the context, the expression 'on active service' as applied to a person subject to military law means whenever he is attached to or forms part of a force which is engaged in operations against the enemy, or is engaged in military operations in a country or place wholly or partly occupied by the enemy, or is in military occupation of any country.

A soldier committing a section 5 offence would undoubtedly know that his actions would not be open to misinterpretation. Other than 5(2), the 'active service' meant here is close to or at the front line, and in the presence of the enemy. There could be no doubt of the *mens rea* of the soldier. This first version of the Defence of the Realm Act (DoRA) was clearly and, arguably, only directed at civilians deliberately acting in support of the enemy. A civilian caught blowing up a bridge or cutting telegraph wires is carrying out an offensive or war-like action and has a clear intent to assist the enemy. Swift summary justice at the hands of the court-martial was the correct means of dealing with such acts, even if the civil courts were open. But was it necessary? The Treason Act, 1842 and the Official Secrets Act, 1911 (OSA) provided perfectly adequate legal powers, and in the former case it also permitted the death penalty, curiously and conspicuously absent from the DoRA. Prosecutions under the OSA required the approval of the Attorney-General but this could have been amended in the emergency legislation sessions.

The Defence of the Realm Act received Royal Assent on 8 August 1914. As with many pieces of primary legislation it was an 'enabling act', which granted powers to provide regulations which provided the specific content of the offences. In the ordinary course of events, legislation passes through several stages in Parliament which include detailed review by both Houses. Notwithstanding the apparent rubber-stamping that was such a feature of the August emergency legislation, the need to return to Parliament each time an amendment was required would have proved too time-consuming; the solution was to use the process of the Order in Council. His Majesty's Privy Council was a body of senior politicians, peers of the realm (including bishops), and naval and military officers. Under the DoRA 'His Majesty in Council has power during the continuance of the present War to issue Regulations', and this power allowed the government, through the Privy Council, to produce extensive regulations without the need to consult Parliament. By the 12 August the first Defence of the Realm regulations were promulgated. They are reproduced here in full:

The Defence of the Realm Regulations, 1914
1914. No. 1231
At the Court at Buckingham Palace, the 12 day of August, 1914.
Present:
The King's Most Excellent Majesty in Council

Whereas by the Defence of the Realm Act, 1914, His Majesty has power during the continuance of the present war to issue Regulations for securing the public safety and the defence of the Realm subject to and in accordance with that Act: Now, therefore, His Majesty is pleased, by and with the advice of His Privy Council, to order, and it is hereby ordered, as follows:–

Part I
General Regulations
  1. The ordinary avocations of life and the enjoyment of property will be interfered with as little as may be permitted by the exigencies of the measures required to be taken for securing the public safety and the defence of the Realm, and ordinary civil offences will be dealt with by the civil tribunals in the ordinary course of law.

The Admiralty and Army Council, and members of the Naval and Military Forces, and other persons executing the following Regulations, shall, in carrying those Regulations into effect, observe these general principles.

  2. It shall be lawful for the competent naval or military authority and any person duly authorized by him, where for the purpose of securing the public safety or the defence of the Realm it is necessary so to do –
     (a) To take possession of any land and to construct military works, including roads, thereon, and to remove any trees, hedges and fences therefrom;
     (b) To take possession of any buildings or other property, including works for the supply of gas, electricity, or water, and of any sources of water supply;
     (c) To take such steps as may be necessary for placing any buildings or structures in a state of defence;
     (d) To cause any buildings or structures to be destroyed, or any property to be moved from one place to another, or to be destroyed;
     (e) To do any other act involving interference with private rights of property which is necessary for the purpose aforesaid.
  3. The competent naval or military authority and any person duly authorized by him shall have right of access to any land or buildings, or other property whatsoever.
  4. The competent naval or military authority may by order require all vehicles, boats, and vessels, and all forms of equipment and warlike stores, within any area specified in the order to be removed from that area within such time as may be so specified, or in the case of military stores incapable of removal to be destroyed, and if the owners thereof fail to comply with the requisition, the competent naval or military authority may himself cause them to be removed or in the case of military stores destroyed.
  5. Where the competent naval or military authority so orders, all person residing or owning or occupying land, houses, or other premises within such area as may be specified in the order, shall furnish within such time as may be so

specified, a list of all or any animals, vehicles, boats, vessels, and warlike stores which may be in their possession or custody within the specified area, stating their nature and quantity, and the place in which they are severally situated, and giving any other details that may reasonably be required.

6. The competent naval or military authority may by order require the inhabitants to leave any area (specified in the order) within or in the neighbourhood of a defended harbour if the removal of persons from that area is necessary for naval or military reasons.

7. The competent naval or military authority may by order require all premises licensed for the sale of intoxicating liquor within or in the neighbourhood of any defended harbour to be closed except during such hours as may be specified in the order.

8. No person shall obstruct or otherwise interfere with or impede, or withhold any information in his possession, which he may reasonably be required to furnish, from any officer or other person who is carrying out the orders of the competent naval or military authority, or who is otherwise acting in accordance with his duty under these regulations.

9. No person shall trespass on any railway, or loiter under or near any bridge, viaduct, or culvert, over which a railway passes.

10. If any person knows that any other person has without lawful authority in his possession or custody, or under his control, any firearms or ammunition (other than shot guns and ammunition for them), dynamite, or other explosives, it shall be his duty to inform the competent naval or military authority of the fact.

11. The competent naval or military authority shall publish notice of any order made by him in pursuance of these regulations in such manner as he may consider best adapted for informing person affected by the order, and no person shall without lawful authority deface or otherwise tamper with any notice posted up in pursuance of these Regulations.

12. If the competent naval or military authority has reason to suspect that any house, building, land, ship, vessel, or other premises are being used for any purpose in any way prejudicial to the public safety or the defence of the Realm, the authority, or any person duly authorized by him, may enter, if need be by force, the house, building, land, ship, vessel, or premises at any time of the day or night, and examine, search, and inspect the same or any part thereof, and may seize anything found therein which he has reason to suspect is being used or intended to be used for any such purpose as aforesaid.

13. Any police constable, officer of customs, or any other person authorized for the purpose by the competent naval or military authority, may arrest without warrant any person whose behaviour is of such a nature as to give reasonable grounds for suspecting that he has acted or is acting or is about to act in a manner prejudicial to the public safety or the safety or the Realm, or upon whom may be found any article, book, letter, or other document, the possession of which gives grounds for such a suspicion, or who is suspected of having committed an offence against these Regulations.

Any person so arrested shall, if he is to be tried by court-martial, be handed over to or kept in military custody, and in other cases shall be detained until he can be dealt with in the ordinary course of law, and whilst so detained shall be deemed to be in legal custody.

No person shall assist or connive at the escape of any person who may be in custody under this Regulation, or knowingly harbour or assist any person who has escaped.

PART II
Regulations specially designed to prevent persons communicating with the enemy and obtaining information for disloyal purposes, and to secure the safety of means of communication and of railways, docks and harbours.

14. No person shall without lawful authority publish or communicate any information with respect to the movement or disposition of any of the forces, ships or war materials of His Majesty or any of His Majesty's allies, or with respect to the plans of any naval or military operations by any such forces or ships, or with respect to any works or measures undertaken for or connected with the fortification or defence of any place, if the information is such as is calculated to be or might be directly or indirectly useful to the enemy.

15. No person shall without the permission of the competent naval or military authority make any photograph, sketch, plan, model, or other representation of any naval or military work, or of any dock or harbour work in or in connection with a defended harbour, and no person in the vicinity of any such work shall without lawful authority have in his possession any photographic or other apparatus or other material or thing suitable for use in making any such representation.

    For the purpose of this Regulation the expression 'harbour work' includes lights, buoys, beacons, marks, and other things for the purpose of facilitating navigation in or into a harbour.

16. No person without lawful authority shall injure, or tamper or interfere with, any wire or other apparatus for transmitting telegraphic or telephonic messages, or any apparatus or contrivance intended for or capable of being used for a signalling apparatus, either visual or otherwise, or prevent or obstruct or in any manner whatsoever interfere with the sending, conveyance or delivery of any communication by means of telegraph, telephone, or otherwise, or shall be in possession of any apparatus capable of being used for tapping messages sent by wireless telegraphy or otherwise.

17. No person shall with the intent of eliciting information for the purpose of communicating it to the enemy or for any purpose calculated to assist the enemy, give or sell to a member of any of His Majesty's forces any intoxicating liquor; and no person shall give or sell to a member of any of His Majesty's forces employed in the defence of any railway, dock or harbour any intoxicating

liquor when not on duty, with intent to make him drunk, or when on sentry or other duty, either with or without such intent.

18. No person shall do any injury to any railway, or be upon any railway, or under or near any bridge, viaduct, or culvert over which a railway passes with intent to do injury thereto.

19. No person shall by the discharge of firearms or otherwise endanger the safety of any member of any of His Majesty's forces travelling on or guarding any railway.

20. No person, without the permission of the competent naval or military authority, shall in the vicinity of any railway or of any dock or harbour be in possession of dynamite or any other explosive substance, but nothing in this Regulation shall be construed as affecting the possession of ammunition for sporting purposes.

21. No person in, or in the neighbourhood of, a defended harbour shall be word of mouth or in writing spread reports likely to create disaffection or alarm among any of His Majesty's forces or among the civilian population.

22. No person shall, if an order to that effect has been made by the competent naval or military authority, light any fire or show any light on any hill within such radius from any defended harbour as may be specified in the order.

23. The competent naval or military authority at any defended harbour may by order direct that all lights, other than lights not visible from the outside of any house, shall be kept extinguished between such hours and within such area as may be specified in the order; and all persons resident in that area shall comply with that order.

24. The competent naval or military authority at any defended harbour may by order require every person within any area specified in the order to remain within doors between such hours as may be specified in the order, and in such case no person shall be or remain out between such hours unless provided with a permit in writing from the competent naval or military authority or some person duly authorized by him.

25. If any person with the object of obtaining any information for the purpose of communicating with the enemy or of assisting the enemy, or with intent to do any injury to any means of communication or to any railway, dock or harbour, forges, alters or tampers with any pass, permit or other document, or uses or has in his possession any such forged, altered or irregular pass, permit of document with the like object or intent, or with the like object or intent, personates any person to whom a pass, permit or other document has been duly issued, he shall be guilty of a contravention of these Regulations and may be tried and punished accordingly; and where in any proceedings against a person for contravention of the Regulation it is proved that he has forged, altered, or tampered with the pass, permit, or other document in question, or has used or had in his possession the forged, altered or irregular pass, permit, or document in question, or has personated the person to whom the pass, permit, or document was duly issued, he shall be presumed to have forged,

altered, or tampered with it, or to have used or had it in his possession, or to have personated such person as aforesaid, with such object or intent as aforesaid unless he proves to the contrary.

26. Any person who attempts to commit, or procures, aids, or abets the commission of any act prohibited by the foregoing special Regulations, or harbours any person he knows, or has reasonable grounds for supposing, to have acted in contravention of such Regulations, shall be deemed to have acted in contravention of the Regulations in like manner as if he had himself committed the act.

27. Any person contravening any of the provisions of the foregoing special Regulations shall be liable to be tried by court-martial and to be sentenced to penal servitude for life or any less punishment;

    Provided that no sentence exceeding three months; imprisonment with hard labour shall be imposed in respect of any contravention of Regulations 22, 23, or 24 unless it is proved that the contravention was for the purpose of assisting the enemy.

    A court-martial having jurisdiction to try offences under these Regulations shall be a general or district court-martial convened by an officer authorized to convene such description of court-martial within the limits of whose command the offender may for the time being be; but nothing in this Regulation shall be construed as authorising a district court-martial to impose a sentence of penal servitude.

    Any person tried by court-martial under these Regulations shall, for the purposes of the provisions of the Army Act relating to offences, be treated as if he belonged to the unit in whose charge he may be; but no such person shall be liable to summary punishment by a commanding officer.

PART III
Supplemental
28. The powers conferred by these Regulations are in addition to and not in derogation of any powers exerciseable by members of His Majesty's naval and military forces and other persons to take such steps as may be necessary for securing the public safety and the defence of the Realm, and the liability of any person to trial and punishment for any offence or war crime otherwise than in accordance with these Regulations.

29. For the purposes of these Regulations the expression 'competent naval or military authority' means any commissioned officer or His Majesty's Naval or Military Forces, not below the rank of commander in the Navy or lieutenant-colonel in the Army, appointed by the Admiralty or Army Council, as the case may be, to perform in any place the duties of such an authority.

    Any harbour declared by order of the Admiralty to be a defended harbour shall for the purposes of these Regulations be treated as such.

30. The Interpretation Act, 1889, applies for the purpose of the interpretation of these Regulations in like manner as it applies for the purpose of the interpretation of an Act of Parliament.

31. These Regulations may be cited as the Defence of the Realm Regulations, 1914.

These regulations follow the spirit of the DoRA itself and in the same way describe a series of offences which when committed by civilians would be construed as assisting the enemy as if on active service. This presumably justified the use of the court-martial for the prosecution of such offences. Sections 2 to 6 are effectively the powers of martial law that the US and Continental systems would recognize, and authorize the competent naval or military authority to take whatever action is required to engage with an enemy force on the land. A number of these regulations provide that the competent naval or military authority was permitted to issue orders; which themselves would then have the force of law.

There are some drafting problems: although 'defended harbours' was a proper description and they were listed by the Army Council,[4] there was a better classification of 'prohibited areas' provided in the Official Secrets Act, 1911 and which was clearly applicable to this legislation. This included 'any work of defence, arsenal, factory, dockyard, camp, ship, telegraph or signal station, or office belonging to His Majesty', as well as 'any place belonging to His Majesty which is for the time being declared by the Secretary of State to be a prohibited place'. Section 21 was intended to prevent the spread of reports likely to cause disaffection or alarm, but only in the area of a defended harbour, so presumably a doom-monger on a soapbox at Speakers' Corner in Hyde Park was perfectly entitled to air their opinions about the war effort. Similarly section 22 prohibited lights on hills near defended harbours, but not on beaches, nor on any hills on the intervening coastline between two such harbours. And residents of sleepy rural towns and villages such as Corton Denham or Wookey might well have wondered what the relevance of the regulations was to them.

The public reaction was muted. The *Huddersfield Daily Examiner* of 6 August 1914 announced that the town of Harwich was in a state of martial law,[5] and a few days later *The Taunton Courier and Western Advertiser* of 19 August 1914 carried an article declaring that England was under a modified form of martial law with a list of 'don'ts' for everybody,[6] but no one appeared sure what this meant, and certainly this language was not used by government nor the competent naval or military authorities who were establishing their areas of control around the country. An Army Order was issued on 18 August giving directions for the trial of civilians by courts-martial,[7] but even while the military and civil authorities were working out the details of the procedures, Viscount Allandale had to return to the House of Lords to apologize for the 'hurriedly drawn' measures and to offer a revised version. The Defence of the Realm (No. 2) Act of 28 August 1914 contained a series of amendments, extending the jurisdiction of military orders beyond 'defended harbours' to a wide range of military installations, and granting extensive powers to acquire or use land.[8] Most of the amendments gave powers to the competent naval or military authority that went further than the mere requirement to conduct warlike activities in the country.

The first court-martial of a civilian took place in Doncaster, at the headquarters of the West Riding Territorial Division on Saturday 19 September 1914. William Sharpe, a colliery worker, was accused under section 16 of being in possession of wireless telegraphy equipment, with an alternative charge that he harboured a person (his son) who was in possession of a complete wireless installation. He entered a 'not guilty' plea. The evidence against him was given by Police Sergeant Roe, who had discovered a tall pole in the rear of the prisoner's premises at 132 Green Dyke Lane on 2 September. The prisoner admitted 'I am doing a bit of wireless telegraphy. I have done it for a hobby. My son bought the machine.' An official from the Post Office stated that, other than the aerial which had not been fixed, the equipment was complete for the purposes of receiving wireless messages, although he described it as a toy set, worth £4 10s. In his opinion it would have been capable of picking up messages from a distance of 200 miles in the right conditions, and he had confiscated the set. Sharpe declined to give evidence, but his son mentioned that he had bought the wireless from a Doncaster man, and that he didn't know Morse code. Sharpe's legal representative, speaking on his behalf, said that he did not know of the regulation about the possession of this equipment. The court found Sharpe not guilty on all charges and he was discharged.[9]

Aaron Maskell and Henry Simmonds appeared before East Grinstead magistrates on 6 October 1914, charged with cutting military telegraph wires at Groombridge. The Assistant Quartermaster-General of the Second Army, Colonel Romilly, appeared on behalf of the military authorities to request that the prisoners be handed over for court-martial, the Kent and Sussex areas being a military district under the Defence of the Realm regulations. The magistrates agreed and the two men left under military escort.[10] They subsequently appeared at a district court-martial at Forest Row Camp, where Simmons was found not guilty, but Maskell was convicted and sentenced to twenty-eight days' imprisonment with hard labour.[11]

Three days later William Bean, motor driver of Shepherdswell, was court-martialled at Dover for circulating a false story, in that he claimed to have witnessed an attack on a sentry at Saltwood Tunnel by an alleged spy, who had fired five times before being shot by the sentry. He was found not guilty.[12]

The application of the DoRA and the military courts to civilians received a particularly severe test in Cardiff in November. Colonel East, the commander of the Severn Defences, was particularly concerned about prostitution, and so he issued a draconian order banning women from all public houses between the hours of 7 pm and 8 am (otherwise unspecified but probably under regulation 24). On 28 November five women were convicted of breaching this order at a district court-martial, and received sixty-two days' detention. The court president pointed out that the sentence needed to be confirmed by the general commanding the district and in the meantime the women would be held in custody. There was a national outcry, particularly when it was revealed that the order had published as a poster, and as some of the women were illiterate they were completely unaware of it. The case was badly reported, and in many it was stated that the order was to prevent any women being out of doors at night, and few noted that the order was directed at women of a certain class. The sentences were confirmed but the women were shortly released, their convictions quashed by order of the Home

Secretary. The *Stirling Observer* was bold enough to point out there was no appeal to ordinary law,[13] and that the higher civil courts had no powers of *certiorari*.

In September a number of regulations had been added by Order in Council, including restrictions on homing pigeons and changes to the powers of arrest of police constables, but by November it was clear that the Defence of the Realm Act and its regulations were not fit for purpose. The Marquess of Crewe, speaking in the House of Lords, asserted that not only was the country under a form of martial law, the different elements of statute law now in place (Defence of the Realm Act and Aliens (Restriction) Act in particular) were enforceable in the one place by the War Office, Admiralty and Army Council, and in another by the Home Office, with a lack of clear boundaries between them, and an overlap in many cases with existing civil law.[14] The Defence of the Realm (Consolidation) Act, 1914 received Royal Assent on 27 November, and the Privy Council issued a completely revised and extended set of regulations on the following day, and which repealed the August regulations. The procedure for prosecutions was drastically overhauled, so that minor offences were to be dealt with in the courts of summary jurisdiction, but the decision as to venue remained with the competent naval or military authority. If, after considering the evidence they felt that the offence was minor, they were to instruct the police accordingly and the matter would be forwarded to the police for the prosecution to proceed to the magistrates' court in the usual way.[15] In response to complaints from senior politicians, section 1(4) of the new Act provided the application of the death penalty if the offence was committed with the intention of helping the enemy.

It is not necessary here to reproduce the text of the Defence of the Realm (Consolidated) Act, but it is worthwhile examining the headings of the new regulations:

General Regulations
1. The ordinary avocations of life and the enjoyment of property will be interfered with as little as may be permitted by the exigencies of the measures required to be taken for securing the public safety and the defence of the Realm, and ordinary civil offences will be dealt with by the civil tribunals in the ordinary course of law.

   The Admiralty and Army Council, and members of the Naval and Military Forces, and other persons executing the following Regulations shall, in carrying these Regulations into effect, observe these general principles.

Powers of competent naval and military authorities, &c.
2. Power to take possession of land, &c.
3. Access to land, &c.
4. Power to use land for training
5. Stopping up of roads
6. Power to require removal of vehicles, &c.
7. Power to requisition output of factories manufacturing arms, ammunition, food, forage or stores
8. Power to take possession of any factory or plant

9. Power to clear areas of inhabitants
10. Power to close licensed premises
11. Power of Secretary of State to require extinguishment of lights
12. Power of naval or military authority to require extinguishment of lights
13. Power to require inhabitants to remain indoors
14. Power to remove suspects from specified areas
15. Power to require census of goods, &c.
16. Schemes of destruction of harbour works, &c.
17. Powers to make byelaws for land in naval or military occupation

Provisions respecting the collection and communication of information, &c.
18. Prohibition on obtaining and communicating naval and military information
19. Prohibition on photographing, sketching, &c., of certain places and things
20. Prohibition on tampering with telegraphic apparatus, &c.
21. Prohibition on possession of carrier pigeons
22. Prohibition on possession of wireless telegraphic apparatus, &c.
23. Power to prevent embarkation of persons suspected of communicating with the enemy
24. Prohibition on non-postal communications to or from United Kingdom
25. Prohibition on signalling
26. Prohibition on displaying lights, use of fireworks, &c.
27. Prohibition on spreading of false or prejudicial reports

Provisions against injury to railways, military works, &c.
28. Penalty on injury to railways, &c.
29. Prohibition on approaching defence works, &c.

Provisions as to arms and explosives
30. Power to prohibit sale of firearms, &c.
31. Prohibition on importation and removal of arms or ammunition
32. Prohibition on discharging firearms
33. Prohibition on possession of firearms, &c.
34. Provision as to the storage of petroleum, &c.
35. Provisions as to celluloid and cinematograph films

Provisions as to navigation
36. Duty of complying with navigation regulations in harbours
37. Duty of vessels to comply with navigation regulations and orders
38. Power to prohibit vessels entering dangerous areas
39. Provision as to the pilotage of vessels

Miscellaneous provisions
40. Prohibition on supplying intoxicants to members of H.M.'s forces
41. Prohibition on unauthorized use of naval, military and police uniforms

42. Prohibition against causing mutiny, sedition or disaffection
43. Obstruction of officers, &c., in the performance of duties
44. Falsification of reports, &c.
45. Forgery and personation, misleading statements
46. False passports, &c.
47. Duty of compliance with orders
48. Aiding and abetting
49. Duty of disclosing contravention of regulations
50. General prohibition on assisting enemy

Powers of Search, Arrest, &c.
51. Power to search premises, &c.
52. Powers to stop and search vehicles
53. Powers of questioning
54. Prevention of conveyance of letters, printed matter, &., into or out of United Kingdom
55. Arrest and bail

Trial and Punishment of Offences
56. Trial of offences
57. Trial and punishment by courts-martial
58. Trial and punishment by courts of summary jurisdiction

Supplemental
59. Saving of other powers
60. Publication of notice of Order; tampering with notices
61. Production of permit for inspection; power to revoke permits
62. Interpretation
63. Short title and application of Interpretation Act

NB further regulations added 24 January 1917
64. Printing and constructions of regulations as amended
65. Construction of references to other documents
66. Operation of revoked and amended regulations

This is a list of the regulations as they were in December 1914. Subsequent regulations were added as sub-headings, so by 1918 regulation 2, for example, had 2A, 2AA, 2AAA, 2B and a total of twenty-eight subsections up to 2UUU.

The process by which the military authorities initiated the prosecution of civilians was gradually revealed in early 1915. As seen in the previous chapter, the court-martial of a soldier is instituted in the first instance by the man's commanding officer, who would have considered the evidence and reached the decision that his summary powers were insufficient and he would then refer the charge and the evidence to a higher authority. Clearly this could not be applied to a civilian offender, so a court of enquiry was formed to provide the initial evidential assessment. The reports of the police and special constables would be considered and the decision to proceed to court-martial, magistrates' court, or discharge followed.[16] William Crocker was one of the first to be prosecuted in Exeter for a breach of the new lighting regulations by having powerful lights on his motor car. In opening the prosecution, Mr Allan explained that under section 11 of DoRA the matter might be tried by court-martial or summarily. Crocker's case had been submitted to Colonel Weston, the competent military authority for that part of No. 8 Army District. He had directed that the matter was minor and should dealt with by summary proceedings, and Staff Captain Godman, of No. 8 District headquarters, produced the authority for the prosecution. The magistrates enjoyed this opportunity to test the workings of DoRA – in order to prove the case, the prosecution had to produce or prove that a lighting order from the competent naval or military authority on behalf of the Secretary of State was in place; there was none. After a one-week adjournment the mayor, in the chair, mentioned that he knew there was such an order, because he himself had given it, to the chief constable, but in the absence of a confirmed copy of the lighting order the case failed, and Crocker was discharged.[17]

The lighting orders under regulation 11 led to a great number of prosecutions (see Chapter 8). By April Major General Hammersley, in Leicester, had reached the stage of simply passing on the prosecutions to the local magistrates with a covering letter,[18] and by July 1915 the police had been given authority to institute proceedings for such breaches.[19] As the magistrates took over more of the DoRA-related offences, it became apparent that there had been a legal oversight. With a conviction under DoRA at a general court-martial carrying the death penalty or penal servitude for life, and the district court-martial able to impose imprisonment with or without hard labour up to two years, the magistrates could impose a prison sentence of up to six months (and more for certain offences), and/or a fine of up to £100. But under section 17(1) of the Summary Jurisdiction Act, 1879, an offender appearing in the court of summary jurisdiction on a matter for which a prison sentence of greater than three months, or fine greater than £25, could be imposed, was entitled to elect a trial by jury at the quarter sessions or assizes; and it was a duty of the magistrates to inform him of this right. A Home Office circular was issued to point out that in section 58 of the Defence of the Realm (Consolidation) Act, 1914, the section 17 right 'shall not apply to charges of offences against the regulations', but it went on to state that the Act now provided for a right to appeal convictions at the quarter sessions.[20]

The right of the defendant to choose the venue of his trial and his right to trial by jury had been recognized in common law for centuries and by statute law in more recent times. Lord Haldane, by now Lord Chancellor, had promised to restore this right and restored the right to jury trial in the Defence of the Realm (Amendment) Act, in March 1915:

Any offence against any regulations made under the Defence of the Realm Consolidation Act, 1914, which is triable by court-martial may, instead of being tried by court-martial, be tried by a civil court with a jury, and when so tried the offence shall be deemed to be a felony punishable with the like punishment as might have been inflicted if the offence had been tried by court-martial.

In the debate around the introduction of this Act, the Attorney-General, Sir John Simon, warned that the government still retained 'the right to maintain the law in its entire severity in an emergency such as an invasion' when ordinary civil tribunals would be unavailable. Sir Edward Carson, soon to succeed Simon, reminded the House that 'when the regular courts are working they ought to be used'.[21] But section 7 of the amended Act made the first reference to invasion, and gave the King the power to make a Proclamation suspending the Act, which was widely interpreted as conferring upon him the authority to declare martial law. Following the restoration of the right to jury trial there were no more district courts-martial of civilians (see table below).

So what of 'martial law'? The French President Poincaré had already declared *l'état de siege* on 2 August, 1914 (two days before receiving the German declaration of war). Although technically in breach of his powers as the French National Assembly was in recess and so could not ratify his decision, this was resolved within days and further extended the state of emergency for the duration of the war. An unusual step was to place the whole country – eighty-six departments, the Belfort, and the three departments of Algeria – on this emergency footing, rather than just the districts and regions actually affected by the German advance and fighting. The French jurist Joseph Barthelemy described *l'état de siege* as a collaboration of the military and civil authorities, rather than a replacement. As a legal system it also provided that the decisions of either authority were still subject to judicial review. Although civil magistrates were supposed to sit with military colleagues, *l'état de siege* allowed that military courts could still be held regardless of the quality of the knowledge of the crime and punishments sections of the French penal code.

The German Kaiser Wilhelm II had decreed a state of war on 31 July 1914, and proclaimed martial law under Article 68 of the German Constitution:

> The Emperor may, if the public safety in the federal territory is threatened, declare every part thereof in a state of war. Until the issue of an Imperial law repudiating the prescription, the form of notice and the effects of such declaration, the provisions of the Prussian law, 4 June 1851, hold good.[22]

The 'state of war' declaration related to frontier controls, protection of railways and communications, prescriptions relating to military personnel and war materials, and, very shortly, food controls.

The question about martial law in this country goes beyond the Defence of the Realm Act, and needs to be considered in the totality of the emergency – and existing – legislation of the time. As seen in previous chapters, the government had extensive powers to mobilize, transport, billet, feed and equip the reserve and Territorial forces. The new legislation added extensive, if vague, powers to seize land and resources, to take control of the output of factories (with compensation) for government purposes. The Aliens (Restriction) Act provided the state with considerable powers to identify and register foreign nationals and, if enemies of His Majesty, to detain them as de facto prisoners of war, which in itself denies the right to *habeas corpus*, and with extremely limited recourse to the courts.

Very few lawyers expressed opinions in writing at the time; the most significant commentary was by Thomas Batty and John Hartmann Morgan (who later defended Roger Casement in his treason trial in 1916). They were both legal academics and they wrote a scathing analysis of the emergency legislation in *War: Its Conduct and Legal Results*,[23] which was published in New York in early 1915 (at the time of going to press, on 5 February 1915, Professor Morgan was already serving in France). Rather pointedly the book was dedicated to the Attorney General Sir John Simon, who they clearly felt was responsible for this poor legislation. They identified that the outcome of the legislation was 'martial law and something more', primarily on the basis that the executive had devolved such substantial powers to the competent naval and military authorities but without any recourse to legal appeal or redress. Most of their substantial concerns, however, such as the right to trial by jury, had been remedied by the time the book was published, but it remains an excellent reference.

Harold M. Bowman was a legal academic in Boston, Massachusetts, and from that distance he was able to consider the wartime legislation. Writing in December 1916, he had been shocked at the speed with which the Defence of the Realm Act had been passed through Parliament, at the absolute lack of critical discussion, and at the number of amendments brought about in subsequent months. He noted, with horror, the introduction of the death penalty which, for the first time, allowed the execution of a civilian without trial by jury.[24] He questioned if the Crown, acting through its ministers, would have had the right in the emergency of 1914 to 'make the rules and bring about the judicial, administrative and military situation among civilians brought about by DoRA', and he believed that it did not and, with the benefit of two years' worth of hindsight, he challenged the notion that that the general security of the inhabitants of the British Isles had been seriously threatened, indeed that the threat of invasion had been overestimated. He concluded that in the absence of a written constitution the powers of the Crown, executive and Parliament had worked together correctly and legally to produce the legislation and regulations required for the public safety and the defence of the realm. He quoted Sir W.R. Adkins MP, who had written that 'the government have at each step taken the country with them ... the government has neither gone ahead of, nor lagged behind, the real national will'.

Lord Loreburn, in the March debates, had identified the major flaw of the original DoRA in that it 'failed to provide that when the civil courts are sitting discharging justice in the normal way and trying to do what is right according to their experience and judgement, they and they alone should try civilians'.[25] He reiterated the principle that serious cases should be tried by juries and simple cases by the justices, particularly in light of the number of new offences that had been created by DoRA. Another Law Lord, Lord Parmoor, followed Halsbury's opinion, that martial law could not arise in this country unless there were actual conditions of warfare, and proposed that DoRA was based not on martial law but on the extension of military law to civilians.[26] It is on this latter point that the test of 'martial law' rests: military courts deal with military offences, civil courts with civil offences. DoRA offences were new and could, by definition, only apply while hostilities lasted. Given that the first DoRA regulations were addressed at civilians potentially carrying hostile activities 'as if on active service', then the military court-martial is the correct venue for the trial of such offences. Insofar as the Defence of the Realm Act continued to allow courts-martial of civilians once the revised regulations had been introduced in December 1914, for matters that clearly were not hostile in nature this must be seen as martial law. This anomaly was rectified with the restoration of the right to trial by jury under the Defence of the Realm (Amendment) Act of 16 March 1915. I would argue that between December 1914 and March 1915 a real form a martial law existed in this country.

Courts-Martial of Civilians

Period	GCM	DCM
Aug 14 – Sep 14		1
Oct 14 – Sep 15	9	34
Oct 15 – Sep 16	35	8
Oct 16 – Sep 17	11	44
Oct 17 – Sep 18	7	146
Oct 18 – Sep 19	25	161
Convictions	72	379

GCM: General Court-martial
DCM: District Court-martial

General Courts-Martial of Civilians

Period	War Treason	DoRA	Death	PS	Imp HL	Imp
Aug 14–Sep 14						
Oct 14–Sep 15	5	3	7	1		
Oct 15–Sep 16	2	19	3	13	4	1
Oct 16–Sep 17	3	9		5	3	4
Oct 17–Sep 18		6		4	2	
Oct 18–Sep 19		23		7	12	4

PS: Penal Servitude
Imp HL: Imprisonment with Hard Labour
Imp: Imprisonment

District Courts-Martial of Civilians

Period	DoRA	Imp HL	Imp	Det	Quash or remit
Aug 14–Sep 14					
Oct 14–Sep 15	12	6	2	1	3
Oct 15–Sep 16	3		3		
Oct 16–Sep 17	41	28	13		
Oct 17–Sep 18	125	63	61		1
Oct 18–Sep 19	139	107	26		6

Imp HL: Imprisonment with Hard Labour
Imp: Imprisonment
Det: Detention

Civilians Tried at District Court-Martials September 1914–March 1915

(District Courts-Martial Records, WO 86/62, 86/63, 86/64, National Archives)

23/09/1914	William	SHARPE	Doncaster	19/09/1914	DORA 16 + 26	NG		
17/10/1914	William	BEAN	Dover	09/10/1914	DORA	NG		
19/10/1914	Henry	SIMMONS	Forest Row	10/10/1914	DORA 16	NG		
19/10/1914	Aaron	MASKELL	Forest Row	10/10/1914	DORA	28 days HL imprisonment		
05/11/1914	Frederick	CHRISTENSEN	Tynemouth	30/10/1914	DORA	24 hrs? HL imprisonment		
10/11/1914	Michael	MURPHY	Fort Westmoreland	04/11/1914	DORA 21	NG		
03/12/1914	Harold	FOCHTENBERGER alias FALCONER	Woolwich	14/11/1914	DORA 2	6 months HL imprisonment	Remitted 3 months 'com. to D'
04/12/1914	James E	PINDER	Codford St Mary	18/11/1914	DORA	1 month HL imprisonment		
04/12/1914	Harold	WEARING	Falmouth	02/12/1914	DORA	84 days HL imprisonment	Remitted 28 days
05/12/1914	Ernest A	GREENWOOD	Colchester	01/12/1914	DORA 2	7 days HL imprisonment		
09/12/1914	Emily	HEMERY	Cardiff	02/12/1914	DORA	56 days HL imprisonment	Quashed 19/12/14
09/12/1914	Lena	MORRIS	Cardiff	02/12/1914	DORA	62 days detention	Quashed 19/12/14
09/12/1914	Kate	FURY	Cardiff	02/12/1914	DORA	62 days detention	Quashed 19/12/14
09/12/1914	Mary	SIMPSON	Cardiff	02/12/1914	DORA	62 days detention	Quashed 19/12/14
09/12/1914	Maggie	ROWLANDS	Cardiff	02/12/1914	DORA	62 days detention	Quashed 19/12/14
09/12/1914	Cassie	COLLINS	Cardiff	02/12/1914	DORA	62 days detention	Quashed 19/12/14
09/12/1914	Mary	THOMPSON	Cardiff	02/12/1914	DORA	56 days HL imprisonment	Quashed 19/12/14
09/12/1914	Emily	THOM	Cardiff	02/12/1914	DORA	56 days HL imprisonment	Quashed 19/12/14

16/12/1914	Archibald G	LOCKS	Hull	05/12/1914	DORA 2	6 months HL imprisonment	commuted 4 months
30/12/1914	Elizabeth	HAYWARD	Cardiff	07/12/1914	DORA 24	62 days detention	Quashed SoS 8/1/15
30/12/1914	Elizabeth	WILLIAMS	Cardiff	07/12/1914	DORA 24	62 days detention	Quashed SoS 8/1/15
30/12/1914	Dorothy	EVANS	Cardiff	07/12/1914	DORA 24	62 days detention	Quashed SoS 8/1/15
30/12/1914	Mary A	MURPHY	Cardiff	07/12/1914	DORA 24	62 days detention	Quashed SoS 8/1/15
30/12/1914	Elizabeth	CONNELLY	Cardiff	07/12/1914	DORA 24	62 days detention	Quashed SoS 8/1/15
30/12/1914	Lorenzos	LEPOCKIBOS (master of SS *Ermine*)	Barry Island	12/12/1914	DORA 36	14 days HL imprisonment	Remitted HL
30/12/1914	William R	LADD (master of SS *Dauntless*)	Barry Island	12/12/1914	DORA 36	Reprimand	Remitted
03/01/1915	Edwin	SINGLE	Jersey	31/12/1914	DORA 21	14 days imprisonment	
03/01/1915	Henry (Harvey)	FRANCIS	Swansea	19/10/1914	DORA 21	NG	
12/01/1915	Richard	GERRARD	Weymouth	05/01/1915	DORA 40	NG	Honourably acquitted
25/01/1915	Frederick	GODDARD	Manchester	06/01/1915	DORA 16 + 22	NG	
05/02/1915	Robert	BRUCE	Invergordon	28/01/1915	DORA 40	28 days HL imprisonment	Quashed SoS 17/2/15
05/02/1915	William	MAIR	Invergordon	28/01/1915	DORA 40	28 days HL imprisonment	Quashed SoS 17/2/15
05/02/1915	David	GURNEY	Cork	29/01/1915	DORA 27 (3)	112 days HL imprisonment	
24/02/1915	William	BUCKLEY	Cork	15/02/1915	DORA 27	NG	
25/02/1915	Janet	MACKENZIE	Cromarty	18/02/1915	DORA 40	21 days imprisonment	

Chapter 6

The Enemy Within

The Isle of Wight occupies a strategic position in the English Channel, protecting the approaches to the Solent and the naval and civilian dockyards at Portsmouth and Southampton on the mainland. An invasion force which could land and establish itself on the island would be in a strong position from which to control shipping movements in the area, as well as to build up forces for an attack on the south coast of the mainland. Although the island has natural defences of its own – from a military perspective the south coast of the island is an almost impenetrable wall of chalk cliffs between Ventnor in the south-east to Freshwater Bay in the west – there are bays and beaches which offered potential landing grounds. The Royal Commission on the Defence of the United Kingdom in 1860 proposed the construction of a number of fortifications around the whole coastline (known as Palmerston forts) and nineteen of these forts were built on the Isle of Wight alone.

One such fort, the Freshwater Redoubt, was built on an outcrop of rock some twenty metres above the sea at Freshwater Bay. The area was popular with holidaymakers and day trippers, with a sweeping promenade behind the semicircular beach and a number of tea rooms, boarding houses and the grand old Albion Hotel. On Thursday, 30 July 1914 Jacob Swets and his young brother Gerard arrived there on a coach excursion from Ventnor. They were spending a couple of weeks on a tour from their home in Wageningen in the Netherlands, which had taken them through Belgium and France, and they had arrived in London on Monday, 27 July, travelling down to the Isle of Wight the next day. Once at Freshwater Bay they enjoyed lunch at the Albion, and afterwards 17-year-old Gerard took his small folding pocket Kodak camera down to the beach to take some holiday snaps.[1] Jacob posed for him, and as a serving officer in the Dutch Grenadiers he was travelling in uniform, which quickly brought the two of them to the attention of a nearby police constable.[2] The Freshwater Redoubt was a 'prohibited place' as defined by section 3 of the Official Secrets Act, 1911, and it was an offence (indeed a felony) under section 1 (b) to 'make any sketch, plan, model or note which is calculated to be or might be or is intended to be directly or indirectly useful to an enemy'. The two brothers were arrested. They appeared before the Ryde magistrates on Saturday, 1 August 1914 and were charged with espionage, by being in the neighbourhood of a prohibited place for the purpose of taking photographs.

The Official Secrets Act (OSA) was introduced in August 1911 and repealed the rather clumsy Act of 1889. It was passed through Parliament in a single day, and identified a number of activities that might be interpreted as being 'for any purpose prejudicial to the safety or interests of the State', which included approaching or being in the neighbourhood of any prohibited place, sketching or making notes, plans or models, or communicating any such sketches, notes, plans or models or anything which was calculated to be or might be or is intended to be directly or indirectly useful to an enemy.

Under section 8 of the OSA the decision to prosecute was that of the Attorney-General, and the details of the case needed to be considered by him, so the Ryde magistrates released the brothers on bail on their own recognizances of £40, with an undertaking not to leave the island. The decision not to proceed was taken swiftly and they reappeared at court on Tuesday morning. The Dutch vice-consul had confirmed their identities and they were acquitted. They immediately left and returned to the Netherlands.[3]

The Swets brothers experienced the spy mania that was rife in the days up to and around the declaration of war. On 3 August Herbert Jankewitz, a Latvian clerk employed at a timber firm in Grimsby, was seen loitering near the Admiralty wireless station at nearby Waltham. The installation was guarded by the men of the 2nd Border Regiment who, after seeing him for the third time in as many days, challenged him and gave chase when he refused to surrender. In the melee that followed Private Filbert received a bayonet wound from a comrade and had to be taken to the hospital, while Jankewitz was arrested and charged with being on the property of His Majesty for the purposes of obtaining information.[4] He appeared at Grimsby county magistrates on 4 August but the police, having searched his lodgings and spoken to his employer, could find no incriminating evidence, so Captain Cholmondley, the officer in charge of the wireless station, agreed that he should be discharged.[5]

Five years before the war the Prime Minister, Herbert Asquith, had created a subcommittee of the Committee of Imperial Defence in response to concerns about the level of foreign espionage in the country. One early outcome was the formation of the Secret Service Bureau, from which evolved the Military Intelligence agencies, and Section 5 (MI5) took on the responsibility of counterintelligence. An early test of the Official Secrets Act and the new agency took place in 1911, when Captain Heinrich Grosse, of the German mercantile marine, was arrested and charged with espionage in Portsmouth and Southsea. He appeared before Colonel Lanyon Owen and the Portsmouth magistrates on 5 December[6] and again the following week,[7] when the bench committed the prisoner for trial at Winchester Assizes. The case was heard on 9 February 1912 before Mr Justice Darling and Grosse was sentenced to three years' penal servitude.[8] On 16 December 1910 three police officers were murdered and two others shot and wounded at a bungled burglary in Houndsditch, east London. Following a major investigation, two suspects, described as Latvian anarchists, were traced to a terraced house at 100 Sidney Street in Whitechapel. In the early hours of 3 January 1911 the police evacuated the residents of the surrounding buildings and at daybreak, following an attempt to enter the property, the suspects opened fire on the police, wounding a sergeant. The senior officers present, Superintendent Mulvaney and Chief Superintendent Stark, realised that they were unable to respond in force and so requested support from the Home Office. Winston Churchill, as Home Secretary, authorized a detachment of 'snipers' from 2 Battalion Scots Guards stationed at the Tower of London (it is interesting to note that the Riot Act was not used). After a gun battle lasting for over an hour and a half the house caught fire and the two men perished inside.[9] The incident highlighted public fears over the level of alien immigration: 'hordes of foreign immigrants, whether criminals or not, settle with us, bringing with them a miserably low standard of living. They herd among our poor, whose wretchedness they increase, and think nothing of thanking us for our hospitality by robbery and murder.'[10] Churchill played to the concerns of the nation by attempting to introduce his Aliens (Prevention of Crime) Bill. Under the Aliens Act, 1905, courts already had largely unused powers to expel aliens convicted of any offence, but Churchill sought to make it mandatory that the convicted alien should provide reasons to the court as to why they should not be deported. Worse still, he demanded 'sureties of good behaviour from certain lawless communities though no proof of actual commission of crime be forthcoming, with the alternative of expulsion'.[11] Aliens would also require special permission from the police to obtain and own weapons. This bill was strongly opposed in Parliament and was eventually withdrawn in December 1911.[12]

The Home Office monitored the number of aliens in the country. Census returns in 1911 suggested that there were around 27,000 Germans resident in London, and another 26,000 in the rest of the country.[13] In 1913 1,709 aliens became naturalized British subjects, with 10,356 in the previous decade.[14] In August 1913 Winston Churchill chaired a committee charged with considering the treatment of aliens in time of war, which established an unofficial 'Aliens Register',[15] compiled from various sources including intelligence reports and police records. Around 11,000 Germans resident in the United Kingdom were 'registered' without their knowledge. MI5 worked closely with the Metropolitan Police, which at the time had the special responsibility of guarding dockyards and other government establishments around the country. Officers of the Special Branch of the Metropolitan Police had been keeping a number of Germans under observation for several weeks, and although the declaration of war did not occur until 11 pm on 4 August, the police and intelligence services worked together to obtain the necessary search warrants. At the close of the final peacetime evening, Chief Inspectors Ward and McBrien, Inspectors Hester, Riley and Buckley, and 'a large force of detectives' raided nearly thirty residences and business premises across London.[16] A number of Germans were charged the following morning at Bow Street police court with offences under the OSA. Karl Ernst, a barber of 402a Caledonian Road, claimed it was a 'ridiculous charge'. August Klenden, of 17 Commercial Road, Spitalfields, became faint and collapsed in court. Alongside them were Frederick Dietrich and Adolf Schneider.[17] Max Laurens, a famous music hall artiste, was also remanded at Bow Street, as was Marie Kronauer, the widow of a German businessman who 'used to send letters for spies'.[18] They were all remanded in custody. Raids took place around the country: in Barrow, Cumbria, Frederick Appel, of 14 Fisher Street, appeared before the Barrow police court, again on OSA charges, and was similarly remanded.[19] Not all were German – Albert Rodriguez Garcia was a Spanish teacher at a Berlitz school in Portsmouth and was believed to be in contact with the German Secret Service.[20] Johannes Engel was arrested in Falmouth, and Max Heinert and Line Heine were detained in Southsea. The convicted spy Heinrich Grosse, who had been released on licence in April, was brought back to Bow Street on a warrant and recommitted to prison, his licence having been revoked by the Secretary of State.[21] William Fisher, a hairdresser of Penarth, Wales, was arrested on an OSA charge of obtaining and selling information to Germany,[22] and Frederick James Ireland, a hairdresser's assistant and formerly a seaman in the Royal Navy, was charged at Swansea with being in possession of notes calculated to be of use to the enemy.[23]

In the House of Commons the next day (5 August) the Home Secretary, Mr McKenna, introduced the Aliens (Restriction) Bill, against the backdrop of the twenty-one arrests made during the night. It was '… a Bill to enable His Majesty in time of war or imminent national danger or great emergency by Order in Council to impose restrictions on Aliens, and make such provisions as may be necessary or expedient for carrying such restrictions into effect'. He pointed out that a key objective was to remove or restrain the movements of undesirable aliens, especially those suspected of espionage. There should be 'as little inconvenience as possible to alien friends'.[24] As with so much legislation brought to the House that day, the Bill was enacted with no comment. A particular feature was section 1(4), which was that the onus of proving that a person was, or was not, an alien, lay with the person himself; further, there was no definition of what an 'alien' actually was (although the grounds for establishing British citizenship was stated in the British Nationality and Status of Aliens Act, 1914, and which provided that an 'alien' is simply a person who is not a British subject). The statute provided that such cases were to be managed under summary jurisdiction so these questions were to be tested and resolved by the magistrates. Persons convicted under the Act were liable to a maximum penalty of a £100 fine or six months' imprisonment, with or without hard labour.

The first Order in Council under this Act was passed on the same day, and it differentiated the 'alien enemy' (an alien whose Sovereign or State is at war with His Majesty), from an 'alien friend' as one which is at peace[25] (note that at this date war had been declared on Germany only). It specified that after 10 August alien enemies would not be permitted to leave the country without a special permit; until then they could only leave through the approved ports:

Aberdeen	North of Scotland and Orkney & Shetland Steam Navigation Wharf outside lock of Victoria Dock
Dundee	Camperdown Jetty
West Hartlepool	Central Dock
Hull	Riverside Quay
London	Tilbury Docks and pontoon
Folkestone	Railway Pier
Falmouth	Outer arm of harbour pier
Bristol	Landing stage, Avonmouth docks
Holyhead	London & North Western Railway quay, east side
Liverpool	Landing stage
Greenock	Prince's Pier
Dublin	North Wall
Rosslare	Railway pier[26]

All aliens were required to register themselves with the police with immediate effect, and to provide details of age, nationality and birthplace, occupation, sex, personal description and photograph, business address, and residence. Any person who had a German residing with them was also required to notify the police. Alien enemies were not permitted to travel more than five miles from their place of residence without a permit, and were prohibited from possessing firearms, ammunition, explosives, equipment capable or intended for signalling, carrier or homing pigeons, and motor cars and motorcycles.[27] The chief officer of police for the district was the registration officer, and the registration district itself was the corresponding police district. An amendment to the order followed the British declaration of war on Austria-Hungary on 12 August 1914, so that 'alien enemies' now included people we would now describe as Poles, Czechs, Slovakians, Romanians, Slovenians, Croatians and Serbs, and some Italians and Ukrainians. Turkey, or rather the Ottoman Empire, entered the war on 5 November 1914, and the list expanded again: Syrians, Iraqis, Afghans, Lebanese, Palestinians and Israelis. Bulgarians were included when they entered the war on 15 October 1915.

The impact of alien registration on the police was enormous, not only in dealing with the queues of foreigners at the police stations, but also in the follow-up interviews for those who sought permits to remain in prohibited areas or to keep prohibited articles, or to travel. Much of this work was carried out by the volunteer part-time special constables who were themselves struggling to familiarize themselves with their new rôle (see Chapter 12). As registration progressed, towns and cities around the country became aware of the numbers of 'alien enemies' living in their midst. Edinburgh discovered it had 'law abiding and peaceful' German community of around 300, with their own church and pastor.[28] Birmingham registered around 500,[29] Huddersfield 31,[30] and Loughborough found about a dozen.[31] London, of course, was the main centre for German immigration with an estimated 30,000 living and working in the capital.[32] The area around Tottenham Court Road was well known for the concentration of German businesses, restaurants and shops, and two out of every three houses were occupied by foreigners. Many of the Austrians and Germans living there and in nearby Charlotte Street were young men seeking the employment opportunities that they could not find at home, and they worked as waiters, hotel servants and clerks. Many of them lost their jobs at the outbreak of war and, unable to obtain benefits or to return home, had to rely on their community for support.[33]

The *London Gazette* of 6 August declared a number of 'prohibited areas' from which German residents would be excluded and, if ordinarily resident, removed, which were primarily the key ports and military garrison towns such as Plymouth, Devonport, Portsmouth, Birkenhead, Chester, Poole, Weymouth, Hartlepool, Jarrow, Colchester, Ipswich, Harwich, Southampton, South Shields, Dover, Chatham, Gravesend, Folkestone, Ramsgate, Newcastle, Great Yarmouth, Brighton, Eastbourne, Lewes, and the whole county of Glamorgan. They were also advised to leave the Isle of Wight.[34] Orders were implemented with local restrictions, so for example, the prohibited area for the county boroughs of Brighton and Eastbourne and the municipal borough of Lewes also included the municipal borough of Hove, the urban districts of Newhaven, Portslade-by-Sea, and Seaford, and the rural districts of Chailey, Eastbourne and

Hailsham (civil parishes of Arlington, Chalvington, Chiddingly, Hailsham, Hellingly, Laughton and Ripe only).[35]

The poster that appeared in Cardiff and Glamorgan on 8 August 1914 was fairly standard:

Notice is hereby given that:

1. Aliens of German nationality, wherever resident, are required to register themselves forthwith.
2. Aliens of German nationality are prohibited from residing in any of the areas specified below without a permit from the chief officer of police.
3. Aliens of whatever nationality residing in any of the areas specified below are required to register themselves.
4. All aliens coming within the foregoing paragraphs should apply immediately to the nearest police station for instructions.

By order of the Secretary of State for the Home Department[36]

The police followed up the notices by visiting all houses known to belong to alien enemies to ensure that they were aware of the Order. Those living in the prohibited areas were given four days to move out; and in most such towns there seemed to be a sense of satisfaction in the chief of police's report that 'not a single permit to remain had been issued'.[37] Many Germans attempted to leave the country, only to find that the Channel ports and ferries were closed to them. A group of sixty Germans was arrested at Folkestone on 10 August, while waiting for a boat to take them home. They were instead marched off to Shornecliffe camp.

The deadline for voluntary registration was Monday, 17 August. The courts were already filling up with offenders who had deliberately or, more commonly, inadvertently breached the new orders. Following the order in Cardiff the crews of the German-registered ships *R.C. Rickmers*, *Carl* and *Schwarzenbeck*, including the captains and their wives, were all charged with residing in Cardiff, a prohibited area, and were remanded for eight days at the Cardiff court.[38] Paul Pitsch, a private teacher of 42 Snargate Street, Dover, was arrested and brought before Dover magistrates charged with failing to notify a change of address. Police Sergeant Fox gave evidence that there were posters all over town requesting all foreigners to register at the Police Station, to which Pitsch had replied: 'I do not take any notice of them'. The Mayor, Councillor E.W.T. Farley, remanded him for a week at Canterbury.[39] The magistrates at Margate police court sentenced Frederick Sudrow to three months' hard labour for registering himself as Swiss, when in fact he was a German reservist.[40] Wilhelm Lerwig, a German hairdresser of no fixed abode, did not endear himself to the North London police court on 19 September. In response to the charge of failing to register, he declared 'I am a German and I wish I was fighting for my country like my brother. I came here three weeks before the war and now I cannot get back.' Mr Hadderwick gave him six months' hard labour.[41] Interestingly, Austrians and Hungarians were given an easier time, probably because they were not associated with the alleged atrocities committed by the Germans in Belgium,[42] nor was there the long-standing military and commercial rivalry as Britain had had with Germany.

A week after the Official Secrets Act raids, those who had been arrested and remanded in custody had to be dealt with. OSA offences had to be tried at the Assizes as felonies or misdemeanours and the preparation for such trials was time-consuming and expensive. At Bow Street it was found that the Home Secretary had come up with a solution. A much simpler option was to issue a deportation order under the Aliens (Restriction) Act, and so Laurens and Cronauer and four others were released from the OSA charges by the magistrate, and they were then promptly rearrested and returned to prison, subject to their deportation.[43]

This process was used on many aliens who breached the Aliens Restriction Order. The problem was what to do with those who were not in breach. Neither the Order nor the Defence of the Realm Act made it an offence simply to be an alien enemy (although there was an existing common law provision known as the '*droit de renvoi*' by which aliens could be returned to their home countries by order of the Sovereign[44]). By 9 September 1914 50,633 Germans and 16,141 Austro-Hungarians had registered. These included men, women and children, many of whom were deemed to be of little threat and if outside the prohibited areas were allowed to go about their normal business. The legal problem was that the civilian alien enemies could not be detained by civil authority unless they had committed a crime, and it could be argued that merely failing to register or to remove from a prohibited area was scarcely grounds for depriving a person of their liberty. Regulation 13 of the first Defence of the Realm regulations provided for the arrest and detention of 'any person', alien or not, 'whose behaviour is of such a nature as to give reasonable grounds for suspecting that he has acted or is acting or is about to act in a manner prejudicial to the public safety or the safety or the Realm', and as such could be handed over to the military authorities, but arrest had to be followed by a prosecution, not by an indeterminate period of detention. The Home Secretary consequently declined responsibility for the system of internment but put his department at the disposal of the War Office in a convoluted arrangement by which the police and civil authorities identified male alien enemies aged between 18 and 42. Both Germany and Austria had compulsory military service, following which the man was placed in the reserves to be called up in times of emergency, wherever he might then be living. At the outbreak of war, many young men of military age living in this country received their call-up papers and this provided the authorities with a clear legal justification for their detention as *de facto* prisoners of war. They were then handed over to the War Office for detention under the Defence of the Realm Act. This demarcation was made clearer by the repeal of the first Defence of the Realm regulations and their replacement with revised regulations under the Defence of the Realm (Consolidated) Act, 27 November 1914, and which came into force on 1 December 1914. The competent naval or military authorities were given a new power:

14. Where a person is suspected of acting, or of having acted, of being about to act in a manner prejudicial to the public safety or the defence of the Realm and

it appears to the competent naval or military authority that it is desirable that such person should be prohibited from residing in or entering in any locality, the competent naval or military authority may … by order prohibit him from residing in or entering any area or areas which may be specified in the order and upon the making of such and order the person shall … leave that area within such time as may be specified by the order, and shall not subsequently reside in or enter any area specified in the order … Any order made as aforesaid may require the person in respect of whom it is made to comply with such restrictions on movements, or otherwise as may be imposed on him, and if any person in respect of whom such an order is made fails to comply with any such condition he shall be guilty of an offence against these regulations.

In the footnotes to the regulation it stated that 'This regulation does not impose upon a court of law the question of whether the competent naval or military authority had reasonable ground for the suspicion' (1916). Whilst very similar to the old regulation 13, it did not require the arrest and charge of the individual and makes clear that any breach of an order will be dealt with as a DoRA offence. But it still applied equally to British subjects and to enemy and friendly aliens.

Government policy concerning enemy aliens not of military age was that they were either deported or repatriated. Deportation was an executive action in which the person had no choice in the matter. Repatriation was of course voluntary and many of the elderly aliens and dependents left the country this way. The Admiralty and the Board of Trade coordinated the deportation or repatriation of enemy aliens via neutral countries such as the Netherlands, Denmark and Spain. The United States of America acted as an intermediary, with the British, German and Austrian governments agreeing to finance those who could not afford the fare. Alien enemies in detention could also apply to be released back into the community, particularly if they had strong family ties or business connections, but military intelligence had to be consulted before the repatriation or release of any person could be considered.

A number of temporary and then more permanent detention centres were created. Germans and Austrians in London were put up at the Cornwallis Road Institution in Islington (a former workhouse), the exhibition hall at Olympia, and at Stratford. Those from the southern counties were sent to Frith Hill, Frimley, in Surrey. This was a huge compound of about 40 acres, with 12-foot high barbed wire fences, the innermost one of a width of 4 feet, with armed guards patrolling between the fences.[45] This was divided into separate sections for the prisoners of war and that for the internees. In the Midlands there were camps at Leoman Road, near York, Lofthouse Park near Wakefield, and Lancaster. The *Royal Edward*, a converted passenger liner, held East Anglian alien enemies at Southend. North Country and Scottish detainees were sent to Stobs Camp in a rather bleak and exposed position near Hawick in the Scottish borders or to Redford in Fifeshire. But for many, the massive camps on the Isle of Man were to be home for the duration. Cunningham's holiday camp on Victoria Road in Douglas held around 4,000 men in tented accommodation. The nearby camp at Knockaloe Moar grew to be an enormous collection of twenty-three compounds, each housing 1,000 men, by 1915.

The Poundbury Camp at Dorchester was held up as an exemplar of the humane way in which these men were held, where each man had a straw palliasse and three blankets and 'in some instances bunks have been constructed'. There were day rooms for 'the better class of prisoner', and it was noted that there was musical entertainment nightly.[46] Although military and naval prisoners of war were always kept separate, the camps held a disparate mixture of men of military age who faced no prospect of deportation, men such as sailors who had been arrested aboard ship, men who had been convicted by the courts (initially of Aliens Restriction Order offences, but later a conviction for any offence was likely to result in detention), and men of all ages who had given themselves up voluntarily. Poundbury held 'merchants, writers, clerks, labourers, musicians, artists, electricians, apothecaries, ships' officers, schoolmasters, and university graduates'.[47] Some men had money and assets and could purchase additional food and some luxuries, others were dependent on earnings from the menial work that was assigned to them. Both here and at internment camps around the country this was potentially explosive mix, and in November 1914 a riot, apparently over food, broke out at the Douglas camp, resulting in five deaths.[48] The next month a riot broke out in the Lancaster internment camp. The offenders, and camp discipline generally, were dealt with by court-martial.

Despite the general excitement of the times, there was surprisingly little civil disorder involving attacks on Germans or their property in the community. The exception was at Peterborough. Messrs Frank & Co was a well-known pork butchers on the Westgate. Frederick Frank had opened it in 1881 and it was now run by brothers Leonard and George Cantenwine, Germans by birth but both naturalized British subjects. On the evening of Friday, 7 August 1914 a large crowd, estimated at in excess of a thousand, collected in front of the shop and pelted the windows with bricks, bottles and stones until all the windows were smashed in. As the Cantenwines made their escape, helped by friends, a section of the crowd broke off and made its way to the family home in Fletton Avenue, three-quarters of a mile away. As the mob passed Frederick Metz's butcher's shop on the way they gave it the same treatment. Seeing that the police were failing to control the situation Chief Constable Slaughter summoned Sir Richard Winfrey, magistrate and MP. At around 10 pm Winfrey stood on the steps of the Bull Hotel in Westgate and, for one of the last times in English history, read the Riot Act. As the crowds had not dispersed within the hour specified by the order, Captain Frank Gilliat, commanding officer of the 1/1 Northampton Imperial Yeomanry, called his men out of their barracks at the Corn Exchange, and they applied 'steady pressure and great forbearance', gradually forcing the crowd back and clearing the streets, and by midnight had restored order to the town.

The following morning the Cantenwines decided to close down the business. The shop windows were boarded up and signs were posted announcing a closing-down auction at 2.30 that afternoon. However, the crowds returned and as people emerged from the shop with their purchases their goods were seized and thrown at the boards and at the police, with 'pork pies and small joints serving as footballs'. The police were in a difficult position, and so the magistrate swore in fifty special constables, who were deployed in Westgate and the Long Causeway. As the crowds passed the Salmon and Compasses public house, owned by Charles Guest who was of German extraction, the rumour went around that he had made disparaging comments about a naval reservist. A brick was thrown through his front window followed by a 'perfect fusillade' of missiles. The fire brigade was called out and, in an apparent attempt to control the crowd, connected a hose to a fire hydrant. The crowd turned on the hapless firemen, seized the pipe and turned the jet onto the police. However, the effects of the additional special policemen and the judicious use of the baton brought some semblance of control by the early hours of Sunday morning.

There were about a dozen arrests and a number of names and addresses were taken, so that twenty-four men appeared before Mr Winfrey and his colleagues at Peterborough police court on Wednesday morning. The charges ranged from 'causing an affray', 'incitement to riot' and 'damaging windows and property'. Noting that the offences were committed 'during the outbreak of patriotic fervour', Winfrey offered them a choice: they could volunteer for active service or be sentenced. Only four accepted his offer and were duly despatched to the recruiting officer. The ringleader was given fourteen days' imprisonment, and a prolific stone-thrower was given a month. The others were either bound over or fined.[49]

A similar incident took place in Deptford High Street on 17 October 1914. Considerable damage was caused to a number of German-owned shops but the police used their common law powers to require 'private persons' to 'assist in dispersing those who are assembled';[50] in this case the private persons were 300 men of the Army Service Corps stationed at the Foreign Cattle Market. The Riot Act was not read.

After the first few months of the war the relationship between alien enemies and their hosts seemed to settle down. Simple breaches of the registration order were a regular feature of the magistrates' court, usually attracting a small fine (20–40s). Spy mania continued, but those arrested found themselves in a detention centre on DoR grounds, rather than being processed through the courts. By October the efforts to round up all men of military age petered out, and in particular when the police began to release men from custody if they could provide two sureties of British nationality.[51] Government policy was that women and children would not be sent to detention camps, and the welfare of these dependents became a problem: in the absence of the breadwinner, they were likely to end up being chargeable to the Poor Law, and under the Aliens Act, 1905 they would be subject to mandatory deportation after six months. In November 1914 the Local Government Board announced that the German and Austrian governments had placed funds at the disposal of the American Embassy for the benefit of distressed nationals in the United Kingdom.[52] The scheme was administered by the local Boards of Guardians and grants were made on condition that the husband was an interned alien and that the wife was of British birth and without sufficient resources. The rates of assistance was 10s/week in London and 8s/week outside. 1s 6d was granted for each dependent child.

'Trading with the enemy' was a new offence on the statute books. A Proclamation prohibiting 'trade or commercial intercourse with any person resident, carrying on business, or being in the German Empire' was announced on 5 August but the legislation, the Trading with the Enemy Act, 1914, was not passed until 18 September. Offences under this Act were classed as misdemeanours and could be dealt with in the magistrates' courts with fines of up to £500 or imprisonment with or without hard labour up to twelve months – a substantial increase in the sentencing powers of the justices. Conviction on indictment to the assizes carried a sentence of penal servitude of between three and seven years. Goods and money in respect of the offence were to be forfeited. Smethwick magistrates dealt with an early case, in December 1914. The firm of Messrs J.A. Phillips, cycle and cycle accessory manufacturers, and its two joint managing directors, Mr Ernest Bohle and Henry Church, along with their company secretary, Otto Hesmer, faced a total of twelve charges, relating to 'attempting to obtain' a supply of 20,000 bicycle handles. Bohle and Hesmer were naturalized British subjects. Between 24 August and 15 September it was alleged that they had dealings with Adler Ltd, a firm based in Amsterdam. They were unaware that the bicycle handles were manufactured by a German company. Fines of £500 and £300 were imposed, along with £100 costs.[53] At the London Guildhall magistrates' court Louis Bartel was found guilty of unlawfully attempting to enter into a commercial contract with Messrs Mueller and Schmidt, of Soligen, Germany. Having previously dealt with the firm he had realized that he could no longer do so directly, and wrote to the firm suggesting that the goods be sent to 'some friends in Holland'. The correspondence had been intercepted and given to the Home Office. Bartel received three months' imprisonment in the second division.

One way a German or Austrian might avoid unwanted attention would be to change his name, or that of his shop or business. The government took a different view and on 8 October 1914 amended the Aliens Restriction (Consolidation) Order to prevent alien enemies from assuming or using any name other than that by which he was commonly known at the date of the commencement of the war. Wendel Jost had a hairdressing business in Greenwich with his name painted on the window. He prudently had this replaced with 'City Toilet Saloon', but in May 1915 Mr Symmons fined him £5 or one months' imprisonment for breaching the order.[54]

By the spring of 1915 it seemed as if the relationship between the alien enemies and the British community in which they lived had reached a stable, if uneasy, equilibrium. From October most had been left relatively undisturbed. But then the late evening newspapers on Friday, 7 May carried a Press Association announcement that the Cunard liner, the *Lusitania*, carrying 1,900 passengers and crew, had been torpedoed and sunk off the coast of Ireland. Although German submarines had been targeting merchant vessels for a few months and there had been Zeppelin raids on London and the east coast since January, this sinking triggered a new and more serious threat to the safety of the Germans and Austrians working and living in the community. Riots broke out across the country, targeting their shops and homes. In Liverpool, home of the Cunard company, there was considerable violence, looting and arson on the Saturday evening.[55] Pork butchers' shops were 'wrecked systematically from Mile End to Rice Lane', and the police, depleted in numbers because of the number of officers serving in the military, were unable to prevent widespread destruction.[56] By Monday the Liverpool police decided to intern all Austrians and Germans for their own safety, but many of them had already sought the protection of the authorities.[57] Sixty-seven men, women, boys and girls appeared at the Liverpool police court on the same day, charged with offences relating to the rioting. The stipendiary magistrate decided on leniency, and several were discharged and others bound over.[58] Riots also broke out in Manchester, Salford, Bradford and Newcastle, but the largest incidents took place in London, and in particular the East End. One unpleasant incident involved a crowd attacking the shop of a baker who had two sons serving in the British Army at the Front.[59] Francis Willmott, a paperhanger, appeared at the Marylebone Police Court charged with breaking a plate glass window at a baker's shop at Allcroft Road, Kentish Town. It was revealed that the baker was English. The magistrate was unimpressed with this and the other examples of 'mob law' he had seen that morning, and ordered Willmott to find a surety or go to prison for fourteen days. The anti-German feeling was not limited by class or calling – the Royal Exchange in the City of London formed a deputation to attempt to influence the government to intern all enemy aliens in the country.[60] A number of commercial associations banned or expelled German members; a notice was posted at the entrance to the Leeds Corn Exchange: 'Members of the Corn Exchange – let Leeds follow London, and expel Germans from this Market.' The two Germans present left while 600 or so members stood and sang 'Rule Britannia'.[61] Mr Joynson Hicks, MP for Brentford, and Lord Charles Beresford presented petitions to the House of Commons each bearing the signatures of 250,000 women, asking the House to 'ensure the safety of their homes by interning all alien enemies'.[62]

In the following week steps were taken for the internment of all male alien enemies. The Prime Minister, Mr Asquith, announced that from the commencement of the war up to the second week of May, 19,000 aliens had been interned, with 24,000 men and 16,000 women still at large.[63] Women and children in suitable cases would be repatriated (but not interned) and principles of humanity and justice would be used in recognition of those who had grounds to remain, with a special advisory body 'of a judicial character' being formed to consider their cases. The definition of military age was also adjusted, to cover the ages between 17 and 55. Naturalized aliens were not beyond suspicion, and if necessary were to be brought before the advisory committee.[64]

On 13 May the Commissioner of the Metropolitan Police issued an order for the curfew and arrest of alien enemies in London. The superintendents of the twenty-four divisions of the force had previously warned the aliens on their local registers of this intention so that they could surrender themselves voluntarily, and Special Branch officers were responsible for compliance.[65] The order read:

Between the hours of 9pm and 5am male alien enemies are required, with effect from May 18, to remain at their registered places of residence unless furnished with a permit from the registration officer of the registration district in which that place of residence is situate.
The police are directed to enforce this restriction.
R. Henry, Commissioner of Police, 15 May 1915

Thousands of men surrendered to their local police stations, with the Tottenham Court Road and Brixton stations being almost overwhelmed.[66] The urgent problem was accommodation, and drafts of internees were sent to Stratford, Southend and Frimley.[67]

Attempts were made to deal with the single men first, giving time to married men and businessmen to settle their affairs. The official censor relaxed the rules to allow newspapers to report that the Special Branch of Scotland Yard was 'in possession of every address, past and present, of every enemy alien in the country'.[68]

Following the Liverpool riots, a contingent of 300 aliens – the 'Pork Butchers' Battalion' – left the city by special train to the camp at Hawick on 12 May. They were escorted from the Bridewell to Lime Street railway station by armed guards of the King's Liverpool Regiment.[69] A further party of 150 left on 15 May, 'of all stations in life and including many elderly people'.[70] Other groups were sent to the Isle of Man by steamer. A party of 300 was brought from London to Frith Hill, Frimley, arriving in torrential rain and marching the two miles from the station to the camp singing 'It's a Long Way to Tipperary'.[71] They had come down by special train from London Waterloo, watched by a large crowd but there 'were no hostile or unseemly demonstrations'.[72] One solution to the problem of accommodating such large numbers of detainees was to send them to Canada, and camps were established at Petawawa and Capuskausing in Ontario, and Spirit Lake in Quebec.[73]

Many Germans and Austrians were willing, grudgingly, reluctantly perhaps, to accept detention, but not all. Heinrich Hauck, of Gledhouse Street, off Regent Street in London, a journeyman tailor, was found dead in the Serpentine on 21 May; the inquest at Westminster considered that a 'dread of internment' was the reason for his suicide.[74]

Regulation 14 of the Defence of the Realm regulations was amended on 10 June 1915. The new section provided that:

14B.   Where on the recommendation of a competent naval or military authority or one of the advisory committees hereinafter mentioned it appears to the Secretary of State that for securing the public safety or the defence of the Realm it is expedient in view of the hostile origin or associations of any person that he shall be subjected to such obligations and restrictions as are hereinafter mentioned, the Secretary of State may by order require that person forthwith, or from time to time, either to remain in, or to proceed to and reside in, such place as may be specified in the order, and to comply with such directions as to reporting to police, restriction of movement, and otherwise as may be specified in the order, *or to be interned in such place as may be specified in the order* ... [author's emphasis].

The grounds offered are vague and subjective, and for the first time it became possible to order the detention of an individual for an indeterminate period of time. The Order does, however, go on to describe mechanisms for appeal to the special advisory committees.

In July Sir John Simon (the new Home Secretary in the first coalition government formed under Asquith on 25 May 1915) was able to report to the House of Commons on the progress of the work of Mr Justice Sankey's Internment Committee. Following the Prime Minister's policy announcements on 13 May, the committee had been formed on 27 May and had sat on forty occasions since, and had practically completed its work. There were 32,440 alien enemies in the detention camps, with internment then proceeding at about 1,000 per week. There had considered 14,117 requests for exemption from internment, of which 7,325 were refused, and 6,092 had been granted. Sympathy had been shown in particular to Poles, Czechs, Italians and others from the various countries within the German and Austro-Hungarian Empires,[75] as it was also observed that British subjects interned in Austria and Hungary had received much better treatment than those Germany (such as in the notorious Ruhleben camp in Berlin).[76]

The Aliens Restriction (Amendment) Order of 1915 was further amended in February 1916. The regulations provided that:

1. All aliens, wherever resident, must register with the police, and report any change of residence, and any person who has an alien lodging with them or living as a member of his household must notify the police of the alien's presence.
2. All aliens staying in hostels, lodging houses, and boarding house must register with the keeper thereof.
3. All aliens living or being within a prohibited area must be provided with an identity book.

For alien enemies there were further requirements:

4. No alien enemy above the age of 17 is allowed to be at large unless he has been exempted by the Secretary of State from internment or repatriation.
5. Alien enemies may not reside in or enter any prohibited area, except by special permission of the chief officer of police.
6. Alien enemies, wherever resident, may not, except by special permission of the chief officer of police, travel more than five miles from their place of residence, or possess certain prohibited articles, such as motor cars, motor cycles, telephones, cameras, etc.[77]

There was a further restriction added that aliens were not permitted to undertake or perform munitions work without the permission of the Minister of Munitions.[78] The identity card (price 1s) was obtained by providing details of:

If present nationality not acquired at birth, state how acquired, and original nationality

Name and nationality of father

Maiden name and nationality of mother before marriage

Nationality before marriage of wife

Whether possessed of a passport

Particulars of last entry into United Kingdom (or has not been absent since 4 August 1914)

Whether applicant previously held an identity book (if lost or destroyed state name of registration or police district in which issued)

Particulars of convictions (if any) of offences against the Defence of the Realm Act or Aliens Restrictions Act or law relating to trading with the enemy

The photographs and fingerprints, if taken, must by identified by the stamp or signature of the police officer

The application had to be attested by two householders of British birth and certified before a police officer.[79]

Registration offences were very common. The Bow Street magistrate sent a Russian ship's fireman to prison for a month to be followed by deportation for making a false entry in a hotel register. His passport was in the name of Mickamanovitch but he had signed the register of the Tavistock Hotel in Covent Garden as Fabian.[80] At the same court, Louise Champion, who kept an apartment house at Guildford Street, and Daisy Halliday, with a boarding house on Endsleigh Street, were fined £5 and 40s respectively for failing to keep registers of aliens staying at their premises.[81] The ports and docks were of course full of foreign seamen and the regulations required the master of the ship to register them with the port Aliens Officer on arrival. Men intending to go ashore were required to have held a passport for at least two years with photo attached. As seen in the Cardiff case, if the vessel remained for twenty-four hours or more in the port the crew were deemed resident in the area, and were required to register.[82]

From very early on there had been issues concerning nationality. Although the British Nationality and Status of Aliens Act was passed on 7 August 1914 it was not part of the emergency legislation and had been planned for some time; it was actually due to come into force on 1 January the following year. The common law approach to British citizenship was that 'any person born within His Majesty's dominions is, from the moment of his birth, a British subject whatever may be the nationality of either or both of his parents and however temporary or casual the circumstances in determining the locality of his birth may have been'.[83] The new Act set out three conditions:

(1) The following persons shall be deemed to be natural-born British subjects, namely:
   a. Any person born within His Majesty's dominions and allegiance; and
   b. Any person born out of His Majesty's dominions, whose father was a British subject at the time of that person's birth and either was born within His Majesty's allegiance or was a person to whom a certificate of naturalization had been granted; and
   c. Any person born on board a British ship whether in foreign territorial waters or not.

The Secretary of State could grant a certificate of naturalization if satisfied that the applicant had resided in His Majesty's dominions for a period of not less than five years, and was of good character and had an adequate knowledge of the English language, and intended to continue to reside in His Majesty's dominions (and paid a fee of £3).

The Act also provided that the wife of a British subject should be deemed to be a British subject and that the wife of an alien was herself an alien, and further recognized that on the death of the husband the nationality does not change. It was also possible for an individual to make a statement either to resume British nationality (in the case of a child born overseas on reaching majority, or the British-born widow of an alien); or to make a statement of alienage, in which a person asserted their foreign nationality and relinquishes any entitlement to British citizenship. A British subject was not entitled to make a statement of alienage (see below). Section 16 provided that when a British subject ceases to be a British subject he should not be discharged from any liability in respect of any act done before he changed his status.

This provided a statutory definition, but was very unsatisfactory in application because the on the Continent and elsewhere nationality was derived from that of the father, regardless of the place of birth, so that the child of a German man, married to an English woman (who would take his nationality on marriage), born in England, would be British in the eyes of English law, but a German under German law. British citizenship, by birth or naturalization, required no further action by the individual. Under some European systems, however, citizenship had to be actively asserted and confirmed, particularly when residing overseas, and it was possible to lose one's original nationality without acquiring British nationality. By March 1916 it was becoming apparent that a number of people were claiming to be of no nationality, and were appearing in magistrates' and the high courts. German legal experts explained the workings of two German statutes of 1870 and 1873 which provided that if a person left the country and resided for ten years abroad, he lost certain of his rights as a German subject, but which could be recovered on his return; and a further law of 1913 allowed the expatriate German to register at his local consulate or embassy every ten years to retain his citizenship. But the concept of losing nationality, or having no nationality, was not recognized in English law. British nationality was determined by the British Nationality and Status of Aliens Act, 1914, and regardless of the laws regarding nationality in other countries, the British view was that any person who had been the subject of a foreign state remained an alien until naturalized under British law.[84]

Alexander Price was a 67-year-old engineer labourer who lived at 26 Wellesley Street, West Gorton in Manchester. His father was Scottish, his mother Welsh, and he himself was born in Bremen in Germany. He had come to England at the age of 13. He had never taken out naturalization papers, and the thought had probably never occurred to him. Why, or how, Inspector Yonge decided that he was an unregistered alien by fact of 'him being born in Germany made him a German subject' and decided to prosecute, will never be known, but the Manchester magistrates sensibly adjourned the matter *sine die*.[85]

Refugee status did not confer any particular rights, and as previously noted those fleeing Belgium, although the recipients of so much care and support from the British government and people, were treated effectively as enemy aliens. The Local Government Board sent a memorandum to the many Local Committees for the Care of Belgian Refugees pointing out that they could not be received in the prohibited areas on the east and south coasts without the consent of the local police authority, and that they must be registered in accordance with the Aliens Restriction Order.[86] In June 1915 Newcastle magistrates heard the case of Rene Gaston Thunus, who was charged with entering the prohibited area of Newcastle without a permit from the Chief Constable. He explained that he was a partner in a Brussels firm of rubber manufacturers and had travelled from Scotland looking for work. He was a lieutenant in the Belgian Civil Guard and had family serving in the Belgian forces. The prosecutor, Mr Bateson, pointed out that so many Belgians claimed to be ignorant of the provisions of the Aliens Restriction Act that the Home Office had given instructions that all such cases should be brought before the magistrates. Thunus informed the court that he had secured employment at the Armstrong Whitworth aircraft factory; the bench treated him sympathetically and bound him over to comply with the regulations.[87] Reginald Talbot of Axminster found himself in front of his local magistrates in September 1915 for failing to register Jeanne Vanderberghe, the Belgian refugee he had taken into his home, and she was charged with failing to register herself. It was the first such case that the bench had dealt with, and they noted that Talbot himself had brought the matter to the attention of the police. Describing it as a technical offence, they were fined 5s each.[88]

Nationality proved a troublesome issue. Robert Terviel worked as a collector at the passenger steamers' station in South Shields. He had lived there for a number of years, at 88, Marine Approach, and was well known in the town through his interest in local politics. He had been born in Emden, near Hanover, fifty-nine years previously but had left Germany at the age of 16 and had moved first to England, and then on to British Columbia, where he was naturalized in 1880.[89] At the outbreak of war he had visited the police station and Detective Inspector Bruce claimed that he had seen him outside the chief clerk's office, 'putting some papers in a wallet' and which he claimed were his naturalization papers. For some reason he had come to the attention of the authorities in August 1915 and the police had asked to see his papers, at which point he claimed that he had given them to a Conservative election agent some twenty years previously, so that his name appeared on the electoral roll. Under the Aliens Restriction Act the onus was on Terviel to prove his nationality and the electoral roll was deemed insufficient evidence. As he was unable to do so, Alderman Readhead and his colleagues found him guilty of being an enemy alien residing in a prohibited area without the permission of the aliens officer. He was fined £5 and ordered to be interned,[90] leaving behind his wife and daughter.

In June 1916 the Home Secretary was able to report that 32,000 alien enemies had been interned in the country and the Isle of Man. With the exception of about 200 they were all German or Austrian and almost all of military age. No women were interned, but about 23,000 (including a small number of British-born children) had been repatriated, and 4,000 had left for other destinations. Excluding the 10,000 or so British-born wives, there were around 22,000 Germans or Austrians who had been exempted from internment or repatriation by the Home Office advisory committee.[91]Eight internment camps or institutions were operated by the War Office, and four by the Home Office.[92]

In late 1916 a Special Commission was appointed to review the position of enemy aliens living under permit in the prohibited areas. In their report in December[93] they noted that some chief constables had been in large part sympathetic to their plight, but had always acted correctly in cases where the military authorities had expressed concerns. The opinion expressed by some chief constables was that it was better to keep an enemy alien in the area where he was well known to neighbours and the police, than to send him away where he could easily become anonymous. The commissioners, Sir Louis Dane and Mr A.J. Sykes MP, noted that in the prohibited areas there were 847 males remaining, 287 of whom were of military age, 548 over and 12 below military age.[94] Of the men of military age, sixty-four were in religious houses or were ministers of religion, including forty inmates of Buckfast Abbey, which was run as an internment camp.[95] A further fifty-seven were Armenians, Poles or Czechs, accepted as sympathetic to this country. One hundred and eighty-eight men were over seventy years of age, thirty-seven blind or bedridden, and fifty-six in workhouses, hospitals or asylums. They identified 494 sons of alien enemies who were serving in His Majesty's forces, a number of whom had lost their lives.[96] There were 2,922 females, of whom 2,031 were British-born.

Not all alien enemies accepted the conditions of internment. Antonius Weber, of 60 Glyn Road, Hackney, was born in Mannheim in 1868 but had left Germany aged 15. After two and a half years in South America he arrived in England in 1901 and had lived and worked here ever since, up until his internment at the London office of a French poultry merchant. His wife was Dutch, his two children were born in London, and neither spoke German. However, in August 1915 the police informed him: 'Take notice that it is intended to intern you as a prisoner of war on Tuesday August 3 1915.' He was taken to an internment camp on the Isle of Wight on 17 August. Under a German statute of 1870, Weber claimed that having left the territory of the German Empire and residing abroad for more than ten years, he lost his German nationality and had no allegiance to the German state. He held that he was not an alien and could not therefore be a prisoner of war, and he issued a writ of *habeas corpus* to challenge the legality of his detention. The case went to the House of Lords on appeal from the Divisional Court, and was heard by the Lord Chancellor and Lords Loreburn and Atkinson. The question of a man having no nationality was not the issue, but whether Weber had done anything to divest himself of German nationality such that he no longer remained a German citizen. They found that Weber would be liable for military service if he were to return to Germany, and so their lordships held that the applicant was an alien enemy and might properly be described as a prisoner of war, and that his arrest and internment was within the Crown's prerogative. The appeal was dismissed.[97]

Arthur Zadig and his brother Caesar owned the firm C.A. Zadig and Company of 73, Queen Victoria Street, London, and manufactured portable railway track and equipment (a 16in gauge similar to the Decauville system used at the Front). Born in Leiben, Arthur had been naturalized in 1905, but his brother retained his German citizenship and was interned in the round-up of June 1915. With the benefit of hindsight, Zadig probably regretted his next actions. Believing his brother to have been wrongly detained, he sent a number of 'foolish letters' to the Home Office, and then wrote to the King, which resulted in his immediate internment by order of the Home Secretary himself.[98] This was an important test case, because unlike Weber who had taken no steps to obtain British citizenship, Zadig clearly had, and was to all intents and purposes a full British subject. He obtained a rule nisi against Sir Frederick Loch Halliday, the commandant of the Islington internment camp, calling on him to show why a writ of *habeas corpus* should not be issued for his release. It was contended that the use of regulation 14B went beyond the powers conferred on the Act. The case went to the King's Bench Divisional Court in January 1916, the matter in question being whether Parliament, in formulating the wording of the Defence of the Realm regulation, intended it to enable to internment without trial of British subjects, which in effect is the suspension of the Habeas Corpus Act. The regulation was issued by Order in Council and not through Parliamentary statute. Although the 'hostile origins or associations' of Zadig was not at issue, the challenge was that the regulation was *ultra vires*. After some considerable discussion, the appeal bench considered:

1. That the regulations should be only during the continuance of the war; and
2. That they should be made for the purpose of public safety.

They agreed that the regulation was within those limits, and Zadig stayed in Islington,[99] and was released from Reading Prison in June 1918.[100]

As the need for conscription began to take on increasing political importance in late 1915 and early the next year, the position of alien friends was considered but the Prime Minister, in a written answer to Will Thorne MP, stated that the forthcoming Military Service Bill would not compel unmarried, unnaturalized aliens of military age to attest for military service.[101] Such men were able to, and did, join the forces: Harry Wagner, serving in the Royal Field Artillery and billeted at St. Annes, found himself in front of the Blackpool magistrates in July 1915 for failing to register as an enemy alien. His father was a German and had been interned, but he explained that he had been born in Yorkshire, and his birth certificate confirmed this. The bench discharged him back to the military authorities.

The first Military Service Act (MSA) came into effect on 2 March 1916, when all single men of military age were automatically entered into the Army Reserve. Frederick Freyberger was the son of Austrian parents, his father being a toxicologist and pathologist, and they lived in a grand apartment at 9, St Mark's Square, Regent's Park, London. His parents were naturalized in 1897 and Frederick himself was born in St Pancras the year before, so he was entered as an infant on his father's naturalization certificate. As the MSA came into effect, the 20-year-old found himself an unwilling member of the Reserves and appealed unsuccessfully to the military tribunals. He was arrested and brought before the magistrates in August 1916 and handed to the Middlesex Regiment. He refused to accept his position, and in September he was court-martialled and imprisoned for refusing to obey military orders. On 23 January 1917 he celebrated his 21st birthday, and exercising his right under section 14 of the British Citizenship and Status of Aliens Act 1914, he made a declaration of alienage, asserting himself to be an Austrian subject as he was at the time of his birth. He subsequently launched a writ of *habeas corpus* against his commanding officer, and the case was heard by the King's Bench Divisional Court on 12 March 1917. The Solicitor-General made several points, not least of which was that for a soldier to divest himself of British allegiance during wartime would be an act of treason. On joining the army he was a British subject and would retain this status until discharge from the army or until the end of war. The Lord Chief Justice and Justices Ridley and Horridge agreed that because Freyberger was already in military service he was not in a position to make a valid declaration, and remained subject to military law. They discharged the application.[102]

The Freyberger case affirmed that declaration of alienage remained lawful, but had to be made but before any liability to military service had arisen. Although magistrates normally had little to do with offences under the MSA, other than to send deserters and absentees back to their units, as will be described in Chapter 9, they did have the judicial function of determining whether an individual was subject to MSA in the first place, and so it was not uncommon for the bench to hear cases from individuals who claimed that, as friendly or enemy aliens, they were exempt for military service. A number of similar cases followed, such as George Funck of 2, Edmund Street, Bradford in December 1916. His father, a German, had been interned at the Wakefield camp for two years. Although born in this country George had been told he was not permitted to live in the prohibited area in Sunderland where the family had resided. He subsequently worked in a munitions factory but was discharged when the police found out, and had ended up in Bradford. He had made a declaration of alienage but only after he had become eligible for military service, and he also tried appealed to the local tribunal that he was a conscientious objector. The stipendiary magistrate held that he was subject to the MSA and the unfortunate man was handed over to the military authorities.[103]

The Military Service Acts reflected the desperate need for manpower, a demand which was felt in the Allied countries: France suffered badly at Verdun, and the Russians were struggling against the Central Powers on the Eastern Front. Recognizing that their countries harboured a number of men of military age who were otherwise exempt from local schemes of conscription, the Military Service (Conventions with Allied States) Act was passed on 10 July 1917. This required all men who would be eligible for military service in their countries of birth to either return to that country on an assisted passage scheme, or to present themselves at the local recruiting office for service in His Majesty's forces. This Act had a disproportionate effect on the Russian community in London, which was very largely Jewish, and the measure was criticized for being anti-Semitic;[104] many of the people affected had come here because of the pogroms, and would face an uncertain reception. There were fears that those electing to join the British army might be gathered into Jewish battalions,[105] but this was expressly proscribed under the Army Act, 1881, which provided a restriction of one alien to fifty British subjects. Clearly there was also a corresponding liability on British subjects residing in Allied states becoming subject to the requirements for local or British military service. As an inducement to alien friends, the Home Secretary announced that on completion of three months' satisfactory service the eligible alien soldier would be naturalized free of cost.[106] The law was enacted on 10 July 1917. The Chief Constable of Preston, Mr J.P.K. Watson, published a notice that any Russian subject of military age in the town who wished to return to Russia should apply at the Central Police Station before 9 August, and be ready at any time after 13 August to leave the country. If they failed to comply with the regulations they would become liable for service in the British Army with apparently no right of appeal to the tribunal. If they preferred to remain they would be deemed to have enlisted and transferred to the reserve, under the MSA.[107]

As would be expected, the rules proved difficult to apply. Abraham Spolansky, of 26, Ellen Street, Whitechapel, applied to be taken to Russia and arrangements were made for his travel. He then changed his mind, with the intention of going before the tribunal for an exemption. The Act only allowed Russians who had elected to stay the right to appeal to the tribunal. In October 1917 the King's Bench Divisional Court decided against Spolansky[108] and he was sent off to join the Royal Fusiliers (a London regiment). On 2 November a number of Russian absentees were charged at the Thames Police Court, all of whom had elected to return to Russia but had failed to do so when given the opportunity. Against the usual tariff of a £2 penalty, these men were each fined £5. It was stated that there were around 3,000 Russian men who had failed to return to Russia, most of whom lived in the East End of London.[109] On 22 March Joseph Kutchinsky, another Royal Fusilier, applied for a writ of *habeas corpus* against his commanding officer on the grounds that on 12 February Mr Litvinoff of the Russian People's Embassy had announced that Russia was no longer at war, and that 'the Bolsheviks will call for the release from service of all men now in the army'.[110] Although the divisional court thought that the application raised some 'nice' questions, they held that having become an enlisted man in the British Army he was subject to the same conditions of service as any other soldier and so could not be discharged except in the same way any other man could be discharged.[111] By 4 June 1918 a further Aliens Restriction Order in Council allowed that 'well disposed' Turkish subjects in certain circumstances could be treated as alien friends, as the fortunes of the Ottoman Empire foundered.

Registration offences continued to the very end of the war. Belgian refugees Alfonse and Julie Lebon, of 76 Tenby Road, Walthamstow, took advantage of the warm August weather with a trip to Brighton. They went to the police station on arrival but were told that they should have notified their own police station of their intention to travel, and had therefore committed an offence, and also merely residing at the hotel in Brighton constituted a change of address in itself. The Stratford magistrates fined them 10s each.[112]

The military intelligence services' activity in the pre-war years had meant that many Germans and others sympathetic to the cause of the Central Powers were identified and known before the conflict, along with many other foreign subjects. The limitations of the Official Secrets Act, 1911 for prosecuting spies in time of war were almost immediately recognized, and the Aliens (Restriction) Act, 1914 was one of the better pieces of emergency legislation. The process of alien registration was effectively and efficiently executed using the new regulations, and clearly the police and courts did much to reassure the public that the 'enemy within' was, if not actually locked up, certainly closely monitored. Undoubtedly the early recognition that alien enemies of military age, by definition therefore 'His Majesty's enemies', could be treated as *de facto* prisoners of war and interned as such, provided a solid legal basis for the State to deprive citizens of their liberty.

Chapter 7

Down at the Old Bull and Bush

Dalton's *Country Justice* (1635) gave a simple working definition of drunkenness: 'a man was not drunk unless the same legs which carry him into the house cannot carry him out again'. A slightly later authority proposed that 'a man was properly carrying his drink until he slid under the table'; and a favourite with the lawyers was that 'it was a question of not being able to lie on the ground without holding on'. In a society in which prolific alcohol consumption was prevalent among all classes and both sexes and directly or indirectly implicated in so much criminal behaviour, the legal standard of what constituted 'drunkenness' was largely subjective and assessed by the police officer in the street. The point was tested in Great Yarmouth police court in 1902, with various dictionary definitions being provided to show that the defendant was more than simply 'cherry-merry'. After some discussion, the learned clerk offered:

Not drunk is he, who from the floor
Can rise again and drink still more
But drunk is he who prostate lies
Without the power to drink or rise

As the court dissolved into laughter the magistrates dismissed the case.[1]

Historically it was an offence merely to be found drunk in any highway or other public place, but the 1902 Licensing Act brought in the test of being 'drunk and incapable', which was simply defined as being unable to care for oneself. Shouting or singing, stumbling or using abusive language, could make up the offence of being drunk and disorderly. The offence was aggravated if the offender was in charge of horses, cattle, or steam engines or other carriages or, from 1902, in charge of a child apparently under the age of seven; the punishment, on conviction, could be a fine of up to 40s or imprisonment for up to a month, with or without hard labour. Unless the court decided otherwise, a pensioner was liable to lose his entitlement to his pension for six months.

The Habitual Drunkard Act, 1879 identified the 'habitual drunkard' as 'a person who, not being amenable to any jurisdiction in lunacy, is notwithstanding, by reason of habitual intemperate drinking of intoxicating liquor, at times dangerous to himself or herself, or to others, or incapable of managing himself or herself, and his or her affairs'. Three or more convictions for drunkenness in the previous twelve months were sufficient to bring an individual under the Act, and magistrates were given powers to detain such persons in licensed retreats for treatment. Further powers were granted with the 1902 Licensing Act such that, if the bench decided not to detain the offender, the notification of the conviction was sent to the police authority along with the drunkard's personal details, which included a list of licensed premises or clubs that they were known to frequent.[2] It then became an offence to purchase or obtain (or attempt to purchase or obtain) any intoxicating liquor at any licensed premises within three years of the conviction. As it was also an offence for the licence-holder to supply intoxicating liquor to the habitual drunkard, these details were circulated in the relevant area in what became known as the Black List. By 1914 the list gave a profile and full-face photograph of the unfortunate individual, but, as Inspector Carter stated at Marylebone Police Court, the publicans were unable to identify the people as there were so many of them.[3]

Repeated convictions for drunkenness were addressed by the Inebriates Act, 1898. Section 1 of the Act dealt with indictable offences heard at the Assizes. If the court was satisfied that either the offence was committed under the influence of drink, or that drunkenness was a contributing cause of the offence, and the offender admitted he was (or was found by the jury to be) an habitual drunkard, and the offence was punishable with imprisonment or penal servitude, the court could order the offender to be detained for up to three years in an inebriate reformatory. Section 2 applied to the magistrates' courts: any person who committed offences of drunkenness and who had been within the preceding twelve months convicted at least three times summarily of any such offence, and who was an habitual drunkard, could consent, on summary conviction, to be detained for three years in an inebriate reformatory (this was considered the minimum time for treatment and rehabilitation). At quarter sessions, on indictment, consent for detention was not required. In October 1915 Janet Thornton pleaded guilty to a charge of having neglected her nine children at the Northumberland Quarter Sessions and was sent to the Brentry Certified Inebriate Reformatory, Bristol, for three years.

By 1914 the system had evolved to include state and certified inebriate reformatories, and reformatory homes and retreats. The annual report of the Chief Inspector under the Inebriates Acts for that year estimated that there were about, 48,000 inebriates in England and Wales, of whom 16,000 were as yet unconvicted in the courts, and 32,000 who were known to the authorities.[4]

State inebriate reformatories	Certified inebriate reformatories
Perth	Aberdeen Seabank
Warwick	Greenock
Aylesbury	Hairmyres, Lanarkshire
	Cattal, York (Yorkshire)
	Langho, Blackburn (Lancashire)
	Ackworth, Pontefract (North Midlands)
	Chesterfield (Midland Counties)
	Lewes (Southern Counties)
	Brentry, near Henbury, Bristol
	Farmfield, Horley, Surrey (London County Council)
	East Harling (Eastern Counties)

Drunkenness and offences related or caused by drunkenness comprised a depressingly large part of the magistrates' work. In the period 1910–14, the annual average of convictions for simple drunkenness (drunk and incapable) was 59,250. Aggravated offences (drunk and disorderly, drunk in charge of a cart etc.) averaged 134,104 a year. In the Becontree Petty Sessions (now Stratford) in the three months July to September 1914 there 385 cases of drunkenness, which made 37.6 per cent of the workload.[5]

In 1913 there were 141,000 licensed beer and spirit shops, which was one for every 330 people. The average annual expenditure on intoxicating liquor was £3 12s 4d per person, with the average consumption of 27 gallons of beer per person. These statistics are not adjusted to exclude non-drinkers or children. Alcoholic drinks were slightly stronger on average than today and alcohol content was reported in a different way, using the measure of proof spirit. 100° proof spirit contained 57.1 per cent of alcohol by volume (ABV, the units we use today). Pre-war beer contained 9 per cent proof spirit. This means 9 per cent of a 57.1 per cent ABV solution, which gives 5.13 per cent ABV, or approximately 5 per cent. Wines were around 13 per cent ABV, and spirits were in the range 35 per cent–45 per cent, and not less than 30 per cent. Out of every 100 gallons of pure alcohol consumed in the United Kingdom in 1913, 77.4 gallons were drunk in beer, 20.6 gallons as spirits, and 2 gallons as wine.[6]

The *Justice's Note-book*[7] acknowledged that the control of the retail liquor trade of the country was almost exclusively in the hands of the magistrates (and in times of peace remained so until the Licensing Act of 2003). There were ten different types of licence, permitting sale for consumption on or off the premises:

1. Victualler's or full publican's licence to sell all intoxicating liquors.
2. Beer-house licence, including cider.
3. Cider licence, including perry.
4. Wine-house licence (refreshment rooms, &c.).
5. Sweets i.e. British wines, mead &c.
6. Beer and cider, off licence.
7. Foreign wines, off licence.
8. Spirits, off licence.
9. Cider and perry off licence.
10. Sweets off licence.

Each year the licensing justices held a General Annual Licensing meeting to grant licences to 'fit and proper persons'. These justices were a subcommittee drawn from the bench (except in boroughs, in which case it would be the whole bench) and had both the duty and pleasure of familiarizing themselves with the various establishments for which they were responsible. This included understanding the level of provision of public houses in a locality, the clientele served and any reports of criminal behaviour. To deal with licensing matters arising during the year a number of 'special sessions' were held (as opposed to petty sessions or quarter sessions).

The closing hours for public houses were defined in the 1910 Licensing (Consolidation) Act and, to modern eyes, are quite astonishing:

Premises within the Metropolis i.e. the administrative county of London, or any area within a four-mile radius of Charing Cross
Saturday, from midnight till 1 pm on Sunday
Sunday afternoon, from 3 pm to 6 pm
Sunday, from 11 pm till 5 am on Monday
Other days, from 12.30 am till 5 am

Premises beyond the Metropolis but in the Metropolitan Police District, and Premises in a Town or Populous Place
Saturday, from 11 pm till 12.30 pm on Sunday
Sunday afternoon, from 2 pm to 6 pm
Sunday, from 10 pm till 6 am on Monday
Other days, from 11 pm till 6 am

Premises not in the Metropolis or Metropolitan Police District, or in a Town or Populous Place
Saturday, from 10 pm till 12.30 pm on Sunday
Sunday afternoon, 2.30 pm till 6 pm
Sunday, from 10 pm till 6 am on Monday
Other days, from 10 pm to 6 am of the following day

Wales: Premises in a Town or Populous Place
Saturday, from 11 pm till 6 am on *Monday* [author's emphasis]
Other days, from 11 pm to 6 am the following day

Wales: Premises not in a Town or Populous Place
Saturday, from 10 pm until 6 am *Monday* [author's emphasis]
Other days, from 10 pm to 6 am the following day.[8]

Local authorities could also apply for exemption from closing in the case of local markets or industries where 'considerable numbers of persons' were attending a location, in which case licensed premises were granted a general order of exemption, with closing hours between 1 am and 2 am only.

It was reasonably straightforward to obtain permission to extend opening hours, but there was little power to vary closing times, other than on Sundays and Bank Holidays. However, any two justices could order the immediate closure of any and all licensed premises if immediate riot or tumult was apprehended.

For those who were unable to survive the four-and-a-half hours that the pubs were closed at night in London, there were other ways of obtaining drink. Then, as now, a licensed person was entitled to supply alcoholic beverages to personal friends after closing time, but there was an interesting class of customer known as the *bona fide* traveller. Provided the place where he lodged the previous night was at least three miles by the nearest public thoroughfare from the premises he was currently lodged, he was entitled to buy a drink at that place at any time.[9] Another exception was that liquor was allowed to be served at any time at a railway station to a person arriving at or departing by train, and a test case proved that this held even if the only reason the person undertook the journey was to get a drink![10]

Another source of out-of-hours liquor was the club. In London this might suggest the exclusive opulence of the gentleman's club, but in fact the working men's club movement was very popular, particularly in the industrial heartlands of the country. In 1907 there were nearly 3,000 such clubs with almost a million members,[11] and the annual meeting of the Association of Conservative and Unionist Clubs represented 1,500 clubs with half a million members.[12] Although there were strong community, educational, recreational, and, in many cases, political and charitable forces behind the clubs, the social aspect was essential. Clubs were required to have a formal rulebook and use of the facilities was reserved only for members and their guests, who had to be signed in. Clubs were required to register with the licensing authority, but having done so were permitted to sell and consume alcohol in the hours of their own choosing.[13]

In London it was not uncommon for the streets to be full of people and noise until the early hours, and much of the crime related to drunkenness occurred in these late hours. One report painted a picture of late night in the metropolis: 'great traffic centres, like the Elephant and Castle ... immense crowds usually lounge around until one o'clock in the morning. The police ... [have to] move on numbers of people who have been dislodged from the bars at 12.30 at night ... the sounds of ribald songs, dancing and quarrelling.'[14]

Before considering the effects of wartime licensing legislation, it should be noted that under the existing licensing acts it was an offence for any person who, during the time at which the premises were directed to be closed, sold or exposed for sale, or opened or kept open his premises for the sale of intoxicating liquors, or allowed any intoxicating liquors, although purchased before, to be consumed after closing hours. This was punishable as a first offence with a fine of £10.[15] In grocer's shops and other shops selling goods in addition to liquor, the alcoholic drinks had to be covered up if the shop remained open during closing hours.

With the outbreak of war there was an early recognition that some restrictions on the sale of intoxicating liquor might be prudent and initially attention turned to the magistrates, and in particular the licensing justices. The general Royal Proclamation of 4 August 1914 conferred powers on the military authorities to 'take all such measures as may be necessary for securing the public safety and the defence of Our Realm', and one of the first military orders was issued in Stirling on Thursday, 6 August closing all public houses and hotels and prohibiting licensed grocers from selling liquor as the 3rd Battalion of the Argyll and Sutherland Highlanders begin mobilizing in the town.[16] On Thursday, 6 August 1914 the St. Helen's justices resolved to order the closing of all licensed premises at 8 pm, including Sundays, and to set the opening time for 9 am.[17] Eastbourne magistrates made a recommendation (not an order) to licensed victuallers in their town to close at 10 pm instead of 11 pm[18] in anticipation of any legislation, but in neither case were the orders enforceable, as in the absence of the 'apprehension of riot or tumult' the magistrates had no powers to close any premises.

The first Defence of the Realm Regulations, passed on 12 August 1914, under the Defence of the Realm Act of 8 August 1914, contained two regulations related to alcoholic drinks:

Regulation 7

The competent naval or military authority may by order require all premises licensed for the sale of intoxicating liquor within or in the neighbourhood of any defended harbour to be closed except during such hours as may be specified in the order.

Regulation 17

No person shall with the intent of eliciting information for the purpose of communicating it to the enemy or for any purpose calculated to assist the enemy, give or sell to a member of any of His Majesty's forces any intoxicating liquor; and no person shall give or sell to a member of any of His Majesty's forces employed in the defence of any railway, dock or harbour any intoxicating liquor when not on duty, with intent to make him drunk, or when on sentry or other duty, either with or without such intent.

As seen in Chapter 5 these regulations were almost immediately amended (and subsequently replaced under the Defence of the Realm Consolidation Act of December 1914), so that 'defended harbour' became 'any area specified in the Order', and the restrictions of sale might apply to all persons or to members of His Majesty's forces, and to any or all of the licensed premises in the area. Regulation 7 is reasonable enough, but regulation 17 is very poorly drafted: it would be very difficult to prove any intent to elicit information to assist the enemy, nor any intent to make a soldier drunk, in which case the regulation merely prohibits the gift or sale of drink to a soldier while on duty.

An order made by the magistrates was enforceable by the local police; an order by the competent military or naval authority could be enforced by the army or navy or by the civilian police. With the authority of the regulations, orders were issued in a number of areas and a reasonable amount of common sense was shown. At Dover on one occasion an order was issued closing all licensed premises within 100 yards of the line of march to the station for an hour and a half before the departure of a particular troop train. In several Yorkshire towns publicans and other licence holders were forbidden to sell bottles of beer, wine or spirits to soldiers for 'off' consumption. In Lerwick the problem was the sale of small bottles of whisky.[19] Lieutenant Colonel A.H. Leith, of the 3rd Gordon Highlanders based at Castelhill Barracks in Aberdeen and guarding the defences of the port, wrote to the editor of the *Daily Journal*:

It has been brought to my notice that drink is being offered to soldiers by civilians. This may be kindly meant, but I must point out that during wartime in a defended harbour soldiers are always on duty, and liable at any moment to be called to their positions in the scheme of defence. It might be extremely serious should every man not turn up sober and alert.

Moreover, civilians committing this offence render themselves liable to court-martial, and an award of penal servitude.[20]

After the flurry of legislative activity in the first weeks of the war, the second batch of emergency legislation was submitted to the House of Commons on 25 August. The Home Secretary, Mr McKenna, begged to move 'that leave be given to bring in a Bill to enable orders to be made in connection with the present War for restricting the sale or consumption of intoxicating liquors'.[21] He reminded the house that licensing authorities at that time could only impose restrictions if riot was apprehended; the new Bill would grant them the power to restrict hours of sale at any time. Unlike the other Bills presented that day and which were passed in quick succession, the proposed Intoxicating Liquor (Temporary Restriction) Bill was adjourned. On 27 August there was some considerable debate about the Bill and a number of amendments proposed. Mr Basil Peto made an interesting comment: 'There is a great distinction between the use of the public house as a part of the everyday life of the whole mass of our population – I believe it to be an absolute necessity at meal times in the middle of the day and the evening – and the keeping of public-houses open until ten or eleven o'clock at night.'[22] Objections were raised that the government in introducing such 'panic legislation' was under the influence of the temperance movement, rather than on behalf of the naval and military authorities.[23]

Finally the amended Bill was brought back to the House on 28 August and received its second and third readings, and became law on 31 August.

Intoxication Liquor (Temporary Restriction) Act, 1914

An Act to enable orders to be made in connection with the present war for restricting the sale or consumption of intoxicating liquor.

Section 1

1. The licensing justices for any licensing district may, if they think fit, upon the recommendation of the chief officer of police that it is desirable for the maintenance of order or the suppression of drunkenness in any area, by order direct that the sale or consumption of intoxicating liquor on the premises of any persons holding any retailer's licence in the area, and the supply or consumption of intoxicating liquor in any registered club in the area, shall be suspended while the order is in operation, during such hours and subject to such conditions or exceptions (if any) as may be specified in the order: Provided that, if any such order suspends the sale, supply, or consumption of intoxicating liquor at an hour earlier than nine at night, the order shall not have effect until approved by the Secretary of State.

2. If any person acts in contravention of, or fails to comply with, any order under this section he shall be liable on summary conviction in respect of each offence to a fine not exceeding fifty pounds. If any person feels aggrieved by a conviction under this section he may appeal therefrom to quarter sessions in accordance with the Summary Jurisdiction Acts.

3. The licensing justices shall have power to make an order under this section at their general annual licensing meeting or at any special sessions held by them

for the purpose of their duties under the Licensing (Consolidation) Act, 1910, or at any meeting specially called for the purpose under this Act.

The clerk to the licensing justices shall specially call such a meeting if an application in writing is made to him for the purpose either by two of their number or by the chief officer of police for this district.

4. In the application of this section to the county of London the committee of the compensation authority appointed under section six of the Licensing (Consolidation) Act, 1910, shall be substituted for the licensing justices.

Section 2 dealt with definitions and the application of the Act to Scotland and Ireland.

The key features of this reasonably well-drafted legislation are that the licensing justices remain the authority to determine any Order, but that they may act on application from the Chief Officer of Police and on the new basis of the maintenance of order or the suppression of drunkenness. Although the Home Secretary admitted that the Act was introduced on behalf of the naval and military authorities they were given no powers, other than those conferred by the Defence of the Realm regulations. Of course they could, and did, make representations to the Chief Officer of Police, who could then apply to the justices on their behalf. It is also notable how the Act used existing magisterial and judicial practices such as the general annual licensing meeting and special sessions. An important aspect of this Act was its application to registered clubs, which closed a loophole and ensured that the new restrictions applied equally to all vendors and consumers of intoxicating liquor.

The Act was well received and was applied gradually. The Home Office was particularly keen to recognize special conditions in different localities at different times and they were adamant that there should be 'no unnecessary restrictions that might fall on any particular class of persons or traders'.[24] However it soon became apparent that having two authorities with separate and different powers was going to cause problems. The naval and military authorities could issue closing orders under regulation 7 of the Defence of the Realm Act but these only applied to licensed premises such as public houses. The magistrates issued their orders under the Intoxicating Liquor (Temporary Restrictions) Act, and these covered all on and off licensed premises, as well as clubs, within their licensing district. Further, regulation 7 orders could only apply to a specific area defined by the military authority, whereas the justices' order could have a broader geographical coverage outside the military areas. A further unanticipated legal confusion was that the regulation 7 order was a 'closing order' and that the licensed premises were obliged to close completely. The magistrates' 'closing order' related only to the sale and consumption of alcohol during the hours specified, so that the publican could continue to serve non–alcoholic refreshments and food. And then regulation 17, concerning serving liquor to a soldier on duty, was rather ambiguous about its general application and appeared to apply only to railways, docks and harbours.[25]

As noted above, the licensing justices remained the only authority to impose orders, but they still could not do so at their own initiative. The police made a recommendation which the magistrates could either adopt or reject, but they had no power to vary.

The London Licensing Authority acted on the recommendation of the Commissioner of Police and imposed an order suspending the sale and consumption of intoxicating liquor at 10 pm each evening from 19 October 1914. This applied to all licensed premises, including clubs and restaurants. However, an exception was permitted for the munitions workers in Woolwich and Greenwich. There the pubs were to close at 9 pm, but they were able to drink alcohol with their meals at the Woolwich Labour Institute between 1 am and 2 am, the night shift mealtime.[26]

On the advice of the Chief Constable of Birmingham, the licensing justices there used their powers to close, for the sale of intoxicating liquor, at 9 o'clock each night starting Wednesday, 4 November:

The Red House, Broad Street
White Hart, Broad Street
Square and Compasses, Broad Street
Hen and Chickens, Broad Street
The Crown, Broad Street
Bingley Hall Hotel, King Alfred's Place
Cambridge Bar, Cambridge Street
Prince of Wales, Cambridge Street

These pubs were all in the neighbourhood of Bingley Hall (the first purpose-built exhibition hall in Great Britain), which was being used by Colonel Cook and the 6th Battalion the Argyll and Sutherland Highlanders. He commented on the misguided kindness of the Birmingham public in giving liquor to his men, which the younger ones in particular found it difficult to refuse. The army had its own way of dealing with the trouble caused, and the colonel mentioned that the 'men's leave had been considerably reduced'.[27]

Private Tommy Atkins, living as he does under the provisions of the Army Act, the *Manual of Military Law*, and the *King's Regulations*, is very good at applying the rules to his own advantage. Some barrack-room lawyer in the Aldershot command knew of the Licensing (Consolidation) Act, 1910. He realized that as a fit young soldier it was actually quite easy for him to march himself and his comrades over three miles or more of public thoroughfare to a public house, and once there to claim their rights as *bona fide* travellers. So successful was this ruse that Major General A.H. Gordon, the Officer Commanding Aldershot, had to issue a DoRA order through the Farnham and Camberley police to the licensed victuallers of the area, that soldiers in uniform or civilian clothes were not to be treated as travellers, nor was intoxicating liquor in bottles to be sold to soldiers or any persons acting on their behalf.[28] Gordon later went on to order that members of HM Forces were to be refused service in any pub in Guildford between 2 pm and 6 pm, although civilians were unaffected.

In November an interesting discussion took place between the Commissioner of Police, Alderman Edward Johnson (chairman of the Board of the Licensed Victuallers' Central Protection Society) and Mr Frank Whitbread, of the London Brewers' Council. With all the turmoil and upheaval in the country and in their trade, they decided that their contribution would be to request that all licence holders in the Metropolitan Police district to stop serving women with intoxicating liquor for consumption on or off the premises before 11.30 am.[29] This brought a protest from Mrs Despard, the suffragette, in a letter to the Prime Minister's private secretary, firstly that women were entitled to spend their allowances how they pleased, and secondly, that any apparent increase in the number of women seen drinking of late was because the pubs were so full of men in uniform that the women couldn't get access, and had to drink outside. One unsympathetic report of her letter ended with a telling comment: 'out of twenty charges at the Thames Police Court yesterday, more than half were against women for drunkenness'.[30]

There was genuine concern that there was an increase in drinking amongst women, and in particular that soldiers' wives were drinking their way through their separation allowances (see Chapter 10). Mr J. Gaskin JP, chairman at the Manchester City Police Court, had to deal with such a case on Monday 9 November, 1914. The young woman before the bench said that her excuse for having been drunk was that she had been to a christening. Her husband was at the Front. 'You are exactly the kind of woman who is causing all this outcry', he lectured. 'There is an agitation to stop all this drinking. You get your 12s 6d a week from the Army, and that is money to keep you and enable you to live decently. Instead you help to get the city a bad name, and other people suffer for it.' He fined her 2s 6d, with costs.[31]

By November a new justification for liquor control had appeared: military efficiency. Lord Kitchener had been appointed the Minister of War in the first week of the war and in the process of recruiting and training his New Army had made a number of indirect requests to the public to ease up or to refrain from plying his soldiers with drinks, and his admonishment to resist the dual temptations of wine and women was printed in every soldier's paybook. But on 6 November the Home Office published a circular in which they noted that it was Kitchener's 'wish' that 'all possible steps be taken to preserve the efficiency and discipline of the new army ... from being impaired through excessive facilities for soldiers and their friends to obtain intoxicating liquor'.[32] He actively encouraged the chief constables to liaise with the military authorities, and was keen to see the imposition of orders by the licensing authorities, particularly by restricting sale during morning hours, because such orders applied equally to soldiers and civilians. At the same time the application of the orders to both licensed premises and clubs was emphasized: a military closing order could only apply to licensed houses, so licensing justices were encouraged to impose their own order, corresponding to the hours of the military order, which would then apply to the private clubs. By drawing the attention of the magistrates to these points the Secretary of State hoped to smooth the way for new orders with such restrictions.[33] This was a strategic act on the part of both the War Office and the Home Office – by setting out the link between liquor control and military efficiency the demon of the temperance movement was sidelined. It was effective and by the end of the year 427 orders had been imposed, across the 1,000 petty sessional divisions in England and Wales.[34]

The Defence of the Realm regulations introduced back in August were revoked at the end of November and on 1 December 1914 were replaced with the sixty-three regulations which are generally more familiar to the historian. The old regulation 7 now appeared in the section 'Control of licensed premises, intoxicants, hours of business, and places of entertainment' as regulation 10 'Power to close licensed premises'. The cumbersome regulation 17 moved into the section 'Intoxicants, Drugs and Malingering' being renumbered as regulation 40 'Prohibition on supplying intoxicants to members of HM forces'.

By early 1915 the legislation – and the courts – were being tested. The magistrates at Pontefract Police Court had a tricky start to the year when they had to decide if an order restricting sale and consumption of intoxicating liquor before 12.30 on Sunday afternoons, made on 28 October, was enforceable. On 9 January 1915, Mr Arthur Lee, the secretary of the Smawthorne Lane Working Mens' Club[35] in nearby Castleford, was charged with selling liquor during prohibited hours. According to the evidence, the police visited the club at 11.15 on Sunday, 20 December, and found fourteen persons in one room, twenty-one in another, and nearly all of them drinking. Lee fully admitted that the order had been served and that he had supplied the drink at the time. He challenged that validity of the order, in that the approval of the Home Secretary had to be obtained for any order in which magistrates suspended sales of liquor before 9 pm. The 12.30 restriction was before 9 pm. The bench were unconvinced and fined him £5 with costs. Lee's representative, Mr Waugh, asked for a statement of case to take to the High Court (see Chapter 1), to which the bench agreed and the penalty was suspended for two months. The chairman insisted that in the meantime the order would remain in force across the division.[36]

In the following weeks a number of similar cases were brought against other clubs in the West Riding and they were all adjourned pending the decision of the Pontefract case;[37] indeed the executive of the Club and Institute Union, which represented 1,600 metropolitan and provincial social clubs, advised its members to ignore all such orders.[38] The case arrived at the Divisional Court of the King's Bench Division on Thursday, 13 May, 1915,[39] before the Lord Chief Justice and Justices Avory and Low.

Mr Tindal Atkinson appeared on behalf of the magistrates and described how the problem had arisen because of 'hurried emergency legislation'.[40] He repeated the proviso from section 1 (1) of the Act, whereby an order which 'suspends the sale, supply or consumption of liquor at an hour earlier than nine at night … shall not have effect until approved by the Secretary of State', and that the question turned on the word 'earlier'. Mr Atkinson suggested that the intention was to set the time at which sales should stop in the evening. The order went on to prohibit sale before 12.30 on the Sunday, which the Lord Chief Justice pointed out was 'earlier' than the nine o'clock proviso. After further discussion he suggested that the intention of the legislation was that sale should be suspended from the time specified until the normal opening time the next morning, and that this order is one the justices were entitled to make. His colleagues agreed and the appeal was dismissed.

In early 1915 the perception was that the effects of drink on the efficiency of the army and navy were largely under control. The focus of attention then shifted to the efficiency of the civilian labour force, and in particular to the munitions workers. Civilians, of course, had a reasonable freedom of movement, and it became apparent that they could simply travel from a restricted hours area to an uncontrolled area with impunity. The Home Secretary was challenged in the House of Commons by Mr Stewart, MP for Wirral, who pointed out that the licensing justices had imposed an order restricting the sale of intoxicating liquor to the hours of 9 am to 9 pm in the rural district, but there were no such restrictions in the adjacent port of Birkenhead. He asked Mr McKenna if the hours could be standardized. The reply was simple, in that the government had left these decisions to the local authorities.[41] The importance of the civilian workforce in the national war effort was becoming increasingly apparent and with the Shell Scandal following the Battle of Loos the whole system of the manufacture and supply of munitions was under intense scrutiny, and the effect of heavy drinking in certain sections of the labour force was identified as being a key factor. Restriction orders certainly helped control drinking in the military, but were easily avoided by industrial workers. Fortunately a spirit of cooperation prevailed in both government, industry and the trades unions and there was a willingness to solve the problem. The Chancellor of the Exchequer, Lloyd George, made a significant speech in Bangor on 28 February 1915 and was unequivocal on the dangers: 'Drink is doing us more damage in the War than all the German submarines put together', and he reiterated the point in a further speech to the Shipbuilding Employers' Federation at the Treasury on Tuesday, 30 March, 'We are fighting Germany, Austria and drink. As far as I see it the greatest of these three deadly foes is drink'.[42]

The problem of drink was viewed with concern by the many religious and social groups promoting regulation and firm liquor control – the Temperance League, Temperance Society, the Band of Hope, the Total Abstinence Council, the British Women's Temperance Association and others were all promoting the virtues of civilian and military abstinence. But there was an inherent suspicion throughout the early months of the operation of the Intoxicating Liquor (Temporary Restrictions) Act that the temperance movement was behind it all, and that the Act was anything but temporary (according to the Act itself it was to last the duration of the war and one month beyond). The Russian example was held as a model for the British government – the Tsar had imposed a total prohibition on the manufacture and sale of alcohol on 31 July 1914, originally as a temporary measure during the mobilization prior to and during the outbreak of hostilities. As the vodka industry was under state control and the spirit was sold at Government liquor shops, and there were no private interests to consider, it was a simple step to enforce a permanent prohibition. On 21 October 1914 it was announced that the ban would remain[43] – and it lasted until 1925. The French also banned the sale of absinthe from 16 August 1914, initially in Paris and the Seine department but it was gradually extended across the whole country, and the sale of alcoholic drinks was immediately banned in the military zone under the regulations of l'état de siege.

But the British government and people seemed unwilling to consider total prohibition. Politically this was undoubtedly due to a strong and influential brewing and distilling trade (daily turnover was estimated at £500,000[44]), and the tax on the sale of intoxicating liquor was an important contribution to the economy – in 1914 the national drink bill was £164,463,000. And as we have seen, alcohol consumption was an integral part of British social life. On Tuesday, 6 April 1915, it was officially announced that 'by the King's command, no wines, spirits or beer will be consumed in any of his Majesty's houses after today' but this had little influence on the public.[45]

Evidence began to come in to illustrate the impact of drink on British industry. Lloyd George was able to report the findings of Admiral Tudor, who was responsible for supply of material to the navy. In reference to the private shipyards working on navy contracts, he stated that 'at the end of March the amount of work put in by the men was much less than would reasonably be expected… the men were doing less work than would be regarded as an ordinary week's work in peace days. The problem was not to increase the normal output of these men, but to get them to do a normal week's work.'[46] He added some statistics:

> During a week in one yard turning out submarines only 60 fitters out of 135 worked a full day on a Monday; on a Tuesday only 90; on a Wednesday only 86; on Thursday only 77, on Friday only 91; and on Saturday [pay day] only 103.
>
> On the basis of an ordinary week's work in times of peace these men should have worked 7,155 hours; the actual hours they did work was 5,533.

The Home Office conducted a series of independent enquiries in the dockyards of the Clyde, the Tyne, Barrow, Sunderland, Stockton and Hartlepool. They found that the streets around the shipyards and docks were full of public houses and men visited them before work and during their breaks. On being paid on Saturday the evening would be spent in the pub, and all day Sunday, with the subsequent hangover keeping them home on the Monday. Because of the high wages being paid, some men realized that they could earn so much on overtime at weekends that they needn't come back to work until Wednesday.[47] Fireman and stokers went on board ship drunk, and were unable to get up the steam for the ship to depart on time. Dockers 'knocked-off' early so that they could get to the pubs before closing time, regardless of the need to load or unload.

The appendix to Shadwell's *Drink in 1914–1922* provides many examples of the problems faced by shipbuilders, ironworks, and the docks.[48] One story stands out: by December 1915 the 1st Division was in urgent need of reinforcements, having been fighting in France since the outbreak of war. On 19 December around a thousand reserves from 3 Battalion Royal Munster Fusiliers, 1 Battalion Black Watch and 1 Battalion Queen's Own Cameron Highlanders were sent from bases in Ireland and Scotland to the Southampton docks. They embarked on the SS *Honorius* and prepared for the voyage across the Channel to Le Havre. As a steamship the boilers for the engines were operated by eleven firemen, but at 3.30 pm only four of them had reported for duty. Steam was raised for a 6 pm departure but the missing crewmen failed to appear. Eventually two of the men arrived at 7 pm, one of them intoxicated. Police shortly informed Captain John Roberts that two more had been detained at the Bargate police station on charges of drunkenness. As the remaining men were tracked down the captain decided that he would be unable to make the crossing that day and the troops were transferred to another vessel.[49]

The seven men were charged under section 225 (e) of the Merchant Shipping Act, 1894, which stated that if a man '… combines with any of the crew to disobey lawful commands, or to neglect duty, or to impede the navigation of the ship or the progress of the voyage, he shall be liable to imprisonment for a period not exceeding 12 weeks'.

At their trial at the Southampton magistrates' court on 21 January 1915 Commander Perfect, representing the naval authorities, made strong representations that this was a serious matter of national importance. The magistrates agreed and had no hesitation in sending the seven men to prison for twelve weeks with hard labour.[50] By 2 June 1915 the Defence of the Realm regulations were updated to include 39A: Neglecting to Join Ship, or Joining in a State of Drunkenness.

Wartime research revealed hitherto unreported drinking practices: the workmen on the Clyde enjoyed a half gill of whisky, followed by a schooner of beer. On the Tyne the popular drink was beer, and unlike his Scottish counterpart the English workman drank consistently throughout the week.[51] There was a particular problem with 'industrial drinking' ('drinking as an aid to muscular work'[52]) in which manual workers, such as miners and shipbuilders, went to the pub in the morning before work and, in the case of steel workers, during their breaks, and drank considerable quantities of beer. There was also the habit of buying rounds, in which each member of the work gang had to buy a drink for all the others, in turn, and it was a serious breach of social etiquette to fail to stand one's round. It was also recognized that industrial inefficiencies had other sources: fatigue from extensive overtime, loss of industrial power from skilled men enlisting, and even a lack of an organized and adequate food supply at or near the factories and yards.

Following considerable debate in the House of Commons and in the press, both prohibition and the punitive taxation of liquor were finally rejected, and on May 19 1915 the Defence of the Realm (Amendment) (No. 3) Act was passed. The preamble stated that:

Where it appears to His Majesty that it is expedient for the purpose of the successful prosecution of the present war that the sale and supply of intoxicating liquor in any area should be controlled by the State, on the ground that war material is being made or loaded or unloaded or dealt with in transit in the area or that men belonging to His Majesty's naval or military forces are assembled in the area, His Majesty has power, by Order in Council, to define the area and to apply to the area the regulations issued in pursuance of this Act under the Defence of the Realm Consolidation Act, 1914.

It also provided for 'the prescribed Government authority' to take control of the supply and sale of intoxicating liquor in the area, including the power to acquire licensed premises.

The use of the DoRA was to be expected. On 16 March 1915 the Defence of the Realm (Amendment) (No. 2) Act gave powers to take possession of factories and workshops for the production of war material. Extending government control to the liquor trade was a logical next step. Magistrates would have been disappointed by this. The Intoxicating Liquor (Temporary Restrictions) Act had been an attempt to control the drink problem by using existing structures and processes for the control of licensing and liquor control but clearly this was insufficient and ineffective. Rather than amending the existing Act and perhaps grant the courts additional powers, the government had decided to take over. To complicate matters, offences relating to drinking might now fall under the existing Licensing (Consolidation) Act, 1910, the Intoxicating Liquor (Temporary Restrictions) Act, 1914 or the Defence of the Realm Act regulations.

The 'prescribed Government authority' was the Central Control Board (Liquor Traffic) and, on its formation on 27 May 1915, drew its membership from the Admiralty, War Office, Home Office, employers of labour, Labour organizations, and 'men of wider interests', under the chairmanship of Lord D'Abernon.[53]

On 10 June 1915 the Liquor Control Regulations were issued under the following headings:

1. Constitution of the Board.
2. Powers of the Board to control sale of liquor.
3. Power of Board to prohibit sale of liquor except by themselves.
4. Power to prohibit treating.
5. Power to establish refreshment rooms.
6. Power to acquire premises.
7. Procedure for compulsory acquisition.
8. Power to acquire businesses.
9. Immunity from licensing laws.
10. Provision of entertainment and recreation.
11. Provision of postal and banking facilities.
12. Provision as to dilution of spirits.
13. Suspension of covenants, etc.
14. Suspension of licences.
15. Power to grant excise licence on authority from the Board.
16. Delegation of powers by resolution.
17. Supplemental powers.
18. Powers of inspectors.
19. Prohibition on obstructing inspectors, etc.
20. Attempts to commit offences.
21. Penalties.
22. Exemption from penalties under licensing law.
23. Notice to be given to Commissioners of Customs and Excise.
24. Enforcement by police.

Regulations 25 to 28 dealt with application of the regulations to Scotland, Ireland, definitions and short title.

The Board was empowered to apply these regulations to defined areas, according to the industrial and military efficiency needs. The work of the Liquor Control Board is admirably recorded in *The Control of the Liquor Trade* by Reverend Henry Carter, a member of the Board. Although a keen advocate of temperance, he fully supported the 'efficiency' ethos of the Board and of the regulations. Carter differentiated the work of the Board into the obvious *restrictive* component but also a positive *constructive* component – it will be noted that a number of the regulations were more concerned with offering alternatives to the public house and the consumption of intoxicating liquor, such as regulation 10 which would require employers to provide on-site canteens for the provision of food and non-alcoholic refreshments, and entertainment.

The existing restriction orders were unaffected and applied either to an area defined by the military authority or to the area controlled by the licensing justices. The areas to which the new regulations were to apply (non-military areas where there was a 'drink difficulty'[54]) had to be brought to the attention of the Liquor Control Board and then defined by an Order in Council. This was done in consultation with local employers, military and naval and civil authorities, and the new government department, the Ministry of Munitions, with a 'careful investigation to satisfy [the Board] of the actual local conditions so that interference is in the interests of the efficiency of the locality for the purposes of the war'.[55] The first areas were:

Newhaven	26 July 1915
Southampton	2 August
Barrow-in-Furness	2 August
Dartford District	6 August
North East Coast	10 August
Bristol and Avonmouth	10 August
Liverpool and Mersey District	16 August
Newport	18 August
Cardiff	18 August
Barry	18 August
Scotland, West Central	23 August
Scotland, East Central	23 August
Scotland, Northern	27 September
London	11 October

Within these areas, defined by Order in Council, the Board could:

1. Close licensed premises or clubs, either for all purposes or the purpose of the sale or supply of intoxicating liquor.
2. Regulate the hours during which licensed premises or clubs might be kept open, for the sale or supply of liquor, or for other purposes.
3. Prohibit the sale by retail or supply of any specified class of liquor.
4. Impose conditions or restrictions on the sale by retail or supply of liquor.
5. Regulate the introduction of liquor into, and its transport within, an area.
6. Require the business carried on in any licensed premises in the area to be carried on subject to the supervision of the Board.
7. Prohibit treating.

Bow Street police court, near Covent Garden, was one of the most famous magistrates' courts in the country. It closed in 2006. (*Essex Police Museum*)

Bow Street police station, which also contained the courtroom. Many people, including the magistrates, were unhappy with the apparent connection between the police and the courts system. (*Essex Police Museum*)

Court stamps were attached to court documents as proof of payment. 2s would pay for a summons. (*Author's collection*)

The Judge. "THREE YEARS."
Optimistic Prisoner. "COULDN'T YOU MAKE IT 'THREE YEARS OR THE DURATION OF THE WAR,' ME LUD?"

Three years' imprisonment was the minimum sentence for the convict prisons. (Punch, *7 June 1916*

WARNING.

Defence of the Realm

Discussion in Public of Naval and Military matters may convey information to the enemy.

BE ON YOUR GUARD.

J. Walker, Printer, Northallerton.

Under regulation 18 it was prohibited to obtain and communicate military information. Under regulation 60 it was an offence to tamper with, or deface, posters such as these that appeared all over the country throughout the war. (*Author's collection*)

Field Marshal Lord Kitchener's recruitment drive encouraged towns and communities to compete against each other in providing recruits. (*British Newspaper Archive*)

The tiny British Expeditionary Force of 1914 was supplemented by reservists and Territorials in the first year of the war. Men responding to Kitchener's appeal didn't arrive in France until late 1915 and early 1916. (*British Newspaper Archive*)

Your King and your Country need you.

A CALL TO ARMS.

An addition of 100,000 men to His Majesty's Regular Army are immediately necessary in the present grave National Emergency.

Lord Kitchener is confident that this appeal will be at once responded to by all those who have the safety of the Empire at heart.

TERMS OF SERVICE.

General service for a period of three years or until the war is concluded. Age of enlistment between 19 and 30.

HOW TO JOIN.

Full information can be obtained at any Post Office in the Kingdom or at any Military depot.

God Save the King!

By the KING.

A PROCLAMATION

Regarding the Defence of the Realm.

GEORGE R.I.

WHEREAS by the Law of Our Realm it is Our undoubted prerogative and the duty of all Our loyal subjects acting in Our behalf in times of imminent national danger to take all such measures as may be necessary for securing the public safety and the defence of Our Realm :

And whereas the present state of public affairs in Europe is such as to constitute an imminent national danger.

Now, THEREFORE, We strictly command and enjoin Our subjects to obey and conform to all instructions and regulations which may be issued by Us or Our Admiralty or Army Council, or any officer of Our Navy or Army, or any other person acting in Our behalf for securing the objects aforesaid, and not to hinder or obstruct, but to afford all assistance in their power to, any person acting in accordance with any such instructions or regulations or otherwise in the execution of any measures duly taken for securing those objects.

Given at Our Court at Buckingham Palace, this Fourth day of August, in the year of our Lord one thousand nine hundred and fourteen, and in the Fifth year of Our Reign.

GOD SAVE THE KING.

The King's Proclamation was issued on 4 August, even before war was declared. The proclamation in itself had no legal effect. (*British Newspaper Archive*)

Civilians would learn much about the military legal system during the war. (*Author's collection*)

" IS YOUR SON GETTING ON ALRIGHT
  IN THE ARMY ?"
" YES, I THINK SO, HE SAYS HE'S IN FOR
  A COURT MARTIAL "

Private Wallace Williams was shot and killed by a comrade during a riot at Upwey Camp in November, 1914. Corporal Wilson was convicted of mutiny by court-martial but the Director of Public Prosecutions decided not to prosecute him for William's manslaughter. (*Melcome Regis Cemetery, Weymouth. Photograph by Sandie Sapsford*)

THE SUPER-STATESMAN.

The Majesty of the Law (to Anti-German rioter). "YOU ARE CHARGED WITH A VERY GRAVE OFFENCE. WHAT HAVE YOU TO SAY FOR YOURSELF?"

Prisoner. "WELL, ME LUD, I DON'T WANT TO BOAST, BUT THEY DO SAY AS I 'VE GIVE THE GOVERNMENT A LEAD.'"

Up until the sinking of the *Lusitania* in May 1915 there was remarkably little anti–German sentiment. (Punch, *19 May 1915*)

Government ale, produced from 1917, had a strength of around 2% ABV. (*Author's collection*)

WARNING TO CIVILIANS.

DRINK MUST NOT BE OFFERED TO

SAILORS AND SOLDIERS.

Civilians are requested on no account to offer drink to sailors and soldiers doing duty in the Fortress. It is an act of mistaken kindness to do anything which may help to unfit members of H.M. Forces from performing their duty to the Empire.

Any publican who serves either a sailor or soldier with an ammount of liquor which is likely to render them unfit to perform their duty will be most severely dealt with by the Fortress Commander under the power conferred upon him. All ranks of society are earnestly desired to observe this notice.

A. T. PENTON, Major-General, Fortress Commander.

A notice under regulation 40 for the people of Cornwall. (*British Newspaper Archive*)

Right: Nottingham followed the example of Norwich and Grimsby by imposing very strict controls of lighting during air raids. (*British Newspaper Archive*)

CITY. OF NOTTINGHAM.

PROTECTION AGAINST RAIDS BY HOSTILE AIRCRAFT.

STRIKING OF MATCHES, &c.

THE PUBLIC are required to especially Note that after the Hooters have sounded an Air raid alarm,

(1) The striking of Matches;

(2) The use of Flash Lights. Hand Lamps, Candles, and other Lights

in the STREETS and other OPEN PLACES is STRICTLY PROHIBITED, and the Police have received explicit orders to promptly enforce compliance with this instruction.

It is also of the greatest importance that all persons in the streets should proceed quietly and quickly to their homes.

Dated this 25th day of September, 1916.

JOHN G. SMALL, Mayor.

JOHN T. McCRAITH, Chairman of the Watch and Local Emergency Committee.

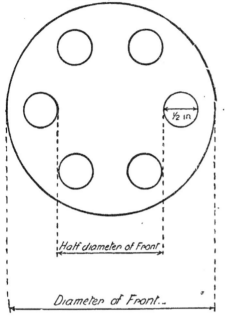

SECOND SCHEDULE.

Illustration of the cap or disc referred to in paragraph (1) of Part III. of the Order.

½ in

Half diameter of Front

Diameter of Front...

An order under regulation 11 was issued in October 1917 which required drivers of motor vehicles to obscure their headlights using this template. (*British Newspaper Archive*)

IN DARKEST LONDON.

" Dropped anything?".   " No."
" What are you looking for, then?"   " Leicester Square."

The lighting restrictions during the First World War were generally less restrictive than those of the Second World War. (Punch, *1 December 1915*)

Air raid warnings ranged from electric hooters, factory sirens, maroons and police officers on bicycles. The 'all clear' was often sounded on bugles by Boy Scouts. (*Essex Police Museum*)

Below: There was a constant demand for skilled manpower for specialist units of the Army. (*British Newspaper Archive*)

The following SKILLED MEN are REQUIRED for the
MECHANICAL TRANSPORT SECTION
OF THE
ARMY SERVICE CORPS:

MOTOR DRIVERS,
STEAM WAGON DRIVERS,
MOTOR FITTERS,
TURNERS,
MOTOR CYCLE FITTERS,
PEDAL CYCLE FITTERS,
MOTOR SMITHS,
MOTOR ELECTRICIANS,
SHEET METAL WORKERS,
PANEL BEATERS,
MOTOR SPARE PART STOREKEEPERS,
TECHNICAL DRAUGHTSMEN (used to Engine Work).
Also Learner Fitters, Turners, Smiths, etc.

A MECHANICAL TRANSPORT OFFICER will INTERVIEW RECRUITS. who should bring references. at
DRILL HALL, CHELMSFORD, on TUESDAY, OCT. 3rd, 1916, at 10.30 a.m.

R.—41

Name of Local Tribunal **CHISWICK.**

Number of Case 77.

MILITARY SERVICE ACT, 1916.

APPLICATION AS TO EXEMPTION.

(The attached duplicate must also be filled up by the Applicant.)

Any person making a false statement or false representation is liable to imprisonment.

1. Man in respect of whom application made :—
   - (a) Name (*in full*) ... ... *George Hagelton Fromow*
   - (b) Age ... ... *27.*
   - (c) Address (*in full*) ... ... *1 Wellesley Road Chiswick*
   - (d) Occupation, profession or business (*Give full and exact details*)
     Nurseryman. Foreman and Salesman. Regular Itinerant Minister. (Strict Baptist Denomination

2. If an employed person :—
   - (a) **Name** of employer ... ... *W. Fromow & Sons*
   - (b) **Address** (*in full*) ... ... *Sutton Court Nursery Chiswick*
   - (c) **Business** ... ... *Nursery.*

3. Ground on which application is made. [*See footnote. It will be sufficient if the letter* (a), (b), (c), (d), (e), (f) *or* (g) (*whichever is appropriate*), *is entered.*]

4. Nature of application. (*A certificate of exemption may be absolute, conditional or temporary. Also, a certificate granted on conscientious grounds may be for exemption from combatant service only, or may be conditional on the applicant being engaged in some work which, in the opinion of the Tribunal, is of national importance.*)

   Absolute exemption from military service

Application may be made:—
  (a) On the ground that it is expedient in the national interests that the man should, instead of being employed in military service, be engaged in other work in which he is habitually engaged; or
  (b) On the ground that it is expedient in the national interests that the man should, instead of being employed in military service, be engaged in other work in which he wishes to be engaged; or
  (c) If he is being educated or trained for any work, on the ground that it is expedient in the national interests that, instead of being employed in military service, he should continue to be so educated or trained; or
  (d) On the ground that serious hardship would ensue, if the man were called up for Army service, owing to his exceptional financial or business obligations or domestic position; or
  (e) On the ground of ill-health or infirmity; or
  (f) On the ground of a conscientious objection to the undertaking of combatant service.
Application may also be made for exemption—
  (g) On the ground that the principal and usual occupation of the man is one of those included in the list of occupations certified by Government Departments for exemption. The official list of the certified occupations may be consulted at the offices of the Local Tribunal or of the recruiting officer.
An application may be made for the withdrawal or variation of any certificate of exemption by the holder of the certificate or by a military representative.
An appeal from the decision of the Local Tribunal lies to the Appeal Tribunal for the area.

[P.T.O.

(b5683) 280M. 2/16 H & S

George Fromow appeared before Chiswick magistrates for failing to report under the Military Service Act. He appealed for exemption and was eventually given non-combatant service. (*www.ancestry.co.uk*)

SINGLE MEN FIRST
HOW THE GROUP SYSTEM WORKS

THE GROUPS	
SINGLE	MARRIED
1st GROUP — Single Men of 18	24th GROUP — Married Men of 18
2nd GROUP — Single Men of 19	25th GROUP — Married Men of 19
3rd GROUP — Single Men of 20	26th GROUP — Married Men of 20
4th GROUP — Single Men of 21	27th GROUP — Married Men of 21
5th GROUP — Single Men of 22	28th GROUP — Married Men of 22
6th GROUP — Single Men of 23	29th GROUP — Married Men of 23
7th GROUP — Single Men of 24	30th GROUP — Married Men of 24
8th GROUP — Single Men of 25	31st GROUP — Married Men of 25
9th GROUP — Single Men of 26	32nd GROUP — Married Men of 26
10th GROUP — Single Men of 27	33rd GROUP — Married Men of 27
11th GROUP — Single Men of 28	34th GROUP — Married Men of 28
12th GROUP — Single Men of 29	35th GROUP — Married Men of 29
13th GROUP — Single Men of 30	36th GROUP — Married Men of 30
14th GROUP — Single Men of 31	37th GROUP — Married Men of 31
15th GROUP — Single Men of 32	38th GROUP — Married Men of 32
16th GROUP — Single Men of 33	39th GROUP — Married Men of 33
17th GROUP — Single Men of 34	40th GROUP — Married Men of 34
18th GROUP — Single Men of 35	41st GROUP — Married Men of 35
19th GROUP — Single Men of 36	42nd GROUP — Married Men of 36
20th GROUP — Single Men of 37	43rd GROUP — Married Men of 37
21st GROUP — Single Men of 38	44th GROUP — Married Men of 38
22nd GROUP — Single Men of 39	45th GROUP — Married Men of 39
23rd GROUP — Single Men of 40	46th GROUP — Married Men of 40

YOU CAN ENLIST NOW

and become at once a Soldier in training

OR

YOU CAN ENLIST UNDER THE GROUP SYSTEM

Under this system you will be enlisted for one day, and at your own request you will be transferred at once to Section B Army Reserve, and allowed to return to your home until the Group in which you are placed is called up for service.

You will be given an Armlet bearing the Royal Crown. Opportunities will be given you of voluntary preliminary drill. You will be given a fortnight's notice before you need actually join your unit.

You will, therefore, be able to continue your usual work until you receive this call, which will allow you time to give notice to your employer, or arrange your affairs.

There are 46 Groups, which are set out at side. The Single Men will be put into the first 23 Groups according to age, and the men entered upon the National Register as Married Men will be put into the following 23 Groups also according to age.

The Groups will be called up in the order of their numbers (but in no case will anyone be called up until he has attained the age of 19 years).

In short,

SINGLE MEN WILL BE CALLED FIRST

Men who have married since their Registration, and Widowers without children, will be regarded as Single Men.

When a Group is called up by Proclamation, any man in that Group will be able, if he so desires, and if there are very special circumstances in his case, to make an appeal to be placed in a later Group.

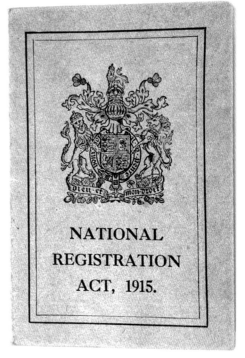

NATIONAL REGISTRATION ACT, 1915.

Lord Derby's Group System was an embarrassing failure. Despite the assurances given by Derby and by the Prime Minister, married men were called up within weeks of the scheme starting. (*Author's collection*)

Following the great National Registration exercise on 15 August 1915, all adults were issued with an identity card. (*Author's collection*)

It is requested that the Admiralty and War Office Forms giving descriptions of Deserters, &c., from His Majesty's Naval and Military Services for insertion in the POLICE GAZETTE, and all communications in connection therewith, shall be addressed to THE EDITOR of the POLICE GAZETTE, New Scotland Yard, London, S.W.

WAR OFFICE, AUGUST 11, 1914.
DESERTERS AND ABSENTEES FROM HIS MAJESTY'S SERVICE.

Office No.	NAME.	REG. NO.	CORPS.	AGE	HEIGHT	COM. PLXN.	HAIR.	EYES.	TRADE.	ENLISTMENT DATE OF	ENLISTMENT PLACE OF	PARISH AND COUNTY IN WHICH BORN	DESERTION OR ABSENCE DATE OF	DESERTION OR ABSENCE PLACE OF	MARKS AND REMARKS.
1	Buckland, Charles	6981	3rd Dragoon G	20	5 7	fresh	brn	blue	ship trmm	6 June '12	Liverpool	Dingle, Liverpool	27 July	Newport	hrt arrw CB l frm
2	Bareroft, J.	5899	E. Cav. Depôt	29	5 6½	fresh	brn	brn	sister	1 July '14	Blackburn	S. Andrews, Darwen	19 July	Woolwich	2 scs bk neck 2 l ed hd
3	Bishop, A.	16105	1st Grenadr G.	19	5 8½	fresh	brn	brn	miller	21 Oct. '12	Nottinghm	Camberwell, London	31 July	London	crossd flags rt frm
4	Gorham, T. A.	5484	E. Cav. Depôt	29	5 6	fresh	brn	grey	carman	4 June '14	Hounslow	Kensington, Middlsx	10 July	Woolwich	sc l knee
5	Bragg, Irving	11768	1st Liverpool R.	19	5 2	sallow	brn	blue	ca'ual labr	6 Dec. '13	Liverpool	Millom, Cumberland	25 July	Aldershot	sc rt al hd star cresnt hrshoe rt frm
6	Buckley, Wilfred	10567	2nd W. Rdg. R.	24	5 3	fresh	brn	blugy	labourer	6 June '14	Huddersfld	Dalton, York	1 Aug.	Dublin	flags rt frm indst tto l
7	Byrne, James	3621	1st Irish Gds.	23	5 5	fresh	brn	blue	farm labr	2 Nov. '10	Dublin	Enniskerry, Wicklw	31 July	London	
8	Cauldwell, J.	23469	R. Garrison Art.	28	5 9½	fresh	tk brn	lt brn	farm servt	21 Aug. '03	Dundee	Boghead, Forfar	30 July	Craigr'thie	2 moles sc l upr arm 6 scs bk scalp
9	Challenger, Thomas	11029	3rd Hussars	20	5 6	fresh	brn	black	collier	13 Mar. '14	Workingtn	Bedwelly, Ebbw Vale	31 July	Shorncliffe	
10	Craig, David	1361	1st Scat. Hghs	19	5 8	fresh	lt brn	grey	coal miner	31 Mar '14	Bathgate	Shotts, Lanark	31 July	Ft. George	fig lady's rt frm claspd hnds wrist
11	Creagh, Peter	19210	2nd Leinster R.	22	5 4	fresh	dk brn	grey	casual labr	16 July '14	Drogheda	St. Mary's, Drogheda	27 July	Cork	
12	Crow, G. W.	17564	R. Field Art.	21	5 4	fresh	brn	brn	labourer	30 Dec. '12	Stratford	Bethnal Green	9 Aug.	Woolwich	3 scs rt side
13	Dunphy, Avlen	10260	2nd R. Irish R.	24	5 9	fair	lt brn	blue	clerk	16 Feb. '14	Waterford	New Ross, Wexford	25 July	Devonport	sc ovr l eyebrow
14	Evans, W. J.	76295	R. Field Art.	21	5 4	fresh	brn	brn	hawker	8 May '14	Woolwich	Deptford, Kent	5 Aug.	Woolwich	sc l sd neck wreath 2 birds rt arm
15	Fay, Water	74969	60th Bty R.F.A.	22	5 4	fresh	brn	brn	valet	13 Nov. '13	Chester	Harrow, Middlesex	4 Aug.	Brighton	sc frnt l shin rt sd nose
16	Flattley, Frank	1308	2nd Mnchstr R.	24	5 5	fresh	brn	grey	gen labr	29 Sept. '08	Ashtn-u-L	S. Augustns, Mnchstr	30 June	Curragh	sc ovr rt eye

Desertion and absenteeism were rife throughout the war. Although in many cases missed trains and connections were to blame, the defaulter's details were circulated in the weekly *Police Gazette*. (*British Newspaper Archive*)

The Silver War Badge was issued to men who had been discharged from the Army or Navy through wounds or infirmity. The badge was accompanied by a certificate, which had to be shown, on demand, to a police constable. (*Author's collection*)

Men who worked in munitions or in particular trades or professions were exempted from military service. (*Author's collection*)

The Farmer. "DON'T YOU KNOW, YOU LITTLE THIEF, I COULD GET YOU TEN YEARS IN JAIL FUR STEALIN' MY APPLES?"
The Boy. "EXCUSE ME, SIR, BUT YOU ARE ABSOLUTELY MISINFORMED. I SHOULD COME UNDER THE FIRST OFFENDERS ACT."

Bind-overs and probation were seen as increasingly ineffective as youth crime increased substantially during the war. (Punch, *5 September 1917*)

Men in civilian clothes were likely to attract negative comment, so munitions factories, dockyards and other national service employers provided badges to show that their employees were engaged on work of national importance. The badges were standardized and controlled from early 1915. (*Author's collection*)

Women involved in munitions work were issued with their own badges. It was an offence to wear a badge if not entitled to do so. (*Author's collection*)

DEFENCE OF THE REALM.
E.P. 6.

MINISTRY OF FOOD.

BREACHES OF THE RATIONING ORDER

The undermentioned convictions have been recently obtained:—

Court	Date	Nature of Offence	Result
HENDON - -	29th Aug., 1918	Unlawfully obtaining and using ration books -	3 Months' Imprisonment
WEST HAM -	29th Aug., 1918	Being a retailer & failing to detach proper number of coupons	Fined £20
SMETHWICK -	22nd July, 1918	Obtaining meat in excess quantities - - -	Fined £50 & £5 5s. costs
OLD STREET -	4th Sept., 1918	Being a retailer selling to unregistered customer	Fined £72 & £5 5s. costs
OLD STREET -	4th Sept., 1918	Not detaching sufficient coupons for meat sold -	Fined £25 & £2 2s. costs
CHESTER-LE-STREET	4th Sept., 1918	Being a retailer returning number of registered customers in excess of counterfoils deposited - - - -	Fined £50 & £3 3s. costs
HIGH WYCOMBE	7th Sept., 1918	Making false statement on application for and using Ration Books unlawfully - - - - - - -	Fined £40 & £6 4s. costs

Enforcement Branch, Local Authorities Division,
MINISTRY OF FOOD.
September, 1918.

The Food Controller, Lord Rhondda, was publicly critical of the leniency of the magistrates in dealing with rationing offences. But perhaps they were right to be so – the Ministry of Food produced a constant barrage of badly-worded orders that the local authorities and courts struggled to understand. (*Author's collection*)

THERE'S A WAR ON!

P.C I.C.U.: " Have they taken any other valuables besides the Matches, Sir ? "

Matches were in short supply and their sale strictly controlled. (*Author's collection*)

Anxious Mother. "NEVER MIND ABOUT YOUR BROTHER, MAUD. 'OLD THE UMBRELLER OVER THE SUGAR!"

Sugar was the first food item to be rationed, in January 1918. (Punch, *24 January 1917*)

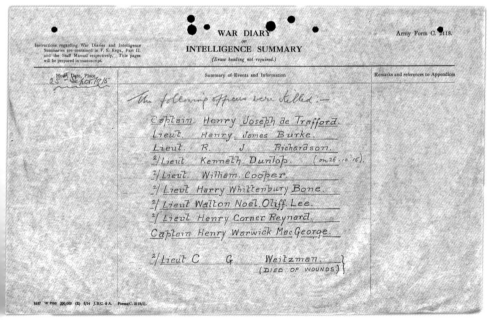

The page from the War Diary of 1 Battalion, South Staffordshire Regiment, recording the deaths of Captain de Trafford and his fellow officers. Only three officers survived. (*www.ancestry.co.uk*)

Lance Corporal John Charles Lane, Wessex Section, Royal Engineers. Served at Winchester and survived the war. (*D\B\ta/42/17 Picture courtesy of Taunton Deane Borough Council and Somerset Heritage Centre. With kind permission of South West Heritage Trust*)

MY DUTIES BRING ME IN TOUCH WITH SOME BIG 'POTS'!

Special constables had a critical rôle in maintaining public order, by supervising the lighting and liquor restrictions and in registering and monitoring aliens. (*Author's collection*)

Special Constable (to suspicious lounger). "NOW, LOOK HERE, IF YOU DON'T CLEAR OFF, I'LL—TELL YOU WHAT I'LL DO— I'LL CALL A POLICEMAN!"

The first special constables were not taken seriously. Ill–equipped and poorly-trained, they often suffered poor morale thanks to tedious duties such as guarding railway stations and reservoirs. (Punch, *14 October 1914*)

Captain Arthur Corbett Edwards, 8 (Service) Battalion, Queen's Own Royal West Kent Regiment. Killed in action along with 550 of his men on 30 August 1915 at Loos. (*British Newspaper Archive*)

Special Constable Herbert Gripper, SC413, of Chelmsford. Gripper's diary and archives of his service as a special can be seen at the Essex Record Office. (*British Newspaper Archive*)

Painted specially for this work] [*By J. P. Campbell.*

CAPTAIN E. N. E. M. VAUGHAN AND HIS MEN DRIVE BACK THE ENEMY FROM AN ISOLATED TRENCH.

When in command of an isolated trench and attacked on front, flank and rear, Captain Eugene Napoleon Ernest Mallet Vaughan (Reserve of Officers), Grenadier Guards, drove off the enemy, killing over 100 of them, and took twenty prisoners. His fine example gave great confidence to his men and he was subsequently awarded the D.S.O. for his conspicuous gallantry.

Captain Eugene Napoleon Ernest Mallett Vaughan, 1 Battalion, Grenadier Guards. Awarded the Distinguished Service Order for conspicuous gallantry in fighting off a German counter-attack on his trench at Ginchy, on the Somme, 10 September 1916. He survived the war and returned to Stafford. (*Author's collection*)

The wartime special constables were issued with a warrant card, an armband and, supplies permitting, a whistle and a truncheon. (*Essex Record Office*)

Lieutenant Colonel Egerton Stanley Pipe Wolferstan, 10 Battalion, Prince of Wales' North Staffordshire Regiment. Served in Okehampton and Cannock Chase. Survived the war. (*With kind permission of Tamworth Castle Museum [6817] (29/5576)*)

8. Direct or permit the dilution of spirits to an extent beyond that allowed under the Sale of Food and Drugs Act.

Oddly the first areas were defined by circles so, for example, the Newhaven controlled area was 'the district within the circumference of a circle with a radius of one and three quarter miles of the Town Railway station'. This flawed approach took no account of existing military areas nor of the jurisdiction of licensing bench or the police authority and produced a patchwork of different orders, much to the annoyance of the police commissioners. This rapidly evolved into a more workable system based on logical administrative boundaries, but of course this would then include areas in which there was no 'drink difficulty'. The previously-mentioned willingness of workers to travel outside restricted areas was addressed by adding a 'protective fringe', and the controlled areas grew larger and eventually merged – Newhaven was incorporated in the South-Eastern controlled area.

A typical order, such as the Order of the Central Control Board (Liquor Traffic) for the Eastern Area,[56] contained the following sections:

1. Limits of Area.
2. Hours during which intoxicating liquor may be sold, on premises and off premises.
3. Additional restrictions as to Spirits.
4. Conditions as to Distribution.
5. Hours of Opening for the Supply of Food and Non-Intoxicants.
6. Saving Provisions.
7. Treating Prohibited.
8. Credit Prohibited.
9. Long Pull Prohibited.
10. Dilution of Spirits, compulsory and permissive.
11. Sale of Light Beer.
12. Explanatory provisions.
13. Exhibition of Order.
14. Commencement of Order.

By 9 September 1915 *The Times* was reporting that the effects of the new regulations on drunkenness was substantial and that there was 'an improvement in both time-keeping and the fitness and efficiency of the men when they come to work'.[57] Reports from Newcastle upon Tyne, Barrow, Middlesbrough, Liverpool and Cardiff attributed this in part to the restriction of hours but more importantly to the prohibition of treating,[58] and *The Times* wanted to see the extension of the regulations to other areas. There were up to 50 per cent reductions in prosecutions and convictions for drunkenness in the controlled areas, and publicans were complaining of a serious drop in takings.[59] By November the Metropolitan Police were reporting that in the three weeks following the no-treating order, average weekly convictions for drunkenness fell from 993 to 695.[60] At the conference of chief constables on 24 September there was unanimous agreement that 'no treating' order was particularly effective at reducing drunkenness.[61]

Average weekly convictions	4 weeks before	First week	Second week
Newcastle	76	36	43
Gateshead	28	9	5
South Shields	19	12	8
Middlesbrough	45	14	17
Liverpool	217	118	
Birkenhead	20	17	

There was a shift in language used by the Board – rather than describing 'closing hours', as used in the licensing acts for the last century, they now referred to 'opening hours'. In the controlled areas the hours varied slightly but in general, weekday opening was between 11.30 am and 2.00 pm, and 6.30–9.00 pm; and Sundays between 12.30–2.30 pm and 6.00–9.00 pm. Off sales ended an hour earlier. The lunchtime hours may be familiar to some readers – they remained until the Licensing Act 2003. The curtailment of hours had a substantial effect, but failed to prevent what we now call binge-drinking, the rapid consumption of large amounts of alcohol. Perhaps the most significant of the new regulations was number 4, the 'No Treating' order, which struck at the heart of British social relationships. One hundred and thirty-six persons convicted of drunkenness in Liverpool in 1915 were interviewed and asked to state the nature of the occasion which led to the offence:[62]

	Men	Women
Treating friends and conviviality, including welcome to friends returning from abroad	49	21
Illness or grief	14	7
Long abstinence from drink before the drinking bout	6	3
No food with drink	3	
No special cause alleged	23	10

Treating – or being treated – was at the top of the list, and the effect of the regulation was immediate. Regulation 4 provided that:

No person shall either by himself or by any servant or agent sell or supply any intoxicating liquor to any person in any licensed premises or in any club to be consumed on the premises unless the same is ordered and paid for by the person so supplied; nor shall any person order or pay for or lend or advance money to pay for any intoxicating liquor wherewith any other person had been or is to be supplied to be consumed on the premises; nor shall any person consume in such premises or club any intoxicating liquor which any other person has ordered or paid for or agreed or lent or advanced money to pay for.

Provided always that is such intoxicating liquor is supplied or served for consumption at a meal supplied at the same time and is consumed at such meal, the provisions of this regulation shall not be deemed to be contravened if the person who pays for the meal also pays for such intoxicating liquor.

A variation of this order subsequently appeared in the Defence of the Realm Manual as paragraph (2) of regulation 10, now amended to 'Power to close licensed premises, and to prohibit treating'.

The first legal challenge to regulation 4 occurred in Cardiff Police Court on the 17 November 1915. Joseph Pearce, the landlord of the Charing Cross Hotel, and his wife Alice Pearce, were summoned for supplying intoxicating liquor to persons to be consumed on the premises, without the same having been ordered and paid for by the person who was supplied by it. In evidence a constable stated that he had seen Mrs Pearce accept an order for three glasses of beer and one of stout from Mr Macdonald. He then handed the drinks to his friends, Mabel Wilkinson, Annie Foley and Mrs Vickery. The stipendiary magistrate, Mr T.W. Lewis, then declared that there was no evidence to show that the defendants were liable. The person who actually supplied the drinks was the man who ordered and paid for them. The magistrate followed the wording of the order exactly: 'no person shall … supply any intoxicating liquor … to be consumed in the premises … unless the same is ordered and paid for by the person so supplied'. The prosecutor, Mr Ensor, claimed that this view would defeat the purpose of the Liquor Control Order but the stipendiary was firm – 'it is not our mistake if it has not been drawn up carefully'. The case was adjourned for a week, and he went on to deal with the next matter, in which Mabel Wilkinson was charged for consuming the intoxicating liquor purchased by another (Mr McDonald). The evidence was that Mrs Pearce had placed the drinks on the table. Mr Lewis held, again, that this did not constitute 'supply' and dismissed the case. The prosecutor wisely offered no evidence against Annie Foley, but managed to secure a conviction against Mrs Vickery because she did consume part of the glass of beer that Macdonald had given her. She was fined 10s or seven days' imprisonment by default.[63]

The stipendiary's decision was confirmed the following week. The drinks in question were handed round by the person who had ordered and paid for them, and they were not 'supplied' by the defendants. The regulation, as it stood, said that the licensed person in effect did not bring himself within the meaning of the order if the liquor was ordered and paid for by the person to whom it was supplied. The summonses against the Pearces were dismissed.[64]

The 'long pull' was an unusual but legal practice where the landlord could give a larger measure than was paid for. A customer asking for a half pint of beer might be served this in a pint glass, which would allow for a generous additional amount. This was prohibited under the first orders. Sales of intoxicating liquor for consumption off the premises was seen as perfectly normal. Indeed the existing Licensing Acts allowed for children as young as 14 to purchase beer and spirits, provided it was in sealed or corked bottle, not less than one pint and taken off site. It was illegal to provide children under 5 with intoxicating liquor, and no children were permitted in the bar area; but apparently it was common to see a row of perambulators and pushchairs lined up in the corridor outside, while the mothers drank inside.[65] It was also common practice to bring your own bottle or container to be filled at the public house, and this was a notorious problem with soldiers travelling on trains. As previously noted, it was possible to obtain alcoholic drinks at a railway station at any time, so the men would take the opportunity to fill their hip flasks with whisky and other spirits. The Liquor Control Board came up with the requirement that the minimum amount that could be purchased for off consumption was the 'reputed quart', which is approximately 757 millilitres or equivalent to the volume of a modern bottle of wine. Orders for such spirits had to be made between 12.00 pm and 2.30 pm on weekdays, and were not permitted at weekends. Such large amounts were unpopular with the soldiers as it was difficult to carry such bottles in a greatcoat pocket or in the haversack. Shortly afterwards the purchase of spirits at railway stations for off consumption was prohibited altogether. The curiosity of the category of the *bona fide* traveller was finally abolished.[66]

Even with the experience of military closing orders, justices' closing orders and the new licensing control regulations, people were still unsure if they were in a controlled area, or if so, by whom it was controlled. Miss F.A. Oakley ran the Castle Hotel in Deganwy and was summoned at Conway on 6 December on a charge of having sold intoxicating liquor to a soldier at a time when such sale to soldiers was prohibited under the Defence of the Realm regulations. The prosecutor read the order as issued by the competent military authority of the St Asaph district, Major General C.G. Macdonald, which directed that soldiers in uniform should not be served with intoxicants between the hours of 2 pm and 6 pm. A copy of the order had been served on Miss Oakley. Her representative pointed out immediately that the order was irregular, as regulation 10 required such orders to state the area to which it applied. Merely serving the order on individual licencees was insufficient. The learned clerk, Mr J. Porter, advised the magistrates the regulation 10 clearly gave the officer power to make such an order 'within any area specified in the order'. There was none, so the magistrates dismissed the case.

A further amendment was made to the Defence of the Realm regulations on 22 December 1915, with the addition of regulation 40A, the 'Prohibition of supplying intoxicants to members of HM's forces undergoing hospital treatment'. This was particularly unpopular. Soldiers and sailors in the military hospitals wore a distinctive uniform of a blue tunic, blue trousers, white shirt and a red tie ('hospital blues') and were a familiar sight in many towns around the country, where there was considerable voluntary effort to support and entertain them. The offence was to give, sell, procure, supply, or offer to give, sell, procure, or supply to any member of any of His Majesty's forces who was undergoing any hospital treatment any intoxicant, and so the ladies of the local relief committees had to restrict themselves to tea, cakes and buns for the boys. Mrs Elizabeth Kirby ran the New Hall Inn as Bowness, and when three soldiers turned up in khaki caps and overcoats on 20 November she asked them if they were from the hospital and they assured her they were not. The Windermere inspector of police arrived and found the men, still in their overcoats, enjoying some drinks. After he questioned them they revealed their hospital blues. On her appearance at Windermere police court on 7 December, the soldiers apologized, 'We're very sorry, missus'. The magistrates dismissed the case.[67]

In the flurry of new orders at the end of 1915 seven new areas came under the control of the Liquor Control Board: the Midlands area, Western Borders, Portsmouth, Pembroke, Plymouth, Falmouth and West Riding.[68] One of the justices' clerks wrote a despondent letter to the *Justice of the Peace* in December, complaining that in only one small corner of his county is there a place where 'war material is made or loaded or unloaded … ' and yet the order was made on the whole county. The editors were pragmatic: 'We do not see any prospect of successfully challenging such an order on the grounds of *ultra vires*; it seems to us that Parliament has seen fit to give the Privy Council carte blanche in the matter, and that there is nothing more to be said.'[69]

There were now offences of selling or supplying, consuming or permitting consumption of intoxicating liquor during prohibited hours, but pubs were allowed to stay open to serve non-alcoholic refreshments and food. Off sales were carefully controlled. The 'no treating' provisions were amended to include the highway, open ground or railway station near the premises or club where the intoxicating liquor was obtained. Under existing legislation, licencees were not to permit drunkenness on the premises, or sell alcohol to a drunken person.

Life as a publican was difficult, and Jesse Boothman, of the Nag's Head, 20 Town Street in Chapeltown, Allerton, was treated very unfairly. He was summoned to Leeds Police Court on Thursday, 1 June 1916 for selling intoxicating liquor after hours, and for permitting treating. Seth Moore, Ned Dowgill, John Milner and William Harrison were all summoned for breaches of the no-treating order. On 16 May police constables Jilbert and Hanson had entered the pub in the evening and ordered themselves a 'nectar split', which is apparently a pint bottle of beer served in two glasses. They watched two of the defendants playing billiards, and one of them ordered a drink for himself and his friend. One of the constables bought another nectar split and shared it with his colleague. At 10.40 pm the billiards game was still in progress, and one of the defendants bought drinks for all three friends. The defence representative, Mr Arthur Willey, contended that the police officers had acted as 'agents provocateurs', in that they had committed offences themselves (the 'nectar split' was, by definition, treating), and they had sat quietly without taking any action as the other offences were committed. The stipendiary magistrate, Mr C.M. Atkinson, felt that it was highly undesirable that the police should behave that way. They were all fined £3.[70]

Having reduced the hours for the consumption of alcohol and dealt with the treating problem, the Central Control Board turned its attention to the strength of the liquor. From 6 June 1916 it was prohibited to sell whisky, brandy, rum or gin unless reduced to at least 25° under proof, and it was permitted to dilute it to 50° under proof. This is a slightly confusing measure compared to the Alcohol by Volume (ABV) standard, and is roughly 1.75 times the ABV. 100° proof was approximately 57 per cent ABV. 25° *under* proof (75° proof) is about 40 per cent ABV. A spirit described at 50° under proof is weaker than one at 75°, as it contains only 28 per cent ABV. Modern spirits are typically in the range 35 per cent–40 per cent ABV.

In January 1917 beer was available in a wide range of strengths, from around 10 per cent ABV in heavy stouts to light beers of around 2 per cent ABV,[71] with most beers being around 5 per cent. Lord Davenport, the Food Controller at the time, was deeply concerned about the national supply of grain. After a 'careful investigation of the resources available for the food of the people' he announced that beer production would be cut to half of its pre-war levels, and that wines and spirits would be released from bond. He summarized his case simply: 'It is a question of bread versus beer.' A reduction in beer production would increase the supply of barley and sugar for human food, and economise on tonnage, transport, labour and fuel.[72] Both the Central Control Board and the Food Controller supported the production and consumption of a much weaker beer, variously known as 'government' or 'munitions' beer. It was particularly promoted in the industrial centres. These beers could be as low as 1 per cent ABV; 'light and palatable' was the Food Controller's description; in Birmingham it was 'hardly on sale because we do not look upon it as beer',[73] even though it cost only 4d a pint.

In April 1917 Lord Rhondda, the new Food Controller, ignored his predecessor's recommendation for a 30 per cent reduction in beer production and passed the Intoxicating Liquor (Output and Delivery) Order, slashing beer production from 26 million barrels to 10 million barrels a year. A number of Food Control Orders were passed in quick succession, restricting or prohibiting the use of brewing ingredients such as malt (April 1917).

Price of a Pint of Beer[74]	
1914	3d
1916	5d
1917	4d (s.g of less than 1036); 5d (s.g less than 1042)
1918	4d (s.g of less than 1030); 5d (s.g less than 1034)

The effect overall on the convictions for offences related to drunkenness are profound. As with crime statistics for the period generally there are many explanations and factors to consider.

Intoxicating Liquor Laws	1914	1915	1916	1917	1918	Annual average 1914–18
Drunkenness, simple	64,225	58,065	39,870	25,208	17,665	44,047
Drunkenness, with aggravation	138,939	72,258	50,199	24,722	13,454	49,951
Unlicenced sale of drink	202	242	240	154	115	238
Habitual drunkards obtaining drink	23	13	4		1	12

Intoxicating Liquor Laws	1914	1915	1916	1917	1918	Annual average 1914–18
Offences by licensed persons						
Permitting drunkenness	652	499	505	247	150	471
Selling drink to children	118	167	186	112	100	136
Selling drink to habitual drunkards	3	1	1			2
Offences against closing regulations	318	873	2,171	1,741	925	1,059
Other offences by licensed persons	208	390	2,124	1,336	689	851
Other offences	2,366	2,684	7,092	4,883	2,737	3,749

Alcohol consumption was seen as a core part of British social life and the government could easily have caused much unrest by introducing prohibition, punitive taxes or nationalizing the liquor industry, all of which had received genuine consideration. Lloyd George, the Minister of Munitions, and the Central Control Board wisely and astutely linked the problems of military and industrial efficiency to the problem of alcohol and in so doing managed to convince the public that a sensible approach to liquor consumption was in the national interest. The Central Control Board had the responsibility 'to secure or sustain industrial activity and naval and military discipline', and through control orders and an imaginative and popular 'hygiene' approach that provided both recreational and dietary alternatives, genuinely changed public attitudes and behaviour concerning consumption. Limitation in production and supply was the domain of the Food Controller, and although in the interests of national economy, Lord Rhondda and his department were to prove less popular, particularly as shortages and rationing began to have an effect in the latter years of the war.

Chapter 8

How Bright is 'Bright'?

Zeppelin VII, the *Deutschland*, was the world's first passenger airship and she made her maiden voyage on 22 June 1910, travelling the 280 miles from Friedrichshafen on Lake Constance, to Dusseldorf 'in considerably less time than would be taken by an express train'.[1] Count Zeppelin was in command, accompanied by a pilot, engineer, two steerers and five fitters. One hundred and sixty yards in length and powered by three 100hp engines, she travelled at an average speed of around 40mph and at a height of up to 600 feet. The airship was delivered to the German Airship Travel Corporation, DELAG, which was to operate a commercial passenger service. Two days later the first passengers boarded for a pleasure flight around the Dusseldorf area. Paying about £10 each, thirty-two passengers, including ten ladies, reported that they were 'delighted with the experience, and had not a moment of discomfort'.[2] A second flight followed and with a favourable tail wind reached the speed of 56mph. The passengers occupied two mahogany-panelled saloons, one of which was fitted with a restaurant.[3] There was considerable interest in the achievement, and the announcement of cheap £5 tickets for a twenty-mile joyride brought crowds to the company offices in Cologne, but over the weekend the weather deteriorated.[4] A flight was reserved for a special cruise for newspaper journalists on Tuesday, 28 June, and a party of twenty left Dusseldorf for a two-hour flight. Ten hours later, having struggled against strong winds and storms, the great airship crashed in the Teutoberger forest and was wrecked.[5] Fortunately there was no loss of life and this high-profile disaster proved only a momentary check: Zeppelin enjoyed the support of the German government and the German people, and was undeterred from his ambitious airship construction and development plans.

The military value of aviation was recognized very early. The Germans believed that the stability, endurance and payload of the Zeppelin, Schütte-Lanz and other dirigibles could be exploited for reconnaissance and potentially offensive purposes. The French, however, believed the future lay in heavier-than-air aviation and began building a fleet of aircraft. But Britain was less sure. Questions were regularly asked in the House of Commons about Britain's commitment to air power and its ability to defend against aerial attack, and as late as 1913 the First Lord of the Admiralty, Winston Churchill, expressed scepticism about the use of airships in particular,[6] and he provided no funding in the Navy Estimates for building large dirigibles.[7] Mr Rowland Hunt, MP for Ludlow, complained that there were few or no guns available for air defence.[8] The Royal Flying Corps, which had been formed from the Air Battalion of the Royal Engineers in May 1912, and the Royal Naval Air Service, which itself was formed from the Naval Wing of the RFC in July 1914, took different views of the future of aircraft in war, with the Army believing in fixed-wing aeroplanes and the Navy in lighter-than-air craft.

At the outbreak of war all the aircraft of the Royal Flying Corps were despatched to France with the British Expeditionary Force, and on 3 September the responsibility for the air defence of the country was given to the Admiralty.[9] The potential of the threat of attack from the air was soon realized in the swift German assault on Belgium, with Zeppelins and aeroplanes dropping bombs on military targets. On 5 August a Zeppelin bombed Liège but was hit by ground fire and destroyed on landing. Two weeks later an airship was lost in action and another damaged. These early attacks exposed some of the weaknesses of the aircraft, and although air-to-air combat was ineffective, the exposure of the large, slow-moving Zeppelins to ground fire in daytime certainly caused a change in tactics, to high altitude and nighttime operations. The first nocturnal raid was on Antwerp on the night of 24/25 August, with further raids in the next few months. The Kaiser initially opposed air raids on Britain but changed his mind in January 1915, permitting attacks on military sites on the east coast but excluding London. The first raid took place on the night of 19/20 January, reaching Great Yarmouth at about 8.30 pm and continuing on to Sheringham and King's Lynn. Four people were killed and sixteen injured and, as proof of the effectiveness of the DoRA reporting restrictions, the newspapers were surprisingly muted, with no mention whatever that there were no British aircraft sent up, nor was there any anti-aircraft artillery, nor, indeed, were there any searchlights. Navigation techniques were primitive and the Zeppelin pilots used visual landmarks such as coastal features and, by night, they flew towards the glow from the towns and cities.

The publication of the first Defence of the Realm regulations on 12 August 1914 provided that the competent naval or military authority could order the extinguishment of all lights at any defended harbour (regulation 23 and later amended to cover any military installation or camp). On Thursday, 17 September the regulation was amended by an Order in Council:

> The Secretary of State may, by order, direct that all or any lights or lights of any class or description, shall be extinguished, or obscured in such manner and between such hours as the order directs, within any area specified in the order and during such period as may be so specified, and if the person having control of the light fails to comply with the order, the Secretary of State may cause the light to be extinguished or obscured as the case may be, and for that purpose any person authorized by the Secretary of State in that behalf or any police constable may enter the premises in which the light is displayed, and to any other act which may be necessary for the purpose.[10]

Rather than being an amendment to regulation 23, this was actually added as 7A, under regulation 7, which restricted the sale of alcohol within specified areas. The power of a police officer to enter *private* premises without a warrant was rather unusual for a non-felony offence.

Almost immediately the Air Department of the Admiralty requested that the Commissioner of Police in the London Metropolitan district should reduce lighting in the streets and shops, and a naval airship was sent over London to observe the effects of street lighting.[11] The 'assistance of the public' was requested:

In order to render more difficult the identification of particular parts of London, it is requested that arc lights, skysigns, illuminated fascias, and powerful lights of all descriptions used outside for advertising or brilliantly illuminating shop fronts be dispensed with.

Where a shop front consists of a considerable area of glass, brilliantly lit from the inside, a reduction in lighting intensity should be effected.[12]

Aberdeen imposed lighting restrictions on 26 September, and Dundee followed on 30 September,[13] along with Scarborough, Hull and many east coast towns.[14] Even though it didn't consider itself a target, Birmingham reduced lighting by one-third in key areas.[15] The good people of Guildford were alarmed by the need for reduced lighting in their town and had to be reassured that although at the time they were not subject to a full lighting order, where necessary steps might be taken locally to reduce 'powerful elevated lights or sky signs', and so the outside lights at the Theatre, Picture Palace and the Cinema had been obscured as a precaution.[16] In October the Home Secretary issued a further order for London which acknowledged that 'while thick fog prevails the normal lighting of the streets may be resumed', and also that lights along the Embankment and the riverside should be masked to prevent reflections on the water.[17]

Edward Nash ran a beer house at 232 High Road, Chiswick and found himself as one of the first lighting offenders before the Acton Police Court on 12 October but the charge was changed to one of obstruction: on the Saturday evening he had three lamps burning in his bar, casting light across the footway and halfway across the road. Two police constables entered and requested that he turn them down, but he refused, so the officers extinguished two of the lights. Nash relighted one of them but his comment, 'Are you the [blank] German Kaiser?' resulted in his arrest. He was fined £5 with costs.[18]

The Home Secretary issued an order for London:

Order of the Secretary of State dated October 1, 1914, under Regulation 7A of the Defence of the Realm Regulations, as to Extinguishment or Obscuration of Lights
In pursuance of the power conferred on me by Regulation 7A of the Defence of the Realm Regulations, I hereby make the following Order:–

1. In all brightly lighted streets and squares and on bridges a portion of the lights must be extinguished so as to break up all conspicuous groups or rows of lights; and the lights which are not so extinguished must be lowered or made invisible from above by shading them or painting over the tops and upper portions of the globes; provided that while thick fog prevails the normal lighting of the streets may be resumed.
2. Sky signs, illuminated facias, illuminated lettering, and powerful lights of all descriptions used for outside advertising or for the illumination of shop fronts, must be extinguished.
3. The intensity of the inside lighting of shop fronts must be reduced.
4. In tall buildings which are illuminated at night the greater part of the windows must be shrouded, but lights of moderate brightness may be left uncovered at irregular intervals.

5. All large lighted roof areas must be covered over or the lighting intensity reduced to a minimum.

6. The lighting of railway stations, sidings and goods yards must be reduced to the intensity sufficient for the safe conduct of business there. The upper half of the globes of all arc lights must be shaded or painted over.

7. Lights along the water front must be masked to prevent as far as practicable the reflection of light upon the water.

8. The lights of trams and omnibuses must not be more than is sufficient to enable fares to be collected, and must be obscured while crossing bridges.

9. The use of powerful headlights on motor cars is prohibited.

10. The aggregation of flares in street markets or elsewhere is prohibited.

11. In case of sudden emergency all instructions given by the Admiralty, or by the Commissioner of Police on the advice of the Admiralty, as to the further reduction or extinction of lights, shall be immediately obeyed.

This order shall apply to the City of London and the whole the Metropolitan Police District, and to the hours between sunset and sunrise, and it shall be in force for one month from this date unless sooner revoked.
Whitehall, 1 October, 1914

The impact was immediate. People found London a sombre place, and missed the brilliance of Leicester Square and Piccadilly Circus. The line of lights along the Embankment from Waterloo to Westminster was extinguished.[19] By November the London orders were widely used as a template for other towns and cities, although it might be sensibly asked why there should be any differences. The Birmingham order initially only had four sections:

1. All sky signs and conspicuous illuminated lettering and powerful external lights used for advertising or the illumination of shop fronts, shall be extinguished.

2. In brightly lighted streets and squares and bridges a portion of the powerful lights shall be extinguished or lowered, and all lights which are not extinguished shall be shaded or obscured so as to cut off direct light from the lamp in all directions above the horizontal.

3. All large lighted roof areas shall be covered over or obscured, or the lighting intensity reduced to the minimum possible.

4. Lights of trams and omnibuses must not be more than is sufficient to enable fares to be collected.[20]

The revised DoRA regulations were issued in December 1914 and lighting control was now the subject of regulation 11. Arguably this had more impact on the lives of British citizens in their private lives than perhaps any other, certainly until the food control orders appeared in late 1917 and, in the same way, affected all classes of society. At first the orders only applied to London, the east coast and certain towns and cities inland, and the darkened streets were seen as a novelty and in most part the restrictions were followed voluntarily. Householders, shopkeepers and businesses switched off lights, fitted blinds and curtains, and attempted to carry on life as normal. One concern was that there would be an increase in accidents but the Home Secretary assured the House of Commons that the returns of the Metropolitan Police up to November 1914 did not support this fear. Mr McKenna even suggested that the restrictions would be relaxed once the Admiralty were satisfied that it was safe to do so.[21] The restrictions actually grew tighter: street lighting was to be broken up so that there were no conspicuous rows or groups of lights. Buses and trams had to have blinds fitted.

In this era shops routinely opened until 8 pm or later, and shopkeepers became concerned that with Christmas approaching and the nights getting shorter customers would be cautious about shopping at night. The Birmingham and District Wholesale and Retail Traders' Association wrote to Winston Churchill to request that the lighting order be varied for the month of December, complaining of a serious falling-off of receipts. Their petition was politely refused.[22] An 'Early Closing Association'[23] had been formed before the war with the objective of ensuring better hours and conditions for shop assistants (they were instrumental in the passing of the Shops Act, 1911, which introduced the 'early closing day') and many believed that, even at this early stage, the change in shopping habits brought about by the lighting controls would help the cause. Shops began closing at six or seven o'clock.[24] The *Manchester Evening News* published a letter from a north-country Territorial battalion which included a number of former drapers and grocers complaining of the 'abominably late hours' in their trades, and welcoming the beneficial health effects of early closing.[25] By February 1915 it was noticed that one effect of the restrictions was that people were starting to shop locally,[26] boosting local businesses.

The first prosecutions were brought under different parts of the regulations. In January 1915 Frank Whibley, a Gillingham outfitter, was fined £10 for breaching regulation 11, apparently after half a dozen warnings from PC Benchley. The stipendiary said he would like to send people who complained of the inconvenience into the trenches for a month. Edward Williams, a photographer in Deal, was charged for displaying a light which might be used as a signal, in breach of regulation 25 which prohibited the display of any light that might serve as a signal, guide or landmark. In his case he claimed he was acting innocently, as he had no knowledge of signalling, and had simply used his bicycle lamp as he fed his rabbits. The bench believed him and discharged him with a warning.[27]

Back in October the Home Secretary passed on a request from the Admiralty to the Chief Constable of Birmingham, Mr C.H. Rafter, asking him to take steps to reduce lighting in the city. By the 23 November Mr McKenna was so unimpressed at the response that he changed his 'request' to an 'order' and the London restrictions were imposed.[28] The Zeppelin raids of late January forced many local authorities to accept that there was a genuine threat of aerial attack. Nottingham followed London and Birmingham on 19 February and Manchester on 1 March.[29] People pointed out inconsistencies: in the suburbs the practice was developing of showing no lights to the street but leaving the garden side of the house in full light.[30] Compliance with the lighting orders was generally good and in the early months the police, and especially the special constables, adopted a good-humoured policy of friendly warnings, but as the London model was applied to more towns and cities the enforcement became far more robust. Aaron Rabinovitch, who owned a jewellery business at 85 North Street, became the first person to be prosecuted in Leeds in April 1915. He was summonsed for 'not having the lights in the interior of his shop screened so as to be invisible from outside'. A copy of the order, dated 24 March, was provided by the town clerk, and PC Doughty gave evidence that he called the defendant's attention to the eight lights in his shop that were visible from outside, and switched off the electricity. He returned later to see the lights back on again. In a defence that must have been offered hundreds of times around the country, Rabinovitch pointed out that there was Corporation arc-lamp in full operation outside his shop. He was fined £10 or a month in default. 'I will pay next week.' 'You will pay today or go to prison.'[31] The first fines were punitive and clearly designed to send a warning to the community.

The reaction of some magistrates to infringements of the lighting orders gave rise to much comment and criticism. On 27 February 1915 five inhabitants of the small seaside town of Bexhill were brought before Hastings County Bench, chaired by the Mayor of Bexhill, Alderman Bond, and all offered the same excuse, that they thought the order had been cancelled. Evelyn Lloyd, of the Sussex Hotel, Alfred Crane, manager of the Maypole Dairy, William Thomas, sweetshop owner, Alfred Mitchell, proprietor of a fried fish shop on Sackville Road, and Henry Sherington, photographer, of 125 Station Road, received fines ranging from £10 to £1.[32] A second batch appeared at Bexhill Police Court a week later and received a similar treatment. The representative of Joseph Collbran, a jeweller, made an application to the bench on behalf of the Bexhill Commercial Association to define 'a reasonable amount of lighting', but the chairman refused.[33] A local editorial expressed the view that the penalties inflicted were out of all proportion to the seriousness of the offences and had given rise to a 'good deal of astonishment and resentment', particularly when it was learned that these were all first offences. There were conflicting orders in place, and no clear definitions, and the financial penalties inflicted were inconsistent with other benches such as Eastbourne, where fines were normally a few shillings.[34]

Infringements of the lighting regulations were breaches of the Defence of the Realm Act and the decision to prosecute initially rested with the competent naval or military authority. In February 1915 Archibald Percival, a hotel owner, successfully challenged a summons before the Worthing magistrates for a breach of the local lighting order, by pointing out that it was for the military authorities to decide to try a case by court-martial or in the civil court. His offence had not been so considered, and so the magistrates had no *locus standi*. They agreed, and dismissed the case.[35] The military authorities clearly had better things to do with their time than consider each case in detail, and it would appear that they simply batched them up and passed them to the magistrates' courts. Brigadier General Nugent was the commandant of the Humber defences, and in March 1915 he authorized the prosecution of twenty-five people at Grimsby Police Court for failing to comply with the regulations. They were 'of various social positions, from Mr Alexander Weddell, surveyor of taxes, to Hing Lee, a typical Chinese laundryman'.[36] On 16 April another fifty-four people were summonsed to the same court. The prosecution reported that measures had been taken to reduce lighting but not sufficient to satisfy the authorities. The object of the order was to secure absolute darkness, and the tradesmen in court were not asking themselves, 'Are my lights so obscured as to promote common safety?', but 'Have I got as much light as I can have without being summoned by the police?' They were all given fines.[37] The next week there were another thirty-two prosecutions, the offenders including a surgeon, a secretary and an electrician.[38] There were often complaints that the military were amongst the worst offenders, with barracks being brightly lit, but as noted, the competent naval or military authority decided if the case was to be heard in the magistrates' court. If the offender was in the army the prosecution took place by court-martial and therefore escaped public attention. This was challenged in Scarborough on 4 August 1915 when Lieutenant Colonel Cookson, officer commanding the Northumberland Hussars headquartered at Broxholm, on the Crescent, was himself prosecuted for a lighting offence. The defence submitted that the magistrates had no jurisdiction unless authorized by the competent military authority, but the Chief Constable Mr H. Windsor drew their attention to the wording of the new order affecting the eastern counties in which infringements became summary offences and the police could take action without consulting the military,[39] and this subsequently became the default mode of prosecution of regulation 11 offences,[40] although the military still retained the authority to consider and prosecute regulation 12 and 26 matters.

On Monday, 12 April 1915 a Home Office order was imposed on lighting in the existing Prohibited Areas from Northumberland to Dorset, which provided that:

1. All lights, whether public or private, which, if unobscured, would be visible from the sea or from the navigable waters of any estuary, shall be extinguished, or, in the case of indoor lights, obscured so as to be invisible from outside. All public light (except any low power lamps, which in the opinion of the police or military authorities are indispensable for the public safety) shall be extinguished, and all lights which are not extinguished shall be shaded or obscured from above, and to cut off direct light from the lamp in all directions above the horizontal.

2. All sky signs and illuminated lettering and outside lights of all descriptions used for advertising or the illumination of the front of any shop or other premises shall be extinguished. The intensity of all the inside lighting of shop fronts shall be reduced, and all windows, skylights, etc., in houses and other premises shall be effectively shaded or obscured so that no bright light is shed outside.

3. In factories and other buildings with lighted areas or numerous windows, roof areas and windows must be covered over or obscured, and outside lights in factory yards must be dispensed with, or, where this is impracticable, the tops and sides of the lamps must be shaded and the lighting intensity reduced to the minimum possible.

4. The intensity of the lighting of railway stations and sidings, goods yards, docks, etc., shall be reduced to the minimum that will suffice for the safe and expeditious conduct of business, and the tops and sides of all arc lamps and other bright lamps which cannot be dispensed with are to be shaded or painted over.

An exception was made in favour of shipbuilding yards, armament yards and other factories engaged in the manufacture of articles required for the fulfilment of Government contracts to such an extent as may be necessary for 'the safe and expeditious progress of work'.[41]

'Prohibited areas' had already been defined in the context of the Aliens (Restriction) Orders of 1914, and it is noticeable that the Home Office recognized existing, known, geographical administrative areas. Part of the confusion over the lighting regulations was that the Home Secretary had broad powers under DoRA regulation 11 to make orders, and the competent naval or military authority had similar local powers under regulation 12. As with licensing orders under the Intoxicating Liquor (Temporary Restrictions) Act, 1914 and the DoRA licensing regulations, this led to a patchwork of general and specific orders. They were often poorly drafted. Lieutenant Douglas Mackay, of the Yorkshire Dragoons, appeared before Norton (East Riding) magistrates for 'having a light on a vehicle other than an oil or candle lamp, contrary to the order of 28 June 1915'. The order was produced in court:

I, Colonel the Lord Basing, being the competent military authority, under powers vested in me by s12 of the Order in Council 10 June 1915, do hereby order that no motor car or other vehicle, when proceeding through any part of the prohibited area, shall use any sort of light except oil or candle lamps, and that they must not be of a greater number or brightness than is necessary for public safety.

Except that regulation 12 provided that 'the competent naval or military authority may by order direct that all lights or lights of a specified class shall be extinguished or obscured in such manner, between such hours, and within such area and during such period as may be specified by the order'. Mr Hall, for the defendant, pointed out that the colonel's order was not an order for extinguishing or obscuring lights, nor did it specify the hours or period to which it applied. The bench agreed, and decided that the order was *ultra vires* and dismissed the summons.[42]

As the days lengthened in April 1915 some of the lighting orders were withdrawn, as at Bradford. The Lord Mayor there announced that he was quite prepared to leave the restrictions to the good sense of the citizens, and should be maintained voluntarily as far as possible.[43] The relaxation of the orders was premature: the next few weeks saw Zeppelin raids on Ipswich, Southend, Dover and Ramsgate, with the first raid on London on 31 May. Lighting orders were rapidly reimposed and extended, and great efforts were put into public awareness – in York the city had been thoroughly placarded and notices sent out privately[44] and in Leicester 4,000 handbills were distributed amongst shopkeepers.[45]

The application of the lighting orders to industry did not always seem equitable. The Consett Iron Company's works were lit at night and local householders believed, to their cost, that they were not required to obscure or extinguish their lights. After numerous prosecutions the officials had to explain that the factory had arrangements in place to rapidly extinguish lights from furnaces and elsewhere in case of emergency, and that neither the company nor the police were able to warn the local population in the same way.[46] Conversely the Tyneside Tramways and Tramroads Company drew much criticism from local shift workers when they announced plans to reduce or cancel services after 9 pm and before 5 am[47] because of the lighting restrictions.

A new lighting order was issued at the end of June 1915 which required 'all windows or shops or rooms in houses in which lights are burning must be either screened by shutters, heavy curtains, or blinds of opaque material which will render it impossible for a light to be seen from outside', which applied to back gardens as much as to street-facing windows.[48] Lieutenant Colonel Thorold, the competent military authority for the Manchester district, complained to the local magistrates that the frequency of the offences was alarming, especially given the number of air raids which had been made, and he felt that sentences were far too lenient.[49] Clearly the message was not going home: at Southend on 24 August 1915 127 residents were summoned for breaches of the lighting regulations, and were fined an average of 5s each. There had been 483 convictions in the previous six months.[50] Nottingham's total was about 150,[51] and the Mayor of Beverley warned that offenders were liable to be dealt with by court-martial.[52]

The language of the regulations caused confusion. The expression 'blackout', as a total extinction of external lighting, was not used at all in the First World War. Instructions to extinguish lights were clear enough, but what was meant by 'subdued', 'obscured', 'shaded', or even 'bright'? The policeman or special constable formed an opinion at the scene, and the notes they wrote formed the evidence on which the prosecution was based. One of the problems faced by the magistrates was caused by the wording of regulation 11 in relation to a person 'having control' of a light. A hotel maid goes into the room of a guest who had gone out, leaving an unshaded light. Who should be prosecuted – the maid, the guest or the proprietor?[53] Mr A.J. Holland, proprietor of the Royal Hotel in Weymouth, was summoned to the Petty Sessions for failing to obscure a light at the rear of his premises in September 1916, with PC Pugh alleging that the naked electric light shining from the window could be seen from West Bay. A servant told the police officer that she was unable to draw the blind as it was out of order. Mr Holland was fined £2.[54] Monsignor Croft, of 34 Broadgate, was fined 10s when his servant neglected to pull the blind down correctly. He took the opportunity to complain to the magistrates that they were rather prescriptive in their treatment of lighting offences: the person was summoned, the case stated and a fine of 10s was imposed regardless of circumstances.[55] But Caroline Carpenter, a domestic, was fined 5s at Portsmouth Police Court for showing a bright light as she opened the front door to a doctor, and did not have the time to switch off the lights after admitting and announcing him before the police called.[56] A commercial traveller, Constantine Evangeline, had gone to his room at the Imperial Hotel in Hull and had fallen fast asleep, leaving his Venetian blinds open and the curtains undrawn. Unfortunately there was an air-raid alert, and staff, including the hotel manager and 'boots', had to use a crowbar to break into his room as they were unable to wake him. The Hull magistrates fined him five guineas (£5 5s).[57] Magistrates were advised to treat 'control' as a matter of fact, and to take into account knowledge and intent in deciding both guilt and seriousness of the offence.

As the second winter of the war set in, the lighting regulations were amended slightly to ensure that all premises not previously specified were now covered (hotels, dwelling houses, lodging houses). Passengers in railway carriages fitted with blinds were to ensure that they were lowered to cover the windows, but were permitted to raise them as necessary when the train was at a standstill in the station.[58] The eastern and south-eastern counties had various orders imposed in February and September but on 15 December 1915 the Home Secretary issued the Lights (East Coast) Order, which swept away with a range of conflicting and overlapping local orders to impose one set of regulations on a clearly-defined area: the portions of the counties of Northumberland, Durham, and Yorkshire (North Riding) which were included in the Aliens Restriction Order, the whole of the East Riding of Yorkshire and the counties of Lincoln, Norfolk, Suffolk, Sussex, Hampshire and the Isle of Wight, and to the counties of Essex and Kent, excluding the parts which were in the Metropolitan Police district. The Lights (West Coast) Order followed, which applied less stringent regulations on Dorset, Cornwall, Somerset, Gloucester, Monmouth, Glamorgan, Carmarthen, Pembroke, Cardigan, Merioneth, Anglesey, Denbigh, Flint, Cheshire, Lancashire, Westmoreland and Cumberland.[59] The regulations did not apply to lights on vehicles, nor to navigation lights, or lights in railway or shipbuilding yards, armament works or other exempted factories.

The Zeppelins tended to follow a route from their bases in northern Germany across the North Sea to make landfall over the distinctive Thames estuary and Essex coastline and these areas bore the brunt of the threat in the early years of the air war,[60] but the raids began to penetrate further inland. Following further Zeppelin raids in late January 1916 the East Coast Order was extended to all of Northumberland and Durham, and the counties of Derbyshire, Nottinghamshire, Leicestershire, Rutland, Northamptonshire and Buckinghamshire. All remaining counties were brought under the West Coast order, so that with the Metropolitan London Order, the whole country was now divided simply into three areas. Simplicity, however, was not a term with much value for the authorities, and lighting restrictions were linked to sunset and sunrise. On the east coast, the restricted hours were from half an hour after sunset to half an hour before sunrise. The Midland counties started an hour after until an hour before, and the western counties a full ninety minutes after and before sunset and sunrise.[61] A few months later the Summer Time Act, 1916 was passed, with the object of 'reducing the number of hours during which artificial lighting was used, and so save a very large amount of coal required for war purposes'.[62] It came into operation on Sunday, 1 May 1916 and the clocks were put forward by one hour, reverting to standard time on 1 October. The farmers of Northamptonshire were among the very few who were unhappy with the new scheme, and requested that farm business be conducted by the 'real time as shown by the sun'.[63] Newspapers already published the times of sunset and sunrise but now began regular listings of vehicle lighting times and the periods of restricted lighting, with a fifteen-minute grace period 'before police action is taken'.[64] Shops began changing their opening hours to fit in with these timings, and even matters spiritual were affected, when the Archbishop of York announced that his service would start at 5 pm,[65] and the parish church at Hadleigh in Suffolk brought its Sunday evening services forward to 6 pm for the same reason.[66]

The burning question of what constituted a 'bright' light was eventually settled. The *Justice of the Peace* noted that a light should be diffused or subdued 'to prevent a point or centre of light to be seen distinctly from outside',[67] and accepted that, provided the source of light was not visible as a naked light, a cream-coloured blind would be acceptable.[68] This interpretation was not generally accepted by the police, so that magistrates had to draw on common sense when dealing with such cases. But in June 1916 rumours circulated that in some eastern counties persons were being prosecuted and convicted for striking matches in the streets.[69] It soon transpired that these rumours were true, when the Chief Constable of Norwich, Mr E.F. Finch, revealed himself as the prosecutor. In the early part of the war he had some friends who were aviators and they had impressed him with their accounts of what they could see flying over Norfolk at night. He subsequently imposed a lighting order on the city that was one of the most stringent in the country – so much so, in fact, that in later years, amendments to the more widespread orders, such as the Lights (East Coast) Order, specifically excluded Norwich from their application! In one account, Norwich was described as the darkest city in the United Kingdom:

> The lighting regulations are exceptionally severe and rigidly enforced. Not a street lamp is lighted, and the striking of matches and use of flash lamps is prohibited. Most of the shops close early and those that remain open (tobacconists and confectioners) have windows and doors heavily curtained. Special constables gave valuable assistance in reporting offenders and magistrates were kept busy with long lines of respectable, law-abiding citizens who through carelessness or neglect had failed adequately to shade their lights. There are fines of £5 but more often of 40s; poor people pay a shilling only.[70]

Other police forces followed. In Hull they were particularly vigilant: Edward Sutton struck a match on Ferriby Road at 10 pm on 5 April 1916. He was fined 9s.[71] Richard Dixon lit his pipe while walking on the Beverley Road on the night of an air raid 'buzzer' alarm and was fined £2 2s, and at the same time Daniel Rawlings was fined £2 18s for striking a light on the same night near Sulcoates Bridge.[72]

During air raids and more frequent alerts it was standard practice for the local chief constable to order the extinguishment all lighting in the local area. But it was not widely appreciated that from an altitude of 10,000 feet, a Zeppelin crossing the coast at Southend would be able to see the lights of Southampton, Birmingham, Nottingham and Leicester. Despite the better alignment of the lighting orders introduced in January 1916 the Home Office was still not satisfied with the situation and so the Lights (England and Wales) Order was introduced on 11 July. This really did simplify matters, as it put the whole country outside London, Norwich and Grimsby under a standard set of eight rules, and included the regional adjustments related to the timings of sunset and sunrise.

1. All lights visible from the sea so obscured as to be invisible from outside.
2. All external lamps, flares, and fixed lights of all descriptions, and all aggregations of lights, extinguished, except such public lights as the Chief Officer of Police directs for public safety. All lights not extinguished to be reduced to the minimum

intensity and so shaded or obscured that direct light is cut off in all directions above the horizontal and no more than a diffused light is cast on the ground.

3. In dwelling houses, hotels, shops, factories, docks, shipbuilding yards, and other premises of all descriptions, all inside lights must be so reduced and shaded, or the windows, roof lighting areas, skylights, glass doors etc. so screened by shutters or dark blinds or dark curtains so that no more than a dull subdued light is visible from any direction outside and no part of the pavement or roadway or any other building or other object is illuminated thereby.

4. Exemption may be granted to naval or military establishments or works of public utility subject to compliance with these orders.

5. These orders do not apply to working lights on railways (including lights in stations and in goods and marshalling yards) nor to navigation, riding or fishing lights, in accordance with Admiralty orders, nor to lights under control of general or local lighthouse authority.

6. Railway passengers are to lower blinds in railway carriages but are permitted to raise them as necessary when the train is standing still at a station.

7. In case of a sudden emergency, all instructions given by the competent naval or military authority or by the Commissioner of Police on the advice of the competent naval or military authority, as to the further reduction or extinction of lights, shall be immediately obeyed.

8. This order comes into effect from 7 August 1916.[73]

The London Metropolitan Police district adopted the same order on 1 September.

Despite the welcome standardization of the lighting regulations there was no corresponding reaction from magistrates, and as regulation 11 offences continued with a depressing frequency there were wide variations in sentencing. Esther David was the manageress of a ladies' costumier and tailoring shop in the North End Road. On the night of 24 August 1916, knowing that an air raid was imminent, PC West noticed two bright rays of light from her shop window. He forced an entry at the back and managed to switch off the lights. He had warned Mrs David to reduce her lights back in June. Mr Fordham, the West London magistrate, felt that this was an extremely serious case and fined her an exemplary £25 or fifty-one days' imprisonment. He added, 'It is my duty to see that nothing is done to assist in guiding German airships, and that there is no doubt that Zeppelins cruise about looking for lights, and when they see a light anywhere they know they are over a town and drop bombs'.[74] The editor of the *Whitby Gazette* had followed this story: 'The above gives lead to our own far-too-lenient bench of magistrates, who, if they backed up the efforts of the police in this and other directions, and thus more greatly encouraged them in the execution of their duties, might effect much more reform in the town and district.'[75]

The Lights (England and Wales) Order of July 1916 was a robust and reliable work that required little further amendment throughout the rest of the war. Its application to fixed lighting was clearly established, but there were minor issues relating to hand-held lights. It became apparent that torches were a source of nuisance, but flashing them in faces or into the sky could, and would, be construed as a regulation 26 offence. Local orders, such as those in Norwich and Nottingham, could prohibit all such handheld lamps and lights.[76] The policing of the lighting orders was an important part of the work of the special constables; it was not an arrestable offence to breach the order, but the offender's name and address had to be recorded along with full particulars of the offending lights. The offender would then be summonsed.

The Lights on Vehicles Act, 1907 replaced the various vehicle lighting byelaws which existed up to that time around the country, and required drivers of motor cars, carts, steam lorries and bicycles to have a lamp or lamps to display to the front a white light visible for a reasonable distance; only drivers carrying loads projecting more than six feet to the rear were required to show a red light.[77] The vehicle rear registration or licence plate was required to be illuminated by white light under the Motor Car Act, 1903.[78] But road users in many areas were often caught out by the new requirement to carry a rear red light. This was introduced in the December 1914 lighting order in which it was explained that 'experience has shown that this is necessary in the present condition of streets to protect vehicles being run into from behind'. It was pointed out that the red glass reflectors widely used by cyclists and others were insufficient. Confusingly, failure to carry a white light was an offence under the 1907 Act, but failure to display a red rear light was a DoRA offence; and a failure on both counted as two separate offences, with separate penalties.[79] Many magistrates found it confusing that a conviction for a lighting offence under regulation 11 should also be marked with an endorsement on the offender's driving licence.[80] Miss Ruth Leng was fined £2 and had her licence endorsed for carrying a light brighter than was necessary for public safety. In evidence PC Davies said that 'Harlech Castle, 550 yards away, stood out clearly'.[81]

Drivers struggled to comply with the rules, especially in the early months of the war when there was a patchwork of orders across the east and south coasts. The driver might find that in one place an order relating to a town was in place, but a mile or two down the road he would find himself in a military area with additional restrictions. The car had to have one or two lamps (if one, it should be fitted to the right or offside), and the red rear light mounted centrally. Not all cars had electric lights, and many were fitted with acetylene or oil lamps, which required regular attention if used for longer periods. Note that the national speed limit was 20mph, and local byelaws permitted restrictions of 10mph, so such lamps provided adequate illumination for travel at what we would consider such low speeds. The use of 'powerful' lights was also prohibited, with the same subjectivity applied by the police as was seen with domestic lighting. However, the Home Office worked in consultation with the Admiralty, War Office and representatives of the motoring organizations to produce the authoritative Lights (Vehicles) Order, implemented nationally, except for the metropolitan area, on 10 January 1916. Part I dealt with the basic requirements:

1. The lighting-up time for all vehicles was to be half-an-hour after sunset.
2. The requirement to carry lights was extended to all vehicles using the roadway, including vehicles drawn or pushed by hand.
3. All vehicles were required to carry a lamp showing a red light to the rear, and a separate lamp carried at the rear was made compulsory for all but hand vehicles.

With the application of the red light requirement to the whole country the Home Office recognized that this might cause a shortage, and so drivers were given until 10 February to comply.[82]

Part II of the Order prohibited the use of headlights in restricted areas and instead permitted the use of sidelights or obscured headlights only. The Engineering Standards Board, report no. 69, had come up with a set of definitions about 'brightness':

a. Electric lamps were to be less than or equal to 12 watts
b. Acetylene lamps were to consume less than 14 litres or ½ cubic foot of fuel per hour
c. Oil lamps were to have a single burner, with the wick trimmed to less than or equal to ¾ inch.
d. If a lens for concentrating the beam was fitted, it was to be obscured by at least one thickness of ordinary white tissue paper.[83]

For reference, a typical filament bulb used in the indicators or brake lights of a modern car is rated at 21 watts.

It had been found that in built-up areas a large number of lighted vehicles (such as the military and naval road convoys that were becoming increasingly common at night) could make the lines of streets visible to aircraft, and so in the east coast districts even the sidelights were further restricted, by the attachment of perforated caps or disks over the lights. The hole had to be less than 4½ inches in diameter. Special signs were to be attached to street lamps to indicate the areas in which the caps had to be used, and Part III of the order listed the towns and cities so affected, and all coastal areas up to six miles inland.[84]

In London a further rule was made concerning cab ranks: if more than five taxis were formed in a queue, only the first two were allowed to leave their lights on.[85] And it didn't take too long for the application of rule 2 to be tested: a common form of a 'vehicle pushed by hand' was the baby's perambulator, so were they required to be fitted with lights? The Hitchin Police Court believed so, white at the front, red at the rear, but they had a problem identifying which end of the pram was the rear. The Home Secretary himself wrote to explain that 'the white light shows in the direction the perambulator is going, and the red light in the reverse direction'.[86] The Middlesbrough stipendiary, Mr T.W. Fry, convicted Ada Robinson, of Wellington Street, for contravening the regulations, but as it was the first case of its kind he imposed no penalty.[87] The Home Secretary subsequently wrote to him to advise that the Lights (Vehicles) Order did apply if the pram was used in the roadway, and had to be fitted with one white light at the front and a red on the back. The lights were not required for prams simply being pushed across the street or on footpaths.[88]

One of the last new lighting regulations was the Lights (Driving of Animals) Order of October 1916, which required anyone driving or leading up to four animals to carry a lamp showing a white light to the front and rear and carried at the rear. For larger herds the same light was required but carried at the front, and on the approach of any vehicle the herdsman was to swing or wave the lamp to indicate an obstacle in the road.[89]

The Advertisement Lights Order of 22 May 1917 prohibited the use of all sky signs, illuminated advertisements or other lights outside shops or places of amusement, at any time, and of these lights inside shops when the shop was closed.

The recognition, or anticipation, of aerial attack and the consequent identification of military targets and landmarks by industrial, domestic and urban lighting at night led to the early measures for lighting controls. Unlike so many of the other Defence of the Realm regulations, under regulation 11 the Home Secretary reserved powers to make orders, maintaining the separate and distinct regulation 12 for orders by the competent or and military authorities. Although the patchwork effect of conflicting or overlapping local and regional orders was seen in the first years, centralized control by the Home Office brought about a sensible and consistent standardization of orders with the Lights (England and Wales) Order of July 1916. Although prosecutions for breaches of the lighting regulations continued right up until the end of the war, it could be held that it was the inconsistent approach to sentencing by the magistrates that led to these continued offences. And unlike the other DoRA regulations, the announcement of the armistice on 11 November 1918 resulted in an immediate and much-welcomed repeal of the restrictions on homes, but with a serious coal shortage commercial and public lighting was not fully restored until the following year.

Chapter 9

What Did You Do in the War, Daddy?

On 29 May 1914 the Canadian Pacific Railway liner the *Empress of Ireland* left Quebec for Liverpool. On board were 1,477 people. At 1.50 am, ten hours out, cruising down the great St Lawrence seaway, the Norwegian collier *Storstad* rammed into the ship which listed heavily to starboard and then sank within fifteen minutes, with the loss of 1,021 lives. The disaster, coming only two years after the loss of the *Titanic*, led to a huge emotional response in Britain and Canada, with distressing scenes of the CPR offices in Liverpool. Two of the victims were Mr John Vincent and his wife Muriel, of Faircross, Wyke Road, Weymouth, returning from a visit to their daughter and son-in-law. Well known in the town as a jeweller in St Mary Street, he had been appointed as a magistrate some eight years previously.[1] The 'Empress of Ireland Disaster Fund' was set up within days at the instigation of the Lord Mayor of London, and collections, band performances, matinees and charitable dinners raised substantial funds for the victims and their families. Bert Towers visited the manager of the Empire Theatre in Leeds and asked for permission to make a collection between the turns, on behalf of the Lord Mayor of Leeds. By passing around small tin boxes, he was able to collect £2 13s 10d at the first performance alone, and he hoped for a similar result in the afternoon. Except that the police recognized him as a military deserter and he was arrested and charged at Dewsbury police court as being absent from 30 Battery, Royal Field Artillery.[2] He was sentenced to three months' imprisonment for the attempt to obtain charitable donations by fraud. While serving this sentence he was taken to Newcastle police court the following month to face two charges of theft of a rifle and theft of £3. He had previous convictions of a similar nature in 1909 in Darlington and in 1912 in Sheffield. Towers (also known as Towse, or Conrad Fraser) was given two sentences of six months' imprisonment, to run concurrently with his current term.[3]

Desertion and absenteeism were the commonest military offences dealt with by the magistrates. Common enough before the war, the numbers soared as more and more men found themselves in uniform either as volunteers or later as conscripts. At the start of the conflict an Army Order was published announcing that the King had approved that pardons should be granted to soldiers who were in a state of desertion on 5 August provided they surrendered themselves before 4 September if in this country, or by 4 October if abroad.[4] On 8 August the War Office requested that military deserters brought before magistrates should be given a railway pass by the police and sent to their depot, with a telegram being sent in each case so that the deserter would be met by the military authorities at his destination.[5] This was shortly followed by a letter from the Home Office:

The War Office and Admiralty have requested that deserters surrendering to the police should be dealt with in the following manner:

> An Army deserter should be allowed to proceed forthwith to his depot, the police showing him into the train and providing him with a voucher under the Cheap Trains Act.
>
> A deserter from the Navy or Marines, if the police are satisfied that he intends to report himself for active service, should be provided with a voucher made out to his home port in the case of a naval deserter, and in the case of a marine to the station nearest his barracks.

Deserters who are arrested in the usual way by the police will be treated in the usual manner, and will have to appear before the magistrates.[6]

According to the *Manual of Military Law*, Chapter III, section 13, the distinction between desertion and absence without leave was that of intention. Desertion was a deliberate act on the part of the soldier either to escape some act of military service or to avoid returning to military service at all. Evidential examples given in the manual include a soldier being found in plain clothes on a steamer bound for America at one extreme, and a man on notice of embarkation concealing himself in his barracks at the other. If a man was missing for twenty-one days or more, a military court of enquiry would be held to formally declare him and convict him as a deserter, at which point all his pay and allowances would be stopped. Once a soldier was believed to be absent without leave, his equipment and clothing would be placed in safe custody, and, according to *King's Regulations* no. 514, his commanding officer was to complete A.F. B 124, a descriptive report of the soldier, and send it to the editor of the *Police Gazette*, at New Scotland Yard, for publication. These lists of deserters were published weekly (later twice weekly[7]) and circulated to all police stations in the country. The first wartime issue, dated 11 August 1914, lists fifty-four deserters and absentees from His Majesty's service, eighty-five from the Special Reserve and twenty-four from the Territorial Force. The Admiralty listed fifty-one men missing from the navy and naval reserve. Each man had his details listed, from name, rank and number, to parish and county of birth, to marks and remarks: James Caldwell, of the Royal Garrison Artillery, and originally from Boghead in Forfar, was 5 feet 9 inches tall, with dark brown hair, light brown eyes, and with two moles and a scar on his left upper arm and six scars on the back of his scalp.[8] At the Stratford Petty Sessions there were eleven military and naval deserters in July 1914, fifteen in August, and twenty-one in September, comprising 3 per cent, 4 per cent and 7 per cent of the monthly caseload respectively.[9]

Desertion was an offence under section 154 of the Army Act, 1881 for regular soldiers or section 15 of the Reserve Forces Act, 1882 for Territorials and later for men who had been transferred to the Army Reserves under the Military Service Act, 1916. Police constables were authorized to arrest anyone suspected of being a deserter and to take them to the magistrates' court, and likewise a justice of the peace could issue a warrant for such an arrest. The court had to be satisfied that the man was a deserter or absentee, either by evidence on oath or, more commonly, by confession, in which case he was to be remanded at the police station or local prison, until he could be delivered into military custody. The legal test to determine whether the soldier was a genuine deserter or merely absent without leave (in naval terms a 'straggler') was carried out by army or navy once the man was back at his unit or ship; the magistrates simply had to ensure that he was lawfully detained in civilian custody. Regular soldiers who fell under section 154 of the Army Act faced no further civil penalty, but on conviction under section 15 of the Reserve Forces Act at the magistrates' court reservists could be sentenced to a fine not less than 40s and not more than £25, with the option of imprisonment in default. In practice the courts were instructed to impose a fine which was then to be deducted from his Army pay – imprisonment in default would simply add a further delay to the man's return to military duty. The standard fine was 40s, nearly six weeks' pay. The magistrates were also allowed to recommend a reward, usually of 5s, for the informant or arresting officer, payable by the Army Council.

The court was required to fill in a 'Descriptive Return' (the Fourth Schedule to the Army Act, 1881, Army Form O 1618), which identified the soldier and the circumstances of his absence, and in particular whether he surrendered or had been apprehended. This form provided all the evidence required by the man's commanding officer and meant that the attendance of witnesses, such as the arresting police officer, was not required. The court would telephone or send a telegram to the military authorities who would then forward this information to the man's regiment who would then despatch a military escort. This usually comprised a non-commissioned officer and one or two soldiers from the same regiment, or from the regimental training depot if the soldier's own unit was overseas. The officer in charge of records at this unit would hold a description of the soldier in the regimental books and would provide a certified extract to the NCO, who would check that it matched the descriptive return supplied by the court when he arrived at the police station or prison where the man was being held. The party would then return to the depot and finally the soldier would be returned to his unit. Not surprisingly it could take some time for the escort to be arranged, and magistrates were concerned about the indeterminate 'remand into custody to await military escort'. The Home Secretary issued guidance that soldiers should be committed to prison for 'such a term as may be reasonably necessary … for the purpose of delivering him into military custody', presumably allowing the man to be released if the escort failed to turn up.[10] There were also grave concerns about the numbers of men tied up in escort duties and travelling around the country. In passing it is worth noting that the acronym 'AWOL', for 'Absent With Out Leave', was not used during the First World War, and first appears in the early 1930s.

The procedure was changed following the introduction of the Group System (the 'Derby Scheme', below) in 1915 and later the introduction of the Military Service Act in 1916. Men in the Derby Scheme attended their local recruitment office and enlisted, but then returned to civilian life to await the call up. Under the MSA the men found themselves 'deemed to have enlisted and transferred to the Reserve'; in neither case had the men been assigned to a regiment and so did not have a description recorded in any regimental book. The district recruiting officer was the commanding officer of such men and so for those who failed to attend at the appointed time and thereby became absentees, he was responsible for the description and the escort.[11] It was not uncommon in the larger towns and cities for an NCO and escort party to attend the court on a regular basis to collect batches of defaulters.

A soldier could easily find himself classed as an absentee by simply missing his train at the end of his leave. Rather than exercising common sense and allowing the man to take the next available transport, he was liable to arrest. The numbers are astonishing – in the seven-month period from October 1916 to April 1917, Stratford Petty Sessions alone dealt with 180 offences, making up a full 30 per cent of the court's work.[12] Even given that Stratford had a large urban population and was a major rail interchange, the figures give a sense of the vast numbers of men on the move. There was some disagreement about the inclusion of these offences in the court register[13] and they do not appear in the national statistics collated by the Home Office each year, but clearly this problem was widespread. In January 1917 Sir John Ball at the London Guildhall Police Court, and Mr Bros at Clerkenwell both raised concerns over the absurdity of the system. They complained that they were dealing with upwards of fifty absentees in each court, and that these technical absentees, whose offence was simply to miss a train, were taken to court and locked up like common criminals.[14] Mr Bros had had to deal with forty men arrested by military police in a concerted roundup of defaulters at the 'World's Fair' exhibition at the Agricultural Hall in Islington on Saturday, 6 January 1917. Despite the involvement of *military* police, the men were held in civilian custody and had to be brought before the civil courts. The assistant provost marshal (the head of military police) offered to take this up with the military authorities.[15] The Under-Secretary of State for War spoke on the matter in the House of Commons on 20 March 1917,[16] and on 5 April 1917 the Army (Annual) Act amended section 154 of the Army Act 1881, so that deserters and absentees who surrendered themselves to the police would be dealt with by the officer in charge of the police station to which they were brought. The police officer completed the descriptive return and forwarded it to the Army Council.[17] The Act also allowed military police to keep such men in their custody in the same way. Men who were arrested, however, were still dealt with by the magistrates. The *Police Gazette* of 12 November 1918 listed 592 Army absentees, 63 naval, and 70 from the Royal Air Force.

On Friday, 7 August 1914, the Secretary of State for War Lord Kitchener issued his famous 'Call to Arms', asking for a new army of 100,000 men. Thousands of volunteers flocked to the recruiting offices up and down the country and had to make an oath of allegiance. The duties of the magistrate in the recruitment process were described in the *Justice's Note-book*:

> Upon the appearance of the candidate for enlistment, the Justice will ask him, in the first place, whether he assents to that step. If so, after cautioning him that any false answer will expose him to punishment, the Justice will read or cause to be read to him the questions in the 'attestation paper', taking care that each question is duly understood; and, after ascertaining that his answers have been properly recorded, will require him to sign the declaration and administer to him the oath of allegiance contained in the paper. The Justice will then attest by his

signature the fulfilment of all the requirements, and deliver the document to the 'recruiter'.[18]

Although in many cases army officers witnessed the declaration, the demand was such that magistrates were asked to help. In Huddersfield they dealt with sixty recruits in one morning alone, with each man making his oath individually.[19] The recruit stated:

> I swear by Almighty God that I will be faithful and bear true allegiance to His Majesty King George the Fifth, his heirs, and successors, and swear that I will, as in duty bound, honestly and faithfully defend His Majesty, his heirs, and successors, in person, crown, and dignity, against all enemies, and will observe and obey all orders of His Majesty, his heirs, and successors, and of the generals and officers set over me. So help me God.

Sir Herbert Ashman presided over a special meeting of the Bristol magistrates on 14 August 1914 at which they arranged the rota so that two justices would always be present at Colston Hall to attest recruits and sign the attestation form, and administer the oath of allegiance. They agreed that they would attend between 8.30 am and 8 pm. They were accompanied by twenty-one 'medical gentlemen', serving in batches of five.[20] The new recruit arrived at Colston Hall, to be met at the top of the steps by Colour Sergeant Young, an old soldier, who inspected his teeth and measured his height. Going upstairs to Lesser Colston Hall he had his physical fitness assessed, and then went back downstairs to see Colonel Burgess and a magistrate for the swearing-in, and to receive a day's pay of 1s. This recruiting office enlisted 256 men between 5 and 18 August, and the main Bristol office accepted 584.[21]

Under section 99 of the Army Act, 1881, a person making a false answer to any question on the attestation paper which had been put to him by the justice of the peace would be tried in the magistrates' court. It the false answer was given to an officer, or came to light at a later stage, the competent naval or military authority had the power to refer the matter to the civilian court or the man could be tried before a court-martial, under sections 32 or 33 of the Army Act. Ernest Harris applied to join the army at the Artillery Barracks at Hull on 19 September 1914. He declared that he was single and that he had never been convicted: both statements were untrue. He was handed over to the police and appeared in front of the stipendiary on 7 October and was sentenced one month's imprisonment with hard labour.[22] A particularly bad case involved John Jones, charged with false attestation and attempting to defraud at Marylebone Police Court. On Friday, 8 January 1915 he had enlisted in the Royal Engineers at Whitehall and was paid the higher rate of 1s 6d. He then made his way to the Marylebone recruitment office and joined the Royal Engineers again. When searched, Major Henry Mansford, the recruiting officer, found the Whitehall papers on him, along with others, dated 5 January, showing that he had enlisted in the Royal Garrison Artillery in Durham, and he was suspected of having done the same elsewhere. He was given six months' hard labour. James Miller, an unregistered American, was described as a 'professional enlister', having signed up six times. For these and other offences the St Helens magistrates sentenced him to twelve months' imprisonment.[23]

Vause Wood had been dishonourably discharged from 9 York and Lancaster Battalion as an 'undesirable character' but had then joined the Royal Horse Artillery at Sheffield without revealing his background. He received a fine of £3.[24] Richard Jobling had served with the 3 Durham Light Infantry for thirty-seven weeks, and had deserted twice in that time. With such a bad conduct sheet in his records, he thought he would have a fresh start by joining the 160 Wearside Brigade Royal Field Artillery. He was charged with false attestation and was sentenced to three months' imprisonment with hard labour by the Houghton-le-Spring magistrates in March 1915.[25] Robert Hutchinson and Joseph Campbell appeared before the Sunderland magistrates on 24 October. They had both enlisted in the Royal Artillery on 28 August but had been discharged on health grounds. They had subsequently joined the Army Service Corps and had denied having been in the military before. They were sent down for two months with hard labour.[26]

Sir James Renals, the son of a former Lord Mayor of London, appeared at Bow Street Police Court in November 1914, charged with making a false statement as to the character of Marcus Barthropp for the purpose of his entry into His Majesty's forces. In September he had signed Barthropp's application for a commission, vouching for his good character during the previous four years. The commission was granted but the police subsequently identified him as a man with seven convictions for fraud between 1903 and 1913, with several periods of imprisonment. He was subsequently cashiered from the Army. Renals had met Barthropp at a West End music hall. He admitted that he had no improper motive but had been rather stupid. The magistrate, Mr Hopkins, fined him the maximum £20.[27] Barthropp was subsequently fined the same amount for the offence of making a false declaration.[28]

A man who was already serving and subject to military law and who then enlisted in another regiment or service committed the offence of fraudulent enlistment. This was a strictly military offence which was dealt with by court-martial under section 13 of the Army Act. The usual basis for this seemingly bizarre action was that a man who was in the regular army and therefore eligible for service overseas would enlist in a Territorial battalion, for home service only. The 'fraudulent' element of the offence was that he was obtaining a free uniform and kit (and presumably defrauding the army out his existing outfit). Cases of false attestation were sometimes mistakenly reported as fraudulent enlistment, and in many cases the offender had been charged with a criminal offence and current or previous convictions for fraudulent enlistment were used as evidence of bad character.

Courtroom etiquette was an early problem. Civilian men were required to remove their hats before the bench, but soldiers claimed that they were required to keep them on. After some correspondence to the *Justice of the Peace* it was finally settled that under *King's Regulations* paragraph 1792 'in a civil court an officer or soldier will remove his headdress while the judge or magistrate is present, except when the officer or soldier is on duty under arms with a party or escort inside the court'.[29]

At some stage it became fashionable to embarrass, if not humiliate, young men not in uniform by handing them a white feather. Lance Bombardier Henry Wilding, of 85

Battery, Royal Field Artillery, was a career soldier and had served in India before being posted to France. He returned home to East Finchley in January 1915 and went out to the pub in his 'civvies'. At some point three local lads put a white feather in his hat, to which Wilding took great exception. He beat up all three of them, knocking Arthur Houghton unconscious. On Monday, 18 January he was brought before the Highgate police court on a charge of grievous bodily harm. He explained that he was due back at the Front on the Wednesday, so the clerk told him to return and 'if the youth got better he would probably hear no more about it, but if the lad died he would have to be fetched home'.[30] As far as we know, the lad survived.

Occasionally magistrates found themselves in a difficult position when hearing evidence about military cases. Mr Clarke Hall, a London police magistrate, found Alfred North, a 'useful looking soldier', before him charged with being an absentee on 13 December 1915. When asked to give his age, he stated that he was 17. He had told the Army he was 19 which was the minimum age to serve overseas. Clarke Hall had previously sent a 15-year-old boy back to his unit, and regretted that it was not for the courts to decide what to do with lads who had lied about their age.[31] William Trower, a 'finely built lad' aged 15, appeared at Clerkenwell Police Court in March 1916 on a false attestation charge. He had recently joined the Royal Fusiliers at Hounslow, stating that his age was 19 and that he had not been in the army before. It then transpired that he had served in the Royal Field Artillery until his father had claimed him out. As the boy was under the age for military service, there could be no offence, so Mr d'Eyncourt released him.[32]

An army uniform offered status and honour, particularly to those who held rank and awards for bravery. Some of those at the bottom were resentful: John O'Connor had been to public school and, since the outbreak of war, had seen his brothers, cousins and school friends win commissions, but he was unsuccessful and had enlisted as a private soldier in the Australian Forces. At one time he had gone to a café with one of his officer friends and they had both been berated by a senior officer, who warned them that officers were not to associate with other ranks. He bought himself an officer's uniform and was regularly seen in places such as Leicester Square and Victoria Station, until he was arrested for impersonating an officer and fined £50 at the Westminster police court in October 1915.[33] Lancelot Dickinson Chapman was a trumpeter in the Royal Field Artillery, and claimed to have been awarded the Victoria Cross and the Belgian Order of Leopold. He took part in a celebratory music hall tableau, and it had been suggested that the Mayor of Camberwell should hold a reception in his honour before his deception was discovered. At Bow Street police court he was sentenced to ten months' hard labour for a number of offences of obtaining money under false pretences. The unauthorized wearing of uniforms or decorations was an offence under regulation 41 of the Defence of the Realm Act regulations, and this also applied to civilians. In early 1915 the Admiralty and the Ministry of Munitions began issuing 'war badges' for civilian men and women employed in Government or munitions work. In a society in which any young man not in uniform was liable to be challenged, if not abused, these badges and their associated certificates were designed to distinguish those involved in work of national importance and to avoid such stigma.[34] Harry Dopson, 16, was fined 7s 6d by Portsmouth magistrates in June 1916, for the offence of wearing his father's Admiralty war badge. The badges also offered protection from the recruiting officers, particularly once conscription began. John Jones, of 173 Steelhouse Lane, Wolverhampton, received his call-up papers in May 1916 and attended the recruitment office wearing a Ministry of Munitions badge. As this provided automatic exemption from military service, the clerk asked for the accompanying certificate but Jones was unable to provide it. First claiming he had left it at home, and then that he had lost it, he admitted that he had borrowed it from Joseph Collins, of 6, Power Street. For the offences of falsely representing himself to be a person entitled to wear and use the badge and for unlawful supply, the two men were fined £5 each.[35] From September 1916 the silver war badge was issued to men discharged from the army or navy 'on account of age, or physical infirmity arising from wounds, or sickness caused by military service'.[36] Joseph Smith was sentenced to four months' imprisonment by Chesterfield Magistrates for his second offence of wearing a silver war badge without authority.[37]

Magistrates sometimes helped with recruitment. A Walworth costermonger, Walter Spencer, was charged with obstruction at the Lambeth Police Court in November 1915. Chester Jones, the magistrate, asked him if there was anything wrong with his health. 'No sir.' 'Well why don't you join the Army?' 'I think I will, sir'. 'Pay 5s and go and join the Army'.[38] A similar offer was made to Rochdale labourer John Hanlon, charged with being drunk and disorderly at Rochdale police court in August 1915. He had been refused admission to his boarding house and had been aggressive. Dr Malin asked, 'Why don't you go and fight the Germans?' 'I will, if you give me the chance.' He was fined 5s but Malin said he would pay the fine for him if he would go and enlist. A police constable escorted him to the recruiting station at the Manor House, but unfortunately Hanlon failed his medical because of a cataract in his right eye. The Chief Constable reported this back to the court before it rose, but the magistrate took it in good part – 'I will pay the fine; he has tried to enlist'.[39]

And sometimes prison was the only option. James Rice, formerly a butcher's assistant, joined the Royal Army Medical Corps at the start of the war. He was brought back from Salisbury to face the Exeter magistrates on a charge of embezzling 13s 3d from his employer. The defence representative proposed that as he had enlisted he should face no further penalty and should be simply bound over. The Chief Constable then pointed out that Rice had several previous convictions of a similar nature and eight other offences which had not been proceeded with. He was sent to prison for six weeks, with hard labour.[40] John Gothard had already been discharged from the army by the time he found himself in front of the Nottingham magistrates in September 1916, accused of stealing £17 and a cheque from the Electrical Stores on Burton Street where he worked as a porter. The military representative, Major McGuire, was present in court and informed the bench that prior to the war such a man would not be wanted, but under the Military Service Act it was probable that he would be called up again, but if he persisted in such conduct he would 'probably spend much of his time in a military prison'. Gothard asked for a chance to rejoin the forces, but he was given four months' hard labour.[41] Boy Scout Percy Turner and his pals Albert Ayton, Herbert Chambers and Reginald Rhodes went camping in Mr Netherclift's farm at Great Ponton. While they were out exploring, Private George Griffiths entered their tent and stole a quantity of their clothing, valued at 37s 6d. Police sergeant Skinner arrested him on the farm and on the way to the police station Griffiths told him, 'I am not soldiering as a machine gunner if I can get 12 months for this'. Grantham magistrates heard from an officer from his unit, telling them that he had been in service for five months and his conduct was execrable, and they had no use for him in the army. He was given three months, with hard labour.[42]

The vast majority of men who volunteered did so for personal, if not patriotic, reasons, but whatever motivated a man to join up it certainly wasn't financial: civilian wages were, generally, higher than army rates of pay. But young, fit, and skilled men left their peacetime jobs and careers to the extent that it became increasingly apparent that the demand for military manpower was conflicting with the demands of industry to manufacture the munitions consumed in vast quantities by the war. Skilled labour was a particularly valuable commodity and the government realized that some means had to be found to balance these competing needs of 'men and munitions'. As early as 31 August 1914 an all-party Parliamentary Recruiting Committee had been formed under the presidency of the Prime Minister, Asquith, Mr Bonar Law and the Leader of the Labour Party, Mr Arthur Henderson, to assist Lord Kitchener's request for 100,000 men. Based around the existing network of party political branches and agents, local recruiting committees were formed. Fears were expressed about the ultimate aims of this recruiting campaign, so in one speech Henderson made it clear that the Labour Party was opposed to conscription and all forms of military service, and that he was confident that a voluntary response would be sufficient,[43] and Kitchener himself, speaking at the Guildhall, 'put it beyond question' that there was any intention for anything other than a voluntary system.[44] Towards the end of October the committee announced a voluntary census of men of military age. The 'Householder's Return' was a form was issued to all whose names appeared on the list of voters, asking for details of name, age, marital status, number of children, occupation, any member of the family or household who had already enlisted, and height, of every man between 19 and 38 living on the premises, stating if they were prepared to enlist.[45] The forms, accompanied by an appeal from the committee and leaflets describing army pay and benefits, were posted out from 21 November 1914 onwards. It was not a success: there were complaints that the forms had not been received in many areas,[46] there was a break in delivery over the Christmas period, and many householders filled them in incorrectly, thinking it was a normal census.[47] There were also suspicions that this census was a prelude to conscription.[48] Four and a half million forms had been sent out by the end of the first week of January 1915, with some 218,000 indicating a willingness to enlist.[49] Letters were sent out in the first week of February to request that the respondents should now join up,[50] but as early as May it was apparent that not only had it failed to produce any significant improvement in recruitment, but the President of the Board of Trade, Walter Runciman, and Lord Derby both protested that a golden opportunity to assess the numbers of men – and women – available for any class of work in the national interest had been missed.[51] The first calls for a national register began to he heard, and the Welsh MP Sir Ivor Herbert declared that 'the State had a right to know what it held in reserve'.[52]

Sir John French, the commander-in-chief of the British Expeditionary Force in France, had begun a campaign of his own, criticising the shortage of munitions available to his army and, through carefully placed leaks to key journalists, provoking the 'Shell Crisis' of 1915. This, along with other political troubles drove Asquith to form his coalition government on 25 May 1915, and one of his first actions was to create a new Ministry of Munitions, appointing David Lloyd George as the minister. The Munitions of War Act was passed at the same time and gave the new ministry and the Board of Trade sweeping powers over industrial relations, wage and strike controls, and excess profits. It also introduced a number of new offences, which would be tried, not by the magistrates' courts, but by munitions tribunals.[53] Section 14 (1) described the constitution of these bodies:

> The munitions tribunal shall be a person appointed for the purpose by the Minister of Munitions sitting with two or some other even number of assessors, one-half being chosen by the Minister of Munitions from a panel constituted by the Minister of Munitions or persons representing employers and the other half being so chosen from a panel constituted by the Minister of Munitions of persons representing workmen.

Section 13 set out five categories of offences, the penalties for which ranged from £3 for failing to comply with regulations in a controlled establishment, to £50 for a general failure to comply with any other provisions of the Act. Sir John Simon, the Home Secretary, explained to the House of Commons that it would be wrong to settle a dispute in the police courts, as a workman found in breach could be sent to prison if he did not pay his fine. The munitions tribunal fine was to be treated as a stoppage from pay.[54] Magistrates had been involved in trade disputes for decades: the Conspiracy and Protection of Property Act, 1875 provided public protection against the effects of disputes, and prevented the intimidation of workers. The Employers and Workmen Act, 1875 provided a 'convenient and effective court of arbitration',[55] and the Trades Disputes Act, 1906 set the boundaries of legitimate strike action. The first appointments, to the General Munitions Tribunal for Wales and Monmouthshire (Chairman Robert Wallace, KC, with Sir Griffith Thomas [employers' representative] and Cllr Tom Griffiths [workers] as assessors), were made on 15 July 1915 against the backdrop of the South Wales miners' strike and 156,000 men standing idle over a demand for a 5 per cent increase in wages.[56] The strikers lost public and political support when it was claimed that the reduction in coal production would affect supplies for the navy, and critics were keen to see how the tribunal would penalise the miners. Lloyd George made a personal intervention in the crisis and the men returned to work the following week, with no further disciplinary action being taken which was perhaps just as well, as some were predicting total fines in excess of £1 million.

The rules for constituting and regulating munitions tribunals were published on 16 July. Local tribunals were to consider matters of employers and workers in breach of the regulations, and the general tribunal with trade disputes, negotiations and arbitration. Complaints were to be made to the chairman, who would then issue notices, by registered letter, to summon individuals. No solicitors were allowed. Fines could not be imposed in absence, and fines, deducted from wages, were to be paid to the clerk to the tribunal. Appeal, to quarter sessions, was only permitted on fines of £20 or more.[57] Given that any fines were to be recoverable as a deduction from wages, it was subsequently noticed that men on strike were not paid, and the question of recovery of fines in such cases had not been considered.[58]

Almost as if to prove that the powers of the tribunals were superfluous to the normal working of the courts, Sheffield magistrates fined Frank Burgess, of 27 Manor Lane, £20 or two months' in default, for defrauding his employers Cammell, Laird & Co of £1 3s 10d. Burgess had paid a small boy 3d a time to 'clock in' and out for him over a specimen period of four days – on one occasion he had clocked in himself but left after half an hour.[59] The first munitions tribunal sat at Barrow on 21 July, to consider the case of twenty-eight employees of the Vickers Naval Construction Works who had left work on the shell presses without referring their cause of complaint to arbitration. Fellow members of the union, the British Steel Smelters' Association, had stepped in to take over the work, so there was no loss of production. Mr John Hodge, the local MP, had returned to the borough from London to get the men back to work, and at the hearing the Vickers representative withdrew the charges.[60] Thirty-two members of the Amalgamated Society of Engineers, working at Craven Brothers of Darnall in Manchester, were not so lucky. A grievance over wages, piece rates and war bonus led to a one-day walkout. The shop steward had been absent on the day and, on his return, had taken the men straight back to work. He pleaded guilty on their behalf, and pointed out that most of them were ignorant of the new Act. The tribunal fined each man 2s 6d, and apportioned costs of £3 3s between them.[61]

Skilled labour was crucial to the plans of the Ministry of Munitions and under the Act restrictions were placed on men (and women) and their employers to prevent unnecessary mobility in the workforce. Men had to obtain a certificate from their company when leaving, and naturally these were not granted easily (itself a source of grievance to be resolved at the tribunal). But more manpower was needed and within a month of the formation of the new ministry the Prime Minister was able to announce a new Bill 'for the registration and subsequent organisation of the national resources',[62] and the following week Mr Walter Long introduced the Bill in the House of Commons, in which there would be compulsory registration of men and women between the ages of 15 and 65, with penalties for non-registration.[63] Mr Asquith repeated the assurances that neither conscription nor forced labour was contemplated.[64] The National Registration Act was passed on 15 July 1915. After various consultations the Local Government Board decided that the date for registration would be Sunday, 15 August 1915. The framework for implementation was essentially the same as the decennial census, last carried out on 2 April 1911, but now on a much shorter timescale. Twenty-five million forms had to be printed and distributed in the 2,000 local authority districts (registration authorities) in the country, and then arrangements made for their collection and assessment by an army of 50,000 volunteers.[65] The forms were delivered between Monday, 9 August and Saturday, 14 August, to be completed by midnight on

Sunday for collection the following week. Forms for men were printed on blue paper, and those for women on white, but they had the same nine questions:

1. Age last birthday.
2. If born abroad and not British, state nationality.
3. State whether single, married, widow or widower.
4. How many children are dependent on you: Under fifteen years? Over fifteen years?
5. How many other persons are dependent on you, excluding employees? Wholly dependent? Partly dependent?
6. Profession or occupation. State fully the particular kind of work done and the material worked or dealt in (if any)?
7. Name, business, and business address of employer.
8. Are you employed for or under any Government department? Say 'Yes', or 'No', or 'Don't know'.
9. Are you skilled in any work other than that upon which you are at present employed, and if so, what? Are you able and willing to undertake such work?

To modern eyes perhaps a rather rambling and badly-phrased document, but a comprehensive set of explanations and commentary accompanied the questionnaire, supported by volunteers ('enumerators') visiting homes during the week to provide guidance and, if necessary, to help complete the forms. The local authorities collected them during the following week and transferred the responses to index cards: blue for men, white for women, and green for those reporting a secondary occupation (question 9). The most important, for many, were the pink cards, on which were recorded the details of all men between 18 and 41 years of age, the so-called 'pink list'.[66]

Naturally there were many forms which had been incorrectly filled in or were incomplete, and in most cases were easily resolved by a further visit from an enumerator or a visit to the town hall. But it soon became apparent than some people were not willing to participate in the registration process at all. Katherine Anne Raleigh, of Park Road, Uxbridge, belonged to a 'militant suffragette society' and, when summoned to Stratford-upon-Avon magistrates' court on 21 August 1915, explained that she had a 'conscientious objection to completing a form which trampled on the liberties of women'. Curiously she relied on a rather genteel defence: the requirement to register applied to people between the ages of 15 to 65, and the prosecution had provided no evidence of her age. The magistrates were unswayed and fined her £3 for failing to register.[67] Another suffragette, Annie Hutty, of Ateha Lodge, Delaval Gardens, West Benwell, appeared at the Newcastle police court on 3 September and told the bench that as a woman she had no vote, and was not therefore a citizen and 'by filling in the form I shall be sacrificing my liberty'. She had neglected to register herself and refused to fill in the form, and she was fined £1 for each offence.[68] Lily Girdlestone, the wife of a Bristol clergyman, stated to magistrates that 'Englishwomen were classed with criminals, idiots, aliens and paupers' by being denied the vote, and that as these classes were exempted from registration so she refused to do so. She was fined 50s.[69]

Amelia Hewitt, of Upper Green, Mitcham, refused to pay a total of £4 12s 6d in fines and costs imposed for the same offence in September.[70] October. When a police sergeant visited her draper's shop to seize goods in default of payment she attacked him and bit his thumb so badly it had to be cauterized. For the assault the Croydon magistrates fined her £5 and ordered her to be held in custody until the money was paid. Her brother subsequently paid the fine and secured her release.[71]

Raleigh, Hutty, Girdlestone and Hewitt all appear in the 1911 census and so their moral objection appears questionable. Under the 1910 Census Act neglecting or refusing to complete the return carried a maximum penalty of a £5 fine, which was the same for the National Registration Act, but the new Act also recognized a continuing offence for which a fine not exceeding £1 a day could be imposed. The offence was non-imprisonable. Prosecutions were undertaken by the local registration authority, formed by the local authority or town council, and generally they were very lenient in dealing with troublesome cases, only referring the matter to court if letters and visits had failed. But the ulterior motive of the registration scheme was challenged. Fred Fouchard, of 6 Ending Rake, Healey, appeared before the Rochdale magistrates on 2 October 1915 for refusing to sign the register. He refused to enter a plea, and had to be told to keep quiet by Superintendent Jump. The evidence was given that the enumerator, Mr Ormerod, had collected the completed forms for Fouchard's mother, brother and sister on 16 August, but there was nothing from Fouchard himself. The town clerk, Mr Owen, had called on him, and then written, inviting him to the council offices. There was no reponse, and a final warning went unheeded, so on the advice of the Local Government Board the decision was taken to prosecute. Unfortunately this was first announced at a council meeting, and a damning report about Fouchard's refusal appeared in the local newspaper, claiming that he was afraid of being called up to join the army and had burned the form. Fouchard challenged the magistrates, claiming that the report was prejudicial, but the chairman reassured him that none of the bench had read it. When asked what had become of the form, he admitted that he had indeed burned it, and that 'I conscientiously object to signing it'. Conscientious objection, up to that time, had been accepted as a legal reason for non-compliance with the Vaccination Act, but this was not allowed under the National Registration Act. The bench decided to fine him £5, but Fouchard pointed out that he was not a householder and had no goods. He was warned that if he failed to pay he would be imprisoned for one month in default, and if he continued to refuse to sign the registration form he would be liable to the continuing fine of £1 a day; and the clerk made it clear that if he was 'so stupid' as to serve the month he would be summoned again on release. Later that afternoon Fouchard was taken to Strangeways gaol.[72] He kept to his principles and despite Owen writing to him that if he were to sign the register on his release there would be no further action, he refused, and was summonsed on 10 December. He had a change of heart and finally signed on 18 December. Two days later he made his final appearance in court, where the continuing offence fines were written off, and he was ordered to pay 5s 6d in costs, with two weeks to pay.[73]

Fouchard appears as a rather truculent and foolish young man. A more reasoned case was made by Harold Pugmire, an assistant master at Bamford Road School in

Heywood, Rochdale. In a scenario that would become common the following year, he was summoned before a sceptical, if not hostile, bench of magistrates at Heywood police court on 20 September 1915. The chairman was Major Lees, accompanied by Mr J.S. Hargreaves. The Mayor, Alderman Grundy, and Councillors Healey and Barrett were also on the bench, but as Pugmire was a council employee they did not take part in deciding the case. The prosecution made much of the fact that Pugmire was a teacher and 'expects absolute obedience from the children, but is not obedient to the law of the land'. He had given two addresses, one at 7 Moss Gardens in Heywood, the other at 95 Elm Vale, Liverpool. Forms had been left at both and he had completed neither. When subsequently written to he had replied: 'I hold the opinion that all war is contrary to the teaching of Jesus. In my judgement the Registration Form has been brought into being owing to the country being at war. Therefore as a Christian I refuse to fight or in any way assist in warlike preparations.' He had nothing further to add. Major Lees was clearly almost incandescent with rage, and was appalled that an educated man could present himself that way. He bitterly regretted that the penalties under the National Registration Act did not include imprisonment, and he fined Pugmire the maximum amount of £5, with forty-eight hours to pay.[74] On 11 October he appeared at the same court on a summons requiring him to show cause why he should not be committed to prison for non-payment of the fine. He made a further declaration about his principles, and asked why a person such as him 'following useful employment, offending no man, doing no wrong, but trying to remove ignorance, pain and trouble from the earth and to follow the teachings of Jesus', should be sent to prison. The clerk reminded him that imprisonment would be for non-payment of the fine, not for the National Registration Act offence. He was sent to prison for twenty-eight days in the second division.[75] Pugmire's troubles didn't end in gaol: on 22 October the Heywood Education committee considered his employment. The minute recorded that due to his absence since 11 October, it was 'resolved that such conduct being incompatible with the due discharge of his duty, and also prejudicial to the interests of the local authority, the said Pugmire to be discharged from the service of the local education authority'.[76] There were several similar stories around the country, of men and women who were willing to risk imprisonment in defence of their principles in relation to the war and whose voices would be heard again in the next year.

One outcome of the National Registration Act was that all persons on the register were issued with a National Registration Card which served as an identity card. This recorded the name, occupation and address of the holder (but no photograph) and although at that time there was no legal requirement to carry it, it was of great use in some of the prohibited areas, to which access was restricted. On 11 October 1915 Brigadier General E. Bickford, the officer commanding the Dover Garrison, issued a special order restricting the entrance and exit to the town by certain roads only, with guards detailed to examine all documents and registration cards. Civilians without cards had to submit reasons for wishing to enter.[77]

The National Registration Cards also provided a code representing the employment category of the holder. Those who were engaged on work of a national importance (munitions, mining, agricultural, and some industrial and commercial, subsequently described as the reserved occupations) had their forms marked with a black asterisk, or star, which led to the term 'starring'. This was often confused with the 'badging' of munitions and government workers, so that a machinist working at the Hoffmann's Ball Bearing works might be badged and starred, and a farm labourer merely starred. The proprietor of the only chemist's shop in a small town might also be starred. The issue of badges was controlled by the Badge Department of the Ministry of Munitions. The identification of particular trades as 'starred' was the work of the Labour Exchange department, and men engaged in such trades were exempted from military service although perfectly free to enlist if they so wished, although this was to change later in the war.

At the request of Lord Kitchener, Lord Derby was appointed Director-General of Recruiting on 6 October 1915, and within five days had submitted a recruiting plan to the Parliamentary and Joint Labour Recruiting committees.[78] On 15 October he revealed his plans to use the National Registration pink forms for military recruitment, exactly as the conscientious objectors had feared. The local Parliamentary Recruiting Committees would be given blue cards based on information from the pink list, and canvassers would visit unstarred men to challenge them 'with utmost tact and discretion' about their intentions to enlist or otherwise, and the excuses recorded on the card, to be retained by the recruiting officer[79] (apparently this system of canvassing was already in use for general elections[80]). As not all areas had completed the indexation of the registration forms Derby set the date of 30 November as the deadline for the canvassing process, and such was the optimism that the canvassers were issued with supplies of railway warrants to hand out to men who accepted the call to enlist. If the man wasn't present they were to call repeatedly at his address until they saw him, and they were told to speak plainly and politely and 'Do not bully or threaten'.[81] This was an astonishing intrusion on privacy, to modern eyes, and a clear abuse of the information provided to the national register, and provided a cover of legitimacy for party agents and others to harass private citizens in their own homes.

Extensive and intrusive canvassing was the first part of Lord Derby's master plan. He revealed his eponymous scheme in a speech at the Mansion House on 19 October 1915, in which he proposed to class all men of military age into forty-six groups, by age and marital status. Perhaps unwisely, he made an undertaking, later repeated in the House of Commons by the Prime Minister, that no married men would be called up until all the single men had enlisted. He recognized that personal circumstances might be such that a man would want to be put back to a later group and anticipated an appeal system. And he concluded, 'This is the last effort on behalf of voluntary service'.[82] The Group or Derby Scheme appeared reasonably attractive: men could attend their local recruiting office and, on presenting their National Registration Card, complete the attestation form, make the oath, undergo a medical examination and collect 2s 9d in pay and subsistence allowance, and then return to work and family life as before. Technically he had joined Class B of the Army Reserve (under (2) of paragraph 1 of the War Office letter 27/General Number/4507, dated 23 October 1915[83]) but was not required to do anything until his group was called up by proclamation. Derby intended that all men, including those badged or starred, should attest, and the latter could then obtain formal exemptions from military service. To deal with exemptions and deferrals a system of appeal tribunals was created, under the control of the Local Government Board and the local authorities. The local tribunals were made up of councillors and other local dignitaries but not necessarily magistrates, and the tribunals were not judicial bodies, being solely concerned with the administration of the volunteers under the Derby Scheme (it should be remembered that these men were now Reservists and subject to the provisions of the Reserve Forces Act, 1882). The tribunals were to decide 'all questions of whether a man's domestic responsibilities or business duties justify placing him in a group to be called up later',[84] and Derby issued further guidance that it was for the State, not the employer, to determine if a man was indispensable, and that a War Office representative should be able to appeal against a man who was starred who ought not to be.[85] Attested men and those rejected as medically unfit were entitled to wear a khaki armlet. They also had to possess Army form B.2505A or B2512A to prove their status.[86]

In a final attempt to avoid compulsory conscription, the King made an appeal to the country on 23 October 1915, asking 'men of all classes to come forward voluntarily and take your share in the fight'. The Group Scheme came into operation on 25 October 1915, after a Royal Warrant was passed to allow men to take the novel step of joining the Reserves.[87] The scheme was initially successful, albeit more so with married than with single men.[88] There were some criticisms that it was not always possible to choose a particular unit,[89] but employers welcomed the scheme because it prevented employees from enlisting in groups because under the scheme they would be called up by age. Derby had originally set a deadline of 30 November to complete the canvass and for men to enlist under the Group Scheme, but this was subsequently revised to 5 and then to 11 December. Men who had not attested by this time would bear the brunt of any compulsory conscription scheme that might then be introduced.[90] By early December Derby himself was disappointed with the results of the scheme, and the Under-Secretary of State for War, Mr Tennant, was raising the possibility of conscription.[91] As the deadline approached there was a sudden increase in recruitment and in many places the military authorities set up temporary recruiting offices to deal with the rush. In Birmingham there were arrangements for men to attest at the factories at which they worked, and the local bench undertook to provide magistrates wherever they were needed.[92] In Coventry recruiting centres were set up at the Rover Company's showrooms, at the Masonic Hall and the Daimler Works.[93] So many men came forward that there was a shortage of the coveted khaki armlets,[94] which helped them avoid the further attention of the canvassers. Late on Saturday, 11 December ('Derby Day') the War Office extended the recruitment period to midnight on the Sunday, and there was a public appeal for magistrates to attend the recruiting stations.[95]

The khaki armlets, embroidered with the royal crown, were proudly worn by those who had attested, and by those who had been medically rejected. George Neal, a carman of Venables Street, Lisson Grove, saw an opportunity for some easy money when he met two young men outside a music hall in London, and offered to sell them two armlets for a 'bob'. The youths refused, and followed Neal until they found a police constable and reported the matter to him. Neal appeared in Marylebone Police Court on Thursday,

20 January 1916 when the magistrate remanded him for a week to seek the opinion of the military authorities. Lord Athlumley, the Provost Marshal himself, produced the authority from the War Office to allow the civil prosecution rather than court-martial, and Neal was fined 40s or twenty-one days' imprisonment.[96] Ben Johnson, a 40-year-old recruiting clerk, was paid £1 by Russell Miller for an armlet and some fake attestation papers. The military authorities asked the East Ham magistrates to take a 'very serious view of the case', and Johnson received a swingeing £30 fine.[97]

Even while the statistics were being compiled, on Saturday, 18 December Lord Kitchener published a proclamation (dated 20 December) announcing the calling-up of the first four groups, with a warning to report on such date and place as directed with fourteen days' notice. The call-up was to commence on 20 January 1916, and would be spread over several days. The first groups were the youngest unmarried men:

Group 2 (age 19–20)   Group 4 (age 21–22)
Group 3 (age 20–21)   Group 5 (age 22–23)

Group 1 (18–19) was not called up because men under 19 were not permitted to serve overseas. Although a letter would be posted to each man with the details of his call-up (Army Form W 3.195), for legal purposes the public poster which appeared on 20 January was sufficient notice.

Exemptions were given to men who had been starred or badged or were working in reserved occupations. Such men, if called-up, had to notify their employers, who would then provide a certificate of employment to the recruiting officer. The first rambling attempt at listing the reserved occupations appeared on 22 October, as:

Class A   Munitions workers.
Class B   Railway and farm workers.
Class C   Agricultural and mining.
Class D   Other occupations: indispensable men in trade and industry.
Class E   Time exempt (i.e. requiring time to wind up affairs, etc).[98]

The Reserved Occupations Committee of the Board of Trade issued a supplemental list on 29 November, on which the headings were:

Jute trade.
Lace making.
Ramie spinning.
Oilcloth, linoleum and floorcloth manufacturers.
Newspaper printing.
China and earthenware manufacture.
Lithographic transfer-making for china and earthenware manufacturers.
Paint, colour and varnish making.
Milk trade.
Machine creameries and condensed milk and milk powder factories.

Fish trade.

Fruit, hop and market gardens.

Ports, docks and wharves.

Public carriers of goods by road and carting contractors in connection with railways, docks, wharves and warehouses.

Horse-shoeing.[99]

The list was further expanded on 18 December and was constantly revised throughout the war.[100]

Attested men were entitled to appeal to be placed in a different group, but not for exemption from military service unless they already held certificates for exemption. Claims for postponement were to be made to the local tribunal by 30 December[101] or within ten days of receiving the call-up letter. There were three forms of appeal: from the man himself, in order to sort out personal or business affairs; from his employer, on the grounds that he was considered individually indispensable in a business (and that the man was willing to continue in employment); and in the third case, on the nebulous grounds that although not starred his occupation should be treated as such, which required the assent of the recruiting officer. There was a 'brisk demand' for appeal forms, especially from employers.[102] The first tribunal meetings were often simply to elect a chairman and to determine the procedures to be used in handling appeals. Rochdale local tribunal first sat on 14 January 1916 at the magistrates' room at the Town Hall. Unusually the committee was made up of four magistrates and a councillor: Alderman Cunliffe JP, Sir James Jones JP, Walter Scott JP and Councillor Davidson. It was reported that about 800 men had attested, of whom 250 were starred or badged, leaving 550 men available. Of these, 200 were appealing! In a gruelling session the tribunal sat from 3 pm to 5 pm, resuming at 6 pm until 9.30 pm and completed thirty-three appeals, at an average of ten minutes per case. Thirteen of the appeals were refused. The tribunal sat again on the Saturday and Sunday, and the next three days. They would have been disheartened to learn that, following the proclamation calling up groups 6, 7, 8 and 9, due to start on 8 February, a further 110 appeals had been handed in to the Town Hall.[103]

But even as the Group Scheme got under way, the inevitable need for compulsory conscription had been realized. Mr Asquith announced his intention to introduce a 'Bill dealing with Military Service' to the House of Commons on 4 January 1916,[104] which triggered the resignation of the Home Secretary, Sir John Simon. The Prime Minister revealed that Lord Derby's campaign had brought forward around three million men willing to serve, which with adjustments for medical and other reasons left around 343,000 single men and 487,000 married men, but there were 651,000 unstarred single men unaccounted for.[105] The Military Service (No. 2) Bill[106] – 'a Bill to make provision with respect to military service in connection with the present war' – was issued on Friday, 7 January 1916. Clause 1 presented an astonishing challenge to individual liberty never before seen in English constitutional law, in which every unmarried male British subject of military age would be deemed to have attested in His Majesty's forces and transferred to the Reserves. The Bill was received considerable attention in Parliament and across the country, and was debated several times in the first weeks of 1916. At a quarter to six on 27 January the Military Service Act, 1916 received the Royal Assent.[107] Section 1 stated:

1. Every male British subject who –

   a. On the fifteenth day of August 1915, was ordinarily resident in Great Britain and had reached the age of eighteen years and had not attained the age of forty-one years; and
   b. On the second day of November 1915 was unmarried or was a widower without any child dependent on him;

Shall, unless he is within the exceptions set out in the First Schedule to this Act, or had attained the age of forty-one years before the appointed date, be deemed as from the appointed date to have been duly enlisted in His Majesty's regular forces for general service with the colours or in the reserve for the period of the war, and to have been forthwith transferred to the reserve.

The Army Act, 1881 and Reserve Forces Act, 1882–1907 would immediately apply to any man so deemed to have been enlisted (with or without his consent). The significance of 15 August 1915 is that it was National Registration day, and the military authorities would have the blue and white cards as evidence of the man's age. The relevance of 2 November is not apparent. The 'appointed day' was Thursday, 2 March 1916.

The Derby Scheme had required no new legislation, other than the Royal Warrant which permitted recruits to join the reserves rather than proceed directly into military service, and likewise the local tribunals, however constituted, had no formal legal powers. The Military Service Act was a much more powerful instrument, and Parliament had carefully written down the procedures for appeals for the granting of certificates of exemption by the new Local Tribunals. Initially four grounds were offered:

   a. On the ground that it is expedient in the national interests that [the man] should, instead of being employed on military service, be engaged in other work in which he is habitually engaged or in which he wishes to be engaged or, if he is being educated or trained for any work, that he should continue to be so educated and trained; or
   b. On the ground that serious hardship would ensue, if the man were called up for Army Service, owing to his exceptional financial or business obligations or domestic position; or
   c. On the ground of ill-health or infirmity; or
   d. On the ground of a conscientious objection to the undertaking of combatant service.

Harold Pugmire would have been delighted to see the recognition of a man's moral and religious principles. Certificates of exemption could be absolute, temporary or conditional, and the conscientious objection could be restricted to exemption from combatant work only, or to perform work of national importance. Certificates could also be granted by certain government departments to men whose work was of national importance. There was a distinction between *exempted* men, in the four categories above, and *excepted* men, such as serving soldiers and sailors, clergymen, and visitors from the Dominions (as specified in the First Schedule to the Act).

The appointed day of 2 March was preceded by a flurry of voluntary recruitment as young men believed that they would have better conditions as volunteers than as conscripts. It was also announced that, despite Lord Derby's written promise, the first married groups, Nos. 25 to 32 were to be called up beginning from 7 April.[108] The government had been prepared for widespread opposition and possible civil disobedience[109] but there was none. That morning 651,160 young unmarried men woke up to find that they were in the Army Reserves, and anxiously awaited the arrival of the yellow form warning them to proceed to the recruiting office.[110] An Army Royal Warrant had been issued just the night before, announcing that men deemed to have enlisted under the Act would receive no emoluments while serving in the Reserve.[111] And yet even as the first 'Derbyites' were joining their units for basic training and the first MSA men awaited the call, the government revisited its recruiting policy. By the end of April a new Bill was formulated which provided for the conscription of all men of military age, married and unmarried, and the Military Service Act, 1916 (Session 2) was passed on 25 May 1916. As well as transferring hundreds of thousands of married men into the reserves, it incorporated elements of Sir John Simon's abortive Military Service (No. 1) Bill, such as time-served former servicemen being brought back into the army, as well as the transfer of men between corps and battalions without their consent.

Military and local authorities braced themselves for a flood of appeals for exemption as it was announced that the Central Tribunal was dealing with a backlog of 16,000 Derby cases.[112] The Derby tribunals, appointed by the local registration committees, were still required, and the new local tribunals were distinct and separate. This did not prevent many local authorities simply adopting a dual committee rôle, but the Local Government Board was keen to see membership drawn from a broader community, to include employers and representatives of labour.[113] Learning from the difficulties inherent in the Derby local tribunal/central appeal model, the Military Service (Regulations) Order of 3 March 1916 set out a three-tiered appeal system of local tribunals, county or area appeal tribunals, and the central appeal tribunal. It was intended from the outset that these tribunals were to follow a standard procedure to 'ensure uniformity of decisions and practice', which experienced magistrates would have found a laudable if unworkable principle.[114] There were to be local tribunals for each local registration district, that is, the same administrative unit used for the National Registration Act (and for general elections). Between five and twenty members were to be appointed, depending on the population of the area. The members of the tribunal were in an invidious position. In contrast to the police courts, the tribunals were seen as partial and often biased, and at one time criticized by the military for being too lenient and at others for being harsh and unsympathetic. Appeals could be heard before any call-up papers were received and many employers acted on behalf of their workers. Although legal representation was permitted, many men from the working classes struggled to present an articulate justification for exemption or deferment and from this time onwards the newspapers are full of pathetic little cameos of the lives of men, attempting to explain the potential impact of military service on their businesses and families.

The Defence of the Realm regulations also covered civilian employment. On 11 May 1916 the new regulation 41A required all employers of one or more male persons over 16 to prepare three statements: one to return the particulars of all such employees who had been employed for a week or more; another for all female employees, and the third covering all male persons employed during the preceding month for less than one week. The forms, obtained from the post office, were to be revised as frequently as necessary, and statements 1 and 2 were to be 'constantly posted up in some conspicuous place' in the employer's premises. Copies were to be delivered to the local recruiting officer in the first week of each month, and additional copies to the Director-General of National Service as directed. Exemptions were available from the Minister of Munitions, the Director-General of National Service, the colliery recruiting courts, and the ports labour committees. Regulation 41AAA required agricultural employers to notify the Board of Agriculture and Fisheries within twenty-four hours of the termination of a man's employment, and particulars (if available) of the man's new employer. Regulation 41AB required an employer to take all reasonable steps to obtain the certificate of exemption or other evidence relating to a potential employee's liability for military service before entering into a contract. Subsections of 41AB put the same obligations on the employee, and even on any person 'who in the ordinary course of his business is in communication with any male person apparently of military age with a view to such person being ... engaged in any employment'. The Newton Abbot magistrates had a field day on 26 June 1917, with a number of the local great and good being summoned for 41A offences, including Colonel Robert Patch, John Mills, Colonel Thomas Shortland, Dr A.W. Chennells, headmaster of Newton College, and Edward Wylie, captain of the local Volunteer Company. All protested that they knew nothing of the order and the chairman of the bench, Dr Ley, appeared to sympathize; all defendants were ordered to pay 4s costs, with no further penalty.[115]

Magistrates and the magistrates' courts had surprisingly little to do with conscription. Mr A. Whitworth JP served as military representative to the Colne tribunal, and Mr W. Goodfellow, a justice on the Truro bench and commandant of the local Volunteer Training Corps, was also a military representative. Appeals and exemptions were nothing to do with the magistrates' courts. Men failing to attend when called up were dealt with as absentees under the Reserve Forces Act, and so, in the usual formula, were fined 40s and detained in custody to await military escort. The procedure for the courts to recover the fines from the War Office was described in a Home Office circular in May 1916. The justices' clerk was to notify the local recruiting officer that the absentee had been convicted and fined; when the full amount had subsequently been deducted from the man's pay it would be forwarded in full to the court by the paymaster of the unit to which the soldier belonged. It tiptoed around a rather delicate point but mentioned that in the event of the soldier being 'discharged on medical or other grounds' before the full amount of the fine had been received, it should not be enforced and should be written off. It further added that the Secretary of State considered that as the law provided for the deduction of the amount from the soldier's pay, it would not be appropriate to imprison in default.[116] Chelmsford Petty Sessions dealt with eleven MSA absentees in 1916, or 1.6 per cent of the total workload. One of them was the lion tamer, Leo Stanley, who had been brought from the Highland Light Infantry camp at Widford. He had originally been detained in Fulham and in uniform had been taken to the camp after he claimed to belong to the regiment. The military authorities subsequently found that he had not joined the army nor had he attested, and that he had bought the uniform in Petticoat Lane, while drunk. He was fined the mandatory £2 and handed over.[117]

Conscientious objectors often used the courtroom to express their views and defend their principles, but it was the wrong forum – the man was in court as an absentee and the magistrates had no powers to release him from his military obligations or to challenge the decision of the tribunal. He could of course plead 'not guilty' to the charge, but would have to provide evidence as to why he was not subject to the Military Service Act. This was decided by the magistrates. The First Schedule to the Act excluded serving ministers from the obligations of the MSA, and so when on 15 April 1916 George Hazelton Fromow, of 1, Wellesley Road, Chiswick appeared at Acton Police Court for failing to report, the military representative, Major Smith, contended on behalf of the military authorities that the bench had to decide if he was a minister of religion and exempt, or a nurseryman and liable to military service. He had originally been visited by a Derby canvasser and had sent in a claim of exemption, as a regular minister at the Strict Baptist Church in Farnborough, and this was confirmed by a letter from the Metropolitan Association of Strict Baptist Churches. However, during the rest of the week he worked at his father's nursery, from which he earned his living. Fromow, on oath, described his ministry as his primary occupation but that his denomination was unable to support him full-time, instead he received a stipend of £2 a month. He admitted he had told the canvasser that he was a conscientious objector. The magistrate decided that he was not a regular minister within the meaning of the Act, and therefore liable to military service. Major Smith invited Fromow to put his claim before the military tribunal[118] His appeal was subsequently dismissed by the London County Tribunal and he was given non-combatant service.

On 2 March 1917 the stipendiary magistrate at Middlesbrough Police Court heard the case of Oscar Allwright, of 9, Oliver Street, South Bank. He was charged with being an absentee. The previous year he had obtained a certificate of exemption from his local tribunal of the grounds that he was a regular minister of a religious denomination, the South Bank Mission, which had 112 members. They described themselves as of the Church of England but separate. They owned a chapel and paid Allwright a salary of £78. He worked exclusively for the Mission, delivering two Sunday sermons and eight weekly meetings. The military representative had appealed the case at the county tribunal, which had decided that Allwright was actually an exception, not an exemption and that they had no jurisdiction. The local tribunal then cancelled his exemption but for some reason then awarded an exemption for non-combatant service only, which he refused. The prosecution contended that he was neither a regular minister nor was the Mission a religious denomination. A test case had gone before the divisional courts (Kipps v Lane, 1917) in which the Lord Chief Justice had expressly refrained from providing definitions, requiring each case to be tested on its merits. The magistrate felt that although Allwright was untrained and had not been ordained, ceremonially or otherwise, he had been appointed to a post which required regular and continuous service. He drew attention to the wording of the MSA which provided for 'men in holy orders or a regular minister of any religious denomination', which clearly differentiates between the two. He concluded that the South Bank Mission was a religious denomination and that Allwright was a regular minister, and he dismissed the summons.[119]

An extraordinary case came before the same court in October 1916. John Gaunt was charged with being an absentee under the MSA but Lieutenant Barlow on behalf of the military authorities wanted a legal decision as to whether he was exempted or excepted. Gaunt had been born in Rhenish Prussia in 1891, of British parents. He had lived in the Netherlands for three years for educational purposes. Other than a couple of short visits to England in 1908 and 1914 he had spent the rest of his life in Germany. His parents still lived there, and according to Scotland Yard had not been interned, but Gould was imprisoned in Cologne in September 1914, where he developed jaundice. He was then sent to the infamous Ruhleben detention camp at Berlin but managed to escape and made his way to England via Holland. He tried to join the Officer Training Corps and the Royal Flying Corps but had been rejected as he was classed as a former prisoner of war – were he to be captured again he would be liable to be shot. He had registered under the National Registration Act and was keen to serve. Lieutenant Barlow held that he was probably exempt as a former prisoner of war, under section 8 of the MSA, 1916 (Session 2). His offence was, in part, technical because his absence had been agreed with the military authorities. The magistrate eventually dismissed the case under section 1 of the First Schedule, that Gaunt was not ordinarily resident in this country.[120]

In ordinary language the expression 'called up' seems a reasonable description of the process by which an attested man or a reservist is brought into military service. In both the Group and MSA schemes, if a man intended to appeal he was required to do so before being called up, but at what moment was he deemed to have been called up? According to section 12 (3) of the Reserve Forces Act it was when the man 'received such directions to attend at the date and time fixed' – the receipt of the letter – but it subsequently suggests that he is not called up until 'at and after that time', when he actually attends. For the purposes of exemption it appeared that the man could apply at any time up to the moment he went to the barracks or recruiting office. The Old Street magistrate attempted to clarify this anomaly in April 1917 by deciding that it was from the moment of receiving the letter.[121]

The constant demand for manpower for the armed forces conflicted with the needs of industry and agriculture for skilled and unskilled personnel. The National Register had the details of the skills, trades and occupations of every adult in the country and by 1917 it had become apparent that government action was required to ensure they were deployed where they were most needed. Neville Chamberlain, resigning his post as Lord Mayor of Birmingham, was appointed the Director General of National Service in December 1916 and the Ministry of National Service Act was introduced on 28 March 1917 'for the purpose of making the best use of all persons, whether men or women, able to work in any industry, occupation, or service'. One objective of the Act was to reduce the number of 'non-essential trades' to provide a substitute source of labour to allow the release of men of military age for military service.[122] Adults between the ages of 18 and 61 were encouraged to complete Form A, available from the post office or employment exchange, and send it to the Minister of National Service. Candidates would be invited for interview and assigned to vacancies anywhere in the country, on a minimum wage of 25s a week and with a subsistence allowance of 17s 6d a week.[123] In May Councillor Robertson was able to report to the Aberdeen Town Council that seventy-three council employees had volunteered for ploughing service, of whom twenty had been accepted.[124] 1,028 National Service Committees were formed nationally, with the task of matching suitable local volunteers to lists of vacancies circulated by the Ministry,[125] and by April there were 232,455 persons enrolled;[126] however, a large proportion were munitions workers who were not actually available for other employment. Departmental conflicts caused problems: the Ministry of Labour operated the labour exchanges and sought to fill vacancies by its own means, and the Ministry of Munitions was anxious to protect its own interests. Political infighting resulted in Chamberlain's resignation in August, but by then the Cabinet had agreed that the Ministry of National Service would take charge of 'both the military and civil side of universal National Service' on behalf of the War Office.[127] Brigadier General Sir Auckland Geddes MP, formerly Director of Recruiting at the War Office, succeeded Chamberlain on 18 August 1917 and the department officially became a ministry. The Military Tribunal system was amended to become the National Service Tribunal, and the remit extended to consider the needs of local industry and agriculture. The original concept of civilian national service was a failure, but the reconstituted ministry was successful in recruiting and placing agricultural workers and, significantly, women.

There was an endless demand for more men, and in April 1917 the Military Service (Review of Exceptions) Act and the Military Service Regulations (Amendment) Order enabled the 'exception from Military Service of Men excepted on the ground of previous rejection, or the previous relinquishment of, or discharge from, Naval or Military Service, or unsuitability for Foreign Service, to be reviewed'. Such men were previously excepted under the First Schedule, but on receipt of a notice to report for medical examination were deemed to come under section 1 of the MSA and had to report within fourteen days. The Military Service (Conventions with Allied States) Act of July 1917 has been considered in Chapter 6.

On 18 April 1918 the Military Service (No. 2) Act extended the upper age limit to 51 and, for holders of certificates of exemption, there was a requirement to join the Volunteer Force and 'attend such drills, undertake such training, and undertake such military duties as may be so prescribed'. Section 3 provided for cancellation of certificates of exemption by proclamation by His Majesty the King in Council. The status of former prisoners of war was also changed, so that only those who had been formally exchanged under the protection of the International Committee of the Red Cross were excepted – the government would have given an undertaking that such men would not serve again. This now made available a number of escaped internees from Germany, Austria and Turkey.[128] Under the 1918 Act all men between 18 and 51 in Great Britain could be placed in one of six classes:

1. Men subject to military law. This class includes all British subjects and all aliens actually serving with the colours or in the naval or air services of the Crown.
2. Reservists: made up of:

   a. Statutory reservists – British subjects and aliens (under the Military Service (Conventions with Allied States) Act, 1917 (see Chapter 3)), by statute deemed to have enlisted and transferred to the reserve.
   b. Attested reservists – the now rapidly diminishing class of Derby recruits, who attested voluntarily.
   c. Men relegated to the reserves: reservists, statutory or attested, who on being called up were not accepted for service but sent back into reserve.
   d. Demobilized men: regulars and territorials, after active service with the colours, demobilized without being discharged and returned to civil life. Includes greater majority of skilled men released from the colours to follow particular occupations in civil life 'on working furlough', i.e. technically still serving with the colours, but absent on leave.

   Any man of these categories can be called up for service, unless he possesses a certificate of exemption. A 'certificate of protection' also exempts, but the recruiting officer who grants it can withdraw it at any moment.
3. British subjects excepted from military service:

   a. Men ordinarily resident in His Majesty's dominions abroad.
   b. Clergymen and ministers.
   c. Certain categories of discharged officers and men.

4. Friendly aliens not liable to service under the Military Service (Conventions with Allied States) Act, 1917.
5. Neutral aliens – liable to special restrictions under the Aliens (Restriction) Act and Orders.
6. Enemy aliens: liable to internment for the duration of the war, as prisoners of war in common law, by virtue of royal prerogative. British-born persons whose parents are enemy subjects are by our law, British subjects, and liable to military service unless prior to the commencement of the war had elected to choose foreign nationality.[129]

The Military Service (No. 2) Act had barely passed through Parliament when on 22 April the King issued a proclamation in response to the large-scale German attacks in Flanders and France. Certificates of exemption for all men between the ages of 19 and 23 were withdrawn, subject to medical grades higher than B3 and C2 and certain farmworkers, mines, transport workers and medical practitioners.[130] In a series of proclamations and orders over the next few days 'hardship' certificates were withdrawn and men between 41 and 44 called up.

By the end of the war every alien enemy and friend had been identified and registered and was known to the authorities. And, under the 'cult of the card index',[131] so was every British adult.

Chapter 10

And What Did You Do in the War, Mummy?

The young Charlie Chaplin had moved to America in 1913 and started his film career at the Keystone Studios in Los Angeles. By February 1914 he had appeared in his first movie, and in the process of rehearsing for his next appearance he assembled an unusual costume from the wardrobe department and his famous character 'the Tramp' was born. He was filming *Mabel's Strange Predicament* at the time, but the first appearance of the bumbling vagrant was in a six-minute comedy called *Kid Auto Races at Venice*.[1] This was released in Great Britain in July 1914 and, as a short 'screamingly funny'[2] 'comic interest' feature, supported such films as *The Afghan Raiders*,[3] *Vampires of the Night*,[4] or *Lights o' London*.[5] These films were in black and white and with musical accompaniment provided on the piano, organ or even an orchestra,[6] and were an extremely popular form of entertainment – even small towns might have had two or more cinemas. Local authorities had control of the licensing of cinemas under the Cinematograph Act, 1909, and in many cases delegated this power to the justices in petty sessions. At this time there was a British Board of Film Censors, appointed by the film industry itself, and presided over by Mr G.A. Redford. In his first annual report in February 1914 he announced that 6,861 films had been passed for universal exhibition ('particularly suitable for children's matinees'), 627 were given an 'A' certificate for public exhibition, and 166 had been sent back for further editing, on grounds such as portrayals of indecorous dancing, medical operations, scenes 'tending to disparage public characters and institutions', 'native customs in foreign lands abhorrent to British ideas' and indecently morbid death scenes. Only twenty-two were entirely rejected.[7]

The 'A' certificate was merely advisory and children could attend both the 'A' certificate and the universal exhibition films. And perhaps unsurprisingly, the 'pictures' were blamed for influencing youth crime. At the quarterly meeting of the Liverpool justices at the Town Hall on 6 April 1914, Sir Thomas Hughes reported that they intended to take away a number of cinema licences in response to an increase in the number of (juvenile) cases dealt with under the Probation Act, 1907, and at the Hawarden Petty Sessions two 12-year-old boys were charged with stealing tobacco from a truck at Shotton Railway Station.[8] One of the lads said that he wanted to get money to go to the picture palace.[9] The two boys were each given six strokes of the birch.

Physical punishment was still in use at this time, but just a few years earlier the Children Act of 1908 was the first separate legislation that recognized that children should not be treated in the same way as adults by the judicial system, and in particular that children under the age of 14 should not be sent to an adult prison. The preamble of the Act stated that it was '... to consolidate and amend the Law relating to the Protection of Children and Young Persons, Reformatory and Industrial Schools, and Juvenile Offenders, and otherwise to amend the Law with Respect to Children and Young Persons', and it showed the comprehensive and ambitious intention to fundamentally reform the way children, and those with responsibilities for children, would be treated by the courts. The section headings themselves show the broad reach of the new legislation:

I   Infant life protection.
II   Prevention of cruelty to children and young persons.
III   Juvenile smoking.
IV   Reformatory and industrial schools.
V   Juvenile offenders.

The society into which these children was born had a number of social norms, assumptions and institutions, inculcated by their parents. The author of *The Shilling Law Book*[10] (1900) intended to place 'within reach of the reader some slight knowledge of those portions of English law which are most likely to concern him in his every-day life'. The first chapter is entitled 'Husband and Wife' and sets out the legal relationship between the couple from the start of their marriage. It begins with a warning about bigamy, the penalty for which is seven years' penal servitude, and then describes the ways in which they can enter the married state: banns, licence, special licence, registrar's licence or registrar's certificate. The possibility of an action for breach of promise of marriage, which would be heard before a judge and jury and could result in substantial damages, helped to ensure that the process of betrothal was not be taken lightly.

And it then went on to describe the personal rights of the husband and wife, which were substantially changed by the provisions of the Married Woman's Property Act, 1882 (with very slight amendments in 1907). Up to that time a man acquired all of his wife's property on marriage but the Act allowed her authority and independence to manage her own property without her husband's interference, and she could sue and be sued in her own right. The husband now had limited 'control and custody' over his wife but was bound to maintain and support her and their children, this obligation ceasing only if she deserted him or went off in adultery. He was obliged to supply her with 'necessaries'; a vague term which depended on the husband's station in life, and included food, drink, lodging, wearing apparel, fuel, washing and medical attendance.

The Summary Jurisdiction (Married Women) Act, 1895 gave new protection to women experiencing abuse. If a woman left her husband because he ill-treated or neglected to maintain her or the children, he still had to support her. A deserted wife and family might otherwise become chargeable to the rates under the Poor Law, potentially ending up in the workhouse. It was difficult to get out of a bad marriage. The rich could afford to get divorced – a costly process managed in the Divorce Courts. The poor had to settle with a judicial separation from the magistrates' court. Lilian Charlotte Angove, of Torquay Road, Newton Abbot, applied for a separation order to Dr J.W. Ley at the Newton Abbott bench on 31 March 1914. Her husband, Richard Angove, was represented but did not appear. It was stated that Mr Angove was a commercial traveller and had they had been married ten years, with four children. From the start he had shown unkindness, which ended with 'assaults and shocking neglect'. Since the previous December he had given her no money, and she had now sold all her furniture and was relying on the generosity of friends. He had made threats to burn her, and to 'do for her', and she was now in fear of her safety. With a number of witnesses corroborating the accounts of abusive behaviour, in which drink played a part, the bench granted the separation order, giving Mrs Angove the custody of the children and ordering Angove himself to pay £1 per week in maintenance, and 18s costs.[11]

Magistrates also had another major responsibility – deciding the paternity of illegitimate children, under the Bastardy Act, 1845 and the Bastardy Laws Amendment Act, 1872. Although Landsteiner had identified the four human blood groups in 1901, their use in proving relationships between individuals had not been given legal attention. Magistrates were in a difficult and daunting position: the objective of the bastardy laws was to have the man rightly contribute to the maintenance of the child he had fathered, but also the man had to be protected against malicious or vexatious allegations. The woman's evidence had to be corroborated, but it was acknowledged that the circumstances around the conception of the child may well have been concealed from those around the couple. Lord Alverstone (1906) sought material evidence in relation to the conduct of the father or to the probability of his being the father; these could be acts of familiarity between the complainant and the putative father at the relevant time. Corroborative evidence could be easily supplied by admission (and this happened with the wealthier classes, in which a settlement could be reached without the intervention of the court) but an interesting argument was offered concerning a man's silence. It was proposed that if two persons have a conversation in which one of them makes a statement to the disadvantage of the other, and the latter does not deny it, this would be evidence of an admission that the statement was correct. Magistrates were to understand that mere silence in response to spoken or written statement was not enough to amount to corroboration unless the nature of the statement was such that 'an ordinary reasonable man would be expected in his own interest to make an answer'.[12] The putative father, if proven, would be liable to make payments in support of the child until he or she was 13 – a substantial financial commitment, and to fail to make representations to the contrary was clearly not the action of a man of good character. Other corroborative evidence were letters, and testimony of witnesses who had seen the couple together.

The mother could make a summons before the birth of the child, or within a year of the birth. If the father left the country within the year, she was entitled to apply within a year of his return. The magistrates would issue the summons for a hearing not less than six days afterwards, for the attendance of the alleged father, and any witnesses the woman might need. If the decision was in favour of the mother, an affiliation order of a sum not exceeding 5s a week could be imposed, to cover the maintenance and education of the child; once determined, it was not permitted to change the amount, even if the man's circumstances greatly improved. The payments were to continue even if the mother married, but should the father die, the child had no claim on his estate (unlike his legitimate offspring). The Affiliation Orders Act of July 1914 specified that the money was to be paid to a collecting officer of the court, rather than directly to the mother. Refusal to pay, in the first instance, would result in his detention in custody until a distress warrant could be executed by the bailiffs (Chapter 1); if this didn't work the magistrates could commit him to imprisonment (without hard labour). A man was allowed to appeal against an order to the quarter sessions but the woman had no such right. This seemingly harsh and unfair situation was justified by the recognition that the sympathies of the justices were likely to lie with the woman,[13] who also had the right to make a second application if she had additional evidence which had not been available when her first application was dismissed.

Legitimate or bastard, under the Vaccination Acts introduced during the previous seventy years the newly born child had to be vaccinated against smallpox and under the 1898 version of the Act this was to be done before the age of six months, using a new form of the vaccine containing a modified form of the cowpox virus in glycerinated calf lymph. Parents originally took the child to the public vaccinating station but now the doctor visited the child at home. Not all parents were convinced of the safety of the process and up until the 1898 Act a parent refusing to permit vaccination was liable to be fined; and if the fine was not paid to be imprisoned in default. There was a substantial national debate about applying criminal sanctions to a legitimately-held belief, whether religious or philosophical or simply health arguments were used. A novel formulation was included in the 1898 Act:

> No parent or other person shall be liable to any penalty under section 29 or section 31 of the Vaccination Act, 1867, if within four months from the birth of the child he satisfies two justices in petty sessions that he conscientiously believes that vaccination would be prejudicial to the health of the child, and within seven days thereafter delivers to the vaccination officer a certificate by such justices of such conscientious objection.

This is the first recognition of the right of an individual to legally refuse to obey a law in British legal history. The magistrates did not have to decide if vaccination was harmful to the child, but whether the parent conscientiously believed that it would be so. As the *Justice of the Peace* suggested, the bench firstly had to determine that the parent genuinely held the belief, 'whether founded on the most absurd prejudice, ignorance, or misapprehension, or on a real intelligent and scientific study of vaccination and its result',[14] and secondly, that the belief was conscientious, meaning that it is honest and not simply an excuse for laziness or neglect. Magistrates, lay and stipendiary, disagreed on how the interview with the parent was to be conducted: a simple declaration in open court, or under oath or affirmation. The legal mind was tested with a parallel case where 'a person objects to taking an oath, and is thereupon allowed to make affirmation on his mere statement that the taking of an oath is contrary to his belief'. As the courts routinely differentiate truth from falsehood by means of a forensic analysis of the facts of the matter based corroborative and contradictory evidence it is perhaps unsurprising that they were so uncomfortable with this key legal test being satisfied by a mere declaration.

The courts were unhappy with this provision, so that it soon fell into disrepute; magistrates would frequently impose adjournments and technical delays so that the limit of four months was reached without the certificate of conscientious objection being granted, which meant that the child would have to be vaccinated within the next two months, thus returning to the previous cycle of court appearances, fines and imprisonment (although in the latter case the bench might show some sympathy to the objector and they were allowed to sentence them to imprisonment in the first division). In 1907 an amendment was introduced so that the parent no longer had to 'satisfy the justices', but instead made a statutory declaration before them – as seen in Chapter 1, a statutory declaration is a formal statement and the magistrates cannot refuse to allow an individual to make one, whatever their opinions about the merits of the application may be. This made the process much easier, so much so that on 11 June 1914 the Rochdale Board of Guardians heard a report that of the 291 births registered in April in the Rochdale Union 137 had been given exemption certificates. Unfortunately in the neighbouring town of Milnrow experienced an outbreak of smallpox in late May and early June, with thirteen cases being hospitalised. Dr Chadwick, the medical officer of health, reported to the council that 400 persons had been vaccinated or re-vaccinated in the previous ten days.[15]

With the outbreak of war family life was to change in many ways. The immediate impact was on the families of men called up for military service, from the Reserves or the Territorial Forces (TF). The reservists reported to their regimental depots ready for deployment to the battlefields in France. Upon the King's Proclamation the Territorials were 'embodied', and they had to leave their civilian jobs and assemble at drill halls around the country. The official rôle of the TF was home defence, and the General Staff had planned and rehearsed the deployment of TF units to specific locations during peacetime (Territorials had to actively volunteer to serve overseas). These were usually some distance from the unit's home towns, to avoid the risk of men drifting back to their homes and families (the South Midlands Brigade, for example, drawn from Birmingham and surrounding areas, was deployed to the Chelmsford area to guard the Essex coast). There were also large numbers of men volunteering to join the army, choosing to leave their homes and families but still facing an uncertain period ahead. All of these men had to be paid, and somehow this pay had to get back to their families, otherwise they would be in severe financial difficulties. Following the King's Proclamation on 3 August, it was announced that each officer, non-commissioned office (NCO), and soldier of the Territorial Force was, on joining his unit, to receive a gratuity of £5 and married men would be entitled to a separation allowance.[16]

The reservists and Territorials were in a slightly better position than the new volunteers in that they already held army paybooks. The soldier was paid in cash at the weekly pay parade from the funds held by the regimental paymaster, but clearly it would be difficult to remit any of this money back to his wife – not impossible, as postal orders could be obtained at the Post Office, if there was one nearby. The army had two methods for making payments to families: the allotment and the allowance. The former was simply an apportionment of the man's pay. The separation allowance was an additional amount paid from army funds to the wife, usually conditional on his setting-up an allotment first. At the time of the mobilization the basic weekly pay for non-specialist soldiers in the lowest rank (privates, gunners, drivers, sappers) was 7s.

If the soldier made a 2s 4d allotment the army would pay a separation allowance of 7s 7d, making the total payable 9s 11s each week. For each daughter under the age of 16 or each boy under 14 and additional 1s 9d was paid. The allotment was a mandatory deduction, but it could be voluntarily increased up to no more than 3s 6d a week.[17]

The Territorial Force Association, a national organization operating in counties and towns (such as the East Riding Territorial Force Association),[18] was to be the vehicle for payments to the wives of the Territorials.[19] But in August 1914 there was no scheme in place to make such a large number of payments across the country to the wives of the men responding to Lord Kitchener's call for volunteers. The Soldiers' and Sailors' Families Association[20] (SSFA) was a charity formed in 1885 by Major Gildea to help the families of military and naval personnel and had branches and offices, with voluntary and paid staff, throughout England, Wales and Scotland. Following discussions, the Army Council decided to use this organization to distribute the funds; payments would be made centrally each month, to be disbursed on a weekly basis to the soldier's wives. The army paymaster needed details of the soldier's name, regiment, regimental number, and rank, together with precise information about the person or bank to be paid; the SSFA branch would issue a receipt when the money was paid.[21]

The army has a concept of the 'establishment', which is the number of men on the regimental roll for the purposes of pay, equipment, accommodation, and rationing. The 'married establishment' deals with the dependents of the married men and in peacetime would be used to budget for married accommodation. It became apparent that the Territorial men, in particular, had been somewhat casual in recording their marital status or the details of their spouses or children. The remedy was to obtain the relevant marriage and birth certificates and submit them to the officer in charge of records for the regiment (most reservists had already done this during their time in service). These certificates were obtained from the local superintendent registrar, officially for a fee of 3s 7d for each copy. Some registrars were apparently willing to reduce or even waive the fee, but an arrangement was reached with the Registrar-General at Somerset House who would provide a verification certificate free of charge if the soldier submitted precise details of date and place of marriage, and of the births of his children. However, although the War Office gave assurances that wives not currently recorded on the establishment were entitled to separation allowance, there was some delay in making the first payments.[22] It was also announced that separation allowance was not to be paid to mothers whose sons had been called up,[23] but a soldier was allowed to make an allotment.[24]

The delay in payments began to cause alarm in certain areas. On 20 August 1914 the Town Clerk in Huddersfield provided some reassurance when he passed on a communication he had received from Mr G. Hellowell, financial secretary to the 5th (T) West Riding Regiment, that the separation allowances for the wives and families of regular soldiers, Territorials and national reservists would be posted from York 'tomorrow' directly to the wives or their representatives, and rather generously covered the period from enrolment to 30 September.[25] The first separation allowances were paid on a monthly basis, which put a very large amount of cash into the wife's hands, and some of the unfortunate outcomes of this appear later in this chapter.

In Burnley a young mother was given a SSFA temporary grant of 3s to bide her over until the funds arrived,[26] and of course it didn't take long for the unscrupulous to sense an opportunity for some easy money. The husband of Jane Heaps, of 8 Alma Square, Chesterfield, had been employed by Chesterfield Corporation until he had been called up. They had continued his pay for two weeks, and on 8 September she informed the Borough Accountant that she was now receiving separation allowance, so, under a fairly common 'top up' arrangement at the time, she was given her husband's pay less the 9s 7d from the army. In the meantime she had visited the Chesterfield War Relief Fund (the local branch of a national charity formed under the patronage of the Prince of Wales) and obtained sums of 3s 6d, 10s, 6s 7d, and 5s. On calling at the War Relief pay room on 18 September she asked if she could have another 5s. In return she was asked if she was had any other income and she replied that she received nothing other than what they gave her. On being asked a second time, she replied she had nothing other than what her neighbours gave her. When she appeared at Chesterfield Borough Police Court on 1 October on a charge of fraud, one of the members of the bench, Mr J. Howson, had to retire, as he was a trustee of the War Relief Fund, and the matter was heard by his two colleagues, Mr W. Murphy and Mr C. Slack. Mrs Heaps pleaded guilty, and when asked why she obtained money by such means she replied, 'Because when your husband is away you want all you can get and you are anxious to get all you can'. The Chief Constable stated that the defendant's husband had deserted, and on one occasion when an officer visited the house most of the adults were drunk. The chairman was clear that a three-month prison sentence would be perfectly reasonable, but instead they bound her over in the sum of £5 to come up for judgement when called upon.[27]

Emily Taylor, of 19 Moss Street, Bolton, tricked the War Relief Fund out of a 5s food ticket and a ticket for a hundredweight of coal, when she was receiving separation allowance. On 20 October 1914 the Bolton magistrates gave her seven days' imprisonment. A new scheme was introduced on 12 October so that separation allowances would be paid to the Post Office nominated by the soldier.[28] The regimental paymaster sent the soldier's wife a certificate of identity, commonly known as the 'ring paper'. She presented it to the post office clerk when she collected her allowance. The clerk's stamp in the 'ring' marked the payment.

With increasing numbers of men joining the army it became clear that the army scheme of allowances failed to recognize the realities of family life. Young unmarried men living at home were often a major financial support for older and ageing parents, as well as to sisters, and although an allotment could be made there was no entitlement to the far more generous separation allowance. The image of the lonely old mother was widely used to press for change, but undoubtedly there were large numbers of women and children in families where the soldier and his partner were not married and which formed the real platform for reform.[29]

On 27 October 1914 a remarkably humanitarian Army Order announced the conditions for the provision of separation allowances to dependents of soldiers. 'Dependents' were 'such members of the soldier's family (other than his wife and legitimate children and stepchildren) as were wholly or in part dependent upon the earnings of the soldier at the time of mobilization or enlistment'. The members of the family included:

a. The soldier's father, mother, grandfather, grandmother, stepfather, grandson, granddaughter, brother, sister, half-brother, half-sister. The illegitimacy of the soldier himself will not affect the position of his parents or grandparents.

b. A woman who has been entirely dependent on a soldier for her maintenance and who would otherwise be destitute; and the children of the soldier in the charge of such a person.[30]

As soldiers may have already been making allotments to these dependents, they were reminded that these must continue. If the allotment was stopped, the War Office would stop the allowance.[31]

This new allowance was intended to provide a level of support similar to that the soldier provided before enlistment, rather than being the standard amount paid as separation allowance. For example, if a soldier who gave his mother 10s a week made an allotment of 2s 11d/week (or 5d/day) then 10s would be paid to his mother, a contribution of 7s 1d.[32] A mother with two or more sons in the army was only entitled to one allowance, however, and this was usually based on the son with the highest rank. Her other sons could, of course, make an allotment.

To prevent fraudulent applications, a sensible amount of red tape was introduced. The soldier filled in Army Form O.1838 with the details of the intended recipient of the allowance. The important part was the description of the amount he contributed to the household before enlistment. The completed form was submitted to his commanding officer and sent to the regimental paymaster. Back at home, the dependent obtained Army Form O.1839 and filled it in the same way, returning it again to the regimental paymaster. He then forwarded both forms to the local Inland Revenue Pensions Officer, who would send Form S. A 6 to the man's former employer to test the accuracy of the statements made, and if satisfied, the dependent would receive an allowance.[33] The possibility of collusion in making false statements is apparent, but soldiers had their mail censored by their officers who would be alert to any mention of allowances. Soldiers were advised to be careful with their paperwork and to make sure that they did not confuse AF O.1838 (Allowances) with AF 418B (Allotments).[34]

Private Herbert Jackson of the 7 Notts & Derby Regiment, applied for, and received, a separation allowance for his wife, who lived at 25 Wollaton Street, Nottingham. Except that this was his mother's address, Jackson and his wife having separated. The 'Grace Jackson' who signed for her allowance each week at the post office was in fact Elizabeth Jackson, the soldier's sister.[35] She collected the money, £6 3s 10d in total, gave it to the mother, who then passed it on to Jackson himself. The magistrates, Mr F. Acton and Mr J. Langham, heard the case on 2 January 1915 as Elizabeth Jackson was charged with falsely impersonating Grace Jackson with intent to obtain her military pay. She was put on probation for twelve months.[36]

Private Arthur Dodson, 2/6 East Surrey Regiment, appeared before Mr Horace Smith at Westminster Police Court on 8 September 1915. He had stated on his AF O.1838 that prior to enlistment he earned 25s a week, of which he gave his mother 18s. His former employers had told the Pensions Officer who had reviewed his case that in fact he was only paid 12s. He was fined £5 or one month in default.[37] At that time about

£40 million a year was being paid in allowances and the offence was viewed as very serious.[38] The offence of attempting to obtain a sum of money by false pretences needs a place, a date, the witnesses and the evidence, and this had become so common by early 1916 that the *Justice of the Peace* reported that one northern county had a system for dealing with them: the venue was the office of the Territorial Association or regimental paymaster where the forms were received, the date of the offence was the date of receipt at the office. The witnesses were the NCO who saw the soldier sign the form in the orderly room, a clerk from the office which received the form, the pension officer, and the employer to prove the soldier's original earnings.[39]

The demand for munitions created extensive and lucrative employment opportunities in munitions and industry generally. Munitions workers, male and female, received high basic pay, good overtime, and 'war bonuses' – a cost-of-living allowance payable on top of normal earnings for the period of the war only (initially awarded to government workers, it was taken up by the private sector as a novel and equitable form of profit sharing). In early 1915 the General Union of Textile Workers negotiated a scheme with local employers, so that for a 55½-hour week workers would be paid at the following rates:[40]

Basic weekly wage	War bonus per week
10s or less	6d
Males 10s up to 20s	1s
Males 20s up to 30s	2s 6d
Males 30s up to 40s	2s
All women workers earning over 10s	1s

The demand for labour drew people into the industrial towns and cities from all over the country and this put pressure on the rented accommodation and housing market. Migrant workers had the option of the lodging house, which simply provided accommodation, and the boarding house which provided meals. The Ministry of Munitions took over many hotels, bed-and-breakfast houses, and hostels to provide accommodation for its workers. The Local Government Board had frozen the funding of new developments introduced under the Housing of the Working Classes Act, 1885, and landlords began to raise rents. In Glasgow not only was there an intense demand for housing, but the quality of the housing stock was low and there had been little investment in years.[41] When the landlords and factors increased rents in late 1915 there was a rent strike and protestors took to the streets. The local magistrates issued ejectment warrants but they were not served, and Mr P.J. Dollen, a Labour councillor, sent a warning to the Minister of Munitions, Lloyd George.[42] He responded that it was beyond his power to take action, but the Secretary of State for Scotland would look into the matter. Lord Hunter and Professor Scott, of Glasgow University, were commissioned by the minister to look at the rents of small properties in the industrial districts of Scotland. By November around 15,000 people had refused to pay the rent increases.[43] By the time the commissioners reported back the problem had escalated beyond Scotland. A Bill was prepared by the government and introduced by the President of the Board of Trade. In the Parliamentary debate which followed MPs from around the country contributed their own experiences of constituency housing problems, in industrial areas, docks and around military camps.[44] As a result the Increase of Rent and Mortgage Interest (War Restrictions) Act, introduced on 24 December 1915, was given a national scope. It made it 'illegal for the proprietor to increase rent at the present time' and allowed him to charge only a 'standard rent', which was the amount obtained in rent on 3 August 1914. This legislation applied to properties in which the annual rental value did not exceed £35 in London and £26 elsewhere. The working classes both built and bought their own homes, using mortgages from the building and friendly societies which were widely established in the period, so this was not merely a middle-class problem. As the rent was usually calculated to repay the mortgage the landlord might hold on the property, the Act also fixed the interest rate to that charged on the same date. The new law did allow the landlord to increase the rent but only with the approval of the tenant, which, of course, was not usually forthcoming. This law was deeply resented by the property-owning community, and it does appear that they were unfairly constrained at a time when both incomes and inflation were rising rapidly. There were some exceptions provided,[45] but as these matters were contractual they were dealt with in the county courts.[46] The right of a landlord to take possession of his property in cases of rent default under the Small Tenements Recovery Act, 1838 remained, but this of course was restricted by the Courts (Emergency Powers) Act, 1914, so that all applications for ejectment had to be heard before the magistrates. These applications regularly appeared in the magistrates' courts registers; at the Thames Police Court there were so many that a separate Small Tenements register was kept.[47]

Many wives were now in a much better financial position than they had been when their husbands were home. Once the 'necessaries' had been covered, some were left with a disposable income that, if the stories were to be believed, was spent in the public house. Unfortunately the War Office chose to believe these reports, and in November 1914 they issued a circular to the police authorities asking them to put soldier's wives under supervision: 'The Army Council desires to have the police in the measures to be taken in the withholding of separation allowances payable to wives and dependents in the event of serious misconduct by the recipient'. This was received with a barrage of criticism from the public and from the police, and Mr Harold Baker, the financial secretary, hastily withdrew the request.[48] However, the matter did not end there – the Home Office shared similar concerns, and in December they tried a joined-up approach using the Board of Education. Realizing that simply asking the police to 'watch out for women spending their money carelessly or extravagantly or in any way acting in a way the police consider unbecoming'[49] was as unworkable as it was unpopular, a new circular asked local authorities, through managers, teachers and attendance officers, to 'keep an eye on children in the charge of persons drawing an Army separation allowance ... and report to the War Office any case of neglect'. The Army Council considered conditions under which the allowance would be suspended or withheld, such as cases of immorality, convictions on criminal charges, gross neglect of children, or persistent drinking which resulted in the neglect or harm of the children. A mechanism was proposed, whereby the teacher, attendance officer, even neighbours, would report their concern to the local education board or local authority, who would then notify the police. A police officer would then make a home visit and report to the chief constable, who ultimately decided if the case should be referred to the War Office. The Army Council were very clear that it would only be the wife's element of the separation allowance that would be suspended; the children's allowance would be unaffected. If the children were removed from the care of the mother the allowance would be paid to the foster parent or other person in trust.[50] Unsurprisingly, the whole scheme foundered and was not taken any further.

Allowances were sometimes stopped but not through the behaviour of the wife. A soldier undergoing military punishment in detention or who was absent without leave for seven days or more, automatically lost his pay for the period. The first his wife would know about it was that there was no money for her at the post office (the pay of a soldier killed in action or dying of wounds continued for six months after his death). This was amended in March 1915 so that the separation allowance continued but the allotment stopped. Soldiers absent for twenty-one days or more were considered as deserters and all pay, allotments and allowances ceased.[51]

There were some surprising revelations when women went to claim their allowances. Agnes Blair, of Canning Street, Newcastle, first met John Thomas Edington in April 1909. After an on-off courtship, she had his child on 1 November 1912 and they married on 1 March 1913 at the Newcastle Registry Office. Edington joined the Durham Light Infantry and went off to the war. Agnes applied for the separation allowance and was refused, and discovered that her husband was already married to a bookbinder in Elswick. This legitimate wedding had taken place in April 1906 and there were four children. Edington had left his wife in January 1911, and the magistrates at the Newcastle Police Court remanded him in custody until the next assizes for the indictable offence of bigamy.[52]

Joseph William Birchall appeared at the Liverpool Assizes on 29 October 1914 on a charge of bigamy. He had married a woman, who had left him, and taken up with a second woman. The first wife only turned up again when she wanted to claim the allowances. Mr Justice Darling bound him over to come up for judgement when called upon, and ordered the police to see that Birchall was sent back to his regiment in Hartlepool without delay.[53] They took him to the railway station, purchased a ticket for him, and put him on board. However, as soon as the train started he jumped out the other side and was eventually caught after a chase. He was taken straight back to the judge who ordered him to be detained as a deserter until the arrival of a military escort. Justice Darling complained about the 'irregular relations' the soldiers were now conducting, with women marrying them simply to get the allowances. The woman who was the wife of the prisoner 'had never troubled about him until she wanted the allowance, and then she suddenly appeared on the scene and displayed close affection for him'.[54]

Not all soldiers wanted to support their wives and families. In the normal course of life couples sometimes separate, and in such cases the woman was entitled to apply to the magistrates for a an order to enforce payment of maintenance without the formality of a summary judicial separation. The justices could order payment of up to £2 a week in family support. Such orders were a reasonably routine feature of court lists at the time, along with summonses for breaches of orders. The complaint had to be brought by the woman herself, and the magistrates could order that the payment be made within a specified period of time, or, as with any financial penalty, the man could be imprisoned by default. The relationship between the wife and the estranged husband was a matter of concern to the courts, particularly in cases of abuse, so a court collecting officer acted as the go-between and was responsible for collecting the money from the husband on behalf of the wife. In wartime a husband might desert his wife by joining the army or navy and refusing to give her his details, so that she would be unable to claim an allowance. However, the merest hint of a regiment or ship's name would be sufficient for the local separation officer to make enquiries with the records office or paymaster and the soldier or sailor, if found, would have the money deducted from his pay. The Assistant Financial Secretary to the War Office stated that 'where a magistrates' order has been obtained against the soldier for the maintenance of a wife, child, or illegitimate child ... that payment shall be made directly to the complainant instead of the collecting officer, and also undertook to provide the court with the man's new address should he be discharged.'[55] However, under section 145 (2) of the Army Act, 1881, the maximum amount which could be deducted from a soldier's pay for the maintenance of a bastard child under the court order was 3d a day. The soldier could make additional voluntary payments if he so wished, and the mother could apply for a further order for any arrears.

Women who found themselves pregnant following relationships with soldiers often had difficulty in getting maintenance orders. If the soldier had returned to his unit, the magistrates' summons had to be served on the man's commanding officer along with a sum of money for a return journey to the court. But, under section 145 (3), if the soldier was under orders for active service overseas (and not necessarily abroad at the time), the summons was not allowed. The woman had to wait until he returned before making another application. Emma Field of 34 Langley Road, Staines, sought maintenance payments from Ernest Langford, a chauffeur of Clarence Cottage, Hartley Wintney, in respect of her illegitimate child, at Spelthorne Petty Sessions on 24 April 1915. The defendant did not appear as he was, by then, serving as a driver in the mechanical transport section of the Army Service Corps headquarters at Grove Park. Warrant Officer Osborne stated that the summons had been properly served on the man in the presence of the commanding officer, but the learned clerk noted that money for the travel costs had not been included; the case was adjourned for correct service.[56]

Robert Holmes, the police court missionary, was able to provide some insights into the new-found wealth of the working classes in Sheffield in November 1915. In one household with which he was familiar, the husband was a labouring man and formerly earned around 25s per week, but now, with overtime, regularly made £3. He had four sons between 16 and 21 years of age, earning between 17s 6d and £2 2s a week; the total household income was nearly £9 a week. A rather sober family, they spent this additional income on a gramophone, a piano, a sewing machine and four bicycles, all purchased on credit. Another skilled workman earned £6 a week, with his 19-year-old son bringing in another £3, and they had also invested in a piano, gramophone, violin and bicycles. Holmes also noticed a change in diet: meat at every meal, with bacon for breakfast, meat for dinner, and boiled ham for tea and supper. Sales of cheap watches and alarm clocks had increased, and wives of munitions workers were reported buying more expensive winter clothing.[57]

Despite the generosity of the military allowances, there were abuses. Sarah Jessie Radford, of Maidstone Street, Haggerston, had seven children. With her husband in the army she received 34s 6d a week in allowances and her eldest son, William (14) gave her 5s from his wages. The National Society for the Prevention of Cruelty to Children were aware of the situation and gave her several warnings about the poor condition of her children. When the inspector visited at 11 am one morning in November 1915 and found her in bed and the young children in a 'filthy condition and were sitting without a fire in a room the windows of which were broken', with practically no food in the house, the decision was taken to prosecute her. Mr Wilberforce, the magistrate at Old Street Police Court, sent her to prison for four months. Sadly there were many similar cases: Sarah Bright and Nellie Holden rented two rooms in Robert Street, Hampstead Road. Here lived Bright's seven children and six of Holden's, and a dog. With their husbands serving in the forces, they had a combined income of over £200 a year, which they spent on drink. A doctor reported that when he visited, 'the stench was unbearable … the children were itching and had swollen glands, and were huddled together on a dirty bed'. The two women received sentences of three and two months' imprisonment, respectively, at the Marylebone Police Court in November 1915.

The unpleasant expression 'common prostitute' entered English law in the Vagrancy Act, 1824. It survived the Town Police Clauses Act, 1847, the Criminal Law Amendment Act, 1885 and the Street Offences Act, 1959, until it was finally removed by the Policing and Crime Act, 2009; although, by mistake, it can occasionally be seen on court lists today. There were 9,808 convictions for prostitution in the magistrates' courts in 1914, but the figures declined year on year with 5,288 in the final year of the war.[58] The penalty for soliciting was typically a fine but imprisonment with or without hard labour was not uncommon. Younger women were often given the option of being sent to a reform school or, depending on the skills of the police court missionary, a 'situation' with a morally upright family might be found.

Gertrude Winnie Smith appeared before the Folkestone magistrates in September 1917, to deny a charge of soliciting and being a common prostitute. She had been 'true' to a Canadian soldier for a number of weeks and when seen by police speaking to another soldier she had been merely 'asking after her young man'. The Chief Constable, prosecuting, pointed out that she was the wife of a man serving at the Front; the bench sentenced her to two weeks' hard labour. Sixteen-year-old Olive O'Leary appeared before the same bench on the same charges but was given three months' probation when she consented to go into a home.[59] Dulcie Vickery appeared at Westminster police court after being seen accosting three men in Wilton Street, Victoria. She was known to the police and had seven previous convictions at the same court. Mr Waddy fined her 40s.[60]

The naval and military authorities were concerned that 'loose women' would be attracted to the camps and docks of the country; Colonel East's failed attempt to ban women from public houses in Cardiff in November 1914 has already been seen (Chapter 5), but the Defence of the Realm regulations were updated to include two restrictions:

Sec 13A Power to prohibit persons convicted of offences against morality, decency, &c., from frequenting the vicinity of camps (January 1916); and

Sec 35C (b) Power to make rules for securing and preserving order and good behaviour in the area... by controlling or regulating the admission to or presence, movements, and behaviour in the area of any person or class of persons whose unrestricted admission to or presence in the area is likely to prejudice the training, discipline, administration, or efficiency of any of HM Forces (April 1917)

The authorities were less concerned with the moral standards of the troops than they were about their efficiency, and in particular their health. Between 1914 and 1918 there were 199,719 military cases of sexually-transmitted disease in the United Kingdom alone, and in the military hospitals in France between January 1915 and May 1918 out of 91,231 admissions for venereal disease 38,562 men reported that they had contracted the disease in the UK. 68 per cent of cases were of gonorrhoea, 27.5 per cent of syphilis, and 4.5 per cent other venereal diseases. Note that these statistics relate to the United Kingdom and do not include the figures for France and other areas of operations.[61]

In the British Army it was not an offence to contract a venereal disease but under section 11 of the Army Act, 1881 a soldier found guilty of concealing an infection could face up to two years' hard labour. King's Regulations paragraph 462 required that the procedure for reporting sick was to be 'read to the unit on parade at intervals not exceeding three months'. Regimental medical officers gave regular lectures about personal hygiene and soldiers were regularly inspected for venereal disease (the 'short-arm inspection'[62]). Sexually-transmitted infections were curable if diagnosed early enough, but in those pre-antibiotic days the treatment required hospitalization: the average time spent in hospital for each patient in 1915 was 28.6 days for gonorrhoea, 37.6 days for syphilis, and 31.3 days for other venereal diseases.[63] Soldiers admitted to hospital for sickness (as opposed to wounds) had 7d a day stopped from their pay; this unpopular policy was abandoned in September 1917 with the exception of admissions for alcoholism or venereal disease[64] (the Australian and New Zealand Army Corps took a much harder line – a soldier hospitalized for venereal disease was classed as absent without leave and had all pay and allowances stopped for the period).

Most men were willing to identify the likely source of their infection but there was no statutory means of enforcement nor was there any legal action that could be taken against the infected woman, other than under one or other of the DoRA regulations, above. This had not always been the case. In 1864 Parliament passed the Contagious Diseases Prevention Act in an attempt to reduce the incidence of venereal disease amongst the military and naval forces in the country. It applied to 'certain naval and military stations',[65] which were listed as Portsmouth, Plymouth, Woolwich, Chatham, Sheerness, Aldershot, Colchester, Shornecliffe and, in Ireland, the Curragh, Cork and Queenstown. It provided that anyone could lay an information on oath that they had 'good cause to believe that a woman is a common prostitute, and that she is living or has visited in or near a place specified in the Act', upon which information the justice could order the woman to undergo a medical examination. If she were found to be diseased she would be confined in a special ('lock') hospital to undergo such treatment until the hospital surgeon certified that she was free of disease. The penalties for non-compliance were severe, with the starting point at one month's imprisonment.[66] Note that the woman did not have to be suspected of carrying disease, merely that she was believed to be a prostitute; nor in the first instance was there any prosecution or conviction. The Act relied on local Boards of Guardians to provide the necessary hospital facilities and the subsequent Contagious Diseases Act, 1866 gave the Navy and the Army the funding to establish these facilities themselves, along with the formal appointment of Visiting Surgeons, and the addition of Devonport and Windsor to the list. It also provided for the mandatory periodic examination of all prostitutes and by this time the Act was being criticized as a form of state-sanctioned prostitution with widespread opposition to both the spirit and implementation of the legislation.[67] By the time of the Contagious Diseases Act, 1869 any police officer could arrest any woman he suspected of prostitution within the specified areas (now extended from a five to a fifteen mile radius), and Gravesend, Maidstone, Winchester, Dover, Walmer, Deal, and Canterbury were now included.[68] After considerable public and Parliamentary debate these unpopular and discriminatory Acts were repealed in April 1888 and the belief that women were the root cause of venereal disease appeared to have been abandoned.

The prevalence of sexually-transmitted disease in the military and public populations remained a concern throughout the war, and the Venereal Diseases Act of November 1917 made it an offence to advertise or provide any:

> Packet, box, bottle, phial ... containing any pills, capsules, powders, lozenges, tinctures, potions, cordials, electuaries, plaisters, unguents, salves, ointments, drops, lotions, oils, spirits, medicated herbs and waters, chemical and officinal preparations whatsoever, to be used or applied exernally or internally as medicines or medicaments for the prevention, cure, or relief of any venereal disease.

Embarrassment and shame, and perhaps fear of the humiliating and painful medical treatment for sexually-transmitted infections, had resulted in an industry of snake oil formulations for those unwilling to seek medical help. Self-treatment was now effectively banned and only *bona fide* medications and treatments from duly-qualified medical practitioners were permitted. The system of education, inspection, early diagnosis, segregation and treatment within the military and the civilian medical communities appeared to offer some degree of control over the disease.

And then, seemingly from nowhere, came Regulation 40D, which was issued by an Order in Council on 22 March 1918, 'without the knowledge of the representatives of the people and in spite of opposition both inside and outside of the House of Commons'.[69] The short title of the regulation was the 'Prohibition on sexual intercourse by diseased women', and it simply stated:

> No woman who is suffering from venereal disease in a communicable form shall have sexual intercourse with any member of His Majesty's forces or of the forces of any of His Majesty's Allies or solicit or invite any member of His Majesty's

forces or of the forces of any of His Majesty's Allies to have sexual intercourse with her.

The regulation provided that a women charged with this offence be remanded for the purpose of such medical examination required to determine if she was suffering from a venereal disease and, if convicted, she could be fined up to £100 or given six months' imprisonment. For the purposes of the regulation 'venereal disease' covered three distinct infections: gonorrhoea, syphilis, and soft chancre (now known as chancroid).

As an apparent return to the indignities and humiliations of the discredited Contagious Diseases Acts, there was widespread public condemnation of this regulation. On 13 April 1918 the Council of the British Women's Temperance Movement unanimously resolved to send a telegram to the Prime Minister and the Secretary of State for War:

> That the present Council of the British Women's Temperance Movement (Scottish Christian Union) calls upon Parliament to insist upon the immediate withdrawal of Regulation 40D of the Defence of the Realm Act, which constitutes a serious menace to the safety of all women, and has been passed without the sanction of Parliament.[70]

Similar resolutions were passed by the Women's Peace Crusade Movement,[71] the Fellowship of Reconciliation, the Association for Moral and Social Hygiene,[72] the Bridgeton Women's Liberal Association[73] and many trades unions and other groups around the country. In response the War Secretary, Ian MacPherson, rather lamely pointed out that a soldier was liable to two years' hard labour if he concealed the fact that he was suffering from venereal disease; if the woman detained under 40D felt aggrieved she should simply notify the man's commanding officer who have him inspected and court-martialled if required,[74] but of course this only applied if he had failed to report the disease. A woman who believed she had acquired a sexually-transmitted infection from a soldier had no real recourse to the military authorities at all.

Given the moral sensibilities of the time, offences under 40D were discreetly reported, with references to 'unlawful relations' and a 'terrible disease'. The Newport Pagnell magistrates dealt with their first 40D cases at a special sitting on 8 May 1918. Lily Maria Holt, a 20-year-old servant, denied the charge, but Superintendent Dibbens proved two previous convictions for immorality at Sheffield court. The girl was sentenced to four months' imprisonment. Alice Maud Cowley followed, but the medical evidence, from Dr Douglas Bull MD, was inconclusive. The bench gave her the benefit of the doubt and dismissed the case.[75] In Eastbourne Ellen Carter, whose husband was serving in France, was sentenced to the full six months' imprisonment ('in the second division') for communicating the disease to two soldiers. Lizzie Davis and Emily Holt were brought on remand from Nottingham prison to the Leicester magistrates, along with certificates from the prison medical officer. Davis received two months' imprisonment, but Holt was discharged, with the bench directing the police 'to see her out of the town' and cautioning her not to return.[76]

The Contagious Disease Act was applied to any woman believed to be a prostitute, but regulation 40D applied to women believed to be suffering from venereal disease, regardless of background or social status. Gertrude Knowles, a 21-year-old married woman, 'well-dressed and of smart appearance' was arrested on the morning of 7 August and immediately brought before the Newport Pagnell magistrates charged with an offence against a soldier. As was her right under 40D she requested to have a private doctor perform the examination and she was remanded for seven days on her own recognizance in the sum of £5.[77] She reappeared on 14 August, in the company of Dr H.T. Wickham of the Clinical Research Society, who confirmed that she was absolutely free from the alleged complaint.[78] The magistrates dismissed the case, but the effect on Gertrude and her husband, family and friends can only be imagined. Another case that demonstrated the iniquitous workings of 40D was that of Sylvia May Williams, aged 18, convicted by Wellingborough magistrates and sentenced to six weeks' imprisonment in the second division. She bravely appealed to the Northampton Quarter Sessions in January 1919 and the case was heard again. Arthur Allen, a wounded soldier, had deposed that he had met Williams on 17 October and had subsequently reported sick. In response to a question he admitted that he had met other women both before and after Williams. Police Sergeant Jones then testified that he had arrested the girl on 19 October; after cautioning her she said that she did not know that there was anything wrong with her. Dr W. Audland had examined her and found her to be suffering from a venereal disease. Mr Campion, representing Williams, made the obvious point that if the woman was ignorant of her condition there were no grounds for prosecution. As if to prove the absurdity of 40D, Mr Allenborough, the prosecutor, claimed if ignorance was a defence then it would be impossible to secure any conviction. Despite Campion's suggestion that it was as likely that the man gave the disease to her as she gave it to him, the appeal was dismissed with costs, but Williams had her sentence reduced from six weeks' imprisonment to a simple fine of 1s.[79]

It is surprising that Williams had to go to the expense of an appeal. Regulation 40D was one of the first to be revoked, on 26 November 1918. By that date 203 women had suffered the indignity of prosecution and 101 of them were convicted. Putting it another way, 102 innocent women had been arrested and subjected to intimate examination on the word of a soldier. As so often, there was existing legislation that could have dealt with this problem in a more sensitive way – the Infectious Disease (Notification) Act, 1889 and the Public Health Act, 1875 provided legal authority for the notification of specified diseases to the local authorities, who could enforce admission to hospital or take other appropriate action. Although both acts were more concerned with environmental and social hygiene than personal, the addition of venereal diseases to the schedule of infectious diseases would have avoided the criminalisation of these unfortunate women.

Parents who failed to send their children to school regularly would be summonsed to court by the school attendance officer under local authority byelaws (Education Act, 1870). These had an interesting additional application: children who appeared at school in an unclean or otherwise unfit condition were deemed to have not attended. The school nurse inspected children at school and there was a system of cards which were given to the children in sealed envelopes, to be taken home to their parents. Children who were in a generally unsatisfactory condition were given a yellow card. This would explain to the parents the remedial actions required, such as washing the hands, or clean clothes. Children with unclean heads were given a white card. With most inspections carried out on Mondays, children were expected to be clean and treated by the time of the Friday repeat inspection. If they failed this, they were separated from the other children in the school and issued red cards, which notified the parents: 'You are required to have the child's head cleansed within one week, otherwise exclusion will take place, and you will be liable to prosecution and fine for not sending the child to school in a fit state.' The local authorities provided cleansing stations for delousing and other treatments – there were twenty-four of these in London alone. The Annual Report of the Chief Medical Officer of the Board of Education for 1914–15 provided some startling statistics: in London 13,969 children were cleansed, 8,793 statutory notices (red cards) were issued, and 378 parents were fined. Prosecutions were either under the attendance byelaws, or in the case of neglect, sections 12 or 122 of the Children's Act, 1908.[80]

In the years immediately before the war the effects of the Probation Act, 1907 and Children Act, 1908, seemed to demonstrate distinct progress in the management of youth crime. Probation, in particular, was seen as a successful intervention in life of the young offender by the police court missionaries and the probation officers. The rôle of reformatory and industrial schools for the intermediate offender was reinforced by the introduction of the Borstal institutions for more serious forms of criminal behaviour (Chapter 1). At the annual meeting of the Birmingham magistrates on 19 January 1914 it was reported that juvenile crime had decreased and they had dealt with 1,071 cases in the year, with only a small number of girls. Mr Arnold Harris commended the absence of corporal punishment.[81] On introducing the Criminal Justice Administration Bill for its second reading in the House of Commons in 1914 the Home Secretary, Mr McKenna, declared that 'short terms of imprisonment [for juvenile offenders] might be punitive and deterrent [but] they could not be reformative and they should seek to avoid familiarising the young offender with prison walls'.[82] Reverend H. Pelham of the Birmingham Street Children's Union, believed that the term 'juvenile' should be extended from 16 to 21. He maintained that no child was born with tendencies to make him an habitual criminal, and that in the majority of cases the parents were the real offenders (but he also spoke in favour of using the whip as a punishment).[83] At the same time the Liverpool magistrates wanted some form of compulsory drill for male first offenders as a form of direct physical punishment, because any fines they imposed were paid by the parents. They listed the commonest offences: 'football playing in the streets, stone-throwing, jostling pedestrians, making of unseemly noises, and making themselves generally a nuisance'. These offences did not merit imprisonment or a fine, but some physical diversion which would use up their 'animal spirits'.[84] Miss E P Philip, of the State Association for Children, gave a talk on 'Some Experiences of Youth Courts': and she quoted an unnamed but 'famous doctor', who had suggested that 'a large percentage of the delinquencies of children was due to underfeeding during early childhood … which left a "kink in the brain" that could not be remedied by subsequent good feeding'. She welcomed the recent changes in summary courts' procedure so that children were treated as offenders, not criminals, and kept away from adults. And she made a plea for the appointment of women magistrates and women police.[85]

The Children Act made provision for the separation of adult and youth courts, but in practice this was achieved by having a separate list for juvenile cases. At Stratford Petty Sessions the list for 14 August 1914 included:

Breaking into warehouse.
Larceny [theft].
Beyond the control of parents.
Stealing fruit from orchard.
Wandering.
Gambling.
Wilful damage.

The offenders ranged from 9 years of age to 16. Amongst the punishments were being sent to Redhill reformatory school, discharged with a caution, mother being bound over in the sum of £5, and six strokes of the birch.[86]

And then the war broke out. Francis Caldwell, Head Constable of Liverpool, presented his annual report to the council in April 1915, mentioned the decrease in juvenile crime reported to the magistrates in the previous year, but added that since the commencement of war it had increased. He attributed this to the 'lamentable lack of discipline and restraint among the children', due to some extent to the absence of so many fathers in the Army and consequent lack of parental control. He also mentioned 'the temptation of the automatic gambling machines' in the city's shops: 65 per cent of children dealt with were first offenders and many confessed to having lost the stolen money in the machines.[87]

Juvenile offenders did not have their names recorded in the newspapers nor were the public allowed into the hearings, but journalists took a keen interest in the workings of the juvenile courts. In January 1916 the police court in the Guildhall was the venue for the trial of the 'Black Hand Gang', nine boys aged between 11 and 13 who had organized a crime spree in the City of London in the previous weeks. They were fully organized, with a captain, a second-in-command, two treasurers and other officials. The objects were to smash the windows of tobacconists and grab whatever they could. They sold cigars at two for a penny, or eighteen for sixpence, which they spent on sweets. The police reported that after they had been brought to the police station they were put into a special room reserved for juvenile offenders to await the arrival of their parents. Two indulged in a wrestling bout, three were found walking on their hands, and the others had got down the hand ambulance (stretcher trolley) and were practicing ambulance drill. As an officer opened the door one shouted the classic 'Are we downhearted?' to which they responded with a rousing 'No!'. Mr Pinhorn, the London County Council schools officer, had interviewed the boys and he told the magistrate that they had seen the wonderful exploits of boys shown at cinema shows, from which they developed the idea of the 'Black Hand'. They were all sent to the Remand Home.[88]

In Burnley it was reported that formerly one juvenile court a fortnight had been sufficient, but by February 1916 there were two such courts almost every week, with ten or more boys brought up each time. The offences were pilfering and shopbreaking, and the excuses offered were that they stole so that they could go to the picture house or to procure cigarettes.[89]

Mr Samuel, the Home Secretary, sent a circular to the justices' clerks in March 1916 with the statistics for juvenile crime for seventeen of the largest towns. Between December 1914 and February 1915 there were 2,686 convictions of juveniles. From December 1915 to February 1916 there were 3,596. He suggested that there should more recruitment and use of women probation officers, and more use of the Probation Act. He also gave an indication that the issue of film censorship was under review, and that where magistrates had been delegated powers under the Cinematograph Act, 1908 they should give special attention to the nature of films shown at children's performances.[90] In July 1916 Alderman Sir John Baddeley wrote an impassioned critique on 'Cinema, Crime, and the Child's Mind' in the *Daily Mirror*. As a magistrate at the Guildhall he complained that otherwise good boys appeared before him with one craze – 'to see the pictures'. He pointed out that some eight million people went to Britain's 6,000 cinemas each week and that there were no current restrictions on children seeing inappropriate films. He recounted the story of three boys charged with stealing a charity box. They had obtained the idea from seeing cinema films. One of them was said to have impersonated Charlie Chaplin in the streets, with a crowd of 80 to 100 children around him (as a distraction while the theft took place). He sent the boys to a reformatory.[91]

A charming letter appeared in reply a couple of days later:

With regard to Baddersley's article on crime and the cinema, I wonder whether the writer had ever been in a children's matinee at this local cinema. If he has, he must have notice how the villain of the piece is always hissed, whilst the hero, detective or policeman is applauded and given such shouted instructions as, 'There he is, guv'nor', 'Look out, he's behind that door', etc. After seeing this perhaps your contributor will take such tales told at his court as 'I saw it at the pictures' with a pinch of salt. One notices that 'I saw it at the pictures' is the usual excuse for the juvenile offender. Why? Because the child is to be pitied and the pictures unjustly blamed. What better excuse does the young criminal want? W G R[92]

Local authorities attempted to understand the reasons behind the rise in juvenile offending. In Liverpool a joint committee of local justices and the members of the council's education committee reported several factors:

1. Lack of parental control, induced or shown by:
   a. Indifference of parents to their children's welfare.
   b. Comfortless homes.
   c. Intemperance.
   d. Lack of religious influence in the home.
2. Disinclination on the part of parents to their children being subjected to proper discipline and punishment.
3. Street trading.

4. Irregular school attendance.
5. Too frequent attendance at cinematograph theatres.
6. Want of sufficient playgrounds or open spaces for recreation.
7. Careless exposure of goods by tradesmen.

Following this sensible analysis the committee took the opportunity to make several rather draconian recommendations:

1. Justices should be given more power, by legislation, to order the whipping of boys up to 16, and double the number of strokes from six to twelve. This power should apply to all offences committed by boys.
2. Section 99 of the Children Act 1908 should be amended to make parents responsible for any damages and fined in all cases, notwithstanding any punishment on the child.
3. Definite statutory provision empowering school masters and mistresses to punish scholars who misconduct themselves *out* of school (and protecting the teachers in the exercise of these powers).
4. No child of either sex under 16 years of age should be allowed to trade in the street.
5. Where desirable, magistrates should introduce, as a condition in the probation order, restrictions as to the attendance of probationers at cinema exhibitions.
6. Every encouragement should be given to movements calculated to multiply the means of healthy recreation of children outside school hours.
7. Lodging house limited to the use of youths up to 18 years of age, under proper management, should be provided or set aside for this purpose.
8. Better provision of reformatory schools for children who are mentally or physically defective should be made by the state.[93]

It is quite odd to see that most of the recommendations fail to address the factors given as causes of offending. How does the whipping of boys make up for a comfortless home, or irregular school attendance?

Even the King and Queen expressed their 'grave concern', and the Home Secretary, at a conference of the representatives of the principal boys' and girls' brigades and clubs of the country in October 1916, passed on His Majesty's hope for a solution.[94] The conference believed that the absence of the fathers was the crucial factor, but that cinemas fostered a 'spirit of lawlessness'. To combat the evil they believed that they should remedy the lack of social workers, provide evening play centres, and recruit more boys to the Boy Scouts.

At the end the year the Home Office, continuing the momentum from the October conference, formed a Standing Committee to be chaired by Mr C.E.B. Russell, HM Chief Inspector of Reformatories and Industrial Schools, and comprising the leaders of many of the youth organizations of the day, including Lieutenant General Sir R. Baden Powell of the Boy Scouts Association, Lady Baden Powell of the Girls Scouts Association, and representatives of Boys' Clubs, the Boys' Brigade (including the Catholic and Jewish organizations), and the Girls' Life Brigade. The Home Secretary did not wish to create a new youth organization but rather to inspire and empower the existing institutions to attract boys and girls to become members. He was also keen to encourage local education authorities to allow the use of school buildings in the evenings and holidays.[95] It took until August 1917 before Mr R.J. Streatfield, the acting District Commissioner of the Mid-East Sussex Boy Scouts, and Vice Admiral C.H.H. Moore, the Assistant County Commissioner of Sussex Sea Scouts, brought to the attention of the East Sussex Education Committee a letter they had received from the Standing Committee, which wanted to bring 'education authorities into closer touch with all units concerned with the social welfare of boys and girls', with a view to 'remedying juvenile delinquency'.[96]

An interesting contribution to the cinema debate was provided by Mr Cecil Leeson, secretary of the Howard Association (now the Howard League for Penal Reform). He proposed that magistrates, in questioning boys about the motivation for their crimes, were providing a self-fulfilling prophecy: if they asked the boy if he was influenced by the pictures, he would invariably answer yes, in order to shift the blame. Likewise, if asked what made him commit the offence, he knew that the 'right' answer was 'the pictures'. He contended that the fascination of the cinema was an indictment of the child's dull home conditions: 'the boy left school at 4 pm. Neither father nor mother was at home; an older sister prepared his tea, or maybe a neighbour. No one really wanted him, and the only interesting thing remaining in his little world was the picture palace and the street it stood in'.[97] Despite the efforts of the voluntary youth organizations crime continued to rise through 1917. There was an increasing recognition that the working mother was becoming a significant factor, with the wide availability of munitions work and the opportunities for women to take over what was traditionally seen as men's work.[98]

The 'Leeds System' gained prominence in the middle of 1917 as a way of managing the probation service for the magistrates' courts. The Leeds justices formed a committee chaired by Sir George Cockburn. They met once a month and reviewed every case on the probation register (an average of 150) to assess progress during the previous month. The probation officers presented their reports and highlighted any issues of concern. They also saw the probationers. Most of the probation cases arose from the juvenile court, which at that time sat once a week and gave the committee its 'gravest anxieties and greatest rewards'.[99]

In Liverpool, which saw 'a disquieting increase' in juvenile offenders, the Diocesan Church of England Temperance Society took an office at 101, Dale Street, near the police courts, so that parents of the youngsters could consult the police court missionaries (Mr H. Gladstone and Mr W. Ralphs) for guidance and assistance.[100] Section 7 of the Criminal Justice Administration Act, 1914 had expressly provided for, and encouraged, the participation of voluntary societies such as these in the provision of probation services for youths, but the war diverted the funds required and the charities had to rely on their own resources.

For some weeks in the autumn of 1917 there was a big problem with unruly youths affecting the 'better class residential thoroughfares of the suburbs of Birmingham', to the distraction of the residents. As night fell, crowds of boys and girls promenaded along the roads, jostling each other and passersby, singing songs, sat on the walls in front of the houses, stood in doorways and entered drives. Fireworks and bombs were thrown. Finally the police launched a raid on a number of roads and the offenders were hauled before the Third Birmingham Police Court on 11 October, receiving fines between 2s 6d and 10s.[101] At Grimsby Police Court the chairman, Mr G S Letten, declared that as birching did not appear to act as a deterrent, the Grimsby magistrates would, from now on, fine the parents in order to 'impress on them the wisdom of exercising supervision'.[102]

But some of the youth of the day turned their lives around. The police court missionary, Robert Holmes, described a number of cases of young men who had come into his care prior to the war and had subsequently gone on to redeem themselves through naval and military service. His book, *My Police Court Friends with the Colours* (1915) recounted the stories of boys from Sheffield (unfortunately with the names changed), who had written to him over the years about the way their lives had turned out – for the better, of course. In his 17th Annual Report of the Sheffield Police Court Mission, in March 1916, he revealed that in the previous twelve months he had received letters from 1,476 former probationers in the service of their country, and a further 29 who were now incapacitated by wounds. He himself wrote an average of 120 letters a week. But 259 of his boys had lost their lives.[103]

By June 1916 there were 19,648 boys who had been sent to reformatory or industrial schools and were now serving in His Majesty's forces. Three of them had won the highest award for valour, the Victoria Cross. Twenty-five had received the Distinguished Conduct Medal, twenty had been mentioned in dispatches and three had received awards from the French government. Eight had been commissioned as officers and many had been promoted as non-commissioned officers, but 530 had been killed in action, 62 died of wounds, and 1,540 had been wounded.[104] The Home Secretary, John Simon, described this as a 'splendid record'.[105] The Borstal institution at Feltham was particularly proud of its contribution. In its evolution from reformatory school for Middlesex to industrial school for the London County Council and now a Borstal,

> ... Under 'the iron hand of restraint and discipline, masked in a glove of sweet reasonableness and persuasion', one of the reasons for success here is employment of an expert staff of instructors, themselves trained in the forces of the Crown ... out of a total of about 400 boys, 212 have during the last eleven months, gone out to the fronts of battle, together with 35 instructors.[106]

In April 1915 a mother received a letter from an officer about her son, who had been released from Borstal the previous September to enlist in the Army:

> L/Cpl [blank] was in my company, and perhaps I had more to do with him that other officers. No one could wish for a better or braver soldier than he. If volunteers were asked for – whether to take out a patrol to the enemy's trenches or to fix up barbed wire in front of our own lines – he was always one of the first to offer his services. He was shot through the head whilst firing over the parapet, and was killed instantly.[107]

Chapter 11

Is Tea a Food?

Isabella Mary Beeton, known to history simply as Mrs Beeton, wrote her *Book of Household Management* in 1861. Far more than just a cookery book, it was 'the guide, philosopher and friend to countless happy homes'[1] and it became a standard wedding present for the young woman starting her career as a housewife. Following her death at the early age of 28 the book was continuously updated to reflect the new technologies and the demands of the modern household. The book always included recipes and menus and, sensitive to the wide readership, covered not only exotic suggestions for ball suppers and luncheon for a shooting party but also recognized the need for economy. The 1915 edition suggested that a frugal week's dining for the family might be:

Breakfast

Sunday	Boiled eggs, cold bacon
Monday	Findon haddock
Tuesday	Scrambled eggs, beef roll
Wednesday	Fish cakes
Thursday	Brawn
Friday	Rissoles of cold meat
Saturday	Broiled fresh herrings

Luncheon

Sunday	Exeter stew, mashed potatoes, apple charlotte
Monday	Pie of cold meat and potato, cabbage, pancakes
Tuesday	Lentil soup, baked fresh herrings, rice pudding
Wednesday	Meat cakes, baked potatoes, boiled bread pudding
Thursday	Liver and bacon, mashed potatoes, boiled rice and golden syrup
Friday	Shepherd's pie, baked potatoes, baked bread pudding
Saturday	Savoury spare rib, mashed potatoes, Betsy pudding

Dinner

Sunday	Cold meat, savoury potatoes, cornflour blancmange
Monday	Meat cakes, fried cabbage, treacle tart
Tuesday	Poor man's goose, baked potatoes, baked apples
Wednesday	Savoury cod, pancakes
Thursday	Sheep's heart, baked potatoes, bread and butter pudding
Friday	Cold boiled bacon, macaroni cheese
Saturday	Savoury spare rib, baked potatoes, rice shape, stewed figs or rhubarb

Each meal would be accompanied by bread, butter and cheese – in fact it is worth noting that at this time bread consumption was far higher than it is today. Mrs Beeton suggested that it was usual to allow 1lb (453g) of bread per day per person (a modern small loaf weighs 400g). This is also seen in the rations to be provided to soldiers in billets:

(a) For breakfast, six ounces of bread, one pint of tea with milk and sugar, four ounces of bacon;
(b) For hot dinner, one pound of meat previous to being dressed, eight ounces of bread, eight ounces of potatoes or other vegetables, one pint of beer or mineral water of equal value;
(c) For supper, six ounces of bread, one pint of tea with milk and sugar, two ounces of cheese.[2]

This amounts to 20 ounces or 1.25lbs (567g) of bread a day. Even in the workhouse the paupers were entitled to around 22oz per day.[3] The standard measure of bread was the quartern loaf, which weighed around 4lbs (1.8kg), but it was usually sold as a half loaf and sometimes quartered.

As fears of war started rising in late July and early August 1914 there were early fears of food shortages, which led to panic buying and sharp rises in the prices of goods such as sugar, flour, wheat and bread.[4] There was a strong grain and meat trade with the Empire and North and South America, but dairy supplies from Russia, Denmark and Holland were suspended.[5] In response to concerns over food supplies and hoarding by retailers and wholesalers, one of the bills rushed through Parliament was the Unreasonable Withholding of Food Supplies Act, 1914, which was passed on 8 August. It gave powers to the Board of Trade to take possession of any supplies of foodstuffs which it believed were being unreasonably withheld from the market, paying appropriate compensation. It was not aimed at individuals. As with so much of the emergency legislation it was very poorly drafted, and was quickly repealed by the Articles of Commerce (Returns, &c.) Act, 1914, which was passed on 28 August. This allowed the Board of Trade to demand information about stocks and inventories of any commercial articles held by persons or firms. It also allowed the Board of Trade to transfer its powers to other government departments, and in February 1916 John Badcock, a hay dealer in Haverhill, was prosecuted by the military authorities over two stacks of hay. After legal argument and an adjournment Mr Lake and the other Bury St Edmunds magistrates decided that there was a technical offence but that no penalty or costs would be imposed.[6] Badcock seems to have had the distinction of being the only person prosecuted for this offence in the entire war.

Food supply was not a significant problem in the first years of the war. Good harvests ensured the supply of bread and other staples. There were occasional shortages but these were often caused by supply and distribution problems. With prices rising regularly the main complaint was that the wealthier classes were able to afford better and more food. 'Food control' in 1915 was more to do with the control of food prices than the supply of food itself.[7]

By March 1916 rumours of the introduction a 'German system of food control' were commonplace.[8] Germany had experienced problems with its food supplies almost from the outbreak of war, with a system of bread tickets introduced in Berlin as early as February 1915, and the baking of pastries and cakes was prohibited.[9] In this country a number of government departments were concerned with food supply: the Local Government Board was trying to encourage the use of wholemeal flour for making bread, as it contained more nutrients than white flour; the Board of Trade was worried about the large quantities of wheat and flour that were being imported at high prices; and the Board of Agriculture was looking at ways to mill grain more efficiently to produce more flour per given quantity of grain. The demands of the armed forces also had to be considered, and there was a recognition that a single government department should be formed to deal with the whole problem of food control.[10] During 1916 the effects of the German submarine campaign began to be felt, and the challenge of using the shipping available to supply both food and munitions to the nation meant that some clear action had to be taken.

When the Defence of the Realm regulations were first drafted there was no real anticipation of any need to control food supplies. Regulation 2 originally gave powers to the competent naval or military authority to take possession of land, buildings and warlike stores and over time a series of subsections were added to extend this to food, forage, stores and fuel, and after the Ministry of Munitions was formed it was also given powers under this section. A new regulation added as late as November 1916 brought the spirit of the Articles of Commerce Act, 1914 into the *Defence of the Realm Manual*:

2F (1) Where the Board of Trade are of the opinion that special measures should be taken in the interests of the public for maintaining the supply of any article of commerce the maintenance of which is important as being part of the food supply of the country or as being necessary for the wants of the public or for the wants of any section of the public, the Board by order may, with a view to maintaining the supply of the article, apply to that article any of the provisions appended to this regulation.

The key feature here was that rather than the military or naval authorities, or the Ministry of Munitions, the power is granted to the Board of Trade, and that this is directed not to military, naval or munitions purposes but for the public.[11] This was followed almost immediately by a new section 2L which gives a sense of the growing recognition for food control. This gave extensive powers to the Board of Agriculture and Fisheries on the grounds of maintaining the food supply of the country by entering on unoccupied land, common land, or land with the consent of the occupier, for the purposes of cultivating the land.[12] This was a serious intrusion into property rights but seems to have attracted little attention. At the end of December Regulation 2Z allowed the Board of Agriculture and Fisheries to authorize local authorities to act on its behalf for the purposes of maintaining the food supply of the country;[13] and the Board wrote to the London County Council and councils of boroughs and urban districts to notify them of this power (it excluded the county councils on the basis that these were agricultural areas). The Board stated that its object was to secure unoccupied urban land in districts where there was sufficient labour available for the cultivation of such land. Councils were asked to assist with the acquisition of land, paying not more than £2 per acre, which could be recouped from rents paid by the cultivators. They were invited to help bring land into use by using their own tractors and machinery, and to provide fencing, implements and seeds, at cost prices. It was hoped that the local authorities would promote the scheme to existing allotment societies and to individuals.

It will be noted that regulation 2L gave powers to the Board of Trade but 2Z to the Board of Agriculture and Fisheries. This anomalous state of affairs was addressed when on 14 December 1916 Mr Bonar Law announced in the House of Commons that a Ministry of Food was to be formed,[14] with Lord Devonport as Minister of Food, a post that was universally known as the Food Controller (the intention to form such a ministry had been anticipated in the New Ministries and Secretaries Act, 1916). Devonport's speech in the House the next day set the tone for his department. He would first determine the country's existing stocks of food and ensure a system of fair distribution. He was the first senior figure to warn of rationing:

If we are to have equal distribution and give every man a fair share, and prevent individuals from being deprived of their share, I am very much disposed to think that possibly the only way to bring that about is by a system of rationing.[15]

By an Order in Council regulations 2F to 2J were assigned to the Food Controller. 2F was considerably expanded to give sweeping powers for:

the making orders relating to production, manufacture, treatment, use, consumption, transport, storage, distribution, supply, sale and purchase or other dealings in, or any measures to be taken in relation to any articles (including orders as to maximum and minimum prices) ... for the purpose of encouraging or maintaining the food supply of the country.

A number of food control orders had been issued by the Board of Trade before it handed over its powers to the new ministry. Between 20 November and 18 December ten orders had been made, the first of which was the Flour and Bread Order, banning the use of white flour from 1 January 1917 – and causing a run on flour as bakers, grocers and housewives promptly bought up all available supplies. Other early orders included the Price of Milk, Waste of Wheat, and a Seed Potatoes Order. The first food orders from the Food Controller were announced on Friday 12 January, 1917. The Bread Order required the addition of at least 5 per cent barley, maize, rice or oat flour to the flour used for breadmaking. The Wheat Order prohibited the use of wheat for anything other than making flour or as seeds. The use of any grains required for food or feeding stuffs as food for game birds was banned under the Feeding of Game Order. The Sugar and Chocolates Order stopped the production of 'extravagant' sweets, and a maximum retail price of 3d an ounce for chocolate and 2d an ounce for other sweetmeats was fixed. The Cakes and Pastry Order prohibited the use of sugar or chocolate for the external covering of cakes and pastries. A further requirement under this order was that no manufacturer could use more than 50 per cent of the sugar or chocolate used for the same purposes in 1915. The Irish Oat Export Order prohibited the export of oats except under licence, and the Potato Order fixed the price to be paid to potato growers at £8 per ton in January and February, rising to £9 later in the year, and the maximum price for the best seed potatoes was £12 ton.[16] This latter order caused a collapse in both wholesale and retail potato prices.[17]

At the end of February Lord Davenport issued an announcement warning that he would take steps to deal with speculative buying or cornering of food supplies and with food hoarding.[18] On 24 February the Potatoes, 1916 Main Crop (Prices) Order (No. 2) stated that no one may 'make or demand and unreasonable charge' or 'impose or attempt to impose any condition relating to any other article'. This was prevent extortion by requiring customers to purchase other items even if they only wanted to buy potatoes. A matter of days later, on 8 March, an East End costermonger by the name of Dora Clark was fined 10s at the Old Street Police Court for attempting to impose a condition that Bessie Rice must buy 'greens' if she wanted the 2lbs of potatoes she had asked for.[19] The Food (Conditions of Sale) Order on 21 March stated clearly that 'except under the authority of the Food Controller, no person shall, in connection with a sale or proposed sale of any article of food, impose or attempt to impose any condition relating to the purchase of any other article'. To avoid any doubt, Lord Devonport defined the term 'article of food' as 'any article used for food by man, and any article which ordinarily enters into the composition or preparation of human food'.[20] The lawyers were to have much sport in challenging this definition in the months to come.

The Potatoes Order also set the prices which could be charged. William Bray, a greengrocer in Longford, found himself before the Coventry County Magistrates on 23 March for selling potatoes by retail at a price exceeding the maximum fixed by the Food Controller. Constable Ashfield saw a young girl buy 10lbs of potatoes for 2s (2.4d per pound); the fixed price being 1½d per pound. He challenged Bray, who told him that they were seed potatoes, not for cooking. However, there was also the Order respecting seed potatoes which had a fixed price of 3d/lb. There was a sign 'Holbach seed potatoes. 5lbs for 1s' and the defendant's son confirmed they were intended as seed potatoes. The magistrates found Bray guilty and the chairman said that heavy penalties could be imposed, but as this was the first prosecution they would fine him 40s.[21]

By the third year of the war the workings of the Defence of the Realm Act and the Defence of the Realm regulations were well known, if not fully understood, by the public and the courts. The need for a mechanism to produce orders without placing huge amounts of legislation before Parliament had been addressed through Orders in Council. Local interpretation and application of orders rested with the competent naval or military authorities. The courts dealt with offences under the regulations. The problems seen with rushed legislation had been recognized and corrected, so one might assume that there would be form of quality assurance in a government department like the Ministry of Food. The difficulty was that the Food Controller had no need to engage with the police, military or naval authorities, or the courts, nor even the trader, shopkeeper or housewife (although he did consult with producers and manufacturers).

Once the new department was established the orders came out with increasing frequency and many were very poorly written.

Ernest and Lena Green, confectioners and bakers at Jordon Place, Walham Green, were summoned to the West London Police Court on 18 May 1917, for selling jam and custard tarts. Police sergeant Goodenough stated that there was jam on the exterior of the tart. Mr Green replied that he had some jam left over, and thought he would use it up. His representative, Mr H. Pierron, argued that order did not apply to short pastry, from which jam tarts were made. Presumably this is the Cake and Pastry Order of 18 April, 1917, section 2 of which prohibits the addition of any 'edible substance to the exterior of the cake mixture or dough after it has been mixed, or to the article during the process of or after baking'. Pierron also mentioned that bakers and confectioners were confused because some of the orders were drawn up in such a way that even lawyers were puzzled. Mr Boyd, the stipendiary magistrate, also found it difficult to interpret the order and he believed that the defendants had acted in good faith, so he placed them on probation.[22]

Other offenders were dealt with more severely. The next week, in the Bromley Police Court, Louisa Heritage of Mason's Hill, Bromley, was the first person to be prosecuted under the Wheat, Rye and Rice (Restriction) Order. George Barnes, her dustman, had found a number of pieces of bread in her bin and a quantity in an old bath by the side of the bin. The slices and crusts amounted to 4lbs of bread. Inspector Burton interviewed the woman, who explained that she was going to make a bread pudding but found the bread so mildewed that 'I would not even give it to the ducks'. On being told that she would be reported to the Food Controller, she replied 'Pooh! It's not stolen. It is bread I have paid for and I can do as I please'. The dustman gave further evidence that about nine weeks previously he had spoken to Mrs Heritage about the amount of fat and bread she threw away. The bench took a very dim view and gave her an exemplary fine of £5 with the option of serving two months' imprisonment in the second division, with three weeks to pay.[23] In the light of this case Dover Town Council instructed that if any dustman found bread in a dustbin he should report it so that they could prosecute.[24]

The Food Controller reached an arrangement with the Local Government Board in May 1917, conferring on local authorities and their officers the powers and duties of enforcing various provisions of the Food Controller's orders. It was suggested that sanitary officers and other officials who routinely travelled around the district could make the appropriate enquiries and investigations. This required an amendment to the Defence of the Realm regulations, so that regulation 2J delegated the relevant powers to enforce regulations 2F and 2G to the local authorities. The Local Authority (Food Control) Order (No. 1), 1917 duly authorized local authorities and their officers to prosecute any offence against the relevant regulations[25] before the courts of summary jurisdiction. The Food Controller certainly needed external help. The order was dated 8 May by which time no fewer than forty-three food control orders had been passed, averaging just over two orders a week.

The Bristol magistrates had a difficult case to deal with on 15 May. The previous Friday Samuel Tidman was fined for being drunk in charge of a horse and cart in Stokes Croft. While the police constable was dealing with him he noticed that the cart was loaded with about a hundredweight (50.8kg) of clean bread. Tidman was able to explain that he collected the bread from local hostels and barracks. Further enquiries led the police to the Nimrod Hotel on St George's Road and to the Mardyke Hotel in Hotwells, both Ministry of Munitions hostels. The managers of both establishments were summoned to the police court, before Mr Frank Moore and Mr Allan McArthur. Thomas Patterson, of the Nimrod, claimed that the bread represented two days' waste and comprised the tops and bottom of 'tin' loaves. Mrs Perkins, of the Mardyke, stated that she had catered for working men all her life but never the class of man she had now (munitions workers). 'If the dinner did not suit them they would just as soon throw it on the floor and stamp on it.' In response to a question from the bench, she confirmed that indeed the navvy objected to eating crusts. Patterson volunteered that seven slices of bread, each an inch thick, were cut for two meals for each navvy. In sentencing the pair Mr Moore declared this to be a 'very gross and wilful waste of the food of the nation. We have been asked to do all we can to increase the food production of the country and you seem to be doing all you can to waste it. It is a very serious case and we have been considering if we ought to send you to prison.' Patterson was fined £50, Mrs Perkins £25 (there was 'better supervision at the Mardyke Hotel').[26]

The magistrates' courts soon filled up with offenders who wittingly or, more often, unwittingly fell foul of the new orders. Harry Poulson, a baker in Collier's Wood, ended up before the magistrates at Croydon for exposing new bread for sale. In mitigation he complained that 'there appeared to be a terrible muddle, and members of the trade did not get the Food Controller's orders direct, and he was too busy to read the newspapers'. The chairman, Mr Arthur Spurgeon, was unimpressed: 'That is where you are wrong.' Mr J.C.M. Kerslake, 'president of the London Master Bakers' Protection Society and an expert adviser to the Ministry of Food', pointed out that food control orders were published in the *London Gazette* and in the newspapers. He confirmed that the Food Controller depended on the newspapers to make the orders known. Poulson was fined £5.[27] Incidentally, the reasonably common offence of exposing new bread for sale related to the requirement that bread made for less than twelve hours must not be sold. This is because the moisture content is such that the bread cannot be thinly sliced.

There was growing discontent with food control orders as legislative tools. *Justice of the Peace* carried an editorial criticizing the orders as 'one of the most troublesome branches of the emergency legislation'. There had been some discussion about the powers of the Food Controller and whether the orders were actually *ultra vires*, but the overarching concern was the poor draughtsmanship of the authors of the orders. They used the Bread Order of 26 February as a particularly egregious example. The bakers had been told that they could only bake two types of loaf: the 'tin' loaf or the 'one piece oven bottom' loaf. Terms such as these should either have a common meaning and therefore require no further explanation, or they were technical expressions understood by those in the trade, or that there was some other meaning that was then explained in the order itself. This particular order failed on each count. A 'tin' loaf was baked in, as its name suggests, a baking tin, producing a loaf with a flat bottom, four flat sides, and a rounded top. But some bakers cooked them upside-down, producing a loaf with six flat sides. The Food Controller actually meant the former. The 'one piece oven bottom', or

Coburg, loaf was one where a lump of dough is placed in the oven and left to rise. But some bakers stretched the dough so that it was longer and narrower, which produced a 'Danish' loaf. Again the Food Controller meant the former. A Coburg loaf could also be scored down the middle to produce a single loaf but which could be easily split into two – a 'twin sister brick'. This was permitted by a general licence in May. But the baker was only allowed to produce one type of loaf, so he had to choose between making all Coburgs or all twin sisters. And a Coburg could be cooked in a shallow dish to produce a 'tin Coburg' or a 'pan Coburg'.[28] Mr Jesse Heyden and his daughter Ellen, of Miserden, were fined 15s and 5s each for selling 'quite new cottage loaves', breaching two regulations at once.[29]

The Bread Order, 1917 also specified that bread was to be sold by weight, with the minimum weight as 1lb and increasing by an even number of pounds. Mr A.B. Perry and Mr H. Hosegood sat at the Bristol Police Court on 5 April and heard that Philip Blackmore, of 61 Chaplin Road, Easton, offered for sale a loaf of bread two ounces underweight. As he had in fact not sold the loaf the magistrates decided that he had not defrauded the public and they bound him over for six months. The next case, Joseph Needham, of 80 West Street, Bedminster, sold a tin loaf which was 3oz short. He was fined £1. The Food Controller appreciated that bread lost weight as it came out of the oven and allowed the bread to be weighed at any time up to thirty hours. But the interesting question was posed: what if a loaf of bread weighed a pound and a half? Is it an underweight 2lb loaf, or an overweight 1lb loaf? It was also noted that the historic Bread Acts allowed bakers to bake bread of any size or weight they wished. The Food Controller's orders were made under the authority of the Order in Council, which themselves derives from powers under the Defence of the Realm Act. But that Act did not give the King in Council the authority to override existing statutes, which again suggests that the Food Controller was acting *ultra vires*.

Further challenges to the system of food control orders soon arose. To prove a breach of an order or regulation posted by government departments the prosecution need to prove that the notice has been served. This proof was either the copy of the *London Gazette* in which it was published, or copy of the order purporting to be printed by His Majesty's Stationery Office, neither of which were widely available.[30] William Coryton was the nurseryman and manager of Lyndon Nurseries in Hampton. Heeding the demands for the cultivation of land for the production of food, he decided that growing potatoes was more important than growing flowers, and so he turned over part of his land to this purpose. Not experienced with potatoes, he planted a crop of King Edward's along with some Queen Mary's. On 4 August he harvested them and sold them to Henry Smith, a greengrocer on the High Street in Hampton Hill. For some reason Smith had doubts and went to PC Smith for advice. The sale of the Queen Mary's (an early variety) was permitted, but sale of the King Edward's was a breach of the recent Potato Crop (Restriction) Order. Coryton was prosecuted at Feltham magistrates' court by a large bench: John Ashby DL, J. Doherty, J.J. Freeman, G. Metcalf and T. Croysdale. The defence representative challenged the police officer for proof that the 'order was brought to the notice of the people in any other way than by the publication in the *London Gazette*'. The officer replied that he was not aware of any other notice, but 'they can have any advice they ask for'. Coryton explained that he had not seen any notice in the press and anyway since his men had joined up he 'had practically no time to read papers'. He had heard nothing from the Food Controller. The bench were sympathetic, and noted the technical offence but only imposed costs of 4s.

One case achieved some notoriety. George Thompson was a well-known farmer and merchant at Lutton Marsh, Long Sutton, and was a pioneer of potato growing, farming some of the best land in Lincolnshire. Between March and May 1917 he had been selling his top-quality potatoes at an average of £15 a ton. In the Potato Main Crop (Prices) Order (No.2) the price for potatoes was fixed at £11 a ton. He had sold a total of 1,320 tons and made a profit of £4,620. He was deeply critical of the Food Controller's policy in which he had to sell his produce at the same price as an indifferent grower (Mr Coryton perhaps). He claimed that many farmers were upset by the regulations which were not brought before Parliament and received no public viewing, but were made 'by a person occupying an autocratic position'. He was clear that the price he charged was paid by the merchants, and because of the regulations the cost was not passed on to the customer. The chairman, who had known Mr Thompson for many years, and his colleagues took thirty minutes to decide to inflict the maximum £100 penalty for each of the fifty-five summonses, totalling £5,500 with £250 costs. Mr Thompson made out a cheque for the full amount before leaving the court.

On 5 April 1917 the Food Hoarding Order was issued. Whether it was because it was immediately before the Easter holidays, or that the public weren't paying attention to the *London Gazette*, it attracted little notice. It took a while for the first prosecutions to arrive in the courts, but when they did they tended to gather a great deal of publicity. One of the first involved a Russian shipping agent, Kriker Tamirantz. The prosecution, at Southport magistrates' court, was taken on the authority of the Food Controller. On 15 May police sergeant Pendlebury, 'acting on information received', attended the defendant's address in Grosvenor Road, Birkdale, and witnessed a large number of goods being carried into the house from a delivery van. Tamirantz visited the police station in the evening with a list of the goods he had purchased from MacSymon's Stores, of Liverpool. He had:

Four 4lb boxes of macaroni
One 28lb box of vermicelli
6 bottles of chutney
12 bottles of pickles
24 bottles of pears
12 bottles of pineapples
12 bottles of apricots
12 bottles of tomato puree
Two 4lb bottles of compressed vegetables
2½lbs of garlic
24 tins of sardines
Three 7lb jars of gooseberry jam
Three 7lb jars of damson jam

Three 7lb jars of raspberry jam
Three gallons of olive oil
14lbs of raisins

The chairman, Alderman Griffiths noted that 'although the defendant was a Russian he was a patriotic citizen of this country' he would be fined £25.[31]

The criticisms of the work of the Food Controller and the ministry were telling.[32] By the start of June there was speculation that there would be a restructuring, and the appointment of a Board of Control, similar to the Central Control Board (Liquor Traffic), with Lord Devonport being moved out,[33] although he actually resigned due to ill-health. Several candidates were suggested, including Lord Rothermere, and Robert Smillie, president of the Miners' Federation. They all turned down the post. On Friday, 15 June 1917 Lord Rhondda, the former president of the Local Government Board, accepted the appointment. Born David Thomas in Aberdare in 1856, he had made his money in mining before entering politics as a Liberal MP, before elevation to the House of Lords in early 1916. A popular man with the common touch, he had the unusual status of being a survivor of the sinking of the *Lusitania* in May 1915.

Rhondda spent some time trying to understand the problems that faced the food supply of the country. He developed three main policies: that supplies must be conserved; that supplies must be shared equally by rich and poor; and that prices must be kept down. In August he issued an invitation to local authorities to set up local Food Control Committees. Lord Devonport had introduced the idea of voluntary committees in April and there were a number of such bodies set up around the country. The objectives were to reduce food consumption by voluntary rationing, but efforts were lacklustre. The proposal for a 'meatless day' foundered when it was revealed that Devonport didn't favour it himself,[34] and because most initiatives were at the local level, there was no overall strategy or focus. Rhondda redesigned the scheme. The local authorities were to set up food control committees drawing the membership from their own members or from outside, to include at least one representative of labour and at least one woman.[35] Their first duty was to protect the interests of consumers. Each committee would appoint a paid chief executive and an office and such staff as may be required. The Food Control Committees (Constitution) Order of 17 August provided the committees with genuine authority under regulation 2J of the Defence of the Realm regulations. The price-setting mechanism was revisited so that a general scale of prices could be set for each layer of the supply chain, allowing for necessary expenses and for a reasonable profit margin for the wholesaler and retailer. The local food control committees were to use their knowledge of local conditions to make recommendations about local price levels.[36]

Once the prices had been fixed the retailers were required to display them in their shops. Edward Watson, a former magistrate and now member of Glasgow Town Council and of its local Food Control Committee, was also a successful butcher. His business had an annual turnover of between £60,000 and £100,000. For the eight months before the Food Controller fixed the price of meat, he had made a net loss of £402, but since fixing he had made a profit of £260. Except that he wasn't charging the fixed prices and had set his own, and refused to display the official prices in his shop. At the Glasgow Sheriffs' Court he contended that he had always bought the best cattle and sheep at the livestock market, and could not profitably sell this meat at the set price. Sheriff Lyell found him guilty of a wilful defiance of the law, and fined him £50 or sixty days' imprisonment in default.[37] Small shopkeepers were under immense pressure to monitor the prices that they had to use and display, and although some foods could be priced nationally there were regional and seasonal variations. Official Food Control price placards were available from newspaper offices, and notices about the price changes often appeared in the small ads section of the local publication, in amongst hundreds of trivial items. Lapses of attention were not permitted and prosecutions often appeared malicious and the result of petty officialdom: Florence Cooper owned a butcher's shop at Westgate in Rotherham. Mrs Sands, an inspector for the local Food Control Committee, visited her shop on 5 December 1917 and noticed that there was no price list on display. Mrs Cooper told her that it had blown down and that she had forgotten to replace it – the list had been folded and put on her desk, where Mrs Sands could see it. But Mr Turner, from the Town Clerk's Office, decided to prosecute, and at Rotherham Borough Court she was fined 40s.[38]

The new Food Controller introduced the *National Food Journal* to provide 'a record of the administrative work of the department and ... articles explanatory of the Food Controller's policies'.[39] Priced at 2d, and published fortnightly, the first edition appeared on 12 September, 1917, with 'sixteen pages full of interesting information, and an eight page supplement of statutory rules and regulations from 22nd August 1917. Every member of the food control committee should subscribe.'[40] The *Daily Record* hoped that it would be 'a bright and cheery contrast to that other government publication, the *London Gazette*'.[41]

Coventry had to wait until January 1918 for its first hoarding case. Messrs Albert Herbert Ltd was a large and prestigious machine tool maker and the chairman of the company, Mr Alfred Herbert, had been appointed as Controller of the Machine Tools Department at the Ministry of Munitions. He left the management of the firm to Oscar Harmer, a prominent local figure who lived in a large house, 'Dalhousie', in Dalton Road, Coventry. Percy Dawes, the executive officer of the local food control committee, and Chief Constable Chersley visited Harmer at work on 18 December. He was shown a search warrant issued by the Ministry of Food and he accompanied them back to his home. He took them to the second landing of the house and showed them a locked room. In the absence of his housekeeper who had the key, he agreed to unscrew the lock. Inside they discovered:

400lbs tea
144lbs sugar
37 tins of sardines
14 hams
26 2½lb tins of tongue
13 1lb tins of butter

He was told of the contravention of the order and he claimed to know nothing of the law. He subsequently produced a number of receipts from Twinings of London and Heenan & Froude of Worcester.

Harmer's court appearance on 19 January 1918 was a big event, with a full public gallery and a number of members of the city council. The magistrates were Dr E. Lynes, Alderman T.A.B. Soden, J. Crompton, and Hugh R. Farren. The prosecutor was Mr Norman Birkett, instructed by the Town Clerk on behalf of the local food control committee. The defence representative was Mr Henry Maddocks, and Harmer entered a 'not guilty' plea to the charge that he 'did unlawfully acquire a certain article of food, to wit, tea, so that the quantity of such article in your possession at any one time exceeded the quantity required for ordinary use and consumption in your household in contravention of the Food Hoarding Order'. Similar charges related to each of the other items.

The prosecution case was very straightforward. At the time there was shortage of tea in Coventry, and yet the defendant had an ample supply. Evidence was offered that the room was definitely a store room, as there was a larder in the house with ordinary household supplies. There were invoices and letters from the suppliers confirming both the purchases and their bulk nature. There were seven persons in the household, being the defendant and his wife, two sons, the housekeeper, cook and housemaid.

Mr Maddocks, for the defence, initially proposed that the order hadn't been published, but then made an interesting change of tactics. Rather than base the defence on the publication or otherwise of the order, he took the opportunity to criticize the Food Controller and the local food control committee.

> Never was there a time since the Napoleonic period when one individual – the Food Controller – was in a position by a stroke of his pen to create an offence in England without consultation with Parliament and without authority from any person; when he might sit down one morning and write an order which would have an effect in a few days, and if it were infringed by a person, even if he did not know about it, that person would be liable to imprisonment. It was admitted that the law was not published in Coventry, not five persons knew about it until these proceedings began …

Maddocks then pulled his masterstroke – he contended that the wording of the order was specifically about 'an article of food'. Surely no one could possibly suggest that tea was a food?

The bench had to retire to consider the point. Eventually they decided against Maddocks, but agreed to provide a statement of case for review by the Divisional Court (Chapter 1). They found the remaining matters proved. After hearing a character reference from Mr Herbert, Dr Lynes conferred with his colleagues and announced that a financial penalty was not enough for a man in Harmer's position, and he would be given one month's imprisonment in each case, to run concurrently. He was also fined £500 with £50 costs. He collapsed in the dock and two of the medical members of the bench gave him assistance. Maddocks lodged an appeal on the point of law about tea as an article of food, and Harmer was fortunately released on bail. The goods were forfeited.[42] Harmer's appeal was heard at the Warwickshire Quarter Sessions on 20 April 1918, before Lord Ilkeston, Veasey Fitzgerald KC, Alderman W.F. Wyley, Mr T. Burbridge, J. Cramp, R. Burns, E. Wootton, G.H. Pickering, W.H. Grant, and W. Johnson Jr. It was decided to leave the tea conviction out pending the Divisional Court decision. The court upheld the convictions imposed by the magistrates on the butter and sugar cases and reduced the penalty to a total fine of £60, and the imprisonment was remitted.[43]

The Harmer case engaged the attention of many. Is tea a food? Even the *Justice of the Peace* seemed at a loss. The editors distinguished three possible categories: an article directly used as food (bread); an ingredient in the substance of which a food is compounded (oats for porridge, or suet for pudding); or may assist in its preparation (lard, with which to fry). Were tea, coffee and cocoa all covered by the order? From other cases in the country it appeared that some benches believed they were, and others that they were not (similar cases were being put on hold until this matter was resolved). Tea leaves are used in the preparation of liquid tea, so although the tea leaves are not consumed the beverage is. With a sideswipe to the casual legislation pouring out of the Ministry of Food, they decided to follow the correct procedure and sought a precedent – was there an existing definition of 'food' on the statute books? And they found the 1875 Sale of Food and Drugs Act which had a slightly vague wording 'every article used as food by man, other than drugs or water'. This had been tidied up by the 1899 Amending Act, to read 'every article used for food or drink by man, other than drugs or water, and any article which ordinarily enters into and is used in the composition or preparation of food; and flavouring matters and condiments'. Section 30 of the 1875 Act directly applied to tea, which could be classified by the inspector as 'unfit for human food'.[44]

Meanwhile another case seemed to resolve the matter. Mrs Ellen Hinde, of Shipton-under-Wychwood, Oxfordshire, had been fined £50 with costs for having an excessive quantity of tea (122lbs). She appealed the conviction and her case was heard before the King's Bench Divisional Court before Justices Darling, Avory and Shearman on 25 April 1918. She was represented by Mr J.B. Matthews, KC, who spent some time explaining that there was no definition in place, but in common English one wouldn't ask a friend to 'eat tea'. Cocoa (and coffee) were different, because it was dissolved in hot water and consumed with the water. Tea leaves were strained off. The court decided that tea was not a food within the meaning of the Food Hoarding Order, and quashed the conviction.[45]

Lord Rhondda wasted little time in closing this loophole. The Food Hoarding (Amendment) Order was published on 3 May 1918 (although, curiously, the Order itself is dated 1 May, before the court made its decision). Section 5 explicitly stated 'For the purpose of this order, the expression "article of food" shall mean every article which is used for food by man and every article which ordinarily enters into or is used in the composition or preparation of food and shall include tea, coffee, and cocoa'. This was in direct contradiction of the decision of the Divisional Court, but received no further challenge.

Food hoards were seized by the police and on conviction the goods were forfeited to the local food control committee, who were empowered to sell the food to the local community. There were so many instances of food hoarding that Lord Rhondda issued an Amnesty Order which was in force between 8 February and 25 February 1918. This allowed people who were holding excess quantities of food to declare the fact to their local food control committee. They would take the surplus and sell it, returning one half of the net proceeds to the owner. The Food Controller also announced that the Food Hoarding Order did not apply to 'stocks of any home-produced food – for example, bacon, jam, bottled fruits or vegetables, preserved eggs and the like'.[46]

The quality of the legal draughtsmanship of the food orders received further challenge. Hugh Gordon Murdoch, steamship manager, lived at 8 Boringdon Villas in Plympton, Devon. The police found 200lbs of flour *and* 156lbs of sugar in a storeroom in his house, along with a large number of other food articles. He was prosecuted under the Food Hoarding Order, and the Plympton magistrates fined him £30 on 30 December 1917. He appealed the conviction and was before the King's Bench Division on 26 March 1918. Mr Justice Darling noted that he had been fined for hoarding flour and sugar. The correct interpretation was that there were *two* offences, one relating to the flour, the other to the sugar. The magistrates had made one conviction for two offences and, the judges agreed, this made the conviction bad and it was therefore quashed.[47] This was an important decision – there was a separate offence for each item hoarded, not merely for the hoard in its entirety, and it was down to the prosecutor to prepare the relevant charges.

The offence under the Food Hoarding Order was that the quantity of food being hoarded was in excess of that required for the 'ordinary use and consumption' of the household. Again, with novel legislation such as this there was no existing definition of 'ordinary use and consumption'. In a number of cases, including Harmer, part of the defence was that it was quite normal for individuals to hold large stocks of foodstuffs (in Murdoch's case he presented receipts showing that some of the items in his storeroom had been purchased as far back as 1905). The emphasis was on the household's usual requirements for eating and drinking (consumption) rather than on 'arrangements for domestic economy' (purchase).[48] The *National Food Journal* gave as rambling a definition as might be expected from the Ministry of Food:

> It is impossible to give any precise and general definition of food hoarding or to lay down an exact standard of supply which householders may reasonably hold of the various articles of food. Each individual case must be judged on its merits. It may, however, be taken as a very rough indication of the view of the Ministry of Food that a fortnight's to three week's supply of any of the staple articles of food is not regarded as excessive. Stocks for a longer period may, in special circumstances, be held by people living in districts remote from the source of supply and subject to exceptional difficulties of transport.[49]

The *Justice of the Peace* dared to express an opinion that the Food Controller and the Ministry of Food were acting *ultra vires*. The powers granted under 2F of the Defence of the Realm regulations specified the taking of steps necessary to conserve the food supply of the nation. The Defence of the Realm Act, as amended, gave His Majesty in Council the power to 'issue regulations for the public safety and the defence of the Realm, expressed in five areas:

1. Information concerning military operations, etc.
2. Safety of ships, railways, ports and harbours.
3. False reports.
4. Navigation of vessels.
5. Otherwise to prevent assistance being given to the enemy or the successful prosecution of the was being endangered.

None of these described food control or food supply. Recall that in order to deal with liquor control (see Chapter 7), a separate Defence of the Realm (Amendment) (No. 3) Act was passed, so the mechanism and precedent existed.

Francis Lake, a dairyman, appeared before West London magistrates in early March, 1918. He was charged that he had several milk cans and one milk bottle bearing the names and addresses of other firms without their consent, in breach of the Milk Amendment Order, 1917. He tried to explain to Mr de Grey, the chairman, that this was normal practice in the trade. 'Only until DORA came along,' he replied, to laughter. He asked if he knew the purpose of the regulation. Lake didn't. Nor did PC Gomm. The chairman: 'They simply make a regulation and give no reason. At any rate, you must obey it, and there is a fine of 10s.' The London News Agency, which covered the story, actually asked the Ministry of Food for an explanation of the order; apparently it was to stop the theft of milk bottles and cans, which could 'dislocate the milk traffic'.[50]

A common national attribute assigned to the English people is the ability to queue but at time of the Great War this social phenomenon was relatively uncommon. Queues were seen outside theatres and, less commonly, cinemas, and were frequently under the control of a police constable – a line of people could obstruct pedestrian and road traffic and constitute an offence under the Town Police Clauses Act, 1847. In a 1909 case Mr Wachter, of the Theatre Reform League, took out summonses against Fred Hart, lessee of the Prince's Theatre in Manchester, for public nuisance and obstructing the highway. Despite the common law basis for the offences, common sense prevailed and the stipendiary dismissed the case.[51] Mr Denman, the Marlborough Street police court magistrate, imposed a fine of 2s 6d on a man who had been employed to wait in a theatre queue.[52] Social class gave precedence in shops, and this applied as much to one's servants who placed and collected orders. And in many cases shopping had a social aspect – I remember my own grandmother patiently waiting to be served by Mrs Bartlett, rather than Mr Bartlett or his boy, simply because she had some news to share.

Food shortages began to impose pressures on the distribution of food and supplies on an equitable basis. There was a severe shortage of potatoes in south Wales in early March 1917 and 'exciting scenes were witnessed in Clifton Street, Cardiff, when a large crowd of shoppers fought amongst themselves and struggled with the police' to obtain the potatoes.[53] On the same day in Swansea local growers tried to take advantage of the demand by selling at a higher price than that permitted by the Food Controller, leading to incidents in which the police had to intervene. Finally three police officers had to assist in the distribution of 2lb bags to the 'eager crowd'.[54] The next month the Birkenhead magistrates had to deal with Anne Jones, a lodging-house keeper of Borough Road, summoned for disorderly conduct. One of the first police women in the area, Glady Williams, had been supervising a potato queue when the defendant tried to force her way in, using very bad language. Jones denied bad language and claimed that she had not had potatoes for eight weeks. She was fined 40s.[55]

By December margarine was in very short supply. By December 1917 queueing had reached 'appalling' proportions, such as at Manchester where the queues around the principal margarine shops formed at around 7 am, composed of women of the poorer classes and boys and girls (often taking time off school). On one occasion a line stretched 'from Deansgate along St. Mary's Gate, Exchange Street, and half way up to St. Anne's Square', and numbered over 1,000 persons. At Weaste, in Salford, a queue a quarter of a mile long formed outside one of the dairies.[56] Sidney Langford, a labourer, appeared at Coventry Police Court on 14 January 1918 on a charge of breaching the peace. According to Special Constable T. Thurston and other witnesses, Langford had demanded entrance to the Maypole Dairy at Broadgate and then forced his way in, using violence. Thurston managed to eject him, whereupon Langford told the crowd to 'raid the shop'. After the bench found him guilty, Inspector Hobley told the court that this was Langford's fifth appearance; he was bound over for six months in the sum of £5, with a £5 surety.[57] In Bootle an angry and impatient queue vented its frustration by stoning the members of the local Food Control Committee.[58]

The unfairness of the queueing system was a source of continuing grievance. There was strong condemnation of people in queues who were not regular customers of the shops and who bought goods at the expense of the regulars, particularly if they had already received their allowance from their own usual store. People were observed to return to the back of the queue once served, to try to go around again. Others sent two or more family members so that they could obtain additional shares of the goods.[59] The police took a census of one queue in Wolverhampton: out of 410 persons 44 per cent came from outside the area, and many were subsequently refused admission to the shops.[60]

Lily Herbert saw an opportunity in the queues. Only seventeen years old she was on the verge of becoming a professional pickpocket before she was caught stealing a purse containing £1 3s 6d from a woman in Cape Hill, Smethwick. Superintendent Campbell told the Smethwick magistrates that when taken into custody she had two more purses, and intended travelling to Birmingham to work the queues there. She was put on probation for two years, with the condition that she remained in a training home.[61]

The newspapers and court records have vast numbers of cases of offences against the food orders in this period. The Ministry of Food were producing new orders almost on a daily basis, and the administration of these orders had been devolved to the local food control committees who struggled to keep up with the flow. By 31 December 1917 there had been 211 orders issued, including amendments and repeals; in the week up to

Christmas there had been seventeen new orders, including the Bacon and Ham Curers (Returns), Margarine (Registration of Dealers), and the British Onions Order. But the Food Controller was more concerned about food shortages.

The food control committees were responsible for the local distribution of meat and other supplies and in general they worked well with the shopkeepers. Benjamin Holten, a butcher of 44 High Road, Willesden Green, was one of many who fell foul of the requirement to display a price list – in this case a breach of the Meat Prices Order – and although this was the first such case before the Willesden magistrates in September 1917, the excuse he offered would be repeated up and down the country: the list had just fallen down, but the officer did not see it, and anyway there was a price list on the pay desk.[62]

Lord Rhondda made a frank and open statement at the Ministry of Food on Friday, 14 December 1917, having completed six months as Food Controller. He was openly critical of the leniency of magistrates, particularly the unpaid justices, which he felt undermined the effectiveness of the food control orders. Perhaps insensitive to the incompetence of those in his department who drafted the orders, he noted that there was a minority (of magistrates) who sought loopholes in the legislation in order to evade them. He also indicated that the machinery to introduce rationing was in place, and this would add considerably to the work of the justices in the months to come.[63]

As with much of the early work in food control, reliance was placed on the voluntary principle and that for patriotic motives individuals and families would seek to impose their own restrictions on consumption. Sir Arthur Yapp, the Director of Food Economy, toured the country endlessly promoting this philosophy. In November 1917 he proposed a new scale of rations, to replace Lord Devonport's earlier scheme (which foundered largely because Devonport himself was not particularly committed to it). The old system was based on food consumption per household and did not recognize individual needs. Yapp suggested as the bread ration per head per week:

Men on very heavy industrial work or on agricultural work	8lbs
Men on ordinary industrial or other manual work	7lbs
Men unoccupied or on sedentary work	4lbs 8oz
Women on heavy industrial work or on agricultural work	5lbs
Women on ordinary domestic work or in domestic service	4lbs
Women unoccupied or on sedentary work	3lbs 8oz

Despite Yapp's sterling efforts, the reality was that supplies of sugar and other necessities were so limited that voluntary control was unworkable. Another great administrative exercise was undertaken, whereby the head of each household had to register with a named grocer for the supply of their food. The grocer was registered with the local food control committee so that the exact requirements of each shop could be known. The sugar registration scheme started as early as August 1917, but the Sugar (Rationing) Order came into operation on Monday, 31 December 1917, and entitled every registered individual in the country to a ration of ½lb (226g) of sugar per week.

Common rationing offences involved the ration cards. Myra Widdowson, of Lydgate Lane, appeared before Sheffield magistrates on 11 April 1918 to answer a charge under the Sugar (Rationing) Order, that she unlawfully retained a sugar ticket bearing the name of her sister, Mrs Alice Gent, of 11 Hobart Street. It appeared that Mrs Gent, a munitions worker, lived at Widdowson's house each week from Monday to Friday and went home at weekends. She was registered for sugar at Stevenson Brothers, Club Garden Road. Mrs Widdowson, however, had signed her sister's name to another application form and from 5 January to 16 February she used it to obtain sugar from the Glossop Road branch of the Sheffield and Eccleshall Cooperative Society. The defendant claimed inadvertence and had cancelled the card when she discovered her sister was registered elsewhere. A fine of 10s was imposed.[64] An interesting problem arose when, in a number of cases, it appeared that food cards were being held for various reasons as a means of control. There were stories of landladies retaining their lodgers' cards for non-payment of rent, as did wives whose husbands didn't give them enough housekeeping money. The usual redress would be for the lodger or the husband to make an application at the magistrates' court for a summons for theft, which was rather heavy handed, or to take the matter to the County Court as a civil matter. A Bolton woman complained to the borough justices when her husband, from whom she had just separated, refused to surrender her food cards. She even had a letter from the Local Food Office directing the husband to surrender the cards, but he countered that his name was on the cards and he was going to keep them. The magistrates were unable to help.[65] Given the huge numbers of orders in force at the time, it took a while for someone to notice that section 1 (d) of the Local Distribution (Misuse of Documents) Order of 2 February 1918 expressly prohibited the retention of any 'application, card, voucher, authorization or other document ...' but this was too late to help with the earlier cases.[66]

The original Order in Council of 10 January 1917 which provided powers for the Food Controller under the Defence of the Realm regulations 2F to 2J also gave the same powers to the Board of Trade under regulation 2JJ in respect of items of commerce.[67] There were hundreds of such orders issued, and small traders and firms were prosecuted in the same way as under the food control orders. And the same absurdities are found – the Board of Trade set up a Tobacco and Matches Control Board, and on 11 September 1917 they saw fit to issue the Match Control Order. Alderman Peter Peacock chaired the Warrington Borough Court on 12 January 1918 to hear a prosecution against Charles Gould, of 7 Wilderspool Causeway, for failing to exhibit a price list and for selling at a price higher that that fixed by the Board. Acting Sergeant Whitby reported that he had gone to the defendant's shop and found that he was selling Swan Vestas at 1½d a box, when the maximum price was 1d/box. And there was no price list displayed. Gould was fined 10s for each offence.[68] William Humphries, of 90 Holme Lane, Sheffield, wanted to ensure that his limited stocks of matches went to his regular customers and wrote words to that effect on the price list in the window of his tobacconist's shop. According to Constable Thompson this was a condition of sale, and so Humphries was fined £2 by Alderman Samuel Osborn and Mr Richard Farron at Sheffield Police Court.

Even as late as June 1918 the magistrates were still finding flaws in the working of the food orders. Bermondsey Food Control Committee brought a prosecution against John Lavis, the licencee of the Stingo Arms beerhouse, in Tanner Street, at Tower Bridge Police Court. They alleged that he had imposed a condition of sale on the sale of food, by requiring a customer to order a drink to accompany his dinner. The defence representative, Mr Hatton, suggested that a 'dinner' was a combination of articles of food, and the order did not apply. Mr Hay Halkett, the stipendiary magistrate, agreed that a dinner was not 'an' article of food and dismissed the case, adding that 'probably within the next week or two there will be a new order to meet the case'.[69]

Specific statistics relating to food control offences are not available. Although court registers do list the cases, in the criminal statistics records which summarize them they are classed as Defence of the Realm offences, which includes lighting, liquor and other matters. From general research it would appear that food hoarding was one of the commonest charges for individuals, and breaches of the pricing rules for the retailers. The Food Supply Manual contains a full list of all orders issued from 20 November 1916 to 31 July 1918. There were 483 orders and amendments to orders. Forty orders were issued in June 1918 alone. This is lawmaking at its worst – large numbers of regulations, rapidly drafted, promulgated in a publication that very few people read, and implemented by local committees with no legal training. No wonder the magistrates and lawyers involved were so deeply critical. In the vast majority of cases the offenders were ordinary people and shopkeepers, and almost invariably people with no criminal intent. But these were difficult times, and with the reality of widespread food shortages the maintenance of an even and equitable food supply appeared to outweigh the need for good and just legislation.

Meat rationing continued until 15 December 1919, butter until 30 May 1920, and sugar did not become freely available until 29 November 1920.

Chapter 12

Business as Usual

Valencia, January 10 1914

Sir,

Having not the honour to know you personally, but merely by hints, my deceased mother, Anna Allen, of your family, did me address me to you by first time and perhaps the last, on account of my health state. I am imploring your protection for my alone daughter, 12 years age, and at the same time under your valuable concours as a person relational to be able to recover the sum of £24,000 which I have deposited in a secure spot. If you accept as I hope the sacred mission I intrust you. I will name you as tutor of my girl, sending her to your home, giving you the 4 part of said amount as just reward. As I am closely watched by my enemies I entreat you to keep the secret about this letter.

Being Staff-Colonel of the Spanish Army in this place, I was detained by political causes, and according to the Attorney-General petition I will be condemned for 18 gaol years and to the payment of the process expenses. As my luggage was seized when I was detained, it is needful to remove it to acquire my property, paying first to court my process expenses.

My only object to the address me to you is to assure under your help the honest patrimony of my dear daughter living after with your family. You will understand that I am unable to realize myself this affair, being in prison, nor I may trust it to any fellow countryman to be not betrayed again.

Fearful this letter don't arrive at your hands I will await your reply, and then I will say you my secret with all the details.

As the local council of this gaol read all the letters prisoners addressed, I beseech you wire me address inclosed person of all my reliance, who will give me it surely and reservedly, of this manner I shall know this letter arrived to your hands safely.

As my health state is very grievous, I am imploring a soon reply.

Waiting yours, I am, sir, your faithfully,

ALEJANDRO DE BEAL

Address: Manuel Gisbert, Juan de Austria, 28 tercero, Valencia (Spain)
Please answer me only these words – 'Accepted yours' – Allan[1]

This remarkably familiar scam was known in 1914 as the 'Spanish Swindle', and the British Ambassador in Madrid, Sir Arthur Hardinge, was obliged to write to *The Times* to warn of 'a gang of ingenious swindlers established in Madrid' who were sending these letters to unwary targets in English provincial towns.[2] Mr James Bruce, of Market

Street, Clay Cross, near Chesterfield, received an updated version in December 1914, concerning a 15-year-old daughter and £34,000, from 'a Belgian citizen who was residing in Brussels at the time of the German invasion, but obliged to leave'.[3] Scotland Yard had to issue a warning in February 1915, as there was a flood of letters from a Belgian, 'who, on the death of his master at the siege of Liège, has fled to Spain with £20,000 worth of Bank of England notes'.[4]

Some of the ordinary crimes took on a wartime dimension. One of the offences under the Vagrancy Act, 1824 was fortune-telling, and in a time which brought death and suffering to homes across the country, many mothers and wives sought assurance about their loved ones. Mrs Edith Hunter lived in a large fashionable house at 363 Oxford Road, close to Manchester University. Over the course of several visits in January and February 1915 Mrs Clarke, the wife of a police sergeant, gathered evidence of Mrs Hunter's activities. She operated out of three rooms in the house and provided private interviews in the afternoons and public meetings in the evenings. For 1s a time, Mrs Hunter was given insights such as that her (living) husband worked in a large building and travelled a lot, or that she saw 'an open grave in which a young flower had recently been buried', and a girl would die on entering womanhood but not to worry until 'the hyacinths are in bloom'. Sergeant Clarke monitored the house and on 15 February he saw thirty-four women and five men visit, and a further seventeen people attended the evening séance. On 17 February he returned and arrested Mrs Hunter and she appeared before Mr Brierly, the Manchester stipendiary magistrate, on 2 March. Her defence lawyer, Mr Dehn, justified his client's actions: 'There is no doubt that a large number of people of the highest repute and highest scientific attainments in this country believe that there is a great deal in [fortune telling].' The magistrate did not share that belief, and fined her £5.[5] Bertha Pixton held regular séances at the Spiritual Hall at 5a Every Street, Ancoats, and she was particularly popular with soldiers' wives. Three times a day on weekdays between thirty and seventy women at a time would pay 2d entry and form in a circle in the hall. They would each give Pixton an article belonging to the fiancé, husband or relative and she would give them a message in return. Dr Jackson, the chairman of the Manchester bench, fined her £10 on 12 November 1915, and refusing her time to pay, he added 'You have been deceiving these people all along and carrying on a wicked game. You are not deserving of sympathy. You must either pay or go to prison.' Her husband paid.[6] An interesting legal point was that the Vagrancy Act offence was 'pretending or professing to tell fortunes', the latter word in the plural; it was not sufficient to have a single instance of the offence, which is why Mrs Clarke made repeat visits, and Pixton was observed on several occasions. Those convicted of this offence might also find themselves deemed 'rogues and vagabonds' (see Chapter 2).[7]

Sergeant Herbert Dandy of the 1/8 Battalion, Manchester Regiment, had been officially reported as missing in action whilst fighting in Gallipoli in June 1915. His wife, Sarah, carried on with the family bakery at 227 Clowes Street, West Gorton, and on 16 July was putting cakes in the shop window when a uniformed man entered and said that he was her husband. He said that he was pleased to be back with his wife and children and started crying. She noticed that he had altered, but he explained that he had been lying out for 72 hours and had a bone removed from his knee. He had no sergeant's stripes on his uniform because he had broken out of Netley Hospital and stolen someone else's clothes. When she asked him 'private things' he claimed he had lost his memory, as well as some tattoos, but for a week they lived together as 'man and wife'. He made a fuss of the four children and even his own sister believed it was Dandy. Neighbours raised doubts about his real identity and Inspector Thomas challenged the man at the Exchange Station, Manchester. He was initially arrested on the Army Act charge of being an absentee, but he was soon unmasked as George Parkin Hall; his wife, Ada Hall, gave evidence that he was her husband and that they had married sixteen years previously, and that she had last seen him on 7 June before he was posted to Penmaenmawr with the Lancashire Fusiliers. At the hearing at the Manchester Petty Sessions in August six men from Dandy's regiment gave evidence that the accused was an imposter. Photographs were exhibited which showed a striking similarity between the two men. The matter was sent up to the Manchester Assizes for trial on 18 November, where the Grand Jury found a True Bill and he was tried, found guilty and sentenced to three years' penal servitude.[8] Dandy's death on 4 June 1915 was confirmed in September 1916; he had been awarded the Distinguished Conduct Medal for his achievements in the campaign.

Deception and fraud were serious crimes, but sometimes it was not clear who was being deceived. The use of the Red Cross emblem was prohibited under the Geneva Convention Act, 1911, and it was reserved to the British Red Cross Society and the naval and military medical services. Red Cross armlets, flags and insignia required the authority of the Army Council and were stamped with an official registration number. Dr John Key advertised his medical consultancy in 7 West Register Street in Edinburgh with handbills and posters bearing the red or Geneva cross on a white background, and he was fined £2 by Bailie McArthy in February 1915,[9] the maximum penalty being £10. This was one of the few offences that needed authorization from the Attorney-General before commencing a prosecution.

The Red Cross Society and the St John Ambulance Brigade were two of the most recognizable medical charities and, along with many other trusts and charitable organizations, worked hard throughout the war to raise funds from the newly-wealthy working classes. One of the first 'good causes' was the Belgian Relief Fund in August 1914, and the public donated generously. So much so that it didn't take long for the unscrupulous to seize an opportunity for easy money, and it was particularly attractive to organized criminal gangs. Jennie Lines, a 24-year-old artist's model, was one of several girls engaged by the Mirrorgraph Company in Albemarle Street to sell leaflets 'to help the poor Belgians' in Leicester Square. Selling for between 2d and 3d each, half the money went to the girls, 45 per cent to the company, and only 5 per cent to the charity. Although her employer attended Bow Street police court to explain that Scotland Yard had told him that they did not need a licence, Lines received a conviction for obstructing the footway and was fined 10s. Unable to pay, she was taken into custody to serve seven days' imprisonment in default.[10] Frances Newton arrested in similar circumstances in Seven Sisters Road, for selling postcards on behalf of Belgian refugees, most of the money going to the War Novelties Company. Mr Hedderwick strongly criticized the actions of such firms and pointed out the objections of the Belgian Legation. Newton paid her own 10s fine.[11] 'Well dressed' Annie Bird and her sister were from a good background, and thought they were doing genuine charity work by collecting on behalf of the National Patriotic Society in the Strand, for which they were paid a bonus of 6s or 7s a week. Mr Hopkins, the magistrate, was concerned that Bird and her father believed that she was arrested for collecting war funds, and he corrected them: 'You were arrested because the streets are full of girls who are employed by people who put the funds that you collect into their pockets.' He released her without penalty. The increase in fraud, misrepresentation and street begging offences led to the War Charities Act of August 1915. It was passed in response to two perceived abuses: the collection of money from the public for some charitable purpose but where the funds ended up in the collector's pocket, as 'expenses' or salary; and where large funds had been gathered but were poorly managed, with no published accounts, and no records or minute books. Under the new Act war charities were required to register with the Charity Commissioners, with the registration being undertaken by local authorities. The charity had to prove that it was correctly constituted and managed. 'Eminent and well known persons' were expected to carry out their own inquiries into the *bona fides* of any charity to which they wished to attach their names.[12]

Nathaniel Austin worked in the munitions factory of Messrs William Beardmore & Co, at the Parkhead Forge in Glasgow. A diligent and efficient machinist, he managed to produce twenty-eight shells per shift at night, and on the day shift he was able to produce thirty. His colleagues averaged fifteen. On his way home on 17 May 1915 he was accosted by two colleagues, James Marshall and Thomas Robertson and, seizing him by his lapels, Marshall delivered a head butt to the face. Giving evidence, foreman Turner explained that Austin was using a newly-adapted machine and was the only man at the firm using it. Sheriff Tomson said that the two men were trying to intimidate Austin from doing his duty, and that if this had happened in Germany, they would 'be taken out, put against a wall and shot'. He regretted that he could not do this here, and instead gave them the heaviest sentence possible, three months' hard labour.

Other working practices changed as women took over many traditional male jobs. Mrs Adams, a war widow, took a job as a tramway car conductor. On a busy service from Cricklewood one afternoon in April 1915, the lower deck was full so she told William Pursey to go upstairs to the open top deck. He used 'objectionable language', and when she took his fare she warned him that she was not there to be insulted and 'I have given a better man than you to the country'. He should think himself lucky that she did not slap him in the face. So he invited her do so, in fairly robust terms, and she did. He then struck her in the face with his fist, giving her a black eye. She was off work for five days and she took out a summons. At Hendon Petty Sessions the magistrates found no excuse for his behaviour and were sorry that they could not send him to prison. He was fined £2, with £1 15s 6d costs.

Theft, assault, shopbreaking, motoring offences: petty crime continued and the police had to deal with these matters as well as a wide range of new responsibilities brought in by the emergency legislation. By August 1915 the impact of the war on the police was beginning to be seen. The *Justice of the Peace* identified some of the factors affecting the efficiency of the service, such as the increase in the urban population as people took up munitions work, the additional new duties for the police, and the increase in the volume and speed of road traffic. Surprisingly, perhaps, it identified the principal factor affecting the workload as the effect of the Police (Weekly Rest Day) Act, 1910, which 'considerably reduced the policeman's working year'[13] – prior to this date police officers were allowed one day off a fortnight! In addition to keeping the peace and preventing and detecting crime, the wartime police now had to deal with:

Posting mobilization notices.
Personally warning reservists.
Billeting Territorial troops.
Assisting army officers in impressing horses, vehicles and mechanical transport.
Safeguarding important public works.
Restrictions on access to railways, fortified works, camps.
Enforcing the provisions of the Wireless Telegraphy Act.
Restrictions on keeping and use of carrier pigeons.
Restrictions on storage of petroleum and celluloid.
Maintaining registers of aliens.
Control of lights.
Restrictions on the sale of intoxicating liquor.
'Watching those suspected of evil intention towards the Realm.'

There were 188 police forces around the country, comprising 58 county and 130 city or borough forces, employing 35,373 officers (for comparison, on 31 March 2015 there were 43 forces with 129,987 officers[14]): 2,624 of these men were army or naval reservists and had been called up, and a further 4,422 had enlisted voluntarily. A police reserve had been formed in 1911, from former police officers or pensioners, and former soldiers, and around 2,000 of these had been given their warrant cards. But this was the hour of the special constable. At the end of 1914 there were around 120,000 men who had volunteered to take over many of the duties of the regular police, with another 30,000 in the London metropolitan area.

The office of special constable was linked closely with the magistracy and the duties of the justices to 'keep His Majesty's peace'. Before the development of the modern police force but even up to the period of the First World War there was a legal duty on all British subjects to assist in the apprehension and arrest of felons and to defend property and person against violence. Unpaid, and often unwilling, men were appointed to the rôle of parish constable but with the formation of the Metropolitan Police in 1829 and the passing of the County Police Act, 1839 these responsibilities were assumed by the professional police force. However it was recognized that there might be occasions of civil unrest or disorder which might overwhelm the uniformed officers and under the Special Constables Act, 1831, any two or more Justices:

… upon sworn evidence that any tumult, riot or felony has taken place, or might be reasonably apprehended, within their jurisdiction, if of the opinion that the ordinary police force is not sufficient for the maintenance of order, may nominate as many as they shall think fit of the householders or other persons, not being legally exempt, residing in the place or neighbourhood to act as special constables for such time as they consider necessary.[15]

Under the great Municipal Corporations Act of 1882, borough justices were permitted to appoint special constables on an annual basis in October each year, who would act under a temporary warrant which would recite that 'in the opinion of the justice the ordinary police force of the borough is insufficient at the date of the warrant to maintain the peace of the borough'. In both forms of appointment the special constable had a time-limited rôle, and once the immediate cause of alarm had passed he stood down and returned to normal civilian life. With war and the threat of invasion, air raids, bombardments and civil strife, neither of the two mechanisms were sufficient, so the Special Constables Act was passed on 28 August 1914, authorizing the appointment of special constables in the absence of tumult, riot or felony. A subsequent circular from the Home Office further stated that the new special constables would be attached to police districts and come under the authority of the local chief of police, rather than to towns or parishes under the control of the magistrates.[16] Originally there were a number of exemptions from service as a special constable (solicitors, for example) but these were waived if the man wished to serve. The Home Secretary specified that holders of a licence under the Licensing (Consolidation) Act were not to be appointed.

  The response to the appeal for volunteers was immediate and there were a number of high-profile appointments. The Right Honourable Laurence Hardy, MP for Ashford, was sworn in as a special constable in Saltwood, Kent,[17] and 'Jack' Gorman, formerly of Wolverhampton Wanderers FC, joined at Halesowen.[18] The clergy were particularly forthcoming – anxious to serve the country but often instructed not to join the colours.[19] Even the thespians of the West End wanted to play their part – Sir Herbert Beerbohm Tree and other leading lights volunteered, with the arrangement that they would start duty at midnight and patrol beats around the theatres.[20]

  On appointment the special constables had to make a declaration before a justice of the peace:

I [name] do solemnly, sincerely and truly declare that I will well and truly serve our Sovereign Lord the King in the office of Special Constable for the parish of Whitstable and the neighbourhood thereof, without favour or affection, malice or ill-will; and that I will to the best of my power cause the peace to be kept and preserved; and prevent all offences against the persons and properties of His Majesty's subjects; and that while I continue to hold the said office I will to the best of my skill and knowledge discharge all the duties thereof faithfully according to the law.[21]

Many of the first appointments were made under the old legislation and legally these special constables had no enduring power, but a further order passed on 28 August 1915 regularized their position.[22]

There was some scepticism about the new recruits. Supplies permitting, they were given a warrant card, an armlet, a whistle and a truncheon, and although put to work very quickly, they were not given as much training in their legal responsibilities as might be expected. In particular their knowledge of their powers of arrest was questioned but, as in so many areas of law at the time, never challenged[23] (there were thirty-three arrestable offences in the Town Police Clauses Act, 1847 alone). Officially the men signed up for eight hours a week, their time to be arranged so as to 'interfere as little as possible with any permanent employment'.[24] At the first drill night of the Chelmsford specials, on Wednesday 23 September at the Friars Council School, one of the local lads threw a stone over the wall striking Councillor Cowell on the side of the head and leaving a 'nasty bruise'.[25] John Gray, a commercial traveller of Malmesbury Road, South Woodford, was given a month's hard labour by the Stratford magistrates for abusing some special constables patrolling Woodford New Road in the early hours of 4 September 1914.[26]

There were some embarrassments. Within hours of being sworn in, Harry White, of Bishop's Stortford, was found drunk and disorderly and appeared before his local bench on 13 August 1914, charged with this and other offences, including using improper language and assault. He was sent to prison for two months.[27] Ralph Uden, of 58 High Street, Whitstable, who was 'deaf and could not have heard a brass band', appeared before Canterbury magistrates for failing to attend for duty between 10 pm and midnight on 1 October 1914. Mr John Riddell, head of the special constabulary, gave evidence that he had delivered the five-week duty roster to Uden and that he had failed to appear without excuse. He explained that the Chief Constable had asked him to report any men who did not do their duty, and there were so many of them that he had supplied him with a list, from which Uden's name was picked at random. As a warning to the others, the bench fined him £2 with 18s 6d costs or a month in default. Uden asked for imprisonment as he had no means to pay, and despite the clerk suggesting a fortnight to pay, he was locked up for a month.

An early task for the new special constables was that of assisting with the registration of aliens, which not only involved an immense amount of paperwork but also personal interviews for those applying for permits to travel or to reside in prohibited areas. Enemy aliens in the detention camps were permitted to apply for release and it was the special constables who made the enquiries in the community on behalf of the Army Council.[28]

In June of 1915 the role of the special constable underwent a further evolution, this time in response to the demands of the secretive county and local War Emergency Committees, which were tasked with the evacuation of the civilian population in the event of invasion. The duties of the special constable were divided into two: Occasional Duties, which meant 'assisting the regular police in the numerous and onerous duties necessitated by war'; and Emergency Duties, in which they supplemented the police force and undertook to carry out the scheme formulated for the 'removal of all inhabitants of the county for their own personal safety and for military purposes, and the collection or destruction of everything that might be of use to a hostile force landing in the County'; in other words they would have the responsibility for the execution of the evacuation plans, as the army and volunteer forces would be fully engaged in military activities.

It would appear that such an essential role failed to impact the routine duties of the specials. In Chelmsford Herbert Gripper, the eldest son of Joseph Gripper the ironmonger, became Special Constable SC413 on 7 September 1914 with a warrant card, armlet and truncheon. He lived at Redcot, 54 New London Road, and was in charge of a section of four men: Mr Freeland, Mr Luckin the accountant, Mr B. Smith and Mr C. Smith. In his logbook he recorded that they had an emergency station at the corner of New London Road and Writtle Road, and they patrolled Writtle Road, Southborough Road, Elm Road, Rothesay Avenue and the top of Wood Street, 'with their dogs if they wished'. They were required to maintain contact with the group patrolling Moulsham Street and the town. One of their routine duties was to ensure that the lighting restrictions were followed. Coastal and estuary towns had lighting controls from very early on in the war, to ensure that no lights were visible from seawards, but inland street and building lighting was permitted as long as it was 'dull and subdued', with covers over the top of street lamps to prevent aircraft from seeing definite road patterns. But in the event of an air raid alert all external lights were to be extinguished and windows were to be covered. Gripper managed to bring a number of offenders to court – in December 1915 he reported Arthur Layton of Danbury, for not having a rear red light on his car (fined 20s).

Most of the work of the special constable was tedious in the extreme. Wykeham Chancellor, son of the architect Frederick Chancellor, was appointed as superintendent of Gripper's company, and his task was to visit the various stations and patrols during the night. One such post was at Chelmsford Railway Station, in the office at the corner of Duke Street and Park Road, from where Viaduct Street was patrolled throughout the war (the army guarded the railway itself). The log book for the period 1 January to 31 March 1917 has survived. The men checked the security of the various sheds, stores and shops under the railway arches from the subway to Mill Road, including Ketley's fruit and vegetable store, where the produce from the Chelmsford and District Branch of the Vegetable Products Committee was stored before the weekly distribution to the navy, the Wells & Perry coal shed off Duke Street, and across the road down to number 45. They dutifully reported missing keys, missing whistles and a bright light shining from the direction of the National Steam Car works. Six men were on duty each night, working two two-hour shifts with a four-hour break in between, when they could sleep. Seventy-seven men are recorded as carrying out guard duty over this period, including Mr Melvin the Town Clerk, Henry Marriage, Leonard Christy, and many other well-known figures in the Chelmsford business community.

The work of the special constable was as onerous as it was tedious: in additional to the 'day job', he had to perform many of the duties of the regular police, such as patrolling roads, keeping observation on suspects for the purpose of preventing and detecting crime and offences against the Defence of the Realm regulations, protecting railway works, public works such as waterworks and gasworks. Many carried out administrative duties as registration clerks and interpreters under the Aliens (Restrictions) Act.

Some magistrates felt that they were not doing enough to support the war effort, and some volunteered as special constables. The *Justice of the Peace* had to warn that, although there was nothing to prevent them from doing so, they would of course be disqualified from adjudicating in any proceedings initiated by them in pursuit of such duties.[29] One clerk was sufficiently concerned about one of his justices, who was a company commander of the special constables, to question whether such a person should adjudicate on any matter prosecuted by the police, but the same journal advised that, in the absence of any statutory disqualification it would be permitted, subject to the facts of any particular case.[30]

By 1916 it was apparent that crime, overall, was decreasing, and the number of prisoners appearing at the Quarter Sessions and Assizes had shown a marked falling off. Various reasons were proposed, including the obvious one that the 'criminal classes' were now serving in the army, but most believed that poverty, the root cause of criminality, was decreasing, with military allowances supporting families at home, and, certainly in urban areas, the opportunities for well-paid work in munitions and industry[31] which resulted in very low levels of unemployment. The rigorous licensing restrictions served to reduce both convictions for drunkenness and also for offences committed under the influence of drink. A centuries-old custom was followed at the Usk Quarter Sessions in May 1915, when the Clerk of the Peace, Mr H.S. Custard, announced that there were no prisoners for trial and the justices and jurors could be dispensed with, and he ceremonially presented the chairman, Sir Henry Mathers Jackson, Bt, with a pair of white gloves. The gloves were tied up in coloured ribbons representing the other countries in the Allies.[32] In December 1915 Mr R. Wallace, KC, in his charge to the Grand Jury at the London Sessions, told them that the list of cases was 'the shortest ever known in the County of London', and he believed was the effect of the drink orders – there was practically no late drinking, and no trouble when people were turned out at closing time.[33]

The preamble to the Criminal Justice Administration Act, 1914 stated that it was an Act 'to diminish the number of persons committed to prison …'. In introducing the Bill for its second reading in April 1914 Mr McKenna, the Home Secretary, had told the House of Commons that in the year ended 31 March 1912 nearly 80,000 people were sent to prison for non-payment of fines, of whom 13,000 paid their fines in part or in full after commitment.[34] Had the option of being given time to pay been available, it would have been likely that many people might avoid prison altogether. The new Act, passed on 10 August in the middle of all the emergency legislation, was not fully implemented until early 1915 and had a striking impact. In addition to the ability to defer payment of fines by at least seven days, the magistrates were also required to enquire into the defendant's means and to adjust the fine accordingly. Another new sentencing option was that of imprisonment of up to five days in police custody. In July 1915 the Home Secretary reported that in the three months to March 1914, 5,878 men had been committed to prison, 2,549 of whom were fine defaulters;[35] he updated the figures later in the year to report that for the year March 1914 to March 1915 53,988 defaulters had been imprisoned, compared to 74,461 in the previous twelve months.[36] It was also acknowledged that the working classes were considerably better off and able to pay any financial penalties.[37]

Prisoners contributed to the national war effort. The Duke of Devonshire reported to the House of Lords that over three million articles of war had been made an issued by October 1915, with work covering more than twenty trades. With most prisoners serving short sentences there was great pressure to provide instruction for them, but the prison commissioners could not speak too highly of the enthusiasm of the prisoners for such work,[38] probably because it relieved them from the tedium of picking oakum.[39]

The Criminal Justice Administration Act, 1914 was believed by many in the judiciary to be responsible for the drop in prisoner numbers (August 1914: 13,580; March 1915 9,188). Prison governors identified three factors:

1. The enlistment of many habitual petty offenders;
2. The restricted hours for the sale of intoxicating liquors;
3. The great demand for labour rendering employment easy and well paid.[40]

The decrease in the prison population, whether due to the decrease in crime or to revised sentencing practices, meant that the prisons could be considered for other uses. On 5 July 1915 the chairman of the Chelmsford Visiting Committee, Colonel G.W. Wood, received a letter from the Home Secretary:

Home Office, 24 June, 1915
Sir, I am directed by the Secretary of State to inform you that at the urgent request of the War Office he has decided to allow His Majesty's Prison, Chelmsford, to be used for the detention of military prisoners; arrangements have been made whereby all prisoners who would in the ordinary course be committed to Chelmsford will, on and after the 1 proxim, be committed to other prisons.[41]

Devizes, Hereford and Lewes prisons were also taken over by the military authorities, along with wings at Stafford, Wandsworth and Wakefield, and a building at Parkhurst, by November 1915. During the following year Brecon, Knutsford, St Albans, and Stafford were closed and lent to the War Office. Reading Prison and the Borstal Institution at Feltham were used for the detention of aliens.[42]

The number of convicted prisoners fell substantially throughout the war:

	1913	1914	1915	1916	1917	1918	1919
Prisoners	139,060	118,829	63,218	45,649	35,097	27,787	31,032

These numbers reflect both the number of men serving overseas in the military, changes in the approaches to sentencing, and the 'time to pay' effect on the imprisonment of fine defaulters. In 1913 75,152 people were sent to prison for this reason; by 1919 only about 8,000.

Statistics were compiled and published annually by the Home Office as Judicial Statistics for England and Wales,[43] providing data about criminal proceedings, police, coroners, prisons, reformatory and industrial schools, and criminal lunatics. Obviously the war years affected the collection and analysis of the returns on which they were based, and in some years the report was not published. The following gives an insight into some of the areas examined in this book:

Statute[44]	1914	1915	1916	1917	1918	1919
Defence of the Realm	83	33,071	121,563	50,506	46,426	13,427
Aliens Restriction	3,226	7,551	14,279	13,606	12,107	4,015
National Registration	NA	50	879	1,192	459	2
'Other' summary offences	6,194	43,646	139,104	67,120	60,434	19,008

Sadly the Defence of the Realm Act offences are not broken down any further and the author of the 1919 tables is himself unsure of their classification. By way of example he notes that all offences relating to lights on vehicles, whether under ordinary law or DoRA, are returned under 'Highway Acts, offences against'. The category 'Other' also appears to include DoRA offences and there appears to be a reasonable correlation between the two lines in the table above. In total there were 251,649 DoRA convictions during the war years, and 316,498 convictions for 'other' offences. A teasing statistic is provided in the 1917 report of the Commissioners of Prisons, who claimed that 'wartime legislation', such as breaches of the Aliens Restriction, DoRA, and National Registration Acts, had added slightly over 2,000 to the prison population, and there had been 3,730 convictions and sentences of imprisonment under court-martials held under the Military Service Act.

	1913	1914	1915	1916	1917	1918	1919
Military and naval	719	1,095	2,299	11,268	6,667	5,812	1,176

Military offences were similarly consolidated and include the absentees and deserters as well as the Military Service Act. The reduction in offences in 1917 and 1918 is likely due to the result of the change to the Army Act which allowed absentees to surrender themselves to the police and avoid an appearance in court.

Youth crime showed a reassuring and early return to normal conditions by 1919:

	1913	1914	1915	1916	1917	1918	1919
Total	37,520	36,929	43,981	47,342	51,323	49,015	40,473

The commonest offences were larceny (theft) and malicious damage.

The rôle of the grand jury was increasingly called into question during the war; even though the property qualification had been abolished it became increasingly difficult to summon sufficient men in the numbers required to form the grand and petty juries, and it was especially irksome when, due to insufficient work, the juries were discharged. These men were often engaged in 'work of national importance' and could ill-afford such calls on their time, and so their quiet but well-placed complaints eventually resulted in the Grand Juries (Suspension) Act, 1917, which came into effect in April of that year. Although the magistrates' courts still reviewed and rehearsed all the evidence before sending the bill to the quarter sessions, the indictment was now presented directly to the appropriate court 'in like manner as if a true bill had been found'.

The Indictments Act, 1915 had changed the way in which legal language was to be replaced by plain English. Descriptions of the offences were to be set out in separate paragraphs to be known as 'counts', the statement of the offence was to be in 'ordinary language', as were the particulars of the allegation. Ordinary language was defined as the popular language, 'so that it can be understood by prisoners, many of whom are of a very limited education'. Another useful piece of legislation was the Evidence (Amendment) Act, 1915, which recognized that under existing law it was permissible for the statements or depositions given to the magistrates to be read at sessions or assizes if they were too ill to attend, or had died in the meantime. The new law allowed the same provision for soldiers and sailors who were absent on active service, so that their evidence could be used in the same way.

And finally then, what of the magistrates themselves?

Alderman Ernest Martineau JP was Lord Mayor of Birmingham in 1914 and was also, since 1909, lieutenant colonel and commanding officer of 1/6 (Birmingham) Battalion, Royal Warwickshire Regiment (Territorial Force). At the start of August he was at Foryd Ferry Camp in Rhyl for the summer exercises and found himself the first magistrate to be called up for active service.[45] His unit was sent to billets in Kelvedon and Billericay in Essex.[46] He returned to Birmingham to pay his 1s fine to resign from the City Council on 8 September and his appearance at the meeting was greeted with 'hearty cheers'.[47] He gave an account of the spirits and health of this men and of the arduous route marches they had undertaken. In October the *Birmingham Daily Gazette* published his request for 1,000 woollen mittens of a 'drab or brown colour, not too dark or light'.[48] Following training the 31 officers and 997 men of the battalion were sent to France on 22 March 1915 as part of the South Midland Division.[49] A week later they were digging trenches near Bailleul and Neuve Eglise, and on 12 April they moved into the front line, taking over Petit Pont (Point 63) on the Messines-Armentieres road. On 17 April Private Edward Crofts of 59 Franklin Road, Bourneville, became their first casualty, killed in the Douve trench.

On 11 May Martineau returned home, after seven weeks in the trenches, suffering from influenza and a heavy chest cold. In an interview with the *Birmingham Mail* he reported on life in France:

We occupy long lines of trenches in an important position on the front, which vary in distance from 140 yards to 500 yards from the trenches of the Germans ... A large proportion of days are spent in the trenches by the Birmingham troops. It is practically day and night duty, though by a rota system the men are, in turn, able to get a fair amount of sleep. For several days together, however, they do not get out of their clothes ... The dug-outs are in appearance more like rabbit hutches than anything else. The soil was rather stiff in character, but latterly the trenches had been fairly dry and reasonably comfortable ... It is really surprising how quickly the mind adapts itself to spirit of the battlefield. The rifle fire and shelling by the enemy become commonplace, a sort of daily routine. One soon settles down to things, and then one goes about one's business in just the same spirit as one would walk down New Street to the office in the morning.

He added that they seldom saw the enemy, but there was intermittent rifle fire and a constant danger from snipers. The Birmingham Territorials had not taken part in any of the major battles in the area, but had heard the heavy bombardment preceding the capture of Hill 60, near Ypres. His billet had once been bombed, and the officers' quarters had been shelled, and on one occasion they had taken bets on the effectiveness of the German shelling on the farm from which they obtained their water, but it remained unscathed. He also described the skylarks and nightingales singing during bombardments, and of the croaking of the frogs.[50]

By now aged 54 his health had been impaired by life at the front and he did not return to France. He was seconded as commanding officer to the 83 Provisional Battalion[51] (subsequently renamed the 10 Oxfordshire and Buckinghamshire Light Infantry), in Ipswich. Martineau was mentioned in dispatches for his services, recommended by Sir John French for gallant and distinguished conduct in the field, and in January 1916 was appointed a Companion of the Order of St Michael and St George.[52] He subsequently resigned his commission and returned to his solicitor's practice in November 1916[53] and to civic life. He was appointed an honorary colonel of the Warwickshires the following year[54] and also received a Secretary of State's mention in the London Gazette for valuable services rendered in connection with the war.[55] He lived with his wife, Margaret, at 43 Augustus Road, Edgbaston, and represented St Martin's ward.[56] His grandfather and father had both been mayors of Birmingham, as were his son, Wilfrid, and grandson Denis. He died on 25 November 1951.

Captain Eugene Napoleon Ernest Mallett Vaughan, of Lapley Park, was a justice of the peace for the county of Stafford and, as a member of the Reserve of Officers, was called up to serve in the 1 Battalion of the Grenadier Guards. On 9 September 1916 his unit was in reserve at Ginchy, on the Somme. After heavy fighting during the day it was discovered that a gap had opened up in the front line between 4 Grenadier Guards and the 1 Welsh Guards, so Vaughan's No. 3 Company was sent up to report to Lieutenant Colonel Murray-Threipland of the Welsh Guards. At 3 am the following morning the Germans launched a counter-attack and Vaughan was sent to the right to support and relieve the battered Royal Munster Fusiliers. Having repulsed the attack Vaughan and his men spent the day improving the defences of the trench, placing machine guns at each end of his sector. At 10 pm that evening the Germans attacked again and in such strength that the Welsh Guards were forced to pull back, leaving No 3 Company surrounded. Vaughan maintained a vigorous defence, bayoneting one party of Germans who entered his trench and leading Sergeant Williams and his bombing section to hold up the enemy's attack on the left. By the time the Welsh Guards fought back and relieved them Vaughan's two fellow officers had been wounded and fifty-six of his men were killed. The *London Gazette* of 20 October 1916 announced that the King had been graciously pleased to appoint Vaughan a companion of the Distinguished Service Order for his conspicuous gallantry in this action, commenting that 'when in command of an isolated trench and attacked on front, flank and rear, he drove off the enemy, killing over 100 of them and taking 20 prisoners' continuing that 'his fine example has given great confidence to his men'.[57] Vaughan survived the war and returned, as Major Vaughan

DSO, to Stafford. He entered local politics and served for many years on Cannock Rural Council, as member for the Bishops Wood district.[58] He died in 1934.

Most magistrates were too old for active service, but many, particularly from the counties, had previous military service or were involved in the county Territorial Associations and were eager to return to the regular army (where they were affectionately known as 'dug-outs'). Lieutenant Colonel Egerton Stanley Pipe-Wolferstan, the very first magistrate mentioned in this book, was typical of this breed. Born into one of the oldest families in Staffordshire at the family estate at Statfold Hall, near Tamworth, on 23 July 1861, he had joined the South Staffordshire Regiment in 1881 as second lieutenant, and served in the Egyptian Expedition of 1882, where he took part in the Sudan campaigns of 1885–6 as part of the Frontier Field Force and earned himself the Queen's medal and the Khedive's Bronze Star. He was promoted to become adjutant of the 4 (Militia) Battalion of the North Staffordshires and was posted with the regiment to the war in South Africa, where he was mentioned in despatches twice and further decorated. He retired on his return to this country but was gazetted as honorary lieutenant colonel of his old battalion in August 1908. In December 1914 he was appointed as commanding officer of the 10 Battalion of the Prince of Wales' North Staffordshire Regiment. After a period in Okehampton the unit became a reserve battalion and moved to Rugely Camp, Cannock Chase, and Wolferstan returned to civilian life and the bench in November 1917.[59]

Several of the magistrates gave their lives. Captain Arthur Corbett Edwards was appointed to the commission of the peace for Folkestone in March 1915. Well known as the captain of the Folkestone Cricket Club, he had served in the Army in Malta during the South African War. At the time of his appointment he had joined the 8 (Service) Battalion of the Queen's Own Royal West Kent Regiment and on 30 August 1915 they left Southampton for France. Twenty-six days later a terse entry in the regimental war diary records their fate:

26 [September] Attack Hulluch, loose [sic] ¾ of Battalion

This was the second day of the Battle of Loos, and the West Kents lost over 550 men and all but one of their officers. Edwards has no known grave and is commemorated on the Loos Memorial.

Captain Henry Joseph de Trafford, barrister, attached to 1 Battalion, South Staffordshire Regiment, sat on the Tamworth bench, and was killed in action the day before Edwards, on 25 September 1915, at Loos. With the objective being the village of Cite St Eloi, the order to advance was given at 6.25 am, and the battalion left the trenches in extended formation, with about three paces between each man. They had to cross a fire zone of some 500 yards, with heavy artillery, machine gun, and rifle fire, and deep barbed wire entanglements. Against these incredible odds they managed to storm the enemy positions and reach the second support line, but by this time this had suffered terrible losses. The 1 South Staffs lost 430 men out of the 729 who went into action, and 18 officers out of 21.[60] De Trafford is also commemorated on the Loos Memorial.

Captain Rudolf Valintine had also served in South Africa, with the Warwickshire Yeomanry. He had returned to take up farming at Heath End, Snitterfield in Warwickshire. He was known as an agriculturalist, a sportsman and a church warden, and was appointed to the Stratford-on-Avon bench. At the outbreak of war he rejoined his unit and was commissioned as quartermaster of 1 Squadron, 1/1 Warwickshire Yeomanry, before they were sent out to Egypt in April 1915. This was followed by a move to Gallipoli, arriving at Suvla Bay in August. In February 1917 the unit was sent to Palestine as part of the Australian Mounted Division. Valintine was wounded at Katia, but recovered to take part in one of the last great cavalry charges in British military history, at Gaza. Here he was wounded again, and died of his wounds on 12 November 1917. He is buried at the Beersheba War Cemetery. He had been mentioned in dispatches on 6 July, and was awarded a posthumous Military Cross in February 1918.

Captain the Hon. William Amherst Cecil, 2nd Battalion Grenadier Guards, was a justice of the peace for Lincolnshire, the liberty of Peterborough and Northampton. He was sent to France as part of the British Expeditionary Force in August 1914, and took part in the strenuous marching as the British and French armies attempted to stem the German advance. In mid-September his unit crossed the river Aisne at Pont Arcy and attacked. On 16 September their positions were heavily shelled by enemy high explosives, and Cecil, along with twenty-seven men, was killed. His efforts did not go unnoticed: he received one of the very first Military Crosses ever awarded, announced in the *London Gazette* on 1 January 1915. In a poignant story, one of Cecil's men, Private W. Scott, was wounded in the same barrage and was evacuated back to Cardiff hospital. He brought with him Cecil's sword, a family heirloom bearing inscriptions of campaigns as far back as Waterloo, and returned it to the family. Cecil is buried at the Soupir Communal Cemetery.

Reginald Fox of Grimstone, Horrabridge, was a banker and a Devon county magistrate and he chaired the Tavistock bench. Aged 47 and on the Army retired list at the outbreak of war he immediately volunteered and was commissioned as a major (subsequently lieutenant colonel) of the 6 Battalion, Devonshire Regiment, and was sent out to India, where he landed on 11 November 1914. The regiment spent the whole of 1915 in Lahore, before being sent to Mesopotamia on 5 January 1916. The 6th (Poona) Division of the British Army had been surrounded by Turkish forces at the town of Kut, on a bend of the river Tigris. Under Lieutenant General Aylmer a relief force was sent to break the siege but the attempt foundered. Several inconclusive battles followed, at one of which, the Battle of Dujaila on 8 March 1916, Fox lost his life. His name appears on the Basra Memorial.

Magistrates also served and survived. Mr Sam Slater, of Woolhanger Manor, Parracombe, was Master of the Exmoor Foxhounds and president of the Lynton Conservative Club, as well as being a member of Lynton Urban Council. He was appointed to the bench in April 1915 and sworn in on 1 June. He joined the 2/1 North Devon Hussars which ended up in Ireland. In July 1916 Colonel T.W. Fraser, Royal Army Medical Corps, was appointed to the Berwick bench. He was in charge of the Voluntary Aid Detachment in the area.

The working classes were also represented. John Charles Lane, whose photograph appears on the cover of this book, lived at 19 Stephen Street, Taunton and worked as a postman. Keenly interested in politics, he was elected as a Labour councillor for East Ward in 1911. Aged 38 at the outbreak of war he had volunteered for military service but due to a recent operation for appendicitis was not passed fit. He tried again under the Group Scheme but it was found that he needed another operation. Finally successful in 1917, he joined the Royal Engineers (Wessex Section) and was posted to Winchester. Somehow Lane came to the attention of the Lord Chancellor and had the unusual distinction of being appointed as a justice of the peace while serving, in February 1918. As Lance Corporal Lane he returned to Taunton on 17 July 1918 to take his oath and take his place on the bench. The chairman, Mr Sibley, congratulated him on his appointment and as a representative of labour, for he thought that all sections of the community should be on the bench. In return he declared that he would 'do his duty as a magistrate fairly and impartially, giving favour to no-one, acting in every way to the best of his ability'.[61] And Lane duly returned to his military duties. He served the community for many years after the war and was elected Mayor of Taunton in 1925. He chaired the housing committee to great success – the Lane Estate in the town is named after him. He died in December 1955.

Some magistrates were called, but found alternative work. Mr Frank Bibby, of Plas-yn-Foel, Cwm, was a magistrate and chairman of St Asaph Rural District Council. He appeared before the local military tribunal in December 1916 to advise them that the previous conditional exemption he had been granted had allowed him to obtain work of national importance, and that he was now employed at a munition works.[62]

Some magistrates did not have a good war. Thomas Stubbins was variously a joiner and wheelwright and a rent and rate collector. He was elected as a Labour councillor to Winterton Urban Council, and subsequently became chairman. At some stage he was appointed as a justice of the peace on the Scunthorpe bench. He was also chairman of the local military tribunal, and he had applied for, and received, an absolute exemption, on the grounds that he was performing work of national importance. In May 1916 he was summoned before his own bench by the military representative, Captain Colquhoun, as an absentee under the Military Service Act. The military representative told the magistrates that he did not recognize the validity of the exemption, but the bench did not accept his argument and dismissed the case. As Stubbins was a healthy single man, aged 37, Colquhoun lodged an appeal. In July 1916 the Appeal Tribunal for the Grimsby section of Lincolnshire reviewed his case, and learned that at the original hearing in February one of his colleagues was in the chair, and although Stubbins claimed not to have influenced the decision, he had been standing alongside, and his case was not actually discussed at all. Unfortunately the appeal had not followed the strict letter of the law and despite a verbal notification at the time the paperwork had not followed. After legal argument the appeal was allowed and the exemption withdrawn, but Stubbins was not satisfied and took the case to the Court of Appeal, which in October 1916 confirmed the dismissal of the exemption. In June 1917 Stubbins appeared at the Grimsby Bankruptcy Court. Without the exemption card he had been unable to obtain employment, and his journey through the appeal courts had resulted in costs of £102 13s 6d.[63] John Jarvis JP, a 'prominent public man', appeared before the Stirling bench on a charge of failing to report for military service when called upon to do so. He received the standard 40s fine and suffered the indignity of being handed over to the military escort.[64]

The wartime laws and regulations affected everybody and magistrates received no special treatment. Although their appearances on the other side of the bench were newsworthy, the press seemed to recognize that, if anything, they would get harsher treatment and there were few instances of adverse comment. The lighting regulations were rigorously applied: Frederick Wheeler was an auctioneer, with a large house in Friars Street in Sudbury. Special Constable Alston was on patrol on the night of 8 April 1916 and saw a light coming from an unshaded hanging gas bracket. Miss Wheeler, his daughter, extinguished the light immediately, but Wheeler was a magistrate and his colleagues fined him 30s.[65] William Stockton JP, described as a senior magistrate and 'father' of the district council, was fined 10s by his fellow justices at Ellesmere Port for failing to obscure the lights in one of his shops.[66] George Letten's maid switched on the hall light to carry tea into the dining room. As a county and borough magistrate the Grimsby magistrates fined him an exemplary 21s. And on a late autumn evening Councillor James Heaton, chairman of the education authority in St Helen's, attended a meeting at the town hall. He switched on the lights in the Mayor's Parlour, not realizing that the same switch illuminated all the lights in the hall outside which were unscreened. He attended the magistrates' court on 24 November 1916, and was fined 2s 6d. Having dealt with his conviction, the chairman then welcomed Heaton to the bench, to which he was that day appointed![67]

Towards the end of the war the offence of food hoarding was seen as a particularly serious breach of the regulations and offenders were treated unsympathetically. Thomas Barton, a magistrate of some twenty-three years' standing, was lucky that Lord Rhondda's amnesty was announced the day before his appearance at Southport – he gave his 240lbs store of flour to the local food control committee and his fellow magistrates ordered him to pay the prosecution costs only.[68] Slough magistrate Dr Robert Charsley was fined £5 for a hoard of 80lbs of flour, 60lbs of jam, 10lbs each of tea, cocoa and coffee, and 28lbs of margarine. The manager of Shepherd's Dairies was fined £5 for supplying the margarine, and Mr G.H. Charsley, the defendant's cousin, resigned from his post as executive officer to the Slough Food Control Committee, finding himself in a 'painful position' in regard to the case.[69]

County magistrates were often men of substance, as farmers and landowners. Frank Chatterton JP of Somerby Hall, a well-known agriculturalist and military representative on the Brigg tribunal, had a very wet twenty-acre field, and in May 1917 he applied to the Lindsay War Agricultural Committee for a permit to grow mustard, having already sowed the land. The committee recognized that the land had produced three straw crops in succession and that the mustard would be a valuable fertilizer so they granted a notice, but only to grow the crop to be ploughed in as green manure or to be grazed by sheep in preparation for its use to grow wheat. The land was heavy and wet and Chatterton let the mustard grow over without harvesting it, and failed to prepare the ground for the next season's wheat crop. In November 1917 the Brigg Police Court fined him £100 with £25 costs for failing to comply with the original notice.[70]

Colonel Thomas Sunderland JP owned a farm at Ravensden Grange near Bedford. In addition to arable farming, he kept 100 pigs, 1,000 pigeons, and 300 fowls, and he fed them the grain he produced from his own land. The Wheat and Rice Restriction Order had been issued from the Food Controller's office on 11 January 1917, whereby corn fit for human consumption was not permitted as animal feed. Police sergeant Palmer and PC Cable had visited the farm several times and had seen men feeding the birds and pigs with grain – one employee admitted that at least a bushel of corn was used every day. There was an exemption for 'tail' corn, which were poor-quality seeds, but the maize and corn seen were above this standard. Although he pleaded guilty, the colonel was upset about this matter, following, as it apparently did, some trouble over 'that dog that I shot'. He claimed not to know of the order to begin with, but had changed the feed once he had been informed. His 'brother magistrates' fined him £100. 'I never heard such a thing in my life!'[71]

Henry Lannoy Cancellor, the London magistrate, wrote a memoir of his time at the Thames police court, which covered the period of the First World War (*The Life of a London Beak*). Many East European and Russian Jews lived in the area, and he was highly critical of the way in which they appeared to prosper at the expense of local businesses whose owners and employees had gone away to the war; and he was also concerned that the younger male members of these families were so unwilling to fight for their adopted country. He seemed particularly pleased when the Military Service (Conventions with Allied States) Act came in to force in July 1917, in which the Russians of military age were given the choice of returning by sea to Russia or become liable for service in the British Army. The date fixed was 7 August, and they were ordered to present themselves at Euston Station for take the boat-train to Liverpool. Many failed to attend and the military authorities and the police launched a major crackdown. Cancellor's court was kept busy for several weeks – 'special vans were daily in the yard of the police station, and went away fully loaded with aliens who had tried to avoid military service either in the Russian or the British Army'.[70]

Cancellor also recalled a daylight air raid in 1918:

Work in court had to cease for an hour. The noise of the bombs and anti-aircraft guns was deafening, business under such conditions was impossible, and police officers had pressing calls to duty in the streets. I went into the chief clerk's office and saw a pitiable sight. Poor women were rushing in frantic haste to collect small children, whose playground was the open space of Arbour Square [Thames Police Court was then on East Arbour Street]. A bomb fell on to a school, within a short distance of the court. Several infants were killed and more were injured by the explosion.

Another air raid followed while working at Old Street police court, in which he and colleagues took shelter in the basement.

Henry Turner Waddy wrote a post-war account of the London police courts (*The Police Court and its Work*) in which he criticized the 'deplorable lowering' of standards of behaviour, particularly amongst the youth, pointing out that in 1913 there were 37,520 children brought before the youth courts; in 1917 there were 51,323. He also believed that men who had witnessed the suffering of war had become desensitized to violence, which they unleashed on family and friends – and strangers – on returning to civilian life. Waddy sat at Westminster police court and, as with so many of his colleagues, was drawn from a certain class and background that perhaps made him believe that what he saw in court was truly representative of the working classes, an attitude that he presents throughout his book. He was particularly critical of the young people before him, with 'young street hooligans aged sixteen' earning twenty to thirty shillings a week, to spend on the 'pictures' and cigarettes; and girls of fourteen giving evidence in cases of indecent assault without embarrassment, familiar with the 'technical language of vice'. Waddy was also resentful of the continuance of wartime legislation beyond the end of hostilities, asking why there should still be a restriction on the hours during which chocolate could be sold in a theatre, or why the opening hours of public houses for the sale of intoxicants could not be restored? (What would he have made of the latter restrictions actually lasting until 2003?).

The bells rang out at 11 am on Monday, 11 November 1918. Cancellor, at work at Thames police court, heard the peal from the local church, which went on so long it disrupted a trial he was attempting to hear. After an hour he despatched a police officer to silence the bells. The policeman returned 'with a broad grin on his face'. The bellringer had locked himself in by mistake, and for the past half-hour had been ringing for attention, hoping that someone would rescue him.

Chapter 13

Lessons Learned

Gossip for the After Dinner Hour – the Female JP: the criminal classes, I'm told, are a good deal perturbed over the rumours that feminine police magistrates may be appointed in the near future. You see, they know what a woman's tongue is like, and they're mortally afraid of long sentences.[1]

A cheap gibe in the *Sunday Mirror* in October 1916, but attitudes to women were changing. There were no female Members of Parliament. Women were not permitted to sit on juries. Women were debarred from practicing as solicitors or barristers. Margaret Dawson and Nina Boyle had founded the Women Police Service in 1914, and although uniformed and acknowledged by the Metropolitan Police they had no formal powers and primarily pursued a policy of rescue work amongst prostitutes, and first aid. The idea of female magistrates had been considered for several years: the new juvenile courts and the recognition of the special needs of the young offender had brought an increasing realization that women might be well suited to participate in the judicial system.[2] South Australia had led the way by appointing Mrs T. Price, widow of the first Labour Premier of the state, to the bench in 1915, along with Mrs E.W. Nicholls, Mrs E. Cullen, and Miss C.E. Dixon. Mrs Arthur Murphy was appointed Police Magistrate for the City of Edmonton in Canada the following year. There was much grassroots support for the idea of women magistrates, with organizations such as the Women's Local Government Society, the Manchester and Salford Women's Citizen Association, and others promoting the involvement of women in public and civic life.[3] In March 1918 the National Union of Women's Suffrage Societies passed a resolution calling for the appointment of women magistrates.[4] The Labour Party in Bradford was invited to submit names for consideration for appointment as justices of the peace and submitted the name of a 'well-known local lady' as late as August 1918, but they were informed by the Lord Chancellor that such an appointment would be illegal.[5]

The Representation of the People Act (6 February 1918) and the Parliament (Qualification of Women) Act (21 November 1918) demonstrated clear political acceptance of the new status of women. In April 1919 Mr Bonar Law was asked if the government had yet considered the appointment of women magistrates, and replied that he could not say when, 'but I suppose it will have to be considered some day. (Laughter)'.[6] Lord Beauchamp subsequently introduced a Bill in the House of Lords, its one clause providing that 'A woman shall not be disqualified by sex or marriage from being appointed or being or becoming by virtue of office, a justice of the peace'.[7] The reaction of the Lord Chancellor was 'astonishingly friendly and sympathetic', suggesting that the government could not but assent to the proposal.[8] The Justices of the Peace (Qualification of Women) Bill passed through the Lords on 25 June 1919, receiving an amendment to raise the minimum age on appointment to 30 (in alignment with the women's voting age), Lord Strachie thinking it undesirable that women of 25 or thereabouts should be sitting with men magistrates for certain cases.[9] Following a reasonably straightforward reception in the Commons, the Sex Disqualification (Removal) Act, as it was renamed, received Royal Assent on 23 December 1919. The Lord Chancellor formed a central advisory committee of women to advise on the appointment of female magistrates. The committee members were the Marchioness of Crewe, the Marchioness of Londonderry, Mrs Lloyd George, Miss Elizabeth Haldane, Miss Gertrude Tuckwell, Mrs Humphrey Ward, and Mrs Sidney Webb. They were immediately placed upon the Commission of the Peace: the first women magistrates.[10] Mrs Ada Jane Summers was elected Mayor of Stalybridge in November 1919; she qualified as a justice of the peace by virtue of her office, and by taking her oath in the borough police court on 31 December she became the first ever woman on the bench.[11]

In February 1917 the *Justice of the Peace* ventured some thoughts about crime after the war. An increase was feared, as millions of men in military and naval service returned to an uncertain future in civilian life. Marital infidelity, real or imagined, the abrupt end of 'war bonuses' and the high levels of income enjoyed by so many, the consequent fall in the standard of living,[12] mass unemployment: a dangerous mix of social and economic factors that could lead to crime and civil unrest. The trigger would be the end of the war. The armistice of 11 November brought the conflict to a close, but it had no real legal status.

In July 1918 a committee had reported to back to the Attorney-General on the legal interpretation of the term 'the period of the war'. Most, if not all, of the emergency legislation enacted since August 1914 had some indication of how long the law would be in effect: 'until the termination of the present war'; 'for the present war'; 'during the continuance of the present state of war in Europe', and for the government and others it was essential to have a legal definition, not least because such laws would be dead. It was also significant for men serving in the forces, in particular those who had joined voluntarily, as it would affect their service and discharge. The government held thousands of contracts for munitions and other works, as well as land and property, all of which needed to be wound up. In the words of the committee, 'The operation of the emergency statutes and orders is so far-reaching, the powers given are so vast, the responsibility of exercising them so serious, that it would be a calamity if there were any real doubt as to when the respective rights and duties come to an end'.[13]

The 'interminable emergency regulations and orders made about almost every subject of national activity', particularly those of the Defence of the Realm Act, were in effect 'during the continuance of the present war', existing only during the existence of the emergency, and such power would be lost on the day of the termination of the war. It was realized that there were separate declarations of war on the different countries comprising the Central Powers, and peace treaties might be made with any or all of them. But would such peace treaties be preceded by armistice, cessation of hostilities, agreement of terms, or any form of agreement? The committee decided that 'the war cannot be said to end until peace is finally and irrevocably obtained, and that point of time cannot be earlier than the date when the treaty of peace is finally binding on the respective belligerent parties, and that is the date when ratifications are exchanged'.[14]

On 21 November 1918 the Termination of the Present War (Definition) Act was passed. Given that so many laws and regulations had been passed for the 'duration of the war' or until so long after the 'termination of the war', and that hostilities had now apparently ceased, it was determined that the date declared should be as nearly as possible the date of exchange of the treaty of peace.

The demise of the Defence of the Realm Act was awaited by the whole country. On 13 November 1918 the Chancellor of the Exchequer, Mr Bonar Law, announced to the House of Commons that a committee had been formed to consider the abandonment of the Act and similar war legislation. On 25 November an Order in Council repealed a number of DoRA regulations, including the prohibition on sketching and photography of the coast (subject to the Official Secrets Act, 1911), regulation 11 lighting orders, the regulation 12 naval and military authority lighting orders, and the wretched regulation 40D. Orders relating to the supply of commodities such as coal, food, and army clothing were to be withdrawn as soon as supplies could be guaranteed. Perhaps most importantly, with a general election looming on 14 December, press censorship was relaxed. Lloyd George's coalition government was returned in a landslide, and immediate legislative concerns focussed on the return of the country to a state of peace.

The War Emergency Laws (Continuance) Bill was brought before the Commons in August 1919 and provided for the continuance in force for a limited period (generally twelve months) after the termination of the war certain emergency acts and DoRA regulations. It proposed that prosecutions could only be made with consent of Attorney-General (as with the Official Secrets Act, 1911), although summary offences could be prosecuted by a police officer or person acting under authority of the government department concerned. The Bill met with a hostile reception and the Act was not passed until 31 March 1920. The new law appeared to suggest that DoRA would cease to be operative on the last day of August 1920, but the government subsequently asserted that it would remain in force until the 'termination of war' had been officially decided by Order in Council.[15] Peace with Germany was officially declared on 20 January 1920, followed by Austria on 16 July 1920. Except for Turkey the First World War officially and legally ended at midnight on 31 August 1921.

The licensing restrictions lasted until September 1921, with the passing of the Licensing Act, 1921. London opening hours were set as 5.30 pm to 11 pm and in the provinces 5.30 pm to 10 pm. The lunchtime hours were 11.30 to 3.00 pm, where they stayed until 2003. Full-strength spirits (35° under proof) were permitted, and the Central Control Board (Liquor Control) was abolished. The Courts (Emergency Powers) Act, 1914 continued, along with the Special Constables Act, 1914, and the Rent Restriction Act was still in force in 1923. The Summer Time Act was re-enacted each year under the annual Expiring Laws Continuance Act.

Politicians and lawyers (and indeed the country as a whole), recognized that the Defence of the Realm Act and its regulations, and its administration, were a legislative and executive disaster. But there had been nothing before, and the circumstances were such that immediate and assertive action was required, 'for the public safety and the defence of the Realm'. No one knew what these terms really meant. But normal procedures and processes for the proper delegation and review of legislation had been overlooked at best, ignored at worst, and the undertaking in section 1 of DoRA was, by 1918, an empty assurance: 'The ordinary avocations of life and the enjoyment of property will be interfered with as little as may be permitted by the exigencies of the measures required.' The competent naval and military authorities had been given sweeping powers over the civil community in Great Britain that they had never before possessed. For a brief period between December 1914 and March 1915, after the introduction of the Defence of the Realm (Consolidated) Act and its regulations, there had been, arguably, martial law – civilians were brought before courts-martial for non-hostile acts and offences. There was no right to appeal and no means of bringing such matters before the higher courts.

Alien enemies and friends were registered and monitored under the Aliens (Restriction) Act, 1914. In the former case the adult males of military age were considered *de facto* prisoners of war and were denied *habeas corpus*, imprisoned for the duration in detention camps, regardless of means, status or family circumstances. The responsibility for aliens sat uneasily with the War Office and the Home Office, with overlapping and conflicting interests in military intelligence and home security. And then British subjects themselves were gradually brought into a grand scheme of official registration, ostensibly for the identification of skills and attributes of use to the nation, but very shortly for the purposes of compulsory national service. Those who objected to participating in either of these schemes found themselves ridiculed and ostracised and, again, with no form of judicial protection, and decisions about military service lay with tribunals, not the courts.

Even for that vast majority of people who voluntarily or ambivalently participated in the war effort, through military service or by working in munitions or other work of national importance, life became increasingly onerous. The lighting regulations under section 11 of DoRA were implemented in a haphazard and piecemeal way by the competent naval and military authorities until finally the Home Secretary took over the responsibility. Even then, it took more than two years to recognize that such orders should be on a national basis, and in the meantime tens of thousands of people found themselves in the courts for minor lighting offences.

Licensing control began in the same way, with conflicting responsibilities of magistrates and the military resulting in a patchwork of orders. The Intoxicating Liquor (Temporary Restrictions) Act, 1914 and a separate Defence of the Realm (Amendment) (No. 3) Act, 1915 for liquor control provided a firm legislative base for the subsequent orders and regulations. For a society which consumed so much alcohol the wisdom and common sense of the Central Control Board turned what could have been an extremely difficult problem into a positive, shared approach in which the watchword was 'efficiency', resonating with civilians and soldiers alike. Although orders were breached, the overall outcome was a big decrease in convictions for drunkenness and for offences in which alcohol was a contributing factor.

Parliament had devolved its primary legislative functions. The naval and military authorities, putting competency to one side, were given powers over the civilian population, with no responsibility. The Home Secretary issued lighting orders. The Central Control Board managed licensing. But the Food Controller demonstrated the incompetence of the executive. Order after badly-written order flowed from this department without challenge or scrutiny. Without the vision, intelligence or sensitivity of the Central Control Board, the local authorities were stretched to provide the resources needed to adequately monitor or police these orders, and the courts had to deal with weak prosecutions in which the exact nature of the offence was not always clear.

The parliamentary and constitutional lawyers learned their lesson. On 29 October 1920, the Emergency Powers Act was passed. It was short and succinct.

1. (1) If at any time it appears to His Majesty that any action has been taken or is immediately threatened by any persons or body of persons of such a nature and on so extensive a scale as to be calculated, by interfering with the supply and distribution of food, water, fuel, or light, or with the means of locomotion, to deprive the community, or any substantial portion of the community, of the essentials of life, His Majesty may, by proclamation, declare that a state of emergency exists.

   No such proclamation shall be in force for more than one month, without prejudice to the issue of another proclamation at or before the end of that period.

Section 2 provided that His Majesty, by Order in Council, could issue regulations for securing the essentials of life to the community, which may confer or impose on any Secretary of State, government department or others, such powers and duties as they may require. There were two important provisos: that nothing should be construed as authorizing regulations for compulsory military service or industrial conscription; nor to make it an offence to take part in a strike. And, crucially, section 2(2) provided that any regulations so made shall be laid before Parliament as soon as they are made and shall not continue in force after seven days unless both Houses consent to them.

Section 2(3) provided for the trial of persons guilty of offences against such regulations by *courts of summary jurisdiction*, with the maximum penalty being three months' imprisonment with or without hard labour, or a fine of £100. This sentencing threshold avoided the election of trial by jury, and there is no mention whatever of military jurisdiction.

The Siege of Sidney Street in 1911 (see Chapter 6) had highlighted the inability of the police force to maintain public order without military assistance. The last use of the Riot Act was in Scotland Road, Liverpool, on 2 August 1919, in response to serious looting and rioting during widespread industrial action and which included a strike by the police.[16] The General Strike of May 1926 drew on the resources provided by the Emergency Powers Act, 1920 to enable the government to use military forces to support the police in maintaining public order, rather than taking control, and from this point the police assumed the now familiar command and control rôle in civil protection during times of emergency.

The interwar legislation reflected a new understanding of the state control of what we would now describe as national security, and its success or otherwise would not be known until circumstances changed. Britain declared war on Germany again on 3 September 1939. The effect of the 1920 Act was that the King in Council was able to introduce the Emergency Powers (Defence) Act, which was passed 'almost unnoticed'[17] on 5 September. This resulted in a large batch of 105 regulations, divided into five sections:

Part I: Provisions for the Security of the State
Part II: Public Safety and Order
Part III: Ships and Aircraft
Part IV: Essential Supplies and Work
Part V: General and Supplementary Provisions[18]

The preamble to the Act explicitly confirmed the intention: public safety, the defence of the realm, and the maintenance of public order and the efficient prosecution of the war. From the outset the powers of those involved in making regulations was clearly delimited, and the rôle of the civil courts was not challenged. These regulations and orders were not restricted to place: the Lighting (Restriction) Order was applied nationally. And, from the outset, the possibility of enemy invasion was recognized. The Defence (War Zone Courts) Regulations and the Defence (Administration of Justice) Regulations allowed for significant flexibility in the administration of justice 'in any places in England in which by reason of recent or immediately apprehended enemy action the military situation is such that criminal justice cannot be administered by the ordinary courts with sufficient expedition'. Special courts were to be formed of a president, who was a judge appointed by the Lord Chancellor, and two advisory members, who were to be justices of the peace. This mixture permitted the court to deal with both summary and indictable matters. Powers were also given for cases to be heard at any court, regardless of where the offence had been committed. All cases dealt with were to be reviewed by a 'reviewing authority' set up by the Secretary of State.

As would be expected there was also a large amount of general emergency legislation passed in the first few months of the new conflict, and much of it is recognizable: Lighting (Restrictions) Order, Military Training Act, National Service (Armed Forces) Act, and a National Registration Act. This time the nation was as ready as it could be, and the legal structures and processes were in place.

So what would happen today?

20. Her Majesty may by Order in Council make emergency regulations if satisfied that the conditions in section 21 are satisfied.

This is section 20 of the Civil Contingencies Act, 2004 and is the direct descendant of the Emergency Powers Act, 1920 and of the Defence of the Realm (Consolidated) Act, 1914. It provides government with powers to protect the civil community in time of emergency, which is defined as:

1. (a). an event or situation which threatens serious damage to human welfare in a place in the United Kingdom,
   (b) an event or situation which threatens serious damage to the environment of a place in the United Kingdom,
   (c). war, or terrorism, which threatens serious damage to the security of the United Kingdom.

The Act sets out the powers, roles and responsibilities of government bodies and agencies ('responders') tasked with civil protection, and includes conditions and limitations of the exercise of such powers. Section 23(4)(c) deals with offences under the emergency regulations, and does not permit punishment in excess of three months or a fine exceeding level 5 (formerly £5,000 but under the Legal Aid, Sentencing and Punishment of Offenders Act, 2012, now unlimited). There are considerable checks and balances provided, to ensure that Parliament exercises its proper responsibilities in respect of regulations passed by ministers or departments on its behalf, including a time limit of thirty days. A senior Minister of the Crown must place the regulations before Parliament as soon as is reasonably practicable, and the regulations will lapse after seven days unless each House passes a resolution approving them. This latter provision was seen in the Emergency Powers Act, 1920, which was itself repealed by this Act in 2004.

It is easy to find apparent absurdities in the Defence of the Realm regulations. Order no. 844, under regulation 12D and dated 14 August 1917, for example, prohibited whistling for cabs in London. Reading further it also prohibited the making any other loud noise for the purpose of summoning cabs, at any hour. But when originally introduced it gave the reasoning behind this:

> 12D. With a view to preventing the disturbance of members of His Majesty's forces suffering from wounds, accidents or sickness, a Secretary of State may by order prohibit or restrict within any area specified in the order, and to such extent and between such hours as may be so specified, whistling and the making of any other noises which appear to him to be calculated to cause such disturbance, and not to be required in the interests of the safety of the public, and if any person contravenes the provisions of any such order he shall be guilty of a summary offence against these regulations (dated 18 August 1916).

The Defence of the Realm regulations were rapidly repealed. The Ministry of National Service revoked many of the regulations controlling recruiting and exemption from military service. The Official Secrets Act, 1911 was reinstated to deal with offences under Regulation 19 (sketching and photography). All Regulation 11 (lighting) orders were cancelled, other than lights on vehicles, animals and advertisements. On 27 November 1918 the *Cambridge Daily News*[19] took great delight in reproducing the list of regulations 'wholly removed' as published in the previous day's *London Gazette*:

2S	Destruction of stray dogs
2T	Restriction on parting with agricultural horses

6	Power to remove vehicles
7A	Prohibition on exhibition prejudicing production of war material
8B	Prohibition on occupier of engineering, &c., factory canvassing, &c., certain employees
9	Power to clear area of inhabitants
9B	Power to prohibit holding of race meetings
9BB	Power to prohibit holding of coursing, &c., meeting
9C	Power to regulate bank or public holidays
9D	Power to prohibit holding of fair
9DD	Prohibition of dog shows
12	Power of naval or military authority to require extinguishment of lights
12B	Prohibition on ringing of bells or striking of clocks in certain areas
12C	Power to prohibit use of sound signals
13	Power to require inhabitants to remain indoors
14D	Restriction on British subject leaving United Kingdom as member of crew of neutral ship
14E	Power to prohibit aliens, &c., from going to Ireland
15B	Power to require particulars of goods held for enemy benefit
18B	Restrictions on publication of inventions and designs
18C	Restriction on publication of works or articles as to training, tactics &c.
19	Prohibition on photographing, sketching, &c., of certain places and things
25	Prohibition on signalling
25A	Prohibition on unauthorised use of authorised signals
26	Prohibition on displaying lights, use of fireworks, &c.
29C	Prohibition on certain persons entering shipbuilding yard
40D	Prohibition on sexual intercourse by diseased women
41A	Duties to be observed by employer of male persons of 16 years or over
41AAA	Duty to furnish information on cesser [sic] of agricultural employment of male person of 16 years or older
41AB	Production of evidence as to liability to military service of man of military age about to be employed
45A	Alteration of or personation or false statement with regard to certificate of exemption from military service
45B	Production of certificate of exemption from military service
45C	Medical examination of holders, &c., of certificates of exemption from military service
45D	False or misleading statement for prevention or postponement of calling up for naval or military service or medical examination
53A	Power to require production of national registration certificate
53B	Testing accuracy of information given as to employees
56B	Prosecutions before Court of summary jurisdiction by officers, &c., of National Service Department

There is, I believe, a parallel between conduct of the war in Western Europe and the implementation of emergency legislation. The generals and the legislators were from the same breed. The generals, clever, experienced, able men, were transfixed by a form of warfare never before seen and on a scale far beyond anything they had imagined; and indeed their collective lack of imagination resulted in four years of strategic stalemate and massive loss of life. The legislators, of similar intellectual calibre, abjectly failed to impose order and responded weakly to the threats and challenges faced by British society. The 'poor bloody infantry' suffered for the generals, and the 'great unpaid' dealt with the casualties of law.

Notes

Introduction

1. *Justice of the Peace*, 29 December 1917.
2. http://www.britishnewspaperarchive.co.uk
3. http://www.bankofengland.co.uk/education/Pages/resources/inflationtools/calculator/index1.aspx. For consistency this calculator has been used throughout this book.
4. Jonathan Swan, *Chelmsford in the Great War*, Pen & Sword, 2015.

Chapter 1: Summary Justice 1914

1. *Tamworth Herald*, 1 August 1914.
2. *Tamworth Herald*, 8 August 1914.
3. *Lichfield Mercury*, 23 October 1914.
4. *Justice of the Peace*, 13 February 1915.
5. Jonathan Swan, 'The First Working Class Magistrates', *The Magistrate*, 2 June 2015.
6. *Exeter and Plymouth Gazette*, 9 April 1906.
7. *Gloucestershire Echo*, 29 December 1906.
8. Royal Commission on the Selection of Justices of the Peace, 1910.
9. *The Times*, 14 July 1910.
10. *Leamington Spa Courier*, 14 July 1911.
11. Royal Commission on the Selection of Justices of the Peace, 1910.
12. *Derby Daily Telegraph*, 25 October 1916.
13. *Yorkshire Post and Leeds Intelligencer*, 25 August 1914.
14. W. Knox Wigram (ed), *Justice's Note-book*, 9th ed., Stevens and Sons, 1910.
15. *Hansard*, 22 April 1907.
16. C.M. Atkinson, *The Magistrates' Practice*, Steven and Sons, 1913.
17. *Justice of the Peace*, 9 February 1918.
18. *Justice of the Peace*, 6 January 1917.
19. W. Knox Wigram (ed), *Justice's Note-book*, 9th ed., Stevens and Sons, 1910.
20. *Justice of the Peace*, 19 October 1918.
21. *Justice of the Peace*, 29 December 1917.
22. *Justice of the Peace*, 15 February 1908.
23. Ibid.
24. Ibid.
25. H.R.P. Gamon, *The London Police Court, today & tomorrow*, J.M. Dent & Co, 1907.
26. Southend Register of Court, D/Bc 1/1/13/1/3, Essex Record Office.
27. *Justice of the Peace*, 24 November 1888.
28. *Justice of the Peace*, 26 May 1917.
29. *Yorkshire Post and Leeds Intelligencer*, 8 April 1914.
30. *Coventry Standard*, 3 July 1914.
31. Report of the Departmental Committee on the Law and Practice of Juries, 1913.
32. *Justice of the Peace*, 26 May 1917.
33. *Western Times*, 30 December 1913.
34. *Nottingham Evening Post*, 6 February 1914.

Chapter 2: Fourteen Days, With Hard Labour

1. *Portsmouth Evening News*, 19 August 1914.
2. Southend Register of Court, D/Bc 1/1/13/1/3, Essex Record Office.
3. Robert Holmes, *My Police Court Friends with the Colours*, William Blackwood and Sons, 1915.
4. http://www.sentencingcouncil.org.uk/the-magistrates-court-sentencing-guidelines/
5. http://www.sentencingcouncil.org.uk/wp-content/uploads/Adult-Court-Bench-Book-April-20161.pdf

6. *Warder and Dublin Weekly Mail*, 10 August 1901.
7. *Sussex Agricultural Express*, 30 June 1916.
8. *Lincolnshire Echo*, 2 March 1908.
9. *Justice of the Peace*, 13 February 1915.
10. Visiting Committee's Minute Book, Q/A Cm 40, Essex Record Office.
11. *Manchester Evening News*, 30 June 1914.
12. R. Gard, 'The First Probation Officers in England and Wales 1906-14', *British Journal of Criminology*, 7 July 2007.
13. 'Police Court Missionaries: review on value of their work', MEPO 2/1267 National Archives.
14. *London Daily News*, 21 October 1907.
15. Cecil Leeson, *The Probation System*, P.S. King and Son, 1914.
16. P/B Ma2, Essex Records Office.
17. Charles Dickens, *The Pickwick Papers*, 1837, Chapter XL.
18. *The Times*, 15 January 1910.
19. *Justice of the Peace*, 3 March 1917.
20. Ibid.
21. H.R.P. Gamon, *The London Police Court, today and tomorrow*, J.M. Dent & Co, 1907.
22. *Surrey Advertiser*, 11 April 1914.
23. *Birmingham Daily Gazette*, 1 June 1918.
24. *Sheffield Independent*, 23 June 1915.
25. *Birmingham Daily Post*, 25 January 1917
26. H.L. Cancellor, *The Life of a London Beak*, Hurst & Blackett, 1930.
27. H.T. Waddy, *The Police Court and its Work*, Butterworth & Co, 1925.
28. H.R.P. Gamon, *The London Police Court, today and tomorrow*, J.M. Dent & Co, 1907.
29. *Justice of the Peace*, 30 December 1916.

Chapter 3: Transition to War

1. *Birmingham Daily Post*, 4 August 1914.
2. *Middlesbrough Daily Gazette*, 4 August 1914.
3. *Birmingham Gazette*, 5 August 1914.
4. *Sheffield Evening Telegraph*, 5 August 1914.
5. *Manchester Courier and Lancashire General Advertiser*, 5 August 1914.
6. *The Scotsman*, 26 March 1909.
7. *Sheffield Independent*, 2 April 1909.
8. *Reading Mercury*, 23 January 1915.
9. *Luton Times and Advertiser*, 4 December 1914.
10. *Justice of the Peace*, 26 September 1914.
11. *Chelsea News and General Advertiser*, 4 September 1914.
12. *Justice of the Peace*, 15 August 1914.
13. *Birmingham Daily Post*, 4 August 1914.
14. *Justice of the Peace*, 15 August 1914.
15. Ibid.
16. *Justice of the Peace*, 26 September 1914.
17. *Dundee Courier*, 12 August 1914.
18. *Birmingham Daily Post*, 25 August 1914.
19. www.parliament.co.uk
20. *Hansard*, 25 August 1914.
21. *Shoreditch Observer*, 28 August 1914.
22. *Manual of Emergency Legislation*, HMSO, 1914.

Chapter 4: Civil, Military and Martial Law

1. *Western Gazette*, 4 December 1914.
2. Williams' grave can still be seen in Melcombe Regis cemetery.
3. *Western Gazette*, 11 December 1914.
4. *Western Gazette*, 15 January 1915.
5. *Justice of the Peace*, 23 January 1915.
6. *Manual of Military Law*, War Office, 1907.
7. Sir W. Blackstone, *Commentaries on the Laws of England*, 1765, Book 1, Chapter 13.
8. A.V. Dicey, *Law of the Constitution*, 8th ed., Macmillan, 1915.
9. Ex parte Vallandigham, 68 US 243, 1864 www.oyez.org

10. Sir Bartholomew Shower, *The Compleat English Copyholder*, 1735.
11. Ex parte Milligan, 71 US 2, 1866 www.oyez.org
12. *London Daily News*, 23 May 1902.
13. *The Times*, 14 December 1899.
14. *The Times*, 19 March 1899.
15. *Hansard*, 6 April 1900.
16. *Hansard*, 9 July 1900.
17. Martial law instructions, WO 32 8176, National Archives.
18. *The Times* Law Reports, Vol. xviii.
19. Ibid.
20. F. Pollock, 'What is Martial Law?', *The Law Quarterly Review*, Vol. LXX, April 1902.
21. *Hansard*, 16 January 1902.
22. *London Daily News*, 23 May 1902.
23. *Hansard*, 18 June 1913.
24. *Manchester Evening News*, 1 August 1914.

Chapter 5: Dear Old DoRA

1. A.V. Dicey, *Law of the Constitution*, 8th ed., Macmillan, 1915.
2. *London Gazette*, 13 May 2016.
3. *Hansard*, 7 August 1914.
4. Defended Harbours: 'Under the powers given by Regulation 29, the Army Council declare the following places to be "Defended Harbours" for the purposes of the Regulations:

Cromarty	Humber	Portland	Mersey	Berehaven
Aberdeen	Thames and Medway	Plymouth	Barrow	Dublin
Tay	Harwich	Falmouth	Clyde	The Orkneys
Forth	Dover	Milford Haven	Lough Swilly	The Shetlands
Tyne	Newhaven	Swansea	Belfast	
Tees and Hartlepool	Portsmouth	Cardiff and Barry	Queenstown'	

5. *Huddersfield Daily Examiner*, 6 August 1914.
6. *Taunton Courier and Western Advertiser*, 19 August 1914.
7. *Birmingham Daily Gazette*, 19 August 1914.
8. *Hansard*, 27 August 1914.
9. *Gloucestershire Echo*, 19 September 1914.
10. *Manchester Evening News*, 6 October 1914.
11. District Courts-Martial Records, WO 86/63, National Archives.
12. *Dover Express*, 9 October 1914.
13. *Stirling Observer*, 8 December 1914.
14. *Hansard*, 25 November 1914.
15. *Justice of the Peace*, 19 December 1914.
16. *Bedfordshire Times and Independent*, 4 December 1914.
17. *Western Times*, 19 March 1915.
18. *Leicester Chronicle*, 17 April 1915.
19. *Newcastle Journal*, 22 July 1915.
20. *Justice of the Peace*, 28 February 1915.
21. *Burnley News*, 27 February 1915.
22. *Liverpool Echo*, 1 August 1914.
23. T. Baty and J.H. Morgan, *War: Its Conduct and Legal Results*, E.P. Dutton and Company, 1915.
24. H.M. Bowman, 'Martial Law and the English Constitution', *Michigan Law Review*, December 1916.
25. *Hansard*, 4 February 1915.
26. Ibid.

Chapter 6: The Enemy Within

1. *Lincolnshire Echo*, 3 August 1914.
2. *Manchester Evening News*, 3 August 1914.

3. *Sheffield Evening Telegraph*, 4 August 1914.
4. *Hull Daily Mail*, 3 August 1914.
5. *Aberdeen Evening Express*, 4 August 1914.
6. *Sheffield Daily Telegraph*, 6 December 1911.
7. *Yorkshire Post and Leeds Intelligencer*, 13 December 1911.
8. *Dundee Courier*, 10 February 1912.
9. *The Scotsman*, 7 January 1911.
10. *Dundee Courier*, 19 January 1911.
11. *The Spectator*, 22 April 1911.
12. *Hansard*, 4 December 1911.
13. *Aberdeen Journal*, 7 August 1914.
14. *Nottingham Evening Post*, 15 May 1914.
15. C. Northcott, *MI5 at War 1909-1918*, Chevron Publishing, 2015.
16. *Aberdeen Evening Express*, 5 August 1914.
17. *Liverpool Echo*, 5 August 1914.
18. *Birmingham Mail*, 8 August 1914.
19. *Manchester Evening News*, 5 August 1914.
20. *Western Daily Press*, 5 August 1914.
21. *Nottingham Evening Post*, 8 August 1914.
22. *Liverpool Echo*, 5 August 1914.
23. *Aberdeen Journal*, 6 August 1914.
24. *Hansard*, 5 August 1914.
25. *Sussex Agricultural Express*, 13 August 1914.
26. *Dover Express*, 7 August 1914; *London Gazette*, 6 August 1914.
27. *Birmingham Mail*, 7 August 1914.
28. *The Scotsman*, 7 August 1914.
29. *Birmingham Daily Gazette*, 12 August 1914.
30. *Huddersfield Daily Examiner*, 13 August 1914.
31. *Leicester Chronicle*, 15 August 1914.
32. *Birmingham Daily Post*, 7 August 1914.
33. *Lichfield Mercury*, 21 April 1915.
34. *Birmingham Mail*, 8 August 1914.
35. *Sussex Agricultural Express*, 13 August 1914.
36. *Western Mail*, 10 August 1914.
37. Ibid.
38. *Western Mail*, 13 August 1914.
39. *Dover Express*, 14 August 1914.
40. *Western Mail*, 15 August 1914.
41. *Justice of the Peace*, 24 October 1914.
42. *The Scotsman*, 19 August 1914.
43. *The Scotsman*, 13 August 1914.
44. *Justice of the Peace*, 19 May 1917.
45. *Surrey Advertiser*, 15 August 1914.
46. *Evening Despatch*, 19 November 1914.
47. Ibid.
48. *Birmingham Daily Gazette*, 23 November 1914.
49. *Hull Daily Mail*, 10 August 1914; *Yorkshire Post and Leeds Intelligencer*, 13 August 1914; *Biggleswade Chronicle*, 14 August 1914.
50. Riot Act, 1714.
51. *Nottingham Evening Post*, 13 May 1915.
52. *Justice of the Peace*, 14 November 1914.
53. *Justice of the Peace*, 2 January 1914.
54. *Newcastle Journal*, 20 May 1915.
55. *Gloucestershire Echo*, 10 May 1915.
56. *Evening Despatch*, 10 May 1915.
57. *Birmingham Mail*. 11 May 1915.
58. *Manchester Courier and Lancashire General Advertiser*, 11 May 1915.
59. *Birmingham Mail*, 12 May 1915.
60. Ibid.
61. *Aberdeen Evening Express*, 12 May 1915.

62. *Birmingham Mail*, 12 May 1915.
63. *Daily Mirror*, 14 May 1915.
64. *North Devon Journal*, 20 May 1915.
65. *Portsmouth Evening News*, 14 May 1915.
66. *Lichfield Mercury*, 21 May 1915.
67. *Wells Journal*, 21 May 1915.
68. Ibid.
69. *Liverpool Echo*, 12 May 1915.
70. *Berwick Advertiser*, 21 May 1915.
71. *Buckinghamshire Herald*, 22 May 1915.
72. *Lichfield Mercury*, 21 May 1915.
73. *Western Daily Press*, 3 August 1915.
74. *Edinburgh Evening News*, 26 May 1915.
75. *Birmingham Daily Post*, 28 July 1915.
76. *Birmingham Mail*, 27 July 1915.
77. *Justice of the Peace*, 4 March 1916.
78. *Justice of the Peace*, 15 April 1916.
79. *Justice of the Peace*, 12 February 1916.
80. *Justice of the Peace*, 2 October 1915.
81. *Justice of the Peace*, 8 January 1916.
82. *Justice of the Peace*, 7 August 1915.
83. *Justice of the Peace*, 29 August 1914.
84. *Justice of the Peace*, 4 March 1916.
85. *Manchester Evening News*, 22 October 1914.
86. *Justice of the Peace*, 14 November 1914.
87. *Newcastle Journal*, 8 June 1915.
88. *Exeter and Plymouth Gazette*, 3 September 1915.
89. *Newcastle Journal*, 3 August 1915. Several biographical details in the story do not match Terviel's records on ancestry.co.uk; the latter have been used here.
90. *Newcastle Journal*, 10 September 1915.
91. *Manchester Evening News*, 29 June 1916.
92. *Manchester Evening News*, 16 September 1916.
93. *Derby Daily Telegraph*, 23 December 1916.
94. Military age: Germans and Turks – 17 to 55; Austrians 17 to 60.
95. *Exeter and Plymouth Gazette*, 28 February 1917.
96. *Birmingham Daily Post*, 26 December 1916.
97. *Justice of the Peace*, 11 September 1915; *Dundee Courier*, 18 April 1916.
98. *The Scotsman*, 12 January 1916.
99. *Justice of the Peace*, 5 February 1916; *Liverpool Daily Post*, 10 February 1916.
100. *Cambridge Daily News*, 4 June 1918.
101. *Justice of the Peace*, 22 January 1916.
102. *Yorkshire Post and Leeds Intelligencer*, 13 March 1917; *Justice of the Peace*, 19 May 1917.
103. *Leeds Mercury*, 21 December 1916.
104. *Yorkshire Post and Leeds Intelligencer*, 9 June 1917.
105. *Daily Record*, 9 June 1917.
106. *Birmingham Daily Post*, 4 July 1917.
107. *Lancashire Evening Post*, 21 July 1917.
108. *Western Times*, 19 October 1917.
109. *Justice of the Peace*, 10 November 1917.
110. *Newcastle Journal*, 12 February 1918.
111. *Justice of the Peace*, 30 May 1918.
112. *Justice of the Peace*, 31 August 1918

Chapter 7: Down at the Old Bull and Bush
1. *Framlingham Weekly News*, 27 December 1902.
2. Order of the Secretary of State, 28 October 1902, prescribing forms under the Licensing Act, 1902.
3. *Driffield Times*, 14 November 1914.
4. *Falkirk Herald*, 4 March 1914.
5. P/B R16 Essex Record Office.
6. *Birmingham Mail*, 11 April 1914.

7. W. Knox Wigram (ed), *Justice's Note-book*, 9th ed., Stevens and Sons, 1910.
8. Licensing (Consolidation) Act, 1910.
9. Ibid.
10. *Williams v McDonald* (1899).
11. *Lancashire Evening Post*, 27 November 1907.
12. *Shoreditch Observer*, 20 April 1912.
13. Licensing (Consolidation) Act, 1910.
14. H. Carter, *The Control of the Drink Trade*, Longmans, Green & Co., 1918.
15. Ibid.
16. *Stirling Observer*, 8 August 1914.
17. *Manchester Evening News*, 7 August 1914.
18. *Daily Herald*, 18 August 1914.
19. H. Carter, *The Control of the Drink Trade*, Longmans, Green & Co., 1918.
20. Daily Journal, in *Aberdeen Journal*, 28 August 1914.
21. *Hansard*, 25 August 1914.
22. *Hansard*, 27 August 1914.
23. Mr J.W. Wilson MP, *Hansard*, 27 August 1914.
24. *Justice of the Peace*, 12 September 1914.
25. *Justice of the Peace*, 14 November 1914.
26. Ibid.
27. *Birmingham Mail*, 4 November 1914.
28. *Surrey Advertiser*, 24 October 1914.
29. *Justice of the Peace*, 14 November 1914.
30. *Yorkshire Post and Leeds Intelligencer*, 5 November 1914.
31. *Manchester Evening News*, 9 November 1914.
32. *Justice of the Peace*, 14 November 1914.
33. Ibid.
34. 'Return as to the Orders made by Licensing Justices up to and including 31 December 1914 under the Intoxicating Liquor (Temporary Restrictions) Act, 1914' in H. Carter, *The Control of the Drink Trade*, Longmans, Green & Co., 1918.
35. Smawthorne Lane WMC is still there.
36. *Justice of the Peace*, 23 January 1915.
37. See Midland Working Men's Club, *Sheffield Evening Telegraph*, 19 February 1915, and Churwell Working Men's Club and Institute, *Yorkshire Evening Post*, 12 April 1915.
38. *Justice of the Peace*, 23 January 1915.
39. *Yorkshire Post and Leeds Intelligencer*, 14 May 1915.
40. Ibid.
41. *Hansard*, 16 November 1914.
42. *Western Gazette*, 2 April 1915.
43. *Sheffield Independent*, 18 September 1918.
44. H. Carter, *The Control of the Drink Trade*, Longmans, Green & Co., 1918.
45. *Western Times*, 6 April 1915.
46. *Sheffield Independent*, 30 April 1915.
47. H. Carter, *The Control of the Drink Trade*, Longmans, Green & Co., 1918.
48. Arthur Shadwell, *Drink in 1914–1922: a Lesson in Control*, Longmans, Green & Co., 1923.
49. *Dundee Courier*, 21 January 1915.
50. Thanks to several members of the Great War Forum for identifying the ship and the units involved in this story http://1914-1918.invisionzone.com/forums/index.php?/
51. Return to the House of Commons, 'Shipbuilding, Munitions and Transport' 29 April 1915, in ibid.
52. 'The Alcohol Question in relation to the alcoholic strength of beverages', *The Lancet* Vol. 185, April 1915.
53. Ibid.
54. Ibid.
55. *Justice of the Peace*, 11 December 1915.
56. Ibid.
57. *The Times*, 9 September 1915.
58. Ibid.
59. *Justice of the Peace*, 21 September 1915.
60. *Justice of the Peace*, 20 November 1915.
61. *Justice of the Peace*, 11 December 1915.
62. *Justice of the Peace*, 20 November 1915.

63. *Justice of the Peace*, 27 November 1915.
64. *The Times*, 25 November 1915.
65. *Justice of the Peace*, 24 March 1917.
66. *Justice of the Peace*, 27 November 1915.
67. *Yorkshire Post & Leeds Intelligencer*, 7 December 1915.
68. Ibid.
69. *Justice of the Peace*, 25 December 1915.
70. *Yorkshire Evening Post*, 1 June 1916.
71. *Burton Daily Mail*, 26 January 1917.
72. *Western Daily Press*, 25 January 1917.
73. *Birmingham Mail*, 6 July 1917.
74. Arthur Shadwell, *Drink in 1914–1922: a Lesson in Control*, Longmans, Green & Co., 1923.

Chapter 8: How Bright is 'Bright'?
1. *Dundee Evening Telegraph*, 23 June 1910.
2. *Dublin Daily Express*, 25 June 1910
3. *Sheffield Evening Telegraph*, 20 June 1910.
4. *Sheffield Evening Telegraph*, 28 June 1910.
5. *Sunderland Daily Echo and Shipping Gazette*, 29 June 1910.
6. *Hansard*, 30 April 1913.
7. *Hansard* 23 April 1913.
8. *Hansard* 30 July 1913.
9. A.V.M. Hunter (ed.), *Defending the Northern Skies 1915-1995*, RAF Historical Society, 1995.
10. Regulation 7A, *London Gazette*, 17 September 1914.
11. *The Scotsman*, 17 September 1914.
12. *Daily Gazette for Middlesbrough*, 10 September 1914.
13. *Dundee Courier*, 1 October 1914.
14. *Hull Daily Mail*, 22 October 1914.
15. *Birmingham Daily Gazette*, 14 October 1914.
16. *Surrey Advertiser*, 24 October 1914.
17. *Western Mail*, 6 October 1914.
18. *Liverpool Daily Post*, 13 October 1914.
19. *Daily Record*, 9 October 1914.
20. *Birmingham Daily Post*, 23 November 1914.
21. *The Era*, 18 November 1914.
22. *Birmingham Daily Post*, 9 December 1914.
23. *Western Times*, 19 November 1913.
24. *Daily Record*, 21 October 1914.
25. *Manchester Evening News*, 19 January 1914.
26. *Shoreditch Observer*, 12 February 1915.
27. *Folkestone and Hythe Herald*, 23 January 1915.
28. *Birmingham Daily Post*, 23 November 1914.
29. *Nottingham Evening Post*, 19 February 1915; *Manchester Evening News*, 19 February 1915.
30. *Birmingham Daily Post*, 12 February 1915.
31. *Yorkshire Post and Leeds Intelligencer*, 14 April 1915.
32. *Bexhill-on-Sea Observer*, 27 February 1915.
33. *Bexhill-on-Sea Observer*, 6 March 1915.
34. Ibid.
35. *Manchester Evening News*, 11 February 1915.
36. *Cambridge Independent Press*, 26 March 1915.
37. *Yorkshire Post and Leeds Intelligencer*, 17 April 1915.
38. *Hull Daily Mail*, 21 April 1915.
39. *Yorkshire Post and Leeds Intelligencer*, 5 August 1915.
40. *Justice of the Peace*, 18 September 1915.
41. *Newcastle Journal*, 12 April 1915.
42. *Justice of the Peace*, 2 October 1915.
43. *Yorkshire Post and Leeds Intelligencer*, 30 April 1915.
44. Ibid.
45. *Leicester Chronicle*, 8 May 1915.
46. *Yorkshire Post and Leeds Intelligencer*, 19 August 1915.

47. *Newcastle Journal*, 14 October 1915.
48. *Whitstable Times*, 3 July 1915.
49. *Manchester Evening News*, 16 June 1915.
50. *Chelmsford Chronicle*, 27 August 1915.
51. *Nottingham Evening Post*, 5 September 1915.
52. *Yorkshire Post and Leeds Intelligencer*, 31 August 1915.
53. *Justice of the Peace*, 12 June 1916.
54. *Western Gazette*, 22 September 1916.
55. *Yorkshire Post and Leeds Intelligencer*, 14 March 1916.
56. *Portsmouth Evening News*, 27 March 1916.
57. *Yorkshire Evening Post*, 23 May 1916.
58. *Justice of the Peace*, 9 October 1915.
59. *Justice of the Peace*, 1 January 1916.
60. A. Simpson, *Air Raids on South-West Essex in the Great War*, Pen & Sword, 2015.
61. *Justice of the Peace*, 12 February 1916.
62. *Cheltenham Looker-On*, 20 May 1916.
63. *Banbury Advertiser*, 25 May 1916.
64. *Coventry Evening Telegraph*, 4 November 1918.
65. *Hull Daily Mail*, 1 October 1915.
66. *Framlingham Weekly News*, 25 September 1915.
67. *Justice of the Peace*, 16 October 1915.
68. *Justice of the Peace*, 3 June 1916.
69. Ibid.
70. *Birmingham Mail*, 10 January 1916.
71. *Hull Daily Mail*, 27 September 1916.
72. *Hull Daily Mail*, 10 September 1916.
73. *Justice of the Peace*, 26 August 1916.
74. *Lincolnshire Echo*, 18 September 1916.
75. *Whitby Gazette*, 15 September 1916.
76. *Justice of the Peace*, 11 November 1916.
77. *Justice of the Peace*, 6 July 1918.
78. *Western Times*, 11 July 1916.
79. *Justice of the Peace*, 25 December 1915.
80. *Western Daily Press*, 19 August 1915; *Justice of the Peace*, 4 July 1918.
81. *Liverpool Daily Post*, 1 October 1915.
82. *Western Daily Press*, 20 December 1915.
83. *Justice of the Peace*, 1 January 1916.
84. *Justice of the Peace*, 8 January 1916.
85. *Justice of the Peace*, 14 October 1916.
86. *Lichfield Mercury*, 28 January 1916.
87. *Aberdeen Evening Express*, 7 March 1916.
88. *Aberdeen Journal*, 18 March 1916.
89. *Justice of the Peace*, 21 October 1916.

Chapter 9: What Did You Do in the War, Daddy?

1. *Western Gazette*, 5 June 1914.
2. *Yorkshire Evening Post*, 4 June 1914.
3. *Newcastle Journal*, 3 July 1914.
4. *Evening Despatch*, 8 August 1914.
5. *Sheffield Evening Telegraph*, 8 August 1914.
6. *Evening Despatch*, 14 August 1914.
7. *Justice of the Peace*, 12 December 1914.
8. A career soldier, Caldwell joined the army in 1905. Following the absence recorded here he rejoined his unit and was sent to France in November 1914. Wounded in May 1918, he survived the war.
9. Essex Record Office, P/B R16.
10. *Justice of the Peace*, 26 June 1915.
11. *Justice of the Peace*, 5 February 1916; *Justice of the Peace*, 18 March 1916.
12. Essex Record Office, P/B R16.
13. *Justice of the Peace*, 5 June 1916.
14. *Justice of the Peace*, 27 January 1917.

15. *Cambridge Daily News*, 16 January 1917.
16. *Hansard*, 20 March 1917.
17. *Justice of the Peace*, 14 July 1917.
18. W. Knox Wigram JP, *The Justice's Note-book*, Stevens and Sons, 1910.
19. *Huddersfield Daily Examiner*, 26 August 1914.
20. *Western Daily Press*, 17 August 1914.
21. *Western Daily Press*, 22 August 1914.
22. *Hull Daily Mail*, 2 October 1914.
23. *Liverpool Echo*, 16 September 1915.
24. *Sheffield Evening Telegraph*, 26 May 1915.
25. *Sunderland Daily Echo and Shipping Gazette*, 12 March 1915.
26. *Sunderland Daily Echo and Shipping Gazette*, 24 October 1914.
27. *Justice of the Peace*, 3 December 1914.
28. *Aberdeen Journal*, 15 December 1914.
29. *Justice of the Peace*, 6 March 1915; *Justice of the Peace*, 27 November 1915.
30. *Liverpool Echo*, 18 January 1915.
31. *Liverpool Echo*, 13 December 1914.
32. *Middlesex Chronicle*, 8 March 1916
33. *Western Daily Press*, 25 October 1915.
34. *Portsmouth Evening News*, 27 February 1915.
35. *Birmingham Daily Post*, 6 May 1916.
36. *Nottingham Evening Post*, 14 September 1916.
37. *Derbyshire Courier*, 8 December 1917.
38. *Evening Telegraph*, 9 November 1915
39. *Manchester Evening News*, 25 August 1915.
40. *Western Times*, 19 September 1914.
41. *Nottingham Evening Post*, 6 September 1916.
42. *Nottingham Evening Post*, 26 July 1917.
43. *Western Daily Press*, 11 September 1914.
44. *Edinburgh Evening News*, 11 November 1914.
45. *Birmingham Daily Post*, 30 October 1914; *Edinburgh Evening News*, 11 November 1914.
46. *Birmingham Daily Gazette*, 7 December 1914.
47. *The Scotsman*, 17 December 1914.
48. *Framlingham Weekly News*, 12 December 1914.
49. *Manchester Courier and Lancashire General Advertiser*, 7 January 1915.
50. *The Scotsman*, 13 February 1915.
51. *Western Mail*, 5 May 1915.
52. *Western Mail*, 22 May 1915.
53. *The Scotsman*, 26 June 1915.
54. *Western Mail*, 29 June 1915.
55. W. Knox Wigram JP, *The Justice's Note-book*, Stevens and Sons, 1910.
56. *Manchester Courier and Lancashire General Advertiser*, 16 July 1915.
57. *Birmingham Daily Gazette*, 17 July 1915.
58. *Manchester Courier and Lancashire General Advertiser*, 17 July 1915.
59. *Sheffield Independent*, 22 July 1915.
60. *Sheffield Evening Telegraph*, 22 July 1915.
61. *Manchester Evening News*, 31 July 1915.
62. *Dundee Evening Telegraph*, 25 June 1915.
63. *Nottingham Evening Post*, 29 June 1915.
64. *Newcastle Journal*, 6 July 1915.
65. *Hull Daily Mail*, 17 July 1915.
66. Jonathan Swan, *Chelmsford in the Great War*, Pen & Sword, 2015.
67. *Evening Dispatch*, 21 August 1915.
68. *Coventry Evening Telegraph*, 4 September 1915.
69. *Diss Express*, 1 October 1915.
70. *Yorkshire Evening Post*, 9 September 1915.
71. *Framlingham Weekly News*, 16 October 1915.
72. *Rochdale Observer*, 2 October 1915.
73. *Rochdale Observer*, 25 December 1915.
74. *Manchester Evening News*, 20 September 1915.

75. *Manchester Evening News*, 11 October 1915.
76. *Rochdale Observer*, 23 October 1915.
77. *Daily Mirror*, 12 October 1915.
78. *Grantham Journal*, 16 October 1915.
79. *Nottingham Evening Post*, 16 October 1915; *Aberdeen Journal*, 7 September 1915.
80. *Liverpool Echo*, 16 October 1915.
81. *Dundee Courier*, 19 October 1915.
82. *Manchester Courier and Lancashire General Advertiser*, 20 November 1915.
83. *Burnley News*, 1 December 1915.
84. *Birmingham Mail*, 28 October 1915.
85. *Birmingham Daily Gazette*, 19 November 1915.
86. *Western Daily Press*, 27 December 1915.
87. *Western Daily Press*, 22 October 1915.
88. *Manchester Evening News*, 3 November 1915; *Birmingham Daily Post*, 9 December 1915.
89. *Birmingham Daily Gazette*, 4 November 1915.
90. *Birmingham Daily Gazette*, 19 November 1915.
91. *Manchester Courier and Lancashire General Advertiser*, 8 December 1915.
92. *Birmingham Daily Post*, 9 December 1915.
93. *Coventry Evening Telegraph*, 9 December 1915.
94. *Reading Mercury*, 25 December 1915.
95. *Sheffield Evening Telegraph*, 11 December 1915.
96. *Dundee Courier*, 21 January 1915; *Portsmouth Evening News*, 28 January 1915.
97. *Taunton Courier and Western Advertiser*, 8 March 1916.
98. *Birmingham Daily Post*, 22 November 1915.
99. *Birmingham Daily Post*, 29 November 1915.
100. *Birmingham Daily Post*, 20 December 1915.
101. Ibid.
102. *Birmingham Daily Post*, 1 December 1915.
103. *Rochdale Observer*, 15 January 1916.
104. *Hansard*, 4 January 1916.
105. *Hansard*, 5 January 1916.
106. Military Service (No. 1) Bill was promoted by Sir John Simon before his resignation. It advocated the compulsory reenlistment of soldiers who had served their contracted time. Asquith laid it to rest in January 1916.
107. *Aberdeen Evening Express*, 28 January 1916.
108. *Sheffield Evening Telegraph*, 2 March 1916.
109. *Justice of the Peace*, 22 January 1916.
110. *Sheffield Evening Telegraph*, 2 March 1916.
111. *Dundee Courier*, 2 March 1916.
112. *Edinburgh Evening News*, 2 March 1916.
113. *Justice of the Peace*, 5 February 1916.
114. *Justice of the Peace*, 19 February 1916.
115. *Western Times*, 27 June 1917.
116. *Justice of the Peace*, 3 June 1916.
117. *Essex Newsman*, 30 December 1916.
118. *Justice of the Peace*, 15 April 1916.
119. *Justice of the Peace*, 10 March 1917; *Yorkshire Post and Leeds Intelligencer*, 3 March 1917.
120. *Justice of the Peace*, 14 October 1916.
121. *Justice of the Peace*, 14 April 1917.
122. *Liverpool Daily Post*, 28 March 1917.
123. *Sheffield Evening Telegraph*, 24 March 1917.
124. *Aberdeen Press and Journal*, 10 May 1917.
125. *Nottingham Evening Post*, 14 August 1917.
126. *Birmingham Daily Post*, 7 April 1917.
127. *Birmingham Daily Post*, 9 August 1917.
128. *Justice of the Peace*, 20 April 1918.
129. *Justice of the Peace*, 27 April 1918.
130. *Daily Record*, 22 April 1918.
131. *Birmingham Daily Gazette*, 22 March 1917.

Chapter 10: And What Did You Do in the War, Mummy?

1. In Great Britain it was released as *Kid's Auto Races*.
2. *Motherwell Times*, 10 July 1914.
3. *Newcastle Journal*, 2 July 1914.
4. *Motherwell Times*, 3 July 1914.
5. *Coventry Evening Telegraph*, 10 July 1914.
6. *Newcastle Journal*, 26 May 1914.
7. *Yorkshire Post and Leeds Intelligencer*, 16 February 1914.
8. *Liverpool Daily Post*, 9 April 1914.
9. *Dundee Courier*, 11 April 1914
10. H. Langford Lewis, *The Shilling Law Book*, Ward, Lock & Co Ltd, 1900.
11. *Western Times*, 1 April 1914.
12. *Justice of the Peace*, 29 April 1917.
13. W. Knox Wigram JP, *The Justice's Note-book*, 9th ed., Stevens & Sons, 1910.
14. *Justice of the Peace*, 20 August 1898.
15. *Rochdale Observer*, 13 June 1914.
16. *Yorkshire Post and Leeds Intelligencer*, 4 August 1914.
17. *Evening Despatch*, 5 August 1914.
18. *Yorkshire Post and Leeds Intelligencer*, 11 August 1914.
19. *Chester Chronicle*, 8 August 1914.
20. Now the Soldiers', Sailors' and Airmens' Families Association (SSAFA).
21. *Justice of the Peace*, 12 September 1914.
22. *Sunderland Daily Echo*, 12 August 1914.
23. *Manchester Evening News*, 18 August 1914.
24. *Gloucestershire Echo*, 14 September 1914.
25. *Huddersfield Daily Examiner*, 21 August 1914.
26. *Burnley News*, 22 August 1914.
27. *Derbyshire Courier*, 3 October 1914.
28. *Hull Daily Mail*, 17 October 1914.
29. *Dundee Evening Telegraph*, 22 October 1914.
30. *Buckinghamshire Advertiser*, 31 October 1914
31. *Manchester Evening News*, 2 November 1914.
32. *Edinburgh Evening News*, 3 November 1914.
33. *Yorkshire Post and Leeds Intelligencer*, 20 April 1915.
34. *Edinburgh Evening News*, 7 September 1915.
35. The newspaper article states that she was his sister-in-law, which makes little sense.
36. *Nottingham Evening Post*, 2 January 1915.
37. *Aberdeen Journal*, 8 September 1915.
38. *Justice of the Peace*, 4 September 1915.
39. *Justice of the Peace*, 12 February 1916.
40. *Huddersfield Daily Examiner*, 19 April 1915.
41. *Dundee Courier*, 27 October 1915.
42. *Daily Record*, 18 October 1915.
43. *Edinburgh Evening News*, 10 November 1915.
44. *The Scotsman*, 26 November 1915.
45. *Coventry Evening Telegraph*, 23 January 1916.
46. *Newcastle Journal*, 9 February 1916.
47. Small Tenements Registers, 1913–1918, Thames Magistrates' Court.
48. *Burnley News*, 14 November 1914.
49. *Manchester Courier* 5 December 1914.
50. *Middlesex Gazette*, 26 December 1914.
51. *Falkirk Herald*, 20 March 1915.
52. *Newcastle Journal*, 1 January 1915.
53. *Liverpool Echo*, 29 October 1914.
54. *Justice of the Peace*, 7 November 1914.
55. *Justice of the Peace*, 23 October 1914.
56. *Middlesex Chronicle*, 24 April 1915.
57. *Yorkshire Evening Post*, 26 November 1915.
58. *Judicial Statistics, England and Wales, 1919*, HMSO, 1921.
59. *Folkestone, Hythe, Sandgate & Cheriton Herald*, 8 September 1917.

60. *Chelsea News & Advertiser*, 17 August 1917.
61. Major T.J. Mitchell and Miss G.M. Smith, *Medical Services: Casualties and Medical Statistics of the Great War*, HMSO, 1931.
62. An expression possibly of Australian origin: https://web.archive.org/web/20071207190226/http://www.anu.edu.au/andc/res/aus_words/wwi/S.php
63. Major T.J. Mitchell and Miss G.M. Smith, *Medical Services: Casualties and Medical Statistics of the Great War*, HMSO, 1931.
64. *The Scotsman*, 7 November 1917.
65. *Aldershot Military Gazette*, 29 October 1864.
66. *Army and Navy Gazette*, 15 September 1866.
67. Ibid.
68. *Nottinghamshire Guardian*, 13 August 1869.
69. *Nottingham Evening Post*, 15 April 1918.
70. *Aberdeen Journal*, 12 April 1918.
71. *Burnley News*, 13 April 1918.
72. *Western Mail*, 30 March 1918.
73. *The Scotsman*, 7 May 1918.
74. Ibid.
75. *Northampton Mercury*, 10 May 1918.
76. *Grantham Journal*, 29 June 1918.
77. *Buckinghamshire Advertiser and Free Press*, 10 August 1918.
78. *Northampton Mercury*, 23 August 1918.
79. *Northampton Mercury*, 3 January 1919.
80. *Justice of the Peace*, 20 November 1915.
81. *Birmingham Mail*, 19 January 1914.
82. *Portsmouth Evening News*, 15 April 1914.
83. *Evening Despatch*, 2 May 1914.
84. *Liverpool Daily Post*, 23 January 1914.
85. *Lincolnshire Echo*, 4 March, 1914.
86. Essex Record Office, P/B Rj1.
87. *Liverpool Daily Post*, 15 June 1915.
88. *Aberdeen Evening Express*, 25 January 1916.
89. *Burnley News*, 5 February 1916.
90. *Birmingham Daily Gazette*, 13 March 1916.
91. *Daily Mirror*, 19 July 1916.
92. *Daily Mirror*, 21 July 1916.
93. *Liverpool Echo*, 14 October 1916.
94. *Aberdeen Journal*, 24 October 1916.
95. *Justice of the Peace*, 16 December 1916.
96. *Sussex Agricultural Express*, 3 August 1917.
97. *Yorkshire Evening Post*, 19 March 1917.
98. *Daily Mirror*, 13 April 1917.
99. *Yorkshire Evening Post*, 30 August 1917.
100. *Liverpool Daily Post*, 19 September 1917.
101. *Birmingham Mail*, 11 October 1917.
102. *Hull Daily Mail*, 15 October 1917.
103. *Sheffield Evening Telegraph*, 15 March 1916.
104. *Huddersfield Daily Examiner*, 25 June 1915.
104. *Western Daily Press*, 25 June 1915.
106. *Middlesex Chronicle*, 3 June 1915.
107. *Justice of the Peace*, 13 November 1915.

Chapter 11: Is Tea a Food?

1. *Mrs Beeton's Book of Household Management*, Ward, Lock & Co. Ltd, 1915.
2. Part I to Second Schedule to the Army Act, 1881.
3. Schedule A, Part II, Poor Law Institutions Order, 1913.
4. *Yorkshire Evening Post*, 1 August 1914.
5. *Yorkshire Post and Leeds Intelligencer*, 3 August 1914.
6. *Buckingham Advertiser and Free Press*, 8 April 1916.
7. *Edinburgh Evening News*, 21 June 1915.

8. *Dundee Evening Telegraph*, 15 March 1916.
9. *Sheffield Evening Telegraph*, 8 February 1915.
10. *Aberdeen Evening Express*, 2 June 1916.
11. *Justice of the Peace*, 25 November 1916.
12. *Justice of the Peace*, 16 December 1916.
13. *Justice of the Peace*, 23 December 1916.
14. *Dundee Evening Telegraph*, 14 December 1916.
15. *Dundee Courier*, 15 December 1916.
16. *Northampton Mercury*, 12 January 1917.
17. *Gloucestershire Echo*, 12 January 1917.
18. *Daily Mirror*, 26 February 1917.
19. *Coventry Evening Telegraph*, 8 March 1917.
20. *Whitby Gazette*, 23 March 1917.
21. *Coventry Evening Telegraph*, 23 March 1917.
22. *Hull Daily Mail*, 19 May 1917.
23. *Exeter and Plymouth Gazette*, 15 May 1917.
24. *Dover Express*, 18 May 1917.
25. *Justice of the Peace*, 19 May 1917.
26. *Western Daily Press*, 16 May 1917.
27. *Bellshill Speaker*, 25 May 1917.
28. *Justice of the Peace*, 26 June 1917.
29. *Gloucestershire Echo*, 23 April 1917.
30. *Justice of the Peace*, 16 June 1917.
31. *Liverpool Echo*, 5 June 1917.
32. *Western Daily Press*, 16 June 1917.
33. *Lancashire Evening Post*, 4 June 1917.
34. *Yorkshire Evening Post*, 4 June 1917.
35. *Justice of the Peace*, 2 August 1917.
36. *Justice of the Peace*, 8 September 1917.
37. *Dundee Evening Telegraph*, 26 December 1917.
38. *Sheffield Evening Telegraph*, 27 December 1917.
39. *Yorkshire Post and Leeds Intelligencer*, 11 September 1917.
40. *Lincolnshire Gazette*, 12 September 1917.
41. *Daily Record*, 11 September 1917.
42. *Coventry Evening Telegraph*, 19 January 1918.
43. *Coventry Evening Telegraph*, 11 April 1918.
44. *Justice of the Peace*, 29 March 1918.
45. *Banbury Guardian*, 2 May 1918.
46. *Dumfries and Galloway Standard*, 13 February 1918.
47. *Western Times*, 28 March 1918.
48. *Justice of the Peace*, 16 March 1918.
49. *Justice of the Peace*, 9 March 1918.
50. Ibid.
51. *London Daily News*, 12 February 1909.
52. *Nottingham Evening Post*, 18 November 1910.
53. *Western Mail*, 5 March 1917.
54. Ibid.
55. *Liverpool Echo*, 3 April 1917.
56. *Manchester Evening News*, 22 December 1917.
57. *Coventry Evening Telegraph*, 14 January 1918.
58. *Liverpool Daily Post*, 28 January 1918.
59. Ibid.
60. *Birmingham Daily Post*, 7 January 1918.
61. *Birmingham Daily Post*, 22 January 1918.
62. *Edinburgh Evening News*, 28 September 1918.
63. *Coventry Evening Telegraph*, 15 December 1917.
64. *Sheffield Evening Telegraph*, 11 April 1918.
65. *Manchester Evening News*, 21 March 1918.
66. *Justice of the Peace*, 4 May 1918.
67. *Justice of the Peace*, 3 February 1917.

68. *Justice of the Peace*, 12 January 1918.
69. *Justice of the Peace*, 15 June 1918.

Chapter 12: Business as Usual
 1. *Aberdeen Evening Express*, 14 January 1914.
 2. *The Times*, 15 January 1914.
 3. *Sheffield Independent*, 18 December 1914.
 4. *Gloucestershire Echo*, 4 February 1915.
 5. *Manchester Evening News*, 2 March 1915.
 6. *Manchester Evening News*, 12 November 1915.
 7. *Justice of the Peace*, 21 April 1917.
 8. *Justice of the Peace*, 28 August 1915; *Edinburgh Evening News*, 18 November 1915.
 9. *The Scotsman*, 16 February 1915.
10. *Liverpool Echo*, 27 October 1914.
11. *Birmingham Daily Post*, 12 January 1915.
12. *Justice of the Peace*, 9 September 1916.
13. *Justice of the Peace*, 28 August 1915.
14. Police Workforce, England and Wales 31 March 2015, at https://www.gov.uk/government/statistics/police-workforce-england-and-wales-31-march-2015-data-tables
15. W. Knox Wigram JP, *The Justice's Note-book*, 9th ed., Stevens & Sons, 1910.
16. *Justice of the Peace*, 24 October 1914.
17. *Yorkshire Post and Leeds Intelligencer*, 20 August 1914.
18. *Birmingham Mail*, 20 August 1914.
19. *Newcastle Journal*, 2 December 1915.
20. *Dublin Daily Express*, 14 August 1914.
21. *Whitstable Times*, 22 August 1914.
22. *Justice of the Peace*, 27 November 1915.
23. *Justice of the Peace*, 8 May 1915.
24. *Wells Journal*, 4 September 1914
25. *Chelmsford Chronicle*, 25 September 1914.
26. *Chelmsford Chronicle*, 4 September 1914.
27. *Essex Newsman*, 15 August 1915.
28. *Justice of the Peace*, 29 August 1915.
29. *Justice of the Peace*, 17 July 1915.
30. *Justice of the Peace*, 4 March 1916.
31. *Justice of the Peace*, 18 March 1916.
32. *Justice of the Peace*, 8 May 1915.
33. *Justice of the Peace*, 11 December 1915.
34. *Birmingham Mail*, 16 April 1914.
35. *Justice of the Peace*, 10 July 1915.
36. *Justice of the Peace*, 16 October 1915.
37. *Justice of the Peace*, 17 April 1917.
38. *Justice of the Peace*, 12 October 1915.
39. *Justice of the Peace*, 13 November 1915.
40. Ibid.
41. Visiting Committee's Minute Book, Q/A Cm 40, Essex Record Office.
42. *Justice of the Peace*, 20 May 1915.
43. Judicial Statistics for England and Wales, HMSO 1914–1919.
44. Judicial Statistics for England and Wales, HMSO 1919 (published 1921).
45. *Evening Despatch*, 1 January 1916.
46. *Chelmsford Chronicle*, 9 October 1914.
47. *Birmingham Daily Post*, 9 September 1914.
48. *Birmingham Daily Gazette*, 14 October 1914.
49. 1/6 Warwickshire Regiment Regimental Diary, WO95/2755.
50. *Birmingham Mail*, 15 May 1915.
51. *Birmingham Daily Gazette*, 14 July 1915; *Evening Despatch*, 5 August 1914; *London Gazette*, 1 January 1915.
52. *Evening Despatch*, 5 August 1914.
53. *Birmingham Mail*, 8 November 1916.
54. *Birmingham Daily Gazette*, 8 May 1917.
55. *Birmingham Mail*, 26 February 1917.

56. *Evening Despatch*, 5 August 1914.
57. *London Gazette*, 20 October 1916.
58. *Staffordshire Advertiser*, 31 March 1934.
59. *Tamworth Herald*, 12 December 1914; *Tamworth Herald*, 27 February 1917; *Tamworth Herald*, 1 December 1917.
60. War Diary, 1 South Staffordshire Regiment.
61. *Taunton Courier and Western Advertiser*, 17 July 1918.
62. *Liverpool Daily Post*, 2 December 1916.
63. *Birmingham Daily Mail*, 27 May 1916.
64. *Dundee Courier*, 23 August 1916.
65. *Chelmsford Chronicle*, 21 April 1916.
66. *Liverpool Echo*, 13 April 1916.
67. *Liverpool Echo*, 24 November 1916.
68. *Western Mail*, 7 February 1918.
69. *Dundee Evening Telegraph*, 6 February 1918.
70. *Hull Daily Mail*, 28 November 1917.
71. *Luton News and Bedfordshire Chronicle*, 24 May 1917.
72. H.L. Cancellor, *The Life of a London Beak*, Hurst & Blackett, 1930.

Chapter 13: Lessons Learned
1. *Sunday Mirror*, 15 October 1916.
2. *Birmingham Daily Post*, 4 October 1916.
3. *Lincolnshire Echo*, 2 July 1917; *Manchester Courier and Lancashire General Advertiser*, 27 February 1915.
4. *Staffordshire Advertiser*, 30 March 1918.
5. *Nottingham Evening Post*, 13 August 1918.
6. *Nottingham Evening Post*, 1 April 1919.
7. *Yorkshire Evening Post*, 19 May 1919.
8. *Derby Daily Telegraph*, 21 May 1919.
9. *Nottingham Evening Post*, 26 June 1919.
10. *Western Daily Press*, 24 December 1919.
11. *Tamworth Herald*, 10 January 1920.
12. *Justice of the Peace*, 17 February 1917.
13. *Nottingham Evening Post*, 9 July 1918.
14. *The Scotsman*, 9 July 1918.
15. *Derby Daily Telegraph*, 24 September 1920.
16. *Hull Daily Mail*, 4 August 1919.
17. *Western Morning News*, 5 September 1939.
18. *Stone's Justices' Manual*, 73rd ed., 1941.
19. *Cambridge Daily News*, 27 November 1918.

Index

264   Law and War

Meat Prices, 213
Milk Amendment Order, 211
number produced 1916–18, 215
Potato, 201
Potatoes, 1916 Main Crop (Prices) Order (No. 2), 201, 205
Price of Milk, 200
promulgation of orders, 203
relationship to existing legislation, 204
Seed Potatoes, 200
Sugar (Rationing), 213, 214
Sugar and Chocolates, 201
Waste of Wheat, 200
Wheat, 200
Wheat, Rye and Rice (Restriction), 202
Food Controller,
creation of post, 200
criticism of magistrates, 213
criticisms of, 206
liquor production and supply, 133
Food hoarding, 201, 205, 207–10
Food Supply Manual, 215
Food, definitions of, 209
Fortune-telling, 217
Fouchard, Fred, 161
Fox, Reginald, 230
Fraser, Colonel T.W, 230
Fraudulent enlistment, 154
Freshwater Redoubt, 90

Gamon, Hugh, 34
General Annual Licencing Meeting, 113
General Munitions Tribunal for Wales, 158
General Strike, 239
Geneva Convention, 55
Geneva Cross, 218
Gonorrhoea, 187
'Government' beer, 132
Grand Jury, 12, 226
'Great Unpaid', xi, 243
Gripper, Special Constable Herbert, 223
Group System, see Derby Scheme

Habeas corpus, 62
alien enemies, denial of right to, 84
Freyberger, under Military Service Act, 108–9
Marais case, 66
prisoners of war, denial of right to, 84
Vallandigham case, 63
Weber, enemy alien, application for, 107
Zadig, application for, 108
Habeas Corpus Act, 108
Habitual Drunkard Act, 1879, 111
Haldane, Miss Elizabeth, 236
Hard labour, 25
Heaton, Councillor James, 232
Herbert, Alfred, 207

Hoarding, definition of, 210
Holmes, Robert, police court missionary, 28, 185, 196
Hospital blues, 130
Household diet, 197
'Householder's Return', 157
Howard League for Penal Reform, 29
Hygiene inspection, school, 190–1
Hygiene, card system, 190–1

Identity cards,
for aliens, 103
National Registration Card, 162
Idle and Disorderly Person, 21
Imperial units, xvi
Imprisonment,
convict prisons, 23
drop in prisoner numbers, 225
first division, 25
hard labour, 21, 25
local prisons, 23–4
penal servitude, 24
police custody, 24, 224
prisoners contributing to war effort, 224–5
second division, 25
third division, 25
Incorrigible Rogue, 21
Indictment, 227
Industrial school, 30–1, 191
Inebriate reformatories, 112
Inebriate statistics, 112
Inebriates Act, 1898, 112
Information, laying of an, 7
Internment committee, 102–3
Internment of aliens, statistics, 106
Intoxicating Liquor (Temporary Restrictions) Act, 1914, 42, 117, 122, 124

Jarvis, John, 231–2
Jervis Act, 1848, 7
Joint Labour Recruiting Committees, 163
Judge Advocate General, 58
Judge-advocate, 58
Judicial Statistics for England and Wales, 225–6
Justice of the Peace, origins and history, xi
Justice of the Peace (journal), x, 9, 12, 33, 41, 53, 143, 154, 177, 182, 203, 209, 210, 219, 223, 236
Justice of the Peace Act, 1906, 2
Justices' Clerks Act, 1877, 31
Juvenile crime, 190–6, 234
Juvenile offences, 191–2
Juvenile offenders, 174
Borstal, 26, 191
effect of cinema, 193, 195
fining parents, 196
industrial school, 30–1, 174, 191